D0118487

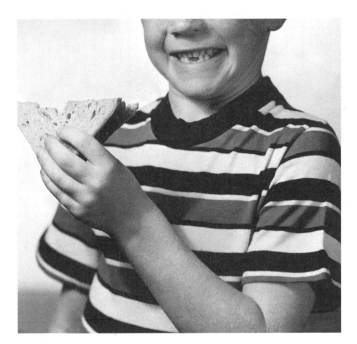

The DevelopMentor Series
Don Box, Editor

Addison-Wesley has joined forces with DevelopMentor, a premiere developer resources company, to produce a series of technical books written by developers for developers. DevelopMentor boasts a prestigious technical staff that includes some of the world's best-known computer science professionals.

*"Works in **The DevelopMentor Series** will be practical and informative sources on the tools and techniques for applying component-based technologies to real-world, large-scale distributed systems."*
　　—Don Box

Titles in the Series:

Essential COM
Don Box
0-201-63446-5

Essential XML
Beyond Markup
Don Box, Aaron Skonnard, and John Lam
0-201-70914-7

Programming Windows Security
Keith Brown
0-201-60442-6

Advanced Visual Basic 6
Power Techniques for Everyday Programs
Matthew Curland
0-201-70712-8

Transactional COM+
Building Scalable Applications
Tim Ewald
0-201-61594-0

ASP Internals
Jon Flanders
0-201-61618-1

Essential IDL
Interface Design for COM
Martin Gudgin
0-201-61595-9

Debugging Windows Programs
Strategies, Tools, and Techniques for Visual C++ Programmers
Everett N. McKay and Mike Woodring
0-201-70238-X

Watch for future titles in The DevelopMentor Series.

Advanced Visual Basic 6:

Power Techniques for Everyday Programs

Matthew Curland

Addison-Wesley

Boston • San Francisco • New York • Toronto
Montreal • London • Munich • Paris • Madrid
Capetown • Sydney • Tokyo • Singapore
Mexico City

Many of the designations used by manufacturers and sellers to distinguish their products are claimed as trademarks. Where those designations appear in this book and we were aware of a trademark claim, the designations have been printed in initial capital letters or all capitals.

The authors and publisher have taken care in the preparation of this book, but make no expressed or implied warranty of any kind and assume no responsibility for errors or omissions. No liability is assumed for incidental or consequential damages in connection with or arising out of the use of the information or programs contained herein.

Copyright © 2000 by Matthew Curland.

All rights reserved. No part of this publication may be reproduced, stored in a retrieval system, or transmitted, in any form or by any means, electronic, mechanical, photocopying, recording, or otherwise, without the prior consent of the publisher. Printed in the United States of America. Published simultaneously in Canada.

The publisher offers discounts on this book when ordered in quantity for special sales. For more information, please contact:

Pearson Education Corporate Sales Division
One Lake Street
Upper Saddle River, NJ 07458
(800) 382-3419
corpsales@pearsontechgroup.com

Visit us on the Web at *www.awl.com/cseng/*

Library of Congress Cataloging-in-Publication Data
Curland, Matthew J., 1970–
    Advanced Visual Basic 6 : power techniques for everyday programs / Matthew Curland.
      p.   cm.
    ISBN 0-201-70712-8
     1. Microsoft Visual BASIC.   2. BASIC (Computer program language)   I. Title.
    QA76.73.B3 C847 2000
    005.26'8—dc21   00-033149

Text printed on recycled and acid-free paper.
ISBN 0201707128
3 4 5 6 7 8   CRS 03 02 01 00
3rd Printing   December 2000

To Lynn and Elizabeth,
the two biggest blessings in my life.
I've missed you.

The significant problems we face cannot be solved at the same level of thinking we were at when we created them.
–Albert Einstein

Contents

Foreword

Writing a foreword is a privilege, especially when the book is by a great author and might easily become a sort of bible for all advanced VB programmers around the world. But when I was asked to write these pages I felt I was privileged in another, far more elementary way: "Hey! This means that I can read Matt's book some months before it gets to the bookstores!" This should give you an idea of how impatient I was to put my hands on what you're reading now.

I won't even try to introduce Matthew Curland. If you have never read one of his BlackBelt Programming columns in *Visual Basic Programmer's Journal*, or heard him speaking at VBITS or other technical conferences, odds are that you never felt the urge to push Visual Basic to its limits. Even if you are new to VB, you are probably unwittingly thankful to him each time you press the dot key and see the list of all the methods and properties of a control or an object. (Matthew was in the team that added IntelliSense to Visual Basic.)

I am especially happy that Matthew finally completed his book, for many reasons. He has written many articles in recent years, but for sure, you can better appreciate these advanced concepts when he doesn't have to squeeze them into a few magazine pages. Being impatient to read later chapters, sometimes I tried to skip over a topic I thought I knew well enough, but I invariably had to go back to fill the holes in my knowledge.

The second reason is that I can finally enjoy only the love side of my love-hate relationship with Visual Basic. As the author explains in his own preface, many advanced VB developers are fond of VB for its simplicity, yet at the same time, they detest it for its lack of power. This book proves that you can do virtually anything with VB. Just as important, it teaches robust and super-optimized coding techniques that will also prove useful in your everyday programming chores. In fact, I have been surprised to find new solutions to challenges I had faced in my recent projects, and I am sure the same will happen to you.

The last reason why I like this book so much is that Matthew has managed to write a layered and reusable textbook. As a developer, you are familiar with the concept of code reuse, but you might be new to the concept of book reuse. Simply stated, a book is *reusable* when you can read it more than once, each time with a different purpose. I realized some time ago that reusable books exist, but finding good examples isn't easy. Because I have already perused what you have just purchased, I can offer you my personal guidelines for getting the most out of *Advanced Visual Basic 6*.

You don't have to carefully read every word in this book the first time you open it. Just enjoy the text between the listings, become familiar with Matthew's way of facing and solving problems, and take note of many undocumented details about VB—they alone can save you many headaches even if you don't plan to use any black-belt programming technique in the immediate future. You can complete this first step in a few hours, even while your 3-year-old child is hanging around.

You are now ready for book reuse. Sit in front of your computer and lock your child out of the room. Go back to page one—OK, skip this foreword—and carefully read everything again, this time paying attention to the portions in Courier as well. This step can take days, but in return you'll learn how to make wonders with your favorite programming language, with or without the great utilities and libraries that Matthew provides.

There is one additional level of book reuse, reserved to the bravest. While you keep the book open on your desk, browse the code on the CD and figure out what each statement does. You will discover many well-kept VB secrets (until today), and you'll learn to write that kind of superb code that only real gurus can teach. To complete this level you'll need to switch off your music player, get several mugs of coffee, and maybe take a few days away from your office as well.

A final warning, coming from my personal experience: This book can be addicting. Don't read it just before going to sleep because you might not sleep at all.

Francesco Balena

Founder, *www.vb2themax.com*
Contributing Editor, *Visual Basic Programmer's Journal*
Author, *Programming Microsoft Visual Basic 6* (Microsoft Press)

Preface

Microsoft Visual Basic has always been positioned by Microsoft as a high-level tool specifically designed to let even inexperienced programmers create Windows applications. VB squarely hits the target of being a high-level language with a rich toolset of rapid-application development features. In addition, VB is also used by a growing number of advanced programmers who make it their language of choice because it gets the job done faster and with fewer bugs than other languages.

This advanced group of VB programmers has a love-hate relationship with VB. They love VB because it takes care of the low-level details and lets them concentrate on their customer's business problems. But they hate VB because it doesn't give them control of their program at a low enough level to fully control the system. Since low-level code generally comprises only a small part of a large application, the love wins out and the programmers tolerate the problems. The vast majority of applications require only a little bit of low-level coding: to provide special UI effects, remove performance bottlenecks, reduce memory usage, and solve other problems. These finishing touches might make up only a small percentage of your application, but they are absolutely essential for shipping a professional software product.

This book focuses on blowing away the wall that many VB programmers hit as they try to polish their application. This is the same wall that managers must consider as they evaluate technologies to apply to new software projects. Managers often choose to code in a lower-level language because they fear that the project cannot be completed in VB. This choice is often unfortunate, because low-level languages are simply not needed for the bulk of today's application development. Precious weeks and months are squandered laboring through mundane C++ code just in case the project requires some low-level code later on.

The easiest way to breach the VB wall is to make use of VB's underlying data types. VB6 works very closely with COM and OLE Automation to do everything from creating objects to managing arrays and strings. Although you don't see the underlying COM types directly in VB, they are always just under the surface: you don't have to dig very far beneath VB's objects, strings, arrays, and Variants in order to find the corresponding IUnknown, BSTR, SAFEARRAY, and VARIANT data types. COM is based on a binary standard, so the memory layout of all COM types is well documented and easily duplicated.

By learning how VB works with COM types, you can open up a whole new world of possibilities in VB. By exploring these data types, I'll break through the thin VB veneer and show you not only what is happening under the surface of normal VB code, but also how to produce your own customized objects. Once you've convinced VB that a piece of customized memory is actually an array or an object, you can use normal VB code to manipulate your data. I am not trying to show you how to write C++ code in VB. I'll show you how to give VB a boost so that VB code runs better and supports otherwise unavailable capabilities.

I have three main goals for readers of this book.

Learn how to write better standard VB code. Even if you come away from this book and decide that you don't want to use the advanced techniques, you will still be able to write VB code that is fundamentally more sound and that performs better.

Learn a new set of advanced VB programming techniques.

Use these programming techniques to enhance your everyday coding productivity by minimizing code reuse and enabling otherwise unavailable algorithms. Following VB's lead, I have made every attempt to package the low-level technology in this book in such a way that you can easily use it without fully understanding what is happening beneath the surface.

Intended Audience

This book is specifically for advanced Visual Basic programmers, but it is also for all VB and COM programmers who want a better understanding of how VB works. I strongly advise that anyone reading this text have a working knowledge of either VB or COM. If you don't have a working knowledge of VB, then please buy another book along with this one.

You will get a lot of value out of this book even if you don't consider yourself an advanced VB programmer and don't understand the low-level manipulations as well as I do. The CD provides easily accessible code that enables common tasks such as subclassing, as well as the previously inaccessible constructs of object aggregation, calls to function pointers, direct memory sharing, and worker thread creation. With just a little bit more of your own code, you get scoped termination events on user-defined types, lightweight object systems that scale painlessly to thousands of objects, custom window creation, and function overriding. You also get three powerful type library add-ins that let you modify both the type libraries VB consumes and the ones it generates.

Although much of the enabling code in this book is very low-level, the book doesn't focus on how to write code at this level. Rather, the goal is to produce a set of tools that you can use repeatedly for everything from full interface implementation reuse to painless hierarchical object models. You can take advantage of the aggregation technologies to greatly improve code reuse by making composite objects that use stock implementations of common interfaces. The longer I use this technology, the more I find myself using it to simplify my day-to-day code. Every VB6 programmer will find code in this book that can be applied to their everyday programming problems.

Future Compatibility

The marketing machine for VB7 is already in motion, so you may already be aware that some of the technology I'll show you is natively available in VB7. For example, VB7 has native support for overriding functions with inheritance, calling function pointers, and providing pointers to class functions. If you make use of the technology in this book to use these design principles now, you can move your application to VB7 simply by replacing the framework calls with the native VB7 equivalents. Only the framework code should change: your design constructs and code logic can remain the same. I'll post more information on VB7 compatibility on the book's web site at *http://www.PowerVB.com* as more information is made available, and I may also be reached via email at Matt@PowerVB.com.

What You're Getting

The book is laid out in sixteen chapters and one appendix. The text alternates between a low-level look at the data underlying array, object, and string types and practical applications of these structures.

1: Building Blocks

Many of the techniques in this book rely heavily on the ability to manipulate the memory underlying VB's array and object types. Reading and writing this low-level data requires direct memory access, otherwise known as "pointer manipulation." VB doesn't provide much explicit support for pointer operations, but it does provide enough to launch us on our journey. The first chapter looks at how VB constantly handles pointers for you, as well as how to access real pointers in VB. You'll also see an introduction to the supporting VBoost objects that come with the book. Many of the samples in the book require VBoost objects, so you need to know how to initialize VBoost before you can run other samples.

2: Leveraging Arrays

I'm starting with arrays, not because I think they're the most commonly used construct in and of themselves, but because they allow you to use standard code to make VB modify arbitrary memory locations. VB's array variables are pointers to an array descriptor structure called a SAFEARRAY. VB automatically allows you to write to the data portion of an array, but you can open up a whole world of direct memory access by reading and writing to the descriptor and the array variable in addition to the data. You'll also see how to best use arrays in straight VB code. The techniques shown in this chapter are used throughout the book to enable and optimize other technologies.

3: IUnknown: An Unknown Quantity

VB is constantly interacting with the COM IUnknown interface, but you never see this interface in normal VB code. IUnknown calls are costly in terms of runtime overhead and code generation so understanding the IUnknown interface is very important. Visual Basic frequently calls IUnknown for you, even though you don't call it yourself. Familiarity with IUnknown is also required to build COM objects from the ground up, as you'll see in later chapters. You can't get very far into customizing VB's COM objects without knowing something about VBs interactions with the QueryInterface, AddRef, and Release functions.

4: Binding Functions to Objects

"Binding" is the general term used to describe how one function calls code in another function. Binding to an object implies that code associated with an object class is applied to a specific instance of that class. You'll see how the VB compiler determines when and how to bind, and how to enable fully dynamic binding at runtime. You'll also see how to bypass the layers that VB puts around a custom control in order to minimize runtime overhead by talking directly to a control's native vtable interface.

5: Object Design Constructs

A well-designed architecture, regardless of the technology employed, is probably the most important factor in the success of your program. You can refer to your program design philosophy as object-oriented, interface-based, optimized for reuse, or all of the above. Regardless of your phraseology, your goal is to write a stable and easily maintained program. This chapter looks at VB approaches to the tried-and-true principles of pluggable components, abstraction, and code reuse. VB natively offers the Implements keyword to provide a shape for your object, and this keyword can take you a long way towards reaching your design goals with interface-based programming. However, you'll find yourself chafing at the inability to achieve easy implementation reuse. I'll take you outside the confines of VB in order to enable full implementation reuse by aggregating existing objects. This gives you the ability to combine multiple implementations into a single object.

6: Circular References

You will run into circular-reference problems almost every time you design an object model. If you know in advance how to handle this situation by using strong references (normal object variables) and weak references (pointers to objects), you will have the tools you need to design object systems without any teardown surprises. To help you compare different approaches, I'll also show you the steps required to solve circular reference problems without pointers (including the pitfalls that make this solution incomplete and overly cumbersome). I'll then apply the weak reference techniques to collections, object ownership, and pain-free hierarchical object models.

7: External Object Creation

All COM objects can be placed within one of two categories: those inside your project and those outside of your project. COM objects are never created directly. Instead, COM uses the registry to create class factory objects, which are then used to create actual class instances. It is surprisingly easy to deal directly with the factory in order to load objects directly from ActiveX DLL and OCX components based on the application path rather than the registry. You'll see how to use aggregation and class factory loading to dynamically specify controls as MDI pages. I'll finish by showing you how to use the CoRegisterClassObject and CoGetClassObject APIs to offer your own application-level singleton objects, creating an easily retrievable context object across multiple components.

8: Lightweight COM Objects

VB creates full-blown COM objects for you, even when you don't need to use all of the COM support. Lightweight COM objects have just enough COM capabilities to be recognized as objects by VB, but not enough to add the large memory overhead of VB-created objects. The only difference between an exciting COM object and a boring (but lightweight) user-defined type (UDT) is a vtable pointer, so you can turn a UDT into a COM object by providing your own vtable to the UDT. You'll see a few simple lightweight objects that give you stack-based local objects, termination code in local- or module-level structures, and the ability to implement arbitrary interfaces that can be aggregated into normal VB objects. Along the way, you'll see all the steps needed to create arbitrary objects: vtable layout, memory-allocation options, reference counting, interface recognition with QueryInterface, and a number of options for generating and handling errors.

9: Large Systems of Objects

VB class modules are perfect for creating a small number of highly complex objects. But the overhead of each object makes it prohibitively expensive to create a large number of very simple objects. Algorithms ranging from scheduling tools to compilers often require thousands of small objects rather than a few large ones. You'll see how to use a custom memory manager to allocate lightweight objects without compromising the coding experience of consuming those objects. When you're done with the objects, you can free them individually or use a single call to reclaim the memory used by the entire object system.

10: VB Objects and the Running Object Table

You can't retrieve VB objects with the GetObject keyword because VB doesn't provide a mechanism for registering public objects in the running object table (ROT). This chapter describes the use and implementation of a lightweight object that lets you place an object in the ROT and automatically remove it when your object terminates. The implementation details look at advanced lightweight objects topics, such as support for multiple interfaces in a single lightweight object and how to hold weak references to secondary interfaces safely.

11: Calling Function Pointers

VB first offered support for proffering function pointers with the addition of the AddressOf operator in VB5. In addition to its primary purpose of enabling a host of Win32 API calls from within VB AddressOf also enables you to create the vtables for lightweight objects. This chapter defines a lightweight object that turns the tables on VB by letting you call a function pointer as well as provide one. Function pointers open the door to a number of possibilities, such as dynamically loading (and unloading) DLLs, writing arbitrary sort routines, using explicit stack allocation in VB, and calling inline assembly code. The ability to call standard function pointers still leaves a couple of holes, so I'll also show you how to associate an object instance with a function pointer (greatly simplifying standard operations, such as subclassing windows), and how to call cdecl functions, enabling you to call entrypoints in MSVCRT and other cdecl DLLs.

12: Overriding Functions

Somewhere in between Implements, which offers no implementation reuse, and aggregation, which offers full implementation reuse, lies partial implementation reuse, which is one of the key benefits of inheritance. The usefulness of inheritance relies heavily on a derived class's ability to override the implementation of specific functions in order to make calls to the base class's functions reach the derived class first. This chapters shows you how to override functions either by using function pointers to redirect calls from the base class or by customizing the aggregation techniques for individual objects in order to override functions without any cooperation from the base class. You have to write a little extra code to use inheritance in VB6, but that's far better than not being able to do it at all.

13: Threads in VB

"VB supports multithreaded components" is a simple statement, but it can mean many things. This chapter tries to make some sense of the term *multithreaded,* and shows you how to make full use of VB's threading capabilities. You'll see how VB runs within the context of COM apartments to initialize itself thread by thread, and you'll see how to spin extra threads in a VB ActiveX EXE project. I'll also show you how to launch worker threads in a DLL with cross-thread object support (offering optimal programming flexibility) or without object support (offering optimal performance).

14: Strings in VB

Visual Basic makes string manipulation very easy. You have a number of operators and string functions at your disposal. However, this does not mean that string manipulation is free. Every string is a block of memory, and larger strings are much more expensive than smaller strings. Automatic string caching can lull you into a false sense of security that vanishes instantly when strings grow beyond the cache size. Learn the true costs associated with VB's String type and how to minimize your string overhead, including how to treat a string as an array of numbers for blazingly fast string algorithms.

15: Type Libraries and VB

Although VB relies on type libraries to compile components and to expose those components to external applications, the day-to-day work of consuming and generating typelibs takes place almost completely behind the scenes. The only direct contact you have with typelibs is through the Project/References dialog. Integrated typelib generation is almost always the right thing, but in most large projects there will be times when you desperately need to get a hand inside a typelib. This chapter shows you how to create typelibs for VB to consume and the reasons why you might want to make custom edits to binary compatibility files and the typelibs that are generated with all ActiveX projects. This chapter does not document the PowerVB Type Library Editor, PowerVB Binary Compatibility Editor, or PowerVB Post-Build Type Library Modifier add-ins included on the book's CD. Instead, it lays out the requirements for the actions you can perform with these tools.

16: Controlling Windows

Most client-side VB programs are built around windows. In fact, VB gained its first foothold in the programming world because it made it so easy to create Windows applications by separating you from the complexities of direct interaction with window objects. But this protective layer brings with it a certain amount of frustration if you try to interact with windows at the level of creation and window procedure. This chapter applies the function pointer, direct memory access, lightweight object, and function overriding techniques from earlier chapters to window objects in general and custom controls in particular. You'll learn about a lightweight and pain-free subclassing approach to control incoming window messages. With subclassing tamed, I'll move on to custom window creation and creating windowless controls that act just like windowed controls.

A: VBoost Reference

The VBoost objects are a small library of functions that provide the base technology pieces required for many of the techniques in the book. The book comes with both a C++ implementation of VBoost (VBoost6.Dll) and a VR implementation in VBoost.Bas, which allows you to remove the external VBoost dependency. Both implementations provide everything you need to perform aggregation, custom

IUnknown hooking, and function overriding. You also get two optimized memory-management variations and a set of assignment and arithmetic functions that greatly simplify the manipulation of pointers in VB. In addition to the code, VBoost includes a set of typelibs categorized by functionality. These typelibs enable easy compilation of all the files in the Code directory on the CD.

Acknowledgments

I would like to thank first and foremost my talented and beautiful wife Lynn for putting her own endeavors on a compressed schedule while this one mushroomed and took on a life of its own. Thanks to my daughter Elizabeth, who has grown during this book from dragging me away from the computer to telling me when it's time to come play. Young children always know what's most important.

Thanks to the tech reviewers who worked through the many details of the book: Troy Cambra, Dan Fergus, Michael Kaplan, Karl Peterson, Ben Wulfe, and especially Brian Harris, who has often been the first user of early (and painfully unrefined) incarnations of many of the techniques shown in this book.

Special thanks goes to Bill Storage for his help in defining the shape for this project, for being a good friend, and for always being so enthusiastic about my work. Bill, I've thoroughly enjoyed working on articles with you and defining the VB black-belt space together.

Thanks to Glenn Hackney, who has endured many unplanned interruptions over the years to act as a sounding board for my new ideas and a rock-solid source of technical direction.

Thanks to my Italian friends Giovanni Librando, for believing in me over two book projects; and Francesco Balena, for writing an unparalleled foreword. It has been an honor to associate with both of you gentlemen.

Thanks to Kristin Erickson, Rebecca Bence, and Jacquelyn Doucette at Addison-Wesley for being friendly and patient as deadlines loomed. Slightly less thanks to Gary Clarke, who talked me into this project a year ago with the lure of a small book. It grew. He knew it would.

Thanks to the birds who've reminded me the last month that it was past time to go to bed. I'll miss the peace at dawn, but not as much as I've missed going to sleep in the dark.

Chapter 1

Building Blocks

In order to make extensions to a system, you have to start within that system. This book offers a number of new programming techniques that you can use in your VB projects, but it is an extension of your existing VB knowledge—not a replacement for it. Just as an addition to a house shares a foundation and walls with the existing structure, these techniques are built on the foundation that VB already has in place. To extend the metaphor, I have also tried to make our new room blend seamlessly with the existing structure.

This chapter is meant only as an introduction to those parts of VB that are used to build all the other extensions in this book. You will feel more at home with the rest of the chapters if you know where I started. The fundamental concept behind all of the extensions is that VB is a COM-based language. VB data types are COM data types, and the COM data types are well documented and easily declared. The techniques used in this book will work as long as VB remains a COM-based product. If VB ever moves away from the COM binary standard, the techniques you see here will have to change as well. Because VB and COM are tied together so tightly, the one guarantee that I can make is that you will rewrite a lot more code than just the pieces you pull from this book if you want to make your program run in a future version of VB that is not based on the COM standard.

Phantom Pointers

Pointers are probably the last things that come to mind when you think about VB programming. In fact, you may be programming in VB in order to avoid the complexities of pointer manipulation inherent in C++. VB doesn't even allow you to define a variable with a pointer type. A pointer is a memory address, so VB has no built-in mechanism to manipulate memory via its address. However, VB does allow you to declare variables with object, array, and string types as well as allow you to pass any variable by reference. Every one of these operations involves pointer manipulation. The only difference between VB and C++ with regard to these common operations is that VB completely hides the pointers from you.

Let's start by looking at the simple case of passing a Long value to two functions, one that expects a ByVal parameter and another that uses ByRef semantics. The equivalent C++ code for both cases will reveal the work VB is doing for you in this very common case (ByRef is the default for all VB parameter types). Both pieces of code are doing the same pointer manipulation, but VB does all of the pointer work for you in both the calling code and the function implementation. All you have to do is specify the ByRef-ness at the parameter.

```
'Pass a parameter by value and then by reference
Sub ByValProc(ByVal Param1 As Long)
    Param1 = 20
End Sub
Sub ByRefProc(ByRef Param1 As Long)
    Param1 = 20
End Sub
Sub Main ()
Dim lValue As Long
    lValue = 10

    ByValProc lValue
    'lValue is still 10

    ByRefProc lValue
    'lValue is now 20
End Sub
```

```
// Equivalent C/C++ code
void ByValProc(long Param1)
{
    Param1 = 20;
}
void ByRefProc(long* pParam1)
{
    *pParam1 = 20;
}
void Main()
{
    long lValue = 10;
    ByValProc(lValue);
    ByRefProc(&lValue);
}
```

In addition to ByRef parameters, some of VB's intrinsic types are also pointer based. Types fall into two categories: In-line types and pointer types. In-line types include Byte, Integer, Long, Single, Double, Boolean, Currency, Variant, user-defined types (UDTs), fixed-size arrays in UDTs, and fixed-length strings. These types store their data at the position they are defined and have variable sizes. For example, a Byte occupies 1 byte of memory, and a Variant takes 16 bytes. Pointer types (which include all object types, variable and fixed-size arrays, and strings) are all variable-length structures that store their data in a different memory location. A 32-bit pointer to this memory (equivalent to four bytes, or one Long variable) is then stored where the variable is defined. Although Variants and UDTs are in-line types, they can contain pointer types, so they occupy memory both where they are defined and in a secondary location.

The difference between in-line types and pointer types is made clearer by defining both a UDT (also called a *structure* or *record* in this book) and a class module with the same members, then trying to look at their byte lengths with the LenB function.

```
'Type definition in a standard (.bas) module
Public Type TwoLongs
    Long1 As Long
    Long2 As Long
End Type
```

```
'Definition of CTwoLongs in a class file
Public Long1 As Long
Public Long2 As Long

'Calling code
Sub Main()
Dim TL As TwoLongs
Dim CTL As New CTwoLongs
    Debug.Print "Structure Length: "; LenB(TL) 'Line 1
    Debug.Print "Class Length: "; LenB(CTL) 'Line 2
End Sub
```

As written, this is not a very satisfying exercise because VB won't compile Line 2. It knows up front that CTwoLongs is an object type and that the length of the memory block associated with an object type is undefined. However, you can declare a second structure with a single CTwoLongs element and verify that the structure has a length of four bytes. Although the LenB and Len functions work on all in-line types, they don't work on pointer types with the exception of String variables. You'll learn why it is easy to get a string length in Chapter 14.

When VB copies an in-line type, it simply copies the data. However, when VB makes a copy of a pointer type, it needs to decide between simply copying the pointer value to the new location or duplicating all the pointed to data and getting a new pointer. Copying just the pointer is known as a *shallow copy;* duplicating the actual data is known as a *deep copy*. VB can always make a shallow copy with object parameters because of COM's reference counting mechanism (which I'll discuss in Chapter 3). However, there is no reference counting mechanism for String or array types, so VB always makes a deep copy when assigning a string or array variable. Deep copies are very expensive in terms of performance and memory, but keep VB a safe language by not allowing you to access memory in locations that you don't own. You'll learn about several techniques for strings and arrays that allow you to minimize deep copies by directly referencing memory that you don't own. Of course, VB has no way of knowing that it doesn't own the memory in a normal variable, so I'll also show you how to clean up your self-managed reference before VB gets hold of it.

Passing a ByVal object type is a source of confusion for some VB developers. Passing an object by value does not mean that you are making a deep copy of the object. Instead, you are simply passing a reference, which means you pass the current pointer value and increase the reference count on the object. The main difference between passing an object parameter ByVal and ByRef is that with a ByRef pass, you can modify the contents of the variable passed to the parameter. However, you have no control over this variable with a ByVal pass. This is the semantic difference between ByVal and ByRef in-line types. There are also some more subtle differences between object types, which we'll discuss in the *Parameters and IUnknown* section in Chapter 3.

Living Pointers

VB hides all its pointer manipulations behind pointer types and ByRef parameters, but it also gives you a built-in (albeit hidden) mechanism to access the actual pointer values of both in-line and pointer types. Once you have a pointer value, you can manipulate it arithmetically just as you would in any other language. Of course, because VB doesn't explicitly support pointer arithmetic and other operations, you step outside VB's guaranteed safe programming environment as soon as you start to use pointers. You also don't get type checking on your pointer operations or compiler help with pointer arithmetic. You are essentially on your own.

Pointers allow you to manipulate memory any way you like. Basic pointer operations allow you to do many things that are otherwise impossible in VB. For example, you can share variables between two class instances without copying them, treat a String as an array of Integers, and create an array from any block of memory. In addition to direct manipulation, this book concentrates on leveraging the known layout of VB's arrays and object types. Once you've constructed an object or array in memory, you can use direct pointer manipulation to assign the array or object to a VB variable. Your goal should always be to get any custom objects and arrays into VB variables as soon as possible so you can use standard VB to make modifications to your data.

The key to memory manipulation in VB is the CopyMemory function. You must provide a declaration for this function in either VB or in a type library. To avoid ANSI/UNICODE string conversion issues (see Chapter 14), we recommend that you use a typelib declare for this function. CopyMemory is a name that has been in common use since the 16-bit days of VB. On 32-bit systems,

CopyMemory is an alias for the RtlMoveMemory entry in the system's Kernel32.Dll. CopyMemory moves an arbitrary number of bytes from one memory location to another. For example, the following snippet moves 4 bytes from one Long variable to another. Note that the VBoostTypes typelib described in the next section contains a CopyMemory declaration and that the VBoost object extensions provide optimized functions for many common operations that would otherwise require CopyMemory.

```vb
'The VB declare statement for demonstration purposes
Declare Sub CopyMemory Lib "kernel32" Alias "RtlMoveMemory" _
    (pDest As Any, pSource As Any, ByVal ByteLen As Long)

'Code to use it
Dim Long1 As Long
Dim Long2 As Long
    Long1 = 10
    'Equivalent to Long1 = Long2
    CopyMemory Long2, Long1, 4
    'Long2 is now 10
```

There are three types of pointers in VB. The first is the memory address of a variable. The second is the address of a string, object, or array pointer type. (Note that pointer-type variables have two pointers: one for the variable and one for the data.) The third is a function pointer. Each of these pointers is retrieved in different ways.

You use the VarPtr function to get the address of any nonarray variable. VarPtr maps to a simple function in the VB runtime that takes a memory address and returns it. Visual Basic's VarPtr function is declared in the VBA typelib and points to the VarPtr entrypoint in the VB runtime DLL. By mapping different function declarations to this single function, you can get the address of different variable types. For example, the *Reading Array Variables* section in Chapter 2 introduces the VarPtrArray and VarPtrStringArray functions. Both are function declarations to call the VarPtr runtime function with different parameter input types. Passing the address of a variable ByVal is equivalent to passing the variable itself ByRef, so the previous CopyMemory call can also be written with VarPtr.

```vb
CopyMemory ByVal VarPtr(Long2), ByVal VarPtr(Long1), 4
```

There are two additional built-in VarPtr-based declarations in the VBA typelib. ObjPtr gets the pointer to the object in any object-typed variable, and StrPtr gets the pointer to the string data in a string variable. ObjPtr and StrPtr differ from VarPtr in that they retrieve the pointer to the actual data rather than the pointer to the variable itself. Although you can also obtain these values with CopyMemory and VarPtr, it is much easier to use the StrPtr and ObjPtr functions directly.

```
'Copy the first seven characters from String1 into String2
Dim String1 As String
Dim String2 As String
Dim pString1 As Long
    String1 = "PowerVB"
    String2 = String$(7, 0)
    'These four operations all do the same thing

    'Try one: this requires a typelib CopyMemory declare
    CopyMemory ByVal String2, ByVal String1, 14

    'Try two: Use StrPtr to guarantee no ANSI/UNICODE munging
    CopyMemory ByVal StrPtr(String2),_
       ByVal StrPtr(String1), 14

    'Try three: Get the string's pointer from VarPtr
    CopyMemory pString1, ByVal VarPtr(String1), 4
    CopyMemory ByVal String2, ByVal pString1, 14

    'Try four: Demonstrate VBoost.Assign instead
    VBoost.Assign pString1, ByVal VarPtr(String1)
    CopyMemory ByVal String2, ByVal pString1, 14
```

The primary use of VarPtr and StrPtr in normal VB code is to enable calls to UNICODE API functions (see *UNICODE Conversions* in Chapter 14). ObjPtr is not needed for API functions, but it is very useful in providing a unique numeric identifier for any object. This enables you to generate a unique key for an object without holding an actual reference to it (see *Weak References and Collections* in Chapter 6). You can also use ObjPtr to track the creation and destruction of your VB-created objects. For example, the following code lets you see when a class instance is created and destroyed.

```
Private Sub Class_Initialize()
    Debug.Print "Create:  "; Hex$(ObjPtr(Me))
End Sub
Private Sub Class_Terminate()
    Debug.Print "Destroy: "; Hex$(ObjPtr(Me))
End Sub
```

The VarPtr function has been part of the Basic language since well before the advent of Visual Basic, and it was moved into the VB runtime when VB was first released. In Visual Basic versions 1 through 3, the undocumented but well-known VarPtr function was accessed via a Declare call into the current version of the VB runtime. The 32-bit VB4 version managed to break most VarPtr-reliant code by performing behind-the-scenes ANSI/UNICODE translations on all string types passed to Declare statement parameters. This effectively meant VarPtr returned the address of temporary variables instead of the data for the real variable. VB5 fixed this by first enabling VB to call void* types in a type library, then adding the (still hidden) VarPtr, StrPtr, and ObjPtr function declarations to the VBA type library. The VarPtr function hasn't changed since VB 1.0; you still call the same entrypoint in the runtime. You just have to use different function declarations to do it.

You can get the address of any function in a standard (.bas) module by using VB's AddressOf operator. AddressOf was primarily designed to provide callback functions for the Win32 API set. For example, getting a list of system fonts and subclassing windows in order to view all incoming messages both require that you provide function pointers to the system. However, VB provides no way to call function pointers; VB can only provide them. I make extensive use of AddressOf in this book for Win32 techniques and for building custom vtables to construct COM objects as described in Chapter 8. I'll also show you, in Chapter 11, how to call a function pointer directly.

The advantages of using pointers make up for the crashes you get along the way. I've already endured many of these crashes for you as I was writing this book. You won't have to experience them. However, as you venture out on your own, you're sure to encounter a few of your own creation, so you should save your work often. You should also be incredibly wary of the IDE's Stop button and the End statement in code. Many of the techniques in this book require cleanup code to run before the program quits. An abrupt End to a program bypasses most termination code, potentially leaving VB in a bad state. You won't always crash if you hit the Stop button, but you *will* crash often enough that you'll stop doing it. Turning off Compile on Demand in the General tab of the Tools\Options dialog will minimize the need to push the Stop button.

VBoost Objects

The core extensions required for this book have been packaged in a component I call VBoost. There are many places in the code samples where you will see a call to VBoost.AssignAddRef, VBoost.AggregateUnknown, VBoost.HookQI, and other functions. These examples all assume that you have a variable called VBoost with a type of VBoostRoot instantiated in your project. VBoost includes three core pieces and several satellite typelibs. You can install these files on your local system by running Setup from the book's CD. You can find full documentation for the VBoost objects and functions in the Appendix.

The VBoostTypes (VBoostTypes6.Olb) type library contains the definitions for all the VBoost objects. It also provides a number of API definitions required by this book. For example, the CopyMemory API function and all the APIs you'll need to perform array manipulation are in this library. VBoostTypes6.Olb is registered under the name "VBoost Object Types (6.0)."

VBoost6.DLL is a C++ implementation of the VBoost objects. This file registers with the name "VBoost Object Implementation (6.0)." Compiling against the objects in this DLL requires type information from the VBoostTypes library, but you don't need to ship VBoostTypes6.Olb with your finished product.

VBoost.Bas provides a VB implementation of all VBoost objects that mirrors the implementation in the DLL. This allows you to use all the techniques in this book without having to ship extra files with your project. VBoost.Bas is a conditionally compiled file that allows you to include only what you need. You can also switch between the VB and C++ implementations by changing the VBOOST_INTERNAL conditional compilation value.

There are several additional typelibs that carry the VBoost name to make them easy to find in the Project/References dialog. These typelibs also use types from the main type library to eliminate redefinition of common types. These files include VBoost: Object Creation and Security (ObjCreate.Olb), VBoost: Ole Type Definitions (OleTypes.Olb), VBoost: Type Library Types and Interfaces (TlbTypes.Olb), VBoost: API declares used for threading (ThreadAPI.Olb), and VBoost: ROT Hook Types (ROTHookTypes.Olb). VBoost itself does not require references to the additional libraries.

You'll need to initialize a VBoost variable before running the samples in this book. This is easily done with the following steps:

Use the Project/References dialog to add a reference to VBoost Object Types (6.0) and VBoost Object Implementation (6.0).

Add the VBoost.Bas file from your local copy of the PowerVB\Code directory on the book's CD.

Call InitVBoost somewhere early in your code. It is easiest to do this from Sub Main, but there is minimal penalty for calling InitVBoost more than once just to be sure.

You are now ready to pull any of the files from the PowerVB\Code directory and write your own code against the VBoost extensions.

Chapter 2

Leveraging Arrays

Arrays are an indispensable tool for any serious programmer. Arrays allow programs to make the quantum leap from acting on a single item to performing the same action against an arbitrary number of items. Arrays also allow you to impose an order on multiple items. As a reader of this book, you should be familiar with arrays, but you may not know how VB handles arrays internally. This chapter is placed very early in the book because understanding how VB uses arrays is required for many other techniques discussed in later chapters.

At its lowest level, an array is simply a block of contiguous memory. This block of memory is divided into a number of equally sized elements. An element in an array is accessed via a zero-based index for the element by adding <Index> * <Element Size> to the starting address of the memory block. Once the memory for a given index has been located in the array, the resulting pointer is then treated as a non-array variable of the same type as the array.

You may think that this definition of an array leaves out multi-dimensional arrays and arrays with a nonzero base index. However, these two cases are simply extensions of the one-dimensional, zero-based indexing system. With a nonzero based array (Dim MyArray(5 To 8) As Long), the lower bound is simply subtracted

Element Number	0	1	2	3	4	5	6
Byte Offset	0	4	8	12	16	20	24
Decimal Value	100000	1000	10	0	-10	-1000	-1000000
Memory	A0 86 01 00	E8 03 00 00	0A 00 00 00	00 00 00 00	F6 FF FF FF	18 FC FF FF	60 79 FE FF

Figure 2.1.   The memory layout of a seven-element array of Longs.

from the index to form a zero-based index, which is then used to locate the element. In a multi-dimensional array (the number of dimensions is also called the *rank* of the array), the vector of indices is used to calculate a zero-based index, which is then plugged into the <ArrayBase> + <Index> * <Element Size> formula. Programming languages support nonzero based and multi-dimensional arrays so that you don't always have to calculate a zero-based index yourself. Since these more complex array types are just thinly veiled versions of a single-dimensional array, I'll concentrate on zero-based, one-dimensional arrays.

Array Descriptors

Although the fundamental building block of any array is the memory block that contains the array's data, a VB array variable is not a pointer to the array's data block. Instead, the array variable points to a structure that describes the contents of the array. This structure is known as an array *descriptor,* and it has the type SAFEARRAY in the C++ headers (the standard OLE Automation structure used to describe an array). SAFEARRAY is called SafeArray in VBoostTypes6.Tlb (SAFEARRAY is a keyword in IDL/ODL, so you can't use it as a type name). By describing its arrays with a SafeArray structure, VB can leverage a wide variety of array-manipulation routines provided by OleAut32.Dll and interoperate easily with external components. For example, VB's ReDim statement maps to the SafeArrayCreate[Ex] API, ReDim Preserve maps to SafeArrayRedim, and Erase maps to SafeArrayDestroy.

The SafeArray descriptor plays the central role in array manipulation. The descriptor holds information about the bounds of the array, the type of data contained in the array, and how the memory for the array was originally allocated. This information not only allows all VB arrays to be managed with the SafeArray* API functions, it also allows arrays to be marshaled correctly when they are passed between COM objects in different threads and processes as parameters or function return values. You can achieve fine-grained control of your arrays by learning what's in the SafeArray structure and how VB and the SafeArray API set respond to the different settings.

Here are the main SafeArray and SafeArrayBound structures as defined in VBoostTypes. They are equivalent to the SAFEARRAY and SAFEARRAYBOUND structures defined by OLE Automation, but these structures are more VB friendly. In practice, a SafeArray structure is always immediately followed in memory by one or more SafeArrayBound structures, depending on the cDims field of the SafeArray. All the other flags and API functions used in this chapter are also included in the VBoostTypes type library.

```
Type SafeArray
    cDims As Integer
    fFeatures As Integer
    cbElements As Long
    cLocks As Long
    pvData As Long
End Type


Type SafeArrayBound
    cElements As Long
    lLbound As Long
End Type
```

You will usually work with a one-dimensional SAFEARRAY. For convenience, VBoostTypes also defines a one-dimensional SafeArray structure with a single inline bound.

```
Type SafeArray1d
    cDims As Integer
    fFeatures As Integer
    cbElements As Long
    cLocks As Long
    pvData As Long
    cElements As Long
    lLbound As Long
End Type
```

Let's look at each of the SafeArray and SafeArrayBound elements individually, as well as the different flags we can apply to the fFeatures field. Although tedious, this exercise is important because we will read these values from VB-created arrays as well as set them in descriptors that we create ourselves.

- **cDims** is the number of dimensions in the array. This must be set to 1 for a one-dimensional array.

- **cbElements** is the number of bytes per element. The memory address for the *Index* element in an array is calculated as pvData + Index * cbElements.

- **cLocks** is a lock count for the array. When an array is locked, you cannot ReDim, ReDim Preserve, or Erase the array. You can change the value of elements in the array, but you cannot modify or destroy the array's structure. VB locks an array when you pass an element of the array to a ByRef parameter or when you use a structure-type array element in a With statement. Trying to Erase or ReDim [Preserve] an array with cLocks > 0 generates an error 10 ("This array is fixed or temporarily locked").

- **pvData** is the element in an array that points to the memory for the array's data. pvData is the main player in the SafeArray structure: All other fields play supporting roles. pvData is stored as a Long value, which has the same length as the void* pointer in the OLE Automation SAFEARRAY definition.

- **cElements** specifies the number of elements allowed per bound.

- **lLbound** is the lower bound of the array dimension. VB's LBound function reads its value directly from this element, while UBound is calculated as lLbound + cElements − 1.

- **fFeatures** is a very important field. The flags set in fFeatures enable the SafeArray* API set to correctly destroy an array and the standard COM marshaling engine to successfully move the array between threads and processes. These flags fall into two categories: they specify either the type of elements in the array or the method used to allocate the memory for the descriptor and the array data itself.

The first group of flags includes three memory flags—FADF_AUTO (&H1), FADF_STATIC (&H2), FADF_EMBEDDED (&H4)—and FADF_FIXEDSIZE (&H10). These flags describe how the array was allocated, and they block ReDim [Preserve]. If any of the memory flags are set, the Erase statement cleans up elements in the array, but it does not free the memory. If FADF_STATIC is set, the memory block for any type is zeroed by Erase. In VB variable-size arrays, none of these flags is set. A fixed-size array has FADF_STATIC and FADF_FIXEDSIZE set, and a fixed-size array in a structure adds the FADF_EMBEDDED flag as well. VB doesn't generate arrays with the the FADF_AUTO flag set, but I'll use it later in the chapter to indicate that the array descriptor is allocated on the stack.

VB plays some nasty little games with the fFeatures flags and local fixed-size array variables. (I had a wonderful time stepping through native assembly code to fully verify this.) Although VB allocates the descriptor for a local fixed-size array variable on the stack, the data for the array is allocated on the heap with SafeArrayAllocData. This method of allocation allows you to create arbitrarily large fixed-size local arrays, by passing the 64K upper limit of fixed-size arrays in structures. However, this means that the array is neither fixed-size nor static in the sense that these flags were intended. VB just uses the flags during the scope of the function or lifetime of the class to prevent other routines from modifying the array. So when a local array variable goes out of scope, VB checks for arrays that are FIXEDSIZE and STATIC (but not EMBEDDED or AUTO). VB clears these flags before calling SafeArrayDestroyData, which then clears and releases the memory block that had been locked by the fFeatures settings.

The next group of flags indicates the type of element in the array. One or none of these flags can be set for an array. FADF_BSTR (&H100) indicates that the array contains Strings, so calling Erase on the array frees each of the string elements with the SysFreeString API, then destroys or zeroes the memory. Similarly, FADF_VARIANT (&H800) forces a call to the VariantClear API for each element, and FADF_UNKNOWN (&H200) and FADF_DISPATCH (&H400) indicate that IUnknown-Release should be called on each nonzero element to release the reference on the object. The array destruction routines are able to free memory associated with all simple types simply by looking at these flags.

The remaining three flags indicate that extra information about the array's type is available in the memory immediately before the SafeArray structure. These values are used to optimize marshaling and to destroy arrays of structures. The first flag, FADF_HAVEVARTYPE (&H80), indicates that the two-byte variant type of the element is stored four bytes before the start of the SafeArray structure. FADF_HAVEIID (&H40) indicates that the 16 bytes preceding the descriptor hold the IID of the type. FADF_RECORD (&H20) indicates that the four bytes preceding the descriptor hold an IRecordInfo reference. FADF_RECORD corresponds to VB6's new support for structures in public interfaces and Variants. VBoostTypes includes a version of IRecordInfo that VB can call.

Reading Array Variables

The goal of this chapter is not to provide alternatives for directly modifying array elements, but rather to provide VB with the appropriate descriptor to enable access array elements with normal code. But in order to make use of an array descriptor, you need to be able to read it from and write it to a VB array variable. Before you can read from or write to an array variable, you need the array variable's address. Determining this address is actually harder than it sounds because there is no built-in function for obtaining the address of an array variable.

VB supports three types of untyped variables in function declarations. The first type, Any, is allowed only in a VB Declare statement and accepts any nonarray type. Data passed to an As Any parameter undergoes automatic UNICODE/ANSI/UNICODE conversion. VB also recognizes the void* type as declared in a typelib. The void* type is treated like Any, except that no string conversion takes place when parameters are passed to the type. Introduced in VB5, void* support enabled a VarPtr declaration that works against any type. The one downside of both Any and void* is that the compiler does not support passing an array to either of these types.

Unfortunately, VB does not support SAFEARRAY(void*) in a type library. Because a SafeArray is actually a type-agnostic structure to begin with, this is doubly unfortunate: There is no way to write a typelib-defined VarPtrArray function that accepts an arbitrarily typed array. In order to humor the compiler, you would have to include definitions for VarPtrLongArray, VarPtrIntegerArray, VarPtrSingleArray, and so on. Of course, including even the full list of intrinsic types wouldn't completely solve the problem because you still couldn't get the address of an array of structures. The good news is that there is an Any equivalent for arrays that comes close to a general solution. The VarPtrArray shown here works for arrays of every type except String. This definition is included in VBoost.Bas.

```
Public Declare Function VarPtrArray _
    Lib "msvbvm60.DLL" Alias "VarPtr" (Ptr() As Any) As Long
```

Applying VarPtrArray to an array variable returns the address of the variable, but that is still only halfway to getting the array descriptor itself. Like String and object types, arrays are pointer types, so the variable's address is a pointer to a pointer to an array descriptor, *not* to an array descriptor itself (SAFEARRAY** in C++ syntax). To get to the actual descriptor, you must dereference VarPtrArray, then copy this value into an array descriptor. The following function gets the array descriptor.

```
Function ArrayDescriptor(ByVal ppSA As Long) As SafeArray
Dim pSA As Long
    'psa = *ppSA
    pSA = VBoost.Deref(ppSA)
    'Make sure we have a descriptor
    If pSA Then
        'Copy the SafeArray descriptor
        CopyMemory ArrayDescriptor, _
            ByVal pSA, LenB(ArrayDescriptor)
    End If
End Function
'Calling code snippet
ReDim VariableArray(0) As Long
Dim FixedArray(0) As Long
Debug.Print Hex$(ArrayDescriptor ( _
  VarPtrArray(VariableArray)).fFeatures)
Debug.Print Hex$(ArrayDescriptor ( _
  VarPtrArray(FixedArray)).fFeatures)
'Output. Both  arrays have FADF_HAVEVARTYPE features set.
'FixedArray also has FADF_FIXEDSIZE and FADF_STATIC set.
80
92
```

You can also use VarPtrArray to look at the additional information stored at the beginning of the array. Generally, you won't need to do this in code, but it is a useful exercise for seeing the layout of the array descriptor. All the support functions shown here are provided with VBoostTypes. VBoost.Deref retrieves the pointer value stored in the array variable, and VBoost.UDif performs pointer arithmetic using unsigned arithmetic.

```
Dim ObjArray() As VBA.Collection
Dim Guid As VBGUID
Dim GuidString As String * 38
ReDim ObjArray(0)
'Read the IID from the memory stored at 16 bytes before
'the beginning of the normal SAFEARRAY descriptor.
CopyMemory _
  Guid, _
  ByVal VBoost.UDif(VBoost.Deref(VarPtrArray(ObjArray)), _
    LenB(Guid)), LenB(Guid)
StringFromGUID2 Guid, GuidString
Debug.Print GuidString

'Output
{A4C46780-499F-101B-BB78-00AA00383CBB}
```

You can verify that this is indeed the IID for a Collection object by using the TLI (TlbInf32.Dll) object library. Adding a project reference to TypeLib Information and running this code in the Immediate window generates the same output as the previous snippet.

```
?TLI.TypeLibInfoFromFile("msvbvm60.Dll"). _
  TypeInfos.NamedItem("Collection").DefaultInterface.Guid
```

VarPtrArray works for every array type except String. For some obscure reason that I have never been able to ascertain, VB actually performs ANSI/UNICODE translation when passing String arrays to a Ptr() As Any or Ptr() As String parameter in a declared function. I find this behavior strange because SafeArray is a UNICODE beast, not an ANSI beast, so passing out a BSTR that contains ANSI characters actually violates the type. At least VB doesn't perform string translation for arrays of structures, so a String in a UDT, unlike strings in a pure String array, is not touched during an API call. In order to look at the array descriptor for a String array, you need a typelib-declared VarPtrStringArray function. If you use VarPtrArray, you actually get the address of a temporary structure, and this causes a crash very quickly when you dereference it. The typelib declaration included with the VBoost type definitions, is shown below. Using the VarPtrStringArray and VarPtrArray functions, you can access an array variable of any type.

```
[dllname("msvbvm60.DLL")]
module StringArray
{
    [entry("VarPtr")]
    long _stdcall VarPtrStringArray (
        [in] SAFEARRAY(BSTR) *Ptr);
};
```

Writing to Array Variables

Reading information about arrays that VB has created adds little to our arsenal of programming techniques. But, being able to read that information through the array variable's address also enables us to write to the same address and modify the data that is already in the provided descriptor. By filling your own array descriptors and assigning them to an array variable, you can not only give your arrays any characteristic you like, you can also point your arrays at arbitrary memory locations. The basic technique is illustrated in the following code, which writes to a Long variable using a Byte array with four elements.

```
Sub FillLongViaBytes()
Dim lVar As Long
Dim Bytes() As Byte
Dim SABytes As SafeArray1d
    With SABytes
        .cDims = 1
        .cbElements = 1
        .cElements = 4
        .fFeatures = FADF_AUTO Or FADF_FIXEDSIZE
        .pvData = VarPtr(lVar)
    End With
    'Assign the address of the SafeArray structure to the
```

```
'array variable. You should remember this code.
'VBoost.Assign is equivalent to CopyMemory xxx, yyy, 4
VBoost.Assign ByVal VarPtrArray(Bytes), VarPtr(SABytes)
Bytes(0) = &H12
Bytes(1) = &H34
Bytes(2) = &H56
Bytes(3) = &H78
Debug.Print Hex$(lVar)
End Sub


'Output (Intel uses big-endian integer layout)
78563412
```

The most important thing to note in this code is how I have taken an arbitrary memory location and applied an arbitrary type to it. I've essentially said "treat the address of the Long variable as four bytes." I could also have told VB to treat the same memory as an array of two Integers (Integers() As Integer, cbElements = 2, cElements = 2), or an array of one Long (Longs() As Long, cbElements = 4, cElements = 1). You can modify the array elements by changing the variable or you can modify the variable by changing the array elements since both the array and the variable point to the same piece of memory. If the array and the variable have the same type, TheArray(0) and TheVariable are equivalent.

By adjusting the array declaration's type and matching the fields in your descriptor to the target type, you have a mechanism for viewing or modifying an arbitrary memory block as a specific type. The ability to view memory in this fashion is used extensively in other parts of this book. For example, with array descriptors you can numerically modify strings and share data between class instances and across threads. Other applications include modifying arbitrary memory, such as an in-memory bitmap, without copying the memory into a VB-allocated byte array.

You should always consider scope when you point VB arrays at arbitrary memory. When the array variable goes out of scope, VB cleans up the array as if it had done all the work of populating it. If an array variable leaves scope with no fFeatures flags set, VB sends the memory for both the data and the descriptor to the heap to be freed. The heap doesn't like to free memory that it didn't allo-cate, and VB will crash. As I mentioned earlier, if only the FADF_STATIC and

FADF_FIXEDSIZE flags are set, VB assumes it is looking at a VB-managed, fixed-size array and sends the data to the heap. This means you can't use these flags alone when pointing an array at arbitrary memory. The safest flags to use are FADF_AUTO Or FADF_FIXEDSIZE. When these flags are set, VB performs only the minimal amount of cleanup.

If you want to use Erase to zero your array, you can add the FADF_STATIC flag. But never use FADF_STATIC without FADF_AUTO. You can see the effects of FADF_STATIC in the following modification of the first routine. With the FADF_STATIC flag added, this routine outputs zero. If you remove FADF_STATIC, you get the desired result.

```
Sub CallFillLongViaBytes()
Dim lVar As Long
    FillLongViaBytes lVar
    Debug.Print Hex$(lVar)
End Sub
Sub FillLongViaBytes(lVar As Long)
Dim Bytes() As Byte
Dim SABytes As SafeArray1d
    With SABytes
        .cDims = 1              '1 dimensional array
        .cbElements = 1         '1 byte per element
        .cElements = 4          '4 bytes to a long
        .fFeatures = FADF_AUTO Or FADF_STATIC Or
          FADF_FIXEDSIZE
        .pvData = VarPtr(lVar) 'Point at the data
    End With
    VBoost.Assign ByVal VarPtrArray(Bytes), VarPtr(SABytes)
    Bytes(0) = &H12
    Bytes(1) = &H34
    Bytes(2) = &H56
    Bytes(3) = &H78
End Sub

'Output
0
```

Of course, the fact that VB cleans up the array data when it goes out of scope means that it's doing work that it shouldn't have to. After all, there is actually nothing to clean up. Although it is safe to leave scope because no memory is being freed, you can do VB a small favor by clearing either the data pointer or the array variable itself before the variable goes out of scope. Clearing the variable leaves the least amount of work for VB to do; Clearing the pvData field is also a viable option. Setting pvData, cDims, or cElements to zero stops the memory from being cleaned up as the array leaves scope. However you modify the array variable or descriptor, you should make a modification that stops VB from freeing or zeroing the array's memory. After all, the array just borrows the memory it uses—it does not own the memory.

```
'Clear the array variable
ZeroMemory ByVal VarPtrArray(Bytes()), 4
'or
VBoost.AssignZero ByVal VarPtrArray(Bytes())


'Change the array descriptor so that it has no data.
'Setting cDims or cElements to 0 is also sufficient.
SABytes.pvData = 0
```

Module-Level Arrays

Modifying local variables provides pretty good control over the array variable, but there are entirely different issues when you deal with module-level variables. The first issue is again a matter of scope. A standard module doesn't have a Terminate event, so you aren't notified when your array is about to go out of scope. Normally, this wouldn't be a huge issue, but VB's module-teardown code does not respect the FADF memory flags. VB makes the (generally reasonable) assumption that it populated its own variable size array variables, so it should always know how to tear them down. So even though the descriptor is flagged as untouchable, VB calls SafeArrayDestroyDescriptor anyway, causing the problems typical of releasing unallocated memory.

You might wonder why you would want to use a module level array/descriptor pair in the first place. If you're calling a function that uses array descriptors a number of times, a module level descriptor makes it unnecessary to fill in and assign the descriptor on every call. You can have an EnsureInit routine in the module, or you can key off a field in the module-level descriptor to test whether you need to initialize the array descriptor. (cDims = 0 works well for indicating an uninitialized array.)

During module teardown VB not only ignores the fFeatures setting, it also ignores error-return values from SafeArrayDestroyDescriptor. There are several work-arounds to the teardown problem. Locking the array by initializing the descriptor with cLocks = 1 stops the unwanted memory destruction dead in its tracks. The disadvantage to this method is that VB still pays attention to pvData during teardown, so you have to make sure pvData is zero whenever you leave local scope. There are three ways to handle this.

- Put your array in a structure and add a termination code to using light-weight objects. The "ArrayOwner Lightweight" section in Chapter 8 shows how this is done.

- Clear the module-level array variable whenever you leave function scope, but leave the structure in place. You might as well use a local descriptor in this case because the savings are minimal.

- Avoid the standard module headaches by creating a class module that allows you to get a termination event automatically. Always clear the array variable in your Class_Terminate, calling Erase to free referenced pointer types if needed.

The ClearArrayData example shown here clears the data in an array without freeing its memory. The routine relies on the simple trick of temporarily setting the array descriptor's FADF_STATIC flag so that a call to SafeArrayDestroyData does not actually release the array's memory block. In order to modify the fFeatures field, I use a module-level descriptor/array pair that enables reading and modification of the descriptor directly. The alternative is to use CopyMemory to get the data into or out of the descriptor. In an FADF_STATIC array, ClearArrayData is equivalent to the Erase statement. Two versions of the routine are shown. The first blocks uses a lock count on the array to block destruction, and the second uses the lightweight ArrayOwner object to clear the array variable as the module tears down.

```
'Version 1 of ClearArrayData. Uses a lock count
'to stop module teardown from freeing memory it shouldn't
```

```vb
Private m_SA As SafeArray1d
Private m_pSA() As SafeArray

Public Sub ClearArrayData(ByVal ppSA As Long)
Dim fOldFeatures As Integer
    With m_SA
        'Initialize the module level variables once
        If .cDims = 0 Then
            .cDims = 1
            .fFeatures = FADF_AUTO Or FADF_FIXEDSIZE
            .cElements = 1
            .cLocks = 1
            VBoost.Assign ByVal VarPtrArray(m_pSA), _
                VarPtr(m_SA)
        End If
        'Change the data pointed to by the helper array
        .pvData = VBoost.Deref(ppSA)
        If .pvData = 0 Then Exit Sub
        'm_pSA(0) is a SafeArray-typed variable that can be
        'used to modify the memory of the SafeArray
        'structure.
        With m_pSA(0)
            'Save the old fFeatures value
            fOldFeatures = .fFeatures
            'Turn on the static flag
            .fFeatures = fOldFeatures Or FADF_STATIC
            'Clear the data
            SafeArrayDestroyData .pvData
            'Restore the old value
            .fFeatures = fOldFeatures
        End With
        'Make teardown safe again
        .pvData = 0
    End With
End Sub

'Version 2 of ClearArrayData. Runs code immediately before
'the array is released, giving us a chance to zero the array
'variable. The ArrayOwner structure needs to be included
'in a second structure with the array variable immediately
'following it.
Private Type SAOwner
```

```
      Owner As ArrayOwner
      pSA() As SafeArray
End Type
Private m_SAOwner As SAOwner

Public Sub ClearArrayData(ByVal ppSA As Long)
Dim pSA As Long
Dim fOldFeatures As Integer
      'Initialize the first time we call this
      If m_SAOwner.Owner.SA.cDims = 0 Then
          'Pass the element size and features.
          'The final False parameter means that
          'pvData is ignored on teardown. Setting
          'the features to zero is OK because this
          'array never makes it to teardown.
          InitArrayOwner m_SAOwner.Owner, _
              LenB(m_SAOwner.pSA(0)), 0, False
      End If
      'We treat m_SAOwner.Owner.SA the same way as
      'm_SA in the previous example
      With m_SAOwner.Owner.SA
          pSA = VBoost.Deref(ppSA)
          If pSA = 0 Then Exit Sub
          .pvData = pSA
          With m_SAOwner.pSA(0)
              fOldFeatures = .fFeatures
              .fFeatures = fOldFeatures Or FADF_STATIC
              SafeArrayDestroyData pSA
              .fFeatures = fOldFeatures
          End With
          '.pvData = 0 not needed because all cleanup is
          'done by the ArrayOwner object.
      End With
End Sub

'Calling code
Dim strArray() As String
  . . .
ReDim strArray(SomeSize)
  . . .
'Clear the array
ClearArrayData VarPtrStringArray(strArray)
```

Here's a generic helper routine that attaches a memory pointer to a single-dimensional array with one element and clears the array variable when we're done. This keeps you from having to write array descriptor code every time you attach a descriptor to an array variable. In this routine, MemPtr is optional; pvData can be left at zero and filled in later. The ElemByteLen parameter is also optional because this field is not needed in an array with one element. You need to specify an element length only if you want to use Erase to zero out all (as opposed to 0 bytes of) your memory. The functions are contained in SafeArray.Bas.

```
Public Sub ShareMemoryViaArray( _
  ByVal ArrayPtr As Long, SA1D As SafeArray1d, _
  Optional ByVal MemPtr As Long, Optional ByVal ElemByteLen _
    As Long)
    With SA1D
        .cbElements = ElemByteLen
        .cDims = 1
        .fFeatures = FADF_AUTO Or FADF_FIXEDSIZE
        .pvData = MemPtr
        .cElements = 1
    End With
    VBoost.Assign ByVal ArrayPtr, VarPtr(SA1D)
End Sub
Public Sub UnshareMemory(ByVal ArrayPtr As Long)
    VBoost.Assign ByVal ArrayPtr, 0&
End Sub
```

With Statements and Reentrancy

Whenever you use a module-level variable instead of a local variable, you run the risk of reentrancy causing problems. For example, in the ClearArrayData routine, the SafeArrayDestroyData API call could actually free a VB object and run a Class_Terminate event, which in turn could call ClearArrayData. This looks like a dangerous situation because there are now two ClearArrayData invocations running on the stack, and both are using the module level m_SA and m_pSA variables. Although this *looks* bad, the With m_pSA(0) clause makes it perfectly safe.

The reason the With statement establishes a lock on an array is that it uses the array descriptor only once to retrieve an element's memory, then places a lock on the array to ensure that the pointer it has retrieved remains valid. At the End

With statement, the array is unlocked. This is relevant to our array code because the pvData field in the array descriptor is not used after the With line, so you are free to change it. You can even point the locked array variable at another memory location. The only requirement after the With statement is that the memory for the original array descriptor must be valid when End With attempts to unlock it. In a normal situation, the lock on the array prevents the memory referenced by the With context variable from being freed. However, in the current case, the lock is merely a harmless side effect. Everything in the With clause references the memory indicated by the state of the SafeArray at the With statement. VB does not look at the SafeArray from within the With block, so it does not see changes to the value of pSA(0). This allows you to modify this value with impunity.

The bottom line is that you can use a module-level descriptor/array pair in reentrant situations if you guarantee that the array descriptor is valid just before accessing an element of the array. Without the With statement, ClearArrayData would require some extra code to be safe. As you can see from the With-less code shown here, it is much easier to use the With statement.

```
With m_SA
    'Change the data pointed to by the helper array
    .pvData = VBoost.Deref(ppSA)
    If .pvData = 0 Then Exit Sub
    fOldFeatures = m_pSA(0).fFeatures
    m_pSA(0).fFeatures = fOldFeatures Or FADF_STATIC
    SafeArrayDestroyData m_pSA(0).pvData
    'Guard against reentrancy, reset .pvData
    .pvData = VBoost.Deref(ppSA)
    m_pSA(0).fFeatures = fOldFeatures
    .pvData = 0
End With
```

Array Options: Beyond Fixed or Variable Size

VB makes you choose between two types of arrays: fixed-size and variable. When you have access to the array descriptor, you can get more flexibility with your arrays by using the best features of each type. I'll first look at the advantages of using fixed-size arrays, then look at enhancing variable-size arrays to get the same benefits. There are three advantages to using fixed-size arrays.

When the array is a local variable, the array descriptor is allocated on the stack. Stack allocation generally performs better than heap allocation, giving fixed-size arrays the advantage here. Only arrays that are dimensioned with the Dim keyword and that specify bounds in the declaration are fixed-size. It is a common mistake to use the ReDim keyword as the primary declaration for the array variable.

```
'Snippet 1, compile error
Dim lArr(0, 0) As Long
lArr(0) = 10 'Wrong number of dimensions

'Snippet 2, no compile error, not a fixed-size array
ReDim lArr(0, 0) As Long
lArr(0) = 10 'Runtime error 9
```

The shape of a fixed-size array cannot be changed when the array is passed to an external function. The FADF_STATIC and FADF_FIXEDSIZE flags lock the size and shape of the array.

The compiler optimizes access for elements of fixed-size arrays declared at the current scope. Because the compiler knows that the array descriptor is on the stack, it also knows exactly where to find pvData. This eliminates the code that determines pvData based on the array pointer (required with variable-size arrays). VB doesn't support fixed-size arrays in parameter lists, so this optimization cannot be performed if the array is passed to another function.

There is no way to gain the compile-time rank checking and other fixed-size optimizations with variable-size arrays. However, with a few simple manipulations, you can lock the layout of your array so that external code can't modify the array's rank and size. In addition to locking the size of your array, you can also reduce the number of heap allocations required to populate a variable-size array variable from two to one, or even to zero.

Array Locking

First, let's look at locking a variable-size array to prevent other code from modifying its shape. In most of the code you write, you shouldn't really care about locking your arrays. You usually pass your arrays to your own code, and you know that the called code won't monkey with the array's structure. However, if you pass the array to external code, as you do when you raise an event in an ActiveX control, you can't rely on the array returning in the same state in which you sent it. In general, you should go out of your way to reduce the vulnerability of your data only when it is passed to untrusted code. You should be able to trust your own code and determine the trust boundary.

You can gain reasonable protection for your array structure by modifying the fFeatures flags. Setting the FADF_FIXEDSIZE flag (which causes a call to ReDim Preserve to raise an error) can lock the size of the array. However, preventing ReDim also requires the FADF_STATIC flag, so your array is only partially protected with FADF_FIXEDSIZE. The problem with FADF_STATIC is that if you don't clear the flag before the array is destroyed, the data memory is not released. In order to use fFeatures to lock the shape of your array, you have to modify fFeatures when the array is first allocated and before it is destroyed. Although this is very doable (just modify the ClearArrayData routine to make the necessary modifications to the array structure), it is a hassle, and there is a built-in locking mechanism that you can use to do this without modifying the flags.

Locking the array is the preferred mechanism for stopping downstream routines from modifying the structure of your array. A lock actually offers slightly more protection than the STATIC and FIXEDSIZE flags because a lock completely blocks the Erase statement. Downstream code can operate only on individual elements in the array, not the array as a whole. If you don't want your array shape to be modified, you must increment the array's lock count before passing the array and decrement the lock count after. If you don't unlock your array after the call, you'll have errors and memory leaks when the array is freed, and you should provide a local error handler when errors are possible. As I mentioned earlier, an array is locked when one of its elements (as opposed to the array itself) is passed to a ByRef parameter or used in a With statement when the element is a structure type. In this way, the With statement provides a simple mechanism for locking arrays that also provides automatic array unlocking. However, you can't use the With statement with arrays of simple or object types. For arrays that aren't structures, you can lock directly with the SafeArrayLock and SafeArrayUnlock API calls.

```
'Lock a Long array during an external call.
Dim lArr() As Long
ReDim lArr(0)
    On Error GoTo Error
    SafeArrayLock VBoost.Deref(VarPtrArray(lArr))
    PassLongArray lArr
Error:
    SafeArrayUnlock VBoost.Deref(VarPtrArray(lArr))
    With Err
        If .Number Then .Raise .Number, _
            .Source, .Description, .HelpFile, .HelpContext
    End With


Sub PassLongArray(lArr() As Long)
    Erase lArr 'Error 10
End Sub


'Lock an object type array during a call
Dim GuidArr() As VBGUID
ReDim GuidArr(0)
    With GuidArr(0)
        PassGuidArray GuidArr
    End With


Sub PassObjectArray(GuidArr() As VBGUID)
    Erase GuidArr 'Error 10
End Sub
```

Alternate Array Allocation Techniques

You need both a descriptor and data in order to have a viable array. VB's ReDim statement uses a separate heap allocation for the descriptor and the array. There are two ways to reduce the number of heap allocations required for a variable-size array. The first is to use the SafeArrayCreateVectorEx API call, which allocates the descriptor and array in a single heap allocation. The second mechanism, applicable to local arrays only, is to use a local descriptor and explicit stack allocation.

The SafeArrayCreateVectorEx API takes a Variant type (such as vbLong or vbInteger) and returns an allocated array. I'll show the Ex version of the API to support creation of arrays with the FADF_RECORD, FADF_HAVEIID, and

FADF_HAVEVARTYPE flags set. You can experiment with creating VT_RECORD and FADF_HAVEIID arrays on your own. As a sample, I'll create a Long array with 10 elements using a single heap allocation. After the array is allocated, it acts just like an array allocated with the ReDim statement.

```
Dim lArr() As Long
VBoost.Assign ByVal VarPtrArray(lArr), _
    SafeArrayCreateVectorEx(vbLong, 0, 10)
Debug.Print Hex$(ArrayDescriptor(VarPtrArray(lArr)).fFeatures)
```

SafeArrayCreateVectorEx lets you allocate an array with one heap allocation instead of two. You can get down to zero heap allocations by using stack allocation along with your own array descriptor. Although it uses a little more code, this variable-size array allocation mechanism is the least expensive. Stack allocations are valid only during the lifetime of the current function, so you can use this type of array only in the current function and any functions it calls directly. The stack allocation routines are described in the "Stack Allocation" section in Chapter 11.

```
Sub UseStackAlloc()
Dim lArr() As Long
Dim SAlArr As SafeArray1d
Dim l As Long
Dim cbExtraStack As Long
    With SAlArr
        .cDims = 1
        .cbElements = 4
        .fFeatures = FADF_AUTO Or FADF_FIXEDSIZE
        .cElements = 500
        cbExtraStack = .cbElements * .cElements
        .pvData = StackAllocZero.Call(cbExtraStack)
        VBoost.Assign ByVal VarPtrArray(lArr), VarPtr(SAlArr)
    End With
    '. . .
    If cbExtraStack Then StackFree.Call cbExtraStack
End Sub
```

I mentioned earlier that a local fixed-size array actually uses heap allocation to support arbitrarily large data blocks. If you know the size of the array you want at compile time and you want to eliminate the extra heap allocation, you can define your own type with a single array element. This gives you much better performance both locally and with fixed-size module level arrays. Also, if a module-level array must absolutely be valid until every line of teardown code in every module has completed, you should use this technique with your array. A fixed-size module-level array loses its data to VB's teardown process fairly early, but fixed-size arrays in module-level structure variables hang on until the bitter end.

```
'One heap allocation
Sub HalfStacked()
Dim Slots(255) As Long
End Sub


'No heap allocation
Private Type Long256
    lArr(255) As Long
End Type
Sub FullyStacked()
Dim Slots As Long256
End Sub
```

Multi-Dimensional Arrays

Up to this point, I've dealt solely with one-dimensional arrays. Multi-dimensional arrays provide a new set of challenges. COM can't specify the required rank of an array at compile time. This means that an incoming array can always have an arbitrary rank at runtime. Combine this with the fact that the number of indices in your code must match the rank of the array and you have a problem. If you want to create a summation routine to combine all the elements in an array, you need to write a separate routine for each rank of array you wish to support.

Writing equivalent support routines for each rank is not the only problem with high-rank arrays. Indexing items in multiple dimensions is much more expensive. The CalcIndex routine shown below is the VB code equivalent to the work required to access a single item in a multi-dimensional array. This calculation is necessary whenever you access an array element.

```
'Calculate the zero-based index for a given item based on
'the array bounds and a set of indices. Both arrays are
'listed with the least-significant (right-most) index first,
'so the first index is in position cBounds - 1
Private Function CalcIndex(Bounds() As SafeArrayBound, _
    Indices() As Long, ByVal cBounds As Long) As Long
Dim i As Long
    CalcIndex = Indices(0) - Bounds(0).lLbound
    For i = 0 To cBounds - 2
        CalcIndex = CalcIndex * (Bounds(i).cElements - 1) + _
                    (Indices(i + 1) - Bounds(i + 1).lLbound)
    Next i
End Function
```

If you write a routine that just wants an array regardless of rank, you should write the routine as if all incoming arrays were one dimensional with a zero lower bound, and then make sure you give the bulk of the routine a normalized array. You can do this by temporarily modifying the current array descriptor or by constructing a second array descriptor to point to the same data. I'll show the first approach and leave the second as an exercise.

In order to normalize an incoming array, you need to turn it into a zero-based, one-dimensional array with the total element count saved in the first dimension. In other words, you change the cDims, cElements, and lLbound items in the now familiar SafeArray1d structure. Just cache the old values, modify the descriptor, and restore the old values when you're done processing the array.

```
Private m_SADesc As SafeArray1d
Private m_pSADesc() As SafeArray1d
Private m_SABounds As SafeArray1d
Private m_pSABounds() As SafeArrayBound

Private Sub InitHelperArrays()
    With m_SADesc
        .cDims = 1
        .fFeatures = FADF_AUTO Or FADF_FIXEDSIZE
        .cLocks = 1
        .cElements = 1
        VBoost.Assign ByVal VarPtrArray(m_pSADesc), _
                    VarPtr(m_SADesc)
```

```
            End With
            With m_SABounds
                .cDims = 1
                .fFeatures = FADF_AUTO Or FADF_FIXEDSIZE
                .cLocks = 1
                .cbElements = LenB(m_pSABounds(0))
                VBoost.Assign ByVal VarPtrArray(m_pSABounds), _
                              VarPtr(m_SABounds)
            End With
        End Sub


'Modify the array descriptor to be one dimensional and zero
'based to enable processing any array as a one-dimensional
'array. Returns True if any changes were made.
Public Function NormalizeArray(ByVal ppSA As Long, _
    Bound0Start As SafeArrayBound, cDimsStart As Integer) _
    As Boolean
Dim i As Long
Dim lSize As Long
    With m_SADesc
        If .cDims = 0 Then InitHelperArrays
        .pvData = VBoost.Deref (ppSA)
        If .pvData = 0 Then Exit Function
        With m_pSADesc(0)
            m_SADesc.pvData = 0
            If .cDims = 1 And .lLbound = 0 Then Exit Function
            cDimsStart = .cDims
            Bound0Start.cElements = .cElements
            Bound0Start.lLbound = .lLbound
            m_SABounds.pvData = VarPtr(.cElements)
            m_SABounds.cElements = .cDims
            lSize = 1
            For i = 0 To .cDims - 1
                lSize = lSize * m_pSABounds(i).cElements
            Next i
            .cDims = 1
            .lLbound = 0
            .cElements = lSize
            m_SABounds.pvData = 0
        End With
    End With
```

```vba
    NormalizeArray = True
End Function


'Undo the temporary damage done by NormalizeArray
Public Sub UnNormalizeArray(ByVal ppSA As Long, _
  Bound0Start As SafeArrayBound, ByVal cDimsStart As Integer)
Dim i As Long
Dim lSize As Long
    With m_SADesc
        Debug.Assert .cDims 'Should call NormalizeArray first
        .pvData = VBoost.Deref(ppSA)
        If .pvData = 0 Then Exit Sub
        With m_pSADesc(0)
            .cDims = cDimsStart
            .cElements = Bound0Start.cElements
            .lLbound = Bound0Start.lLbound
        End With
        .pvData = 0
    End With
End Sub


'Calling code
Public Function TotalItems(Values() As Currency) As Currency
Dim fNormalized As Boolean
Dim Bound0Start As SafeArrayBound
Dim cDimsStart As Integer
Dim i As Long
    fNormalized = NormalizeArray( _
      VarPtrArray(Values), Bound0Start, cDimsStart)
    On Error GoTo Error
    For i = 0 To UBound(Values)
        TotalItems = TotalItems + Values(i)
    Next i
Error:
    If fNormalized Then
        UnNormalizeArray _
          VarPtrArray(Values), Bound0Start, cDimsStart
    End If
    With Err
        If .Number Then .Raise .Number, _
```

```
            .Source, .Description, .HelpFile, .HelpContext
        End With
    End Function
```

There's just one more twist to the normalized array story: none of the nor-
malization code you see here is necessary in a natively compiled executable
when bounds checking is turned off. In compiled code, you won't get an out-of-
range error if you specify an invalid index value. You also won't get an error if you
specify the wrong number of indices, although the program will crash if you
specify too many indices. When bounds checking is off, the only field the runtime looks at is the ILbound of each SafeArrayBound. cDims and cElements are
ignored. So for a compiled executable, your code can simply ignore the fact that
you have a multi-dimensional array. You simply need to know the lower bound of
the first dimension and the total number of items in the array. There is no need
to modify the array descriptor. I'll use a reduced version of NormalizeArray called
CountArrayElements to determine the element count.

```
Public Function CountArrayElements(ByVal ppSA As Long) As Long
Dim i As Long
Dim lSize As Long
    With m_SADesc
        If .cDims = 0 Then InitHelperArrays
        .pvData = VBoost.Deref(ppSA)
        If .pvData = 0 Then Exit Function
        With m_pSADesc(0)
            m_SADesc.pvData = 0
            m_SABounds.pvData = VarPtr(.cElements)
            m_SABounds.cElements = .cDims
            lSize = 1
            For i = 0 To .cDims - 1
                lSize = lSize * m_pSABounds(i).cElements
            Next i
            m_SABounds.pvData = 0
        End With
    End With
    CountArrayElements = lSize
End Function
```

```
'New, simplified calling code. Note that the error
'trapping is no longer necessary as the error handler
'was needed only to restore the array descriptor.
'This works for multi-dimensional arrays only
'when bounds checking is turned off.
Public Function TotalItems(Values() As Currency) As Currency
Dim i As Long
Dim LowerBound As Long
    LowerBound = LBound(Values)
    For i = LowerBound To _
            CountArrayElems(VarPtrArray(Values)) +
                            LowerBound - 1
        TotalItems = TotalItems + Values(i)
    Next i
End Function
```

Miscellaneous Tips for Using Arrays

There are a few more general comments on arrays I'd like to make that defy categorization. The end of the chapter is a good place to put them.

Returning Arrays from Functions

In VB, the name of a Function or Property Get procedure is also a local variable name within the same procedure. As a way of avoiding data duplication, I encourage you to use this implicit variable name in the main body of your code instead of just once at the end of the function. For example, if you have a function that returns a structure, you should use the first snippet shown below, not the second.

```
'Good code
Function FillStruct() As Struct
    With FillStruct
        'Fill in data
    End With
End Function

'Wasteful code, unnecessary copy
Function FillStruct() As Struct
Dim tmp As Struct
```

```
    With tmp
        'Fill in data
    End With
    FillStruct = tmp
End Function
```

It would be great if we could apply this principle to functions that return arrays. However, VB overloads parentheses so heavily that this is virtually impossible in practice.

There are three things you can do to an array: Pass it to another procedure, ReDim it, or access an array element. You can pass the implicit function name variable, but you cannot use the variable with ReDim or to access an array element. Both of these operations require parentheses, which VB interprets as a call to the function, not an index into the local array variable of the same name. This all but forces you to use a temporary array variable that you assign to the function name before returning.

The problem with assigning the temporary array variable to the function name is that you can end up copying the entire array. There are two ways to avoid this, one provided by VB, and one by VarPtrArray. If you assign a local array to the implicit function name variable immediately before an Exit Function/Property or End Function/Property statement, VB automatically transfers the array instead of copying it. If there is an intervening instruction (End If included, comments excluded), the array is copied instead of transferred.

Use the following code at any point in the function to avoid a full array copy by explicitly transferring ownership of the array to the function-name variable.

```
'tmp must be a variable-size array to ensure that the
'descriptor and data are on the heap instead of on the stack.
VBoost.AssignSwap _
    ByVal VarPtrArray(FuncName), ByVal VarPtrArray(tmp)
```

Cost of UBound and LBound

As mentioned earlier, the VB compiler performs quite a few optimizations when it operates on fixed-size arrays. However, these optimizations do not include compiling in the values of UBound and LBound. The compiler generates calls into the VB runtime for these functions. This is a good place to perform your own optimizations. You can use constant values for the bounds instead of UBound and LBound.

The Importance of *No Bounds Checking*

To keep your array access very fast, always select Remove Array Bounds Checks in the Advanced Optimizations dialog. Checking array bounds on every access is incredibly expensive. Error 9 (Subscript out of range) is also an error that should never occur in your production code. This is clearly a useful error during debugging, but there is absolutely no excuse for production code accessing an out-of-bounds element. If you don't turn off bounds checking, you're wasting a lot of cycles checking for an error that never actually happens. Selecting Remove Integer Overflow Checks and using Long variables to index your arrays also improves the access speed on your arrays.

Determining Element Size

Although you'd think that the element size for an array would be immediately apparent after looking at the element type of the array, it is not. LenB returns the number of bytes required by a type, but this value does not include any padding that might be used between array elements in order to keep the elements aligned on a 4-byte boundary. This wouldn't be a problem if all types were actually aligned on this boundary, but padding is used only if it is required to align the elements in the structure. It is not arbitrarily applied to all structures. For example, a structure with {Long, Integer} has a LenB of 6 and a cbElements of 8, but {Integer, Integer, Integer} has a LenB of 6 and a cbElements of 6 as well. The easiest way to determine the element count is to ask the array itself: look at the cbElements field, or use the SafeArrayGetElemsize API. You can also calculate the element count by using the formula VBoost.UDif(VarPtr(1), VarPtr(0)). The one thing you can't assume is that the element size and LenB are equivalent for anything other than simple types.

Memory Layout of Multi-Dimensional Arrays

SafeArrays use a row-major layout, unlike C++, which uses a column-major layout. This means that incrementing the last index moves to the closest array element. You can use the following code snippet to see the memory layout. This code outputs a sequentially ordered list of memory addresses.

```
Dim Bytes() As Byte
Dim i As Long, j As Long, k As Long
ReDim Bytes(1, 2, 3)
    For i = 0 To 3
        For j = 0 To 2
            For k = 0 To 1
                Debug.Print Hex$(VarPtr(Bytes(k, j, i)))
            Next k
        Next j
    Next i
```

The SafeArray API set and the descriptor layout do nothing to help clear up the confusion about memory layout. SafeArrayCreate takes an array of SafeArrayBound elements in row-major (VB) order, but the descriptor itself stores the list in reverse order, which is really column-major (C++) order. SafeArrayGetElement and other APIs also take the indices in reverse order. So in order to get the element that is Bytes(1, 2, 3) in VB, you pass indices of {3, 2, 1} to SafeArrayGetElement, and use ((unsigned char*)psa->pvData)[3][2][1] in C++.

C++ and SafeArrays

I've talked to many C++ developers who do not like to use SafeArrays. Whenever I hear this, I ask which SafeArray API functions they use. Invariably I get a very long list: SafeArrayCreate, SafeArrayAllocDescriptor, SafeArrayAllocData, SafeArrayPutElement, SafeArrayGetElement, SafeArrayAccessData, and so on. None of these calls is necessary in Win32. In C++, you can simply use a stack-based SAFEARRAY descriptor, fill in the fields, and point your pvData to the appropriate block of memory, which can be stack allocated with _alloca if you don't already have one. In Win32, pvData is also valid without locking the array or using SafeArrayGetElement. Simply cast pvData to the appropriate type and use it as a normal C-style array. If you stay away from the API set and populate your own structure, you'll stop cursing the complexities of SAFEARRAY integration.

Chapter 3

IUnknown: An Unknown Quantity

VB creates and consumes COM objects. All COM objects are derived from the IUnknown interface. However, IUnknown is not synonymous with VB's Object keyword. In VB, As Object is actually synonymous with IDispatch*, that wonderfully versatile interface that we all support but rarely use. (You're all vtable binding, right?) IUnknown* has no corresponding native type in VB. The fact that VB doesn't allow you to declare a variable with a native IUnknown type causes a variety of subtle complications when you deal with low-level object manipulations, such as the weak referencing and the aggregation techniques described in this book. This chapter takes a close look at VB's use of the IUnknown interface, and at how to pass, declare, and call the IUnknown interface in VB.

Any discussion of an interface must first define what the interface's member functions do. IUnknown has three functions: QueryInterface, AddRef, and Release. Let's look first at AddRef and Release. AddRef is called when you obtain a reference to an object, and Release is called when the reference is no longer needed. AddRef increments an internal reference count, and Release decrements the same count. When the internal reference count reaches 0, Release calls the object's Terminate event and then frees the object's memory. The AddRef and Release functions take no parameters and return the current reference count on the object. Although the return value is generally the internal reference count, you cannot rely on this number to reflect the inner reference count for all object implementations. If Release returns 0, you know that the object has been destroyed. If it returns anything else, the object is still alive.

QueryInterface (QI for short) is used to ask a COM object for references to specific interfaces. This involves passing an interface identifier (IID), which is what a Globally Unique IDentifier (GUID) is called when it's used to identify an interface. If the COM object supports the interface, a pointer to the implementation of the interface is returned. If the IID is not supported, an error is returned. If a pointer is returned successfully, then AddRef or an internal equivalent is called on the object before QueryInterface returns. Consumers of COM objects manage an object's lifetime by balancing all successful QueryInterface calls and all AddRef calls with a corresponding call to Release. If all the consumers follow the rules, everything goes smoothly. But if Release is not called often enough to balance all the QI and AddRef calls, you end up with memory leaks. If you call Release too often, VB will most likely crash. Except in the case of circular references (see Chapter 6), VB balances the IUnknown calls automatically without a hitch.

The QueryInterface VB provides for a standard class supports the IUnknown and IDispatch interfaces, and the VB-generated IID for the interface implicitly defined by the public procedures in a class. As you add Implements statements, QI becomes smarter and supports the additional interface implementations as well. If you add features to your object, such as by making it public or by supporting persistence, VB adds support for interfaces such as IExternalConnection, IProvideClassInfo, IPersistStream, IPersistStreamInit, IPersistPropertyBag, and so on. If you create a UserControl class, VB also adds support for IOleObject, IOleControl, IOleInPlaceObject, IOleInPlaceActiveObject, IQuickActivate, and so on. In other words, VB makes your objects a persistable class, ActiveX control, or ActiveX document by adding support for additional interfaces. QueryInterface is the key to the entire process.

With all these references being returned and QI returning different pointers for different IIDs sent to the same QI call, how can all these references be identified as the same COM object? COM has two rules for establishing object identity across multiple references. First, when you QI any of the returned references for IID_IUnknown, you always get the same pointer back. Second, if any reference supports an IID, the same IID must be supported by all references that the object returns. Support for both of these COM identity rules generally involves implementing a "controlling IUnknown" object. Every returned reference includes an internal reference to the controlling IUnknown, and all QI calls are simply forwarded to the controlling IUnknown. The controlling IUknown object then maps the requested interface to a specific object.

VB and IUnknown

All VB variable types are compatible with the Variant types defined by OLE Automation. Among the Variant types, there are three object types that VB can handle: VT_DISPATCH, VT_UNKNOWN, and VT_USERDEFINED. A VT_DISPATCH type corresponds to VB's Object type. This type of object supports IDispatch (that is, late binding). VT_UNKNOWN does not have a corresponding type in VB, but VB *can* call functions with this parameter type. VT_USERDEFINED covers all other object types. VT_USERDEFINED also has type information associated with it, such as the object's IID and information about the IID's base interfaces.

VB interacts with the IUnknown interface when you use the Set statement, when you pass an object variable to a parameter during a function call, and when you use the Is or TypeOf…Is operators. Let's first look at the Set statement.

Set and IUnknown

A VB object variable can have two states: Is Nothing (no current reference) and Not Is Nothing (a current reference). Not surprisingly, Is Nothing corresponds to a 0 value in the underlying variable, which you can verify by checking ObjPtr(Nothing). The simplest use of the Set statement is the Set ObjVar = Nothing statement. Set ObjVar = Nothing does nothing if ObjVar Is Nothing. Otherwise, it calls the IUnknown.Release function on ObjVar and assigns a 0 value to the variable. VB automatically calls the Release function for all object variables that go out of scope with a nonzero value.

Using Set to assign a current reference to an object variable is definitely more interesting. You might think that a Set assignment always calls QueryInterface, but it doesn't. In fact, many Set statements simply perform an AddRef rather than a QueryInterface. VB prefers a simple, fast AddRef over an expensive QI. When the VB compiler encounters a Set statement, it examines the types of the variables on both sides of the expression. (Although you can't declare a VT_UNKNOWN in VB, I'm including VT_UNKNOWN in the table for the imminent discussion on parameter passing.)

In this table, the variable's type is shown to the left of the equals statement going down, and the type of the right-hand side expression going across. The types represented fall into five categories.

- UNK=VT_UNKNOWN type
- DISP=VT_DISPATCH
- USER:DISP= VT_USERDEFINED with IDispatch support
- USER:UNK=VT_USERDEFINED with no IDispatch support
- RHLS=LHS means that the type of the left-hand variable is exactly the same as the right-hand expression

Notice how assigning to VT_UNKNOWN never performs a QI, and assigning to the same user-defined type never performs a QI. Assigning to an As Object variable (VT_DISPATCH) only performs a QI if the type on the right is not derived from IDispatch. If you assign between VB-defined object types, which are always derived from IDispatch, VB never performs a QI when assigning to an As Object variable, nor does it perform a QI when assigning to a variable of the same type. VB performs a QI when you assign between different types, which generally happens only when you try to get an implemented interface from an object.

Table 3.1   Determining when a Set statement uses QI or AddRef

LHS ⇓, RHS ⇒	RHS=LHS	UNK	DISP	USER:DISP	USER:UNK
UNK	A	A	A	A	A
DISP	A	QI	A	A	QI
USER:DISP	A	QI	QI	QI	QI
USER:UNK	A	QI	QI	QI	QI

For the sake of discussion, let's look at what would happen with polymorphic objects (a fancy term for objects with multiple-interface support) if VB were to perform a QueryInterface when assigning to an As Object variable. In this scenario, Class1 implements Class2, and Class2 has a Test method.

```
Dim Cls2 As Class2
Dim Obj As Object
Set Cls2 = New Class1 'QI for IID__Class2
Set Obj = Cls2 'Hypothetical QI for IID_IDispatch
Obj.Test 'Late bound call to Test fails
```

Why does the late-bound test call fail in this hypothetical scenario? It fails because the QI call for IDispatch is passed back to the controlling IUnknown, which can return multiple interfaces with IDispatch support. QI ignores the ambiguity inherent in the IID_IDispatch request and returns its primary interface: Class1, not Class2. Class1 doesn't have a Test method, and the IDispatch call fails. This example shows that if VB actually performed an arbitrary QI for IDispatch, it could not support late-bound calls on secondary interfaces. Attempting to retrieve the IDispatch from a secondary interface actually retrieves the IDispatch for the primary interface.

Parameters and IUnknown

Passing a variable or expression to a parameter is a lot like assigning the variable or expression to a variable of the same type as the parameter. Multiplying the two types of Set statement assignment (AddRef and QI) by the parameter modifiers (ByVal and ByRef) yields four permutations that VB must handle when passing to object parameters. We'll examine each of these permutations in terms of the IUnknown functions called in order to make it possible to pass the parameter.

ByVal, QI Required

Caller: **QI** the passed variable for the parameter's type and store the result in a temporary object variable. If the incoming variable is Nothing, initialize the temporary variable to Nothing. Pass the temporary variable.

Callee: **AddRef** the incoming ByVal parameter at the top of the function (VB-generated code does this, but COM objects written in other languages might not).

Callee: **Release** the parameter when it leaves scope.

Caller: **Release** the temporary variable.

ByVal, No QI Required

Caller: **AddRef** the original variable and pass it.

Callee: **AddRef** when entering the function.

Callee: **Release** when exiting the function.

Caller: **Release** the original variable.

ByRef, QI Required

Caller: **QI** to get the correct type, and store the result in a temporary variable. Pass the address of the temporary variable.

Callee: Nothing to do.

Caller: If the temporary is not Nothing, QI the current reference in the temporary variable for the type of the passed parameter. Place the return reference in a second temporary variable.

Caller: **Release** the first temporary reference.

Caller: **Release** the reference in the original variable.

Caller: Move the value from the second temporary to the original variable.

ByRef, No QI Required

Caller: Pass the address of the variable (that's all).

Obviously, if you pass items of the same type, it makes the most sense to use ByRef passing, especially within your own project. Although IUnknown's overhead is not great, you need to be aware of the other implications of ByRef object parameters. If you pass ByRef to untrusted code, you give the callee the chance to invalidate your data. This isn't always a good idea. Also, if you pass an object to a method of an object in a different thread, don't use ByRef: this forces the marshaler to move your object in both directions. Of course, if you're retrieving an object instead of sending it, you need the ByRef parameter.

ByRef calls that involve mismatched types are clearly disastrous. I've rarely seen a case in which the developer really needs this capability. In most cases, the callee doesn't actually change the incoming reference, so you end up running a lot of unnecessary code, just in case. The QI that comes after the function call seems really bizarre because it happens after the function returns. If the extra QI isn't enough to scare you away from such calls, the amount of code generated in order to handle them should be. In the case of ByVal calls, the AddRef/Release call happens in the callee, so there is no extra IUnknown work to be done by the caller. However, in the case of ByRef calls, the entire IUnknown burden falls on the caller, so the code is generated everywhere the function is called with a mismatched type. The code required for a mismatched ByRef call is roughly twice the size of the code required for a mismatched ByVal. Avoid this construct unless you are truly using the parameter as a ByRef.

I didn't put the As Any and void* parameter types in the chart because they're not very exciting. Although As Any (used in VB Declare statements) and void* (used in typelib declarations) behave differently with respect to strings, they behave the same with respect to object types, so I'll address them together. When passing an object to a ByRef As Any parameter, VB passes the address of the object variable. When passing to a ByVal As Any, VB passes the value of the object variable. The caller never makes an IUnknown call in this case. (I told you it wasn't very exciting.) The lack of a QI with As Any types is a boon that I'll take advantage of to handle weak and circular references.

Is and TypeOf...Is Operators

Because a single COM object can return multiple references with different pointer values, it is not possible to tell if two object references belong to the same COM object just by checking their pointer values. If ObjPtr(x) = ObjPtr(y), then x and y are clearly part of the same COM object. However, ObjPtr(x) <> ObjPtr(y) does not indicate that x and y are *not* part of the same COM object.

VB provides the Is operator for making definitive identity equivalence tests for two object references. The Is operator uses the COM identity rule that says all references obtained from the same COM object return the same controlling IUnknown pointer. The Is operator performs a QI on each reference for

IID_IUnknown, compares the returned IUnknown pointers, and calls Release on each IUnknown pointer to balance the QI-generated reference. If the IUnknown pointers are the same, Is returns True. Is also returns True if both references are Nothing.

VB also provides the TypeOf...Is operator as a test to determine whether an object supports a particular interface. TypeOf *x* Is *y* performs a QI against *x* for the *y* interface. If the QI succeeds, Release is called on the returned reference, and TypeOf...Is returns True. I don't recommend using TypeOf...Is: A QI can be an expensive operation, especially when an object is created in response to the QI. In the following code, you end up running the QI/Release cycle twice.

```
Dim x As SomeClass
Dim pIFoo As IFoo
If TypeOf x Is pIFoo Then 'QI now/Release now
    Set pIFoo = x 'QI now/Release later
End If
```

The alternative to this code is to use a Set statement with error trapping code. Although this code isn't as pretty, it is more efficient because you only perform one QI for IFoo. Even with the error-trapping overhead, this alternative beats the other code by about 15 percent; potentially much more if the object supports a lot of interfaces.

```
Dim x As SomeClass
Dim pIFoo As IFoo
On Error Resume Next
Set pIFoo = x
On Error GoTo 0
If Not pIFoo Is Nothing then
    'Process against IFoo
End If
```

Declaring IUnknown and Calling Its Functions

At the beginning of this chapter, I said that you can't declare a variable with an IUnknown type in VB. You may think this statement is false because you've declared a variable As IUnknown in your code, or you may have seen it done in published code. The subtle distinction here is that VB treats As IUnknown as a VT_USERDEFINED type with an IID of IID_IUnknown and not as a true VT_UNKNOWN.

If you can't declare a variable as IUnknown and compile, your project has no reference to the stdole (OLE Automation) type library, contained in stdole2.tlb. Use the Project/References dialog to add this library if the project doesn't have it already. At this point, the compiler recognizes the IUnknown type, but you still don't see it in the statement completion list: IUnknown is a hidden type. If you *really* want to see it, open the Object Browser's context menu and make sure that *Show Hidden Members* is selected.

You can easily tell that the IUnknown reference you get from stdole.IUnknown is not a VT_UNKNOWN because assigning to a VT_ UNKNOWN does not generate a QueryInterface call. When you assign a VB-defined class instance to an IUnknown variable, checking the object's pointer indicates that you are looking at a different interface. This makes it clear that a QI has taken place. This also demonstrates that the VB class's controlling IUnknown and its primary interface are not the same.

```
'In Class1
Private Sub Class_Initialize()
Dim pUnk As IUnknown
    Set pUnk = Me
    Debug.Print Hex$(ObjPtr(Me)), Hex$(ObjPtr(pUnk))
End Sub

'Output
19D988        19D9A4
```

If you use IUnknown types when you generate type libraries (as shown in Chapter 6), you can take advantage of VB's different treatment of VT_UNKNOWN and stdole.IUnknown. For example, VBoost provides a function called CreateDelegator (see "IUnknown Hooking" in Chapter 5). The first parameter takes a stdole.IUnknown type (shown as **IUnknown** in the Object Browser), and the second parameter has type VT_UNKNOWN (shown simply as *Unknown*). CreateDelegator's first parameter needs the controlling IUnknown of the object from VB, but the second parameter does not. By using stdole.IUnknown in the typelib definition, I'm able to omit the QI for IID_IUnknown in the CreateDelegator routine itself because I know VB has already made the call for me.

If you want to assign to an IUnknown variable without performing a QI, you can use one of two functions defined by VBoost. The first, AssignAddRef, works just like the Assign function, copying the pSrc parameter to the pDst. After assigning pSrc to pDst, AssignAddRef calls AddRef to increase the reference count. There is no QI call since the parameters are declared As Any. The second function, SafeUnknown, takes a VT_UNKNOWN parameter and returns a stdole.IUnknown. Unlike AssignAddRef, SafeUnknown can be used inline.

```
'In Class1
Private Sub Class_Initialize()
Dim pUnk As IUnknown
    VBoost.AssignAddRef pUnk, Me
    Debug.Print Hex$(ObjPtr(Me)), Hex$(ObjPtr(pUnk)), _
    Hex$(ObjPtr(VBoost.SafeUnknown(Me)))
End Sub

'Output
19D988        19D988        19D988
```

Now that you have a variable with type IUnknown, you're probably just itching to call QueryInterface, AddRef, and Release. However, when you type "punk.", you don't get a statement completion list. The list is missing because all three of the IUnknown methods are marked as restricted, so the VB compiler doesn't let you call them. Restricting these methods was a deliberate decision of the OLE Automation/VB designers: VB wants to manage IUnknown interaction for you without having you throw a wrench in the works, and restricting the IUnknown methods locks you out quite effectively. Before I show you how to work around the lock, I must say that you will rarely need to do this. The designers of VB were correct in keeping IUnknown under wraps: Calling AddRef and Release explicitly leads to an unstable system, especially during debugging.

In order to call the IUnknown methods, you have to define yet another type with the same IID as stdole.IUnknown. I've provided such a type in VBoostTypes6.Olb called IUnknownUnrestricted. The parameter definitions in this rendition of

IUnknown make it ideal for use while implementing wrapper objects whose own IUnknown implementations defer to inner objects. For example, the UnknownHook and ROTHook objects shown later use IUnknownUnrestricted to call the IUnknown functions on wrapped inner objects.

The AddRef and Release definitions look just like the native function definitions, except they return Long instead of unsigned long values. QueryInterface, however, is modified to return a long instead of an HRESULT. This means that VB doesn't raise an error automatically when the call fails. The output parameter is also changed from a void** to a ByRef Long: VB can't do much with a void**. Here are a couple of sample snippets that use IUnknownUnrestricted. Once again, please don't interpret this as an endorsement of the frequent use of this interface.

```vb
'Check the current refcount of an object by reading
'the return values from IUnknown.Release. This is a
'handy debugging function, but not one you should
'rely on in production code.
Function RefCount(ByVal pUnkUR As IUnknownUnrestricted) As Long
    'Balance the pending Release
    pUnkUR.AddRef
    'Reduce the value returned by Release down 2
    'because pUnkUR is itself holding a reference, and
    'the implicit temporary variable in the calling
    'function also holds a reference.
    RefCount = pUnkUR.Release - 2
End Function

'Calling code: output is 1 for a VB class module
Dim cls1 As New Class1
Debug.Print RefCount(cls1)

'Call QueryInterface to get an IDispatch object. This is
'equivalent to setting an As Object variable to a type that is
'not derived from IDispatch
Function GetDispatch(ByVal pUnkUR As IUnknownUnrestricted) As Object
Dim IID_IDispatch As VBGUID
Dim pvObj As Long
Dim hr As Long
```

```
IID_IDispatch = _
    IIDFromString("{00020400-0000-0000-C000-000000000046}")
hr = pUnkUR.QueryInterface(IID_IDispatch, pvObj)
If hr Then Err.Raise hr
VBoost.Assign GetDispatch, pvObj
End Function
```

The moral of the GetDispatch function: If you know the IID at compile time—which you almost always do—just use the Set statement.

Chapter 4

Binding Functions to Objects

Once you've used the New, CreateObject, or GetObject keywords to create an object, you invariably want to call a method or read a property on the object. After all, an object isn't much good if you can't do anything with it once you have it. In order to call a member function on an object, VB must perform an operation known as *binding*. I'll define binding as "the process of determining the location of a specific function based on the pointer to the object."

All types of binding use static compile-time data together with the dynamic runtime value of the object's pointer to find the function to call. All binding falls into two categories. In the first category, generally referred to as "vtable binding," the compiler generates code that applies a simple formula that locates the function based on the pointer to the object and a static function offset. In the second category, called "IDispatch" or "late binding," there is not enough compile-time information to locate the function directly, so the compiler turns control over to a helper function on the object. The helper function, called "Invoke," then locates and delegates to the real function.

The formula for locating a vtable-bound function relies on the running objects *virtual function table* (which is what "vtable" stands for). The vtable is an ordered array of function pointers. By convention, the vtable pointer is stored in the object's first item. As you'll see later in the discussion on lightweight objects, this leading vtable member is in fact the only difference between a COM object and a normal structure. Here is the function for determining a function pointer given a function offset. The function offset is the zero-based position of the function in the vtable array multiplied by the size of a function pointer—4 in Win32.

```
Function VTableEntry( _
    ByVal pObj As Long, ByVal Offset As Long) As Long
        With VBoost
            .Assign VTableEntry, ByVal .UAdd(.Deref(pObj), Offset)
        End With
End Function


'Calling code. 24 is the 7th function, which is
'the standard IDispatch::Invoke entry for any
'object that supports IDispatch
Debug.Print VTableEntry(ObjPtr(SomeObj), 24)
```

The compiler retrieves a function offset from the type library that describes the type. The offset is then compiled into the code along with information for providing parameters to the function and reading its return value. If you reduce the VTableEntry formula to assembly code with a constant offset, you can see why vtable binding is very fast, especially when compared to the IDispatch binding I look at next.

	Members			Functions Pointers	Group
O	pVTable	→	**V**	QueryInterface	IUnknown Functions
	cRefs			AddRef	
b	etc.		**T**	Release	
				GetTypeInfoCount	IDispatch Functions
j			**a**	GetTypeInfo	
				GetIDsOfNames	
e			**b**	Invoke	
				FirstMethod	Custom Functions
c			**l**	SecondMethod	
				ThirdMethod	
t			**e**	etc.	

Figure 4.1. The first member of any COM object is pointer to the vtable for that class of object. The vtable itself is a list of function pointers.

IDispatch binding is also a vtable-based mechanism, but the vtable entries called by VB are not the target functions. The vtable entries used to IDispatch bind are GetIDsOfNames and Invoke on the IDispatch interface. These functions reside at the vtable offsets of 20 and 24 bytes, respectively. IDispatch uses an ID base system, where each function has a long numeric identifier, known as a MEMBERID or DISPID. Invoke also takes an INVOKEKIND parameter, which controls how the function is called: as a normal function (with the function to the right of an equals sign, or without getting a return value), as a Property Get (which is like a function, except you can't ignore the return value), as a Property Let (the function name is to the left of the equals sign), or as a Property Set (the function name is to the left of the equals sign in a Set statement). The ID and INVOKEKIND uniquely identify the function. The Invoke function also takes an array of parameters stored in a Variant array in reverse order, the return type as an output Variant, and a variety of parameters for returning error information. Clearly, it is a lot more work to bind with the generic Invoke function than with a direct vtable call.

There are actually two types of IDispatch binding. The first type, called "early-id binding," occurs when the compiler has type information about the object from a type library, but the object does not support a vtable beyond the IDispatch entries. In such a case, the compiler can look up the ID at compile time, verify the parameters being passed to the function, and provide IntelliSense lists and function descriptions. In fact, early-id binding is indistinguishable from vtable binding from within the VB IDE. You have to examine the typelib to determine whether you're vtable bound. Currently, the only common objects that don't support vtable binding are custom controls on a form, which we'll look at later in this chapter.

In the second type of IDispatch binding, called "late binding," the compiler can't retrieve information about the function at compile time. In practice, this happens when the variable or expression you're binding to returns Variant or Object (this is Object with a capital O, meaning As Object, as opposed to "an object type," which means any object type). When you're coding, it is obvious when you're adding a late-bound call to your code: You get no IntelliSense information.

Unlike early-id binding, late binding requires a name lookup as well as a call to the Invoke function. A name is translated into an ID using the

IDispatch.GetIDsOfNames function. The name/ID translation adds significant overhead to the call, especially in cases in which you make cross-thread or cross-process calls. The Implements keyword (discussed in Chapter 5) leaves little excuse for using late binding in your code. If you use late binding, you're asking for performance degradation and runtime bugs that the compiler would have caught had you used hard-typed object variables. The exception to this rule is scenarios that require name binding at runtime (see "Name Binding at Runtime" in this chapter).

When Are Objects Bound to?

Apart from avoiding late binding, there is little you can do to affect how VB binds objects to functions. However, you can affect *when* VB binds. Clearly, VB binds a function to an object whenever you use the dot operator between an object variable or expression and a function call. But you don't actually have to use a dot in your code in order to make VB generate a bound-function call.

The first place where VB generates binding code for you automatically is with application objects. When a type library specifies the appobject attribute on a creatable class, VB automatically declares an implicit As New variable with the name and type of the class. The compiler then attempts to bind unqualified names to the implicit variable. For example, the DBEngine class in the DAO object model is flagged as an application object, so VB automatically provides the following declaration for you.

```
Public DBEngine As New DBEngine
```

This implicit declaration has project-level scope. The compiler resolves names to this scoping level after it tries local, module-level, and global scope. In the first two lines of the following code snippet, the library name works as a name-resolution operator that tells the compiler which library to bind to. This qualifier lets the compiler bypass the name search in higher-priority scoping levels and in referenced libraries with priorities above DAO. However, specifying the library name does not generate extra code. Since DBEngine is an application object, it always binds to the Workspaces function, regardless of whether you actually typed the DBEngine name. The four lines shown below generate exactly the same code.

```
Dim iCount As Integer
iCount = DAO.DBEngine.Workspaces.Count
iCount = DAO.Workspaces.Count
iCount = DBEngine.Workspaces.Count
iCount = Workspaces.Count
```

VB has its own application object called Global. App, Screen, Forms, and other objects are all retrieved from methods on Global. When you use App.Title, you're actually using VB.Global.App.Title, which is two bound calls. When working with application objects, VB not only generates code that calls the implicit vtable function, it also generates code that ensures that the variable has been instantiated in response to the As New declaration. The code you don't see before App.Title performs the following tasks and repeats those tasks whenever you reference the global App object directly.

```
Dim tmpGlobal As VB.Global
If VB.Global Is Nothing Then Set VB.Global = New VB.Global
Set tmpGlobal = VB.Global
tmpGlobal.App.Title
Set tmpGlobal = Nothing
```

The second type of object to which you bind automatically is the Me object. For example, when you place a command button on a form and enter Text1.Text = "Power VB", Text1 is a function call, not a variable. Unlike application objects, the implicit Me object is guaranteed to be instantiated and easily accessible as a local variable. This results in less overhead for a function bound to the Me object than for a function bound to an application object.

The third type of hidden dot calls a default method or property. To continue with the DAO example, Workspaces has an Item object as its default member function. Workspaces(0).Name is actually three bound calls: DBEngine. Workspaces, Workspaces.Item, and Workspace.Name. If you watch the Intelli-Sense windows as you type, you can recognize default members as those with names that don't correspond to the name on which the window is anchored. Typing Workspaces(opens a tip window that says "*Item*(**Item**) As Workspace". Moving the cursor one character to the left changes the window to "**Workspaces** As Workspaces". Since the bound name is different before and after the opening parenthesis, you can tell that a call to Item is generated automatically when you put a nonempty parameter list after Workspaces.

As a general rule, your code's speed is inversely proportional to the number of bound calls you make. There are several things you can do to reduce the number of bound calls you force the compiler to make.

- Don't hesitate to cache results in local variables. Behind the scenes, VB creates hidden locals for you for holding the return values of method and property calls. You might as well hang onto the values and use them again. The following code snippets select all the text in Text1. The snippets accomplish the same thing, but the second snippet binds to Text1 only once. Although you don't gain anything for one call, it eliminates n-1 calls to the Text1 function if you set n properties on the Text1 object.

```
'Use Text1 for each call
Text1.SelStart = 0
Text1.SelLength = &HFFFF&

'Use a local variable
Dim txtTmp As TextBox
Set txtTmp = Text1
txtTmp.SelStart = 0
txtTmp.SelLength = &HFFFF&
```

- Remember that using a With statement against an object is equivalent to assigning the object a local variable. With statements offer many other benefits: You don't have to declare the variable, you have less code to type, and the code is nicely organized. If you access application objects in a With statement, you eliminate all but one of the extra implicit Is Nothing checks and method calls that happen implicitly when you use the method name directly. The one disadvantage of a With statement is that you can have only one active With context at a time.

```
With App
    .Title = "I'm Back"
```

```
        .TaskVisible = True
End With
```

- Don't repeat the same call chain in the same function unless you expect a different result. I see this type of code far too often, and I cringe every time. The following code is slow, hard to read, and hard to maintain. You would never write code like this in C++: It takes too long to generate code that does this much. Just because you can write the code quickly in VB doesn't mean that VB can run the code quickly.

```
TreeView1.Nodes.Add , , "P1", "ParentNode1"
TreeView1.Nodes.Add _
   TreeView1.Nodes("P1"), tvwChild, "P1C1", "ChildNode1"
TreeView1.Nodes.Add _
   TreeView1.Nodes("P1"), tvwChild, "P1C2", "ChildNode1"

'Repaired code: cuts bound calls from 15 to 5
'and is a lot easier to read.
Dim ParentNode As Node
With TreeView1.Nodes
    Set ParentNode = .Add(, , "P1", "ParentNode1")
    .Add ParentNode, tvwChild, "P1C1", "ChildNode1"
    .Add ParentNode, tvwChild, "P1C2", "ChildNode1"
End With
```

Reducing the number of bound calls helps you in three ways. First, VB doesn't have to generate binding code multiple times. Second, the objects you call don't have to run the same code repeatedly. And third, the size of the generated code is reduced significantly. In many cases, the size of the code may have the biggest effect on your application's performance. Loading code into memory is expensive. The less you have to load, the better off you'll be.

I'm not claiming that vtable-bound calls to objects in the same thread perform poorly and cause bottlenecks in your application if you call too many of them. In fact, the performance is very good. However, you generate thousands of bound calls in a typical application, and the overhead *does* add up. Simply by using local variables and With statements, and by writing code once instead of multiple times, you can make a big difference in the overall performance of your application.

Name Binding at Runtime

In some specialized applications, you may want to code against objects that weren't available at compile time. For example, a data-driven application can dynamically create objects, determine the methods and properties from a database or from the objects themselves, and then call the object through IDispatch. Although such a practice is infinitely flexible, it carries with it a performance penalty, absolutely no compilation checking, and a lot of extra code. See the November 1999 *Visual Basic Programmer's Journal* for the article "Inspect Dynamic Objects."

VB6 provides the CallByName function that allows you to make the actual call at runtime, but you'll hit a wall if you use it for very long. Any parameters for such a call are passed in the Args parameter, which is a ParamArray. This means that you need to know the number of parameters your as-yet-undefined method will have. If you knew the parameter count, you'd know the function name and probably wouldn't be using name binding in the first place.

CallByName also forces you to pass the same name every time instead of passing a MemberID. If you call the same member function a number of times, you double the overhead by repeatedly calling GetIDsOfNames to translate the name into a MemberID. Calling objects in a different thread, process, or machine is very expensive, and doubling the number of calls for no good reason is simply a bad idea.

IDispatch is not a particularly VB-friendly interface, but you *can* call it. IDispatch's interface and all its methods are restricted, so you can't declare a variable of type IDispatch in VB, nor can you call any of its methods. In addition, many of the types used are not VB-friendly as defined in stdole2.Tlb (OLE Automation), and calling a function pointer is often required to populate error information.

The VBoostTypes library solves all of the declaration problems by defining an IDispatchCallable interface and VB-friendly versions of EXCEPINFO and DISPPARAMS. There's also a function pointer prototype defined that enables deferred filling of the rich error information (see Chapter 11 on calling function pointers).

Using the IDispatchCallable definitions in VBoostTypes, I've coded replacement functions for CallByName. The first function, GetMemberID, translates a name into a MemberID, which is then passed to CallInvoke. CallInvoke works much like CallByName, except it accepts only a MemberID, not a name. Also the parameters must be specified in reverse order: the order that IDispatch.Invoke requires. There are three more versions of CallInvoke that I'll discuss later. The GetMemberID and CallInvoke functions shown here are included on the book's CD-ROM. You can find them in CallDispatch.Bas, and you'll need to add FunctionDelegator.bas to your project.

```
'Shared variables and constants
Private GUID_NULL As VBGUID
Private Const DISPID_PROPERTYPUT As Long = -3
Public Const VT_BYREF As Long = &H4000
Public Enum DispInvokeFlags
    INVOKE_FUNC = 1
    INVOKE_PROPERTYGET = 2
    INVOKE_PROPERTYPUT = 4
    INVOKE_PROPERTYPUTREF = 8
End Enum


'GetMemberID Function, calls GetIDsOfNames
Public Function GetMemberID( _
  ByVal pObject As Object, Name As String) As Long
Dim pCallDisp As IDispatchCallable
Dim hr As Long
    VBoost.AssignSwap pCallDisp, pObject
    hr = pCallDisp.GetIDsOfNames( _
      GUID_NULL, VarPtr(Name), 1, 0, VarPtr(GetMemberID))
    If hr Then Err.Raise hr
End Function


'CallInvoke Function calls Invoke
Public Function CallInvoke( _
  ByVal pObject As Object, _
  ByVal MemberID As Long, _
  ByVal InvokeKind As DispInvokeFlags, _
  ParamArray ReverseArgList() As Variant) As Variant
Dim pSAReverseArgList() As Variant
    'Swap the ParamArray into a normal local variable to enable
    'passing it to CallInvokeHelper. This is done by reading
    'the VarPtr of the stack's previous variable. This is
```

```
             'possible because InvokeKind is a simple type and passed
             'ByVal, so its VarPtr points to the area of
             'the stack used for the initial incoming function
             'parameters. For ByVal String and Object types, VarPtr
             'refers to a local variable that is a copy or reference
             'to the location on the stack, so you can use this
             'trick only for normal parameters. This is required because
             'VB doesn't let you pass a ParamArray to a normal array,
             'including the array parameter defined by VarPtrArray.
             With VBoost
                 .AssignSwap _
                     ByVal VarPtrArray(pSAReverseArgList), _
                     ByVal .Deref(.UAdd(VarPtr(InvokeKind), 4))
             End With
             'Call the helper with pVarResult set to the address
             'of this function's return value.
             CallInvokeHelper pObject, MemberID, InvokeKind, _
                 VarPtr(CallInvoke), pSAReverseArgList
         End Function


         Private Sub CallInvokeHelper(pObject As Object, _
             ByVal MemberID As Long, ByVal InvokeKind As Integer, _
             ByVal pVarResult As Long, ReverseArgList() As Variant)
         Dim pCallDisp As IDispatchCallable
         Dim hr As Long
         Dim ExcepInfo As VBEXCEPINFO
         Dim uArgErr As UINT
         Dim FDDeferred As FunctionDelegator
         Dim pFillExcepInfo As ICallDeferredFillIn
         Dim lBoundArgs As Long
         Dim dispidNamedArg As DISPID
         Dim Params As VBDISPPARAMS

             'Fill the fields in the DISPPARAMS structure
             lBoundArgs = LBound(ReverseArgList)
             With Params
                 .cArgs = UBound(ReverseArgList) - lBoundArgs + 1
                 If .cArgs Then
                     .rgvarg = VarPtr(ReverseArgList(lBoundArgs))
                 End If
```

```
        If InvokeKind And _
            (INVOKE_PROPERTYPUT Or INVOKE_PROPERTYPUTREF) Then
            dispidNamedArg = DISPID_PROPERTYPUT
            .cNamedArgs = 1
            .rgdispidNamedArgs = VarPtr(dispidNamedArg)
            'Make sure the RHS parameter is not VT_BYREF.
            VariantCopyInd ReverseArgList(lBoundArgs), _
                        ReverseArgList(lBoundArgs)
        End If
    End With


    'Move the incoming variable into a type we can call.
    VBoost.AssignSwap pCallDisp, pObject

    'Make the actual call
    hr = pCallDisp.Invoke(MemberID, GUID_NULL, 0, _
      InvokeKind, Params, pVarResult, ExcepInfo, uArgErr)


    'Handle errors
    If hr = DISP_E_EXCEPTION Then
        'ExcepInfo has the information we need
        With ExcepInfo
            If .pfnDeferredFillIn Then
                Set pFillExcepInfo = _
                    InitDelegator(FDDeferred, .pfnDeferredFillIn)
                pFillExcepInfo.Fill ExcepInfo
                .pfnDeferredFillIn = 0
            End If
            Err.Raise .scode, .bstrSource, .bstrDescription, _
              .bstrHelpFile, .dwHelpContext
        End With
    ElseIf hr Then
        Err.Raise hr
    End If
End Sub
```

You can refer to MSDN to get most of the details on calling IDispatch. However, there are a couple of lines of code in the CallInvoke implementation that need further explanation. First, the incoming pObject variable is transferred to the pCallDisp variable using VBoost.AssignSwap. As I discussed in the "Set and IUnknown" section of Chapter 3, using a QueryInterface for IDispatch can have nasty side effects. Despite the fact that they have the same IID, IDispatchCallable and Object are considered different types, so assignment with a Set statement causes a QueryInterface for IID_IDispatch.

The second seemingly off-the-wall line of code is the VariantCopyInd API call. This call is required on the first parameter sent to an INVOKE_ PROPERTYPUT (Property Let in VB) or to an INVOKE_PROPERTYPUTREF (Property Set) function. Most IDispatch implementations can't pass a ByRef parameter to the value property, so a full copy of the data is required. If the incoming parameter is not ByRef, VariantCopyInd does nothing.

CallInvoke Variations

As I mentioned earlier, there are three CallInvoke variations: CallInvokeSub, CallInvokeArray, and CallInvokeSubArray. CallInvokeSub is a Sub rather than a function, and it does not request a return value. Most IDispatch implementations handle a return value request for a Sub by simply emptying the return value. However, some IDispatch implementations fail in this scenario so you need a specific mechanism for not requesting a return value. The *Array variants of these functions remove the ParamArray keyword from the last parameter. The functions are almost identical to CallInvoke except that they don't require special code to forward the array to CallInvokeHelper.

The array versions of the functions allow you to pass an arbitrary number of parameters by adjusting the number of parameters dynamically. However, you lose a key feature ParamArray: the ability to pass a ByRef variant. When you pass a nonvariant type in a call to a ParamArray function, VB passes a Variant with the VT_BYREF flag set. VT_BYREF is combined with the type of the pointed to data and VB then stores a pointer to the data, but not the data itself. If you assign items to a normal Variant array, VB always copies the data and removes the VT_BYREF bit. This means that you have to do extra work to use Call-InvokeArray with ByRef arguments.

```
'Call a sub named "Simple" with 1 ByRef Long parameter
Dim Args(0) As Variant
```

```
Dim pObj As Object
Dim lData As Long
    Args(0) = VarPtr(lData)
    VBoost.Assign Args(0), VT_BYREF Or vbLong
    CallInvokeArray pObj, GetMemberID("Simple"), _
      INVOKE_FUNC, Args
```

VT_BYREF has the interesting side effect of locking a Variant's type. When VB assigns to a VT_BYREF Variant, it first attempts to convert underlying data to the correct type and fails if the conversion can't be completed. Then VB frees the current pointed to data (as indicated by the type) and assigns the new value to the pointer. The VT_BYREF flag is not disturbed, and the pointed to memory is updated through the Variant. The one caveat to this mechanism is that VB assumes all local- and module-level variables are not VT_BYREF. It checks for the VT_BYREF flag on Variant arguments only.

VTable-Binding Custom Control Interfaces

I mentioned earlier that custom controls placed on a form support only IDispatch binding. However, the control objects in most OCX files support vtable binding. There are two compelling reasons for digging into the control and finding the vtable. The first is the obvious performance gains made possible by moving from an IDispatch call to a vtable call. The second is that the specific IDispatch implementation VB uses is generated dynamically in your development machine's OCA file, making it a machine-bound implementation. If you want to pass controls between components and successfully deploy them on someone else's machine, you can't use the private IDispatch interface. So unless you want to settle for fully late-bound helper components, you'll need to get a reference to the true vtable as defined in the OCX.

Before I show you how to get to the vtable, you need to know a little more about how VB handles custom controls. The control definition you see in VB is not the same as the control definition in the OCX. If you select a control library from the Object Browser's dropdown list, the description pane shows a reference to something called an OCA file. A reference to the OCX is nowhere to be found.

The OCA file, which includes the type library seen in the Object Browser and some other data, is generated automatically when you add a custom control to the toolbox. The objects described in the OCA type library include all the properties, methods, and events of the native control in the OCX. However, the native function sets have been extended to include additional properties, methods, and events specific to the VB control container. For example, you'll see Top and Left properties on every control you drop onto a form. To see a superset of the items that VB might add, select the VBControlExtender object in the Object Browser.

The extended object described in the type library is implemented at runtime as an IDispatch wrapper around the native and VB-provided objects. The extended object is a composite that routes incoming Invoke calls to either the IDispatch implementation of the native OCX or to VB's control extender object. No vtable is provided, and the native object also receives requests through IDispatch::Invoke.

The double Invoke system implemented by VB's extender object works reasonably well when you're responding to events at user speed (click, type, think, drink, spill, wipe), but it is a performance hindrance when calling code makes lots of calls to the underlying control. For example, if you're manipulating a graphics-generation control or populating a grid, the individual calls may be very fast once the native OCX takes control, but the calls bottleneck badly in all of the IDispatch work. In the case of controls, calling the vtable directly cuts the call overhead by more than two orders of magnitude (13000 percent in my measurements). All you have to do is find the vtable within the extender wrapping.

VB's extender object includes the Object property, which returns a reference to the unwrapped, inner control. Getting a reference to the object is a step in the right direction, but you will hit a wall because the Object property returns type Object: All you can do is make late-bound calls against it. The point of the exercise is to get a vtable-enabled object reference. But the type for this reference is in the OCX type library, which your project doesn't reference. In fact, you often can't even use Project|References|Browse to add a reference to the OCX because it can have the same library name as the OCA. Even in cases where the

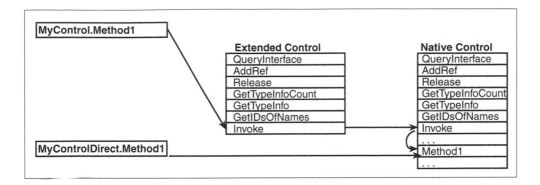

Figure 4.2. Take the direct route to a control's methods by bypassing two Invoke calls.

library names are different, you end up with two complete sets of identical object names, just adding to the confusion.

In order to vtable-bind the native object returned by the Object property, your project must include a reference to a type library whose type looks like the native interface recognized by the runtime control. Using OCXDirect.Dll, an add-in included with the book, you can generate such a library automatically. OCXDirect.Dll walks through all your project's references, finds the OCA files, determines which types have been extended, and creates a type library of aliases to the classes as defined in the native OCX files. The steps are simple.

1. Make sure you've copied OCXDirect.DLL to your machine and registered it with regsvr32.

2. Select "Direct OCX Type Generator (VB6)" in the Add-In Manager dialog.

3. Save your project.

4. Select "Generate Direct OCX Types" on the Add-Ins menu. (The add-in automatically generates a file called *ProjectName*DirectOCXTypes.tlb and adds the library to your project references.)

5. Repeat step 4 whenever you change the set of referenced controls. The Tlb file will be deleted and regenerated.

For every extended control referenced in your project, you now have a type defined with the same name with Direct appended to the end. For example, if RichTextBox1 is a control on your form and you want to vtable bind to it, run the add-in and add the following code.

```
Dim RTDirect As RichTextBoxDirect
Set RTDirect = RichTextBox1.Object
'RTDirect is a direct reference to the native control
```

The *Direct types are defined as simple aliases to the native OCX. Generating this library by hand is not difficult, and seeing it can be very useful. The body of the library block is shown below. Just add an import for each library and a new typedef line for each control in each library.

```
importlib("c:\\winnt\\system32\\RichTx32.Ocx");
typedef [public] RichTextLib.RichTextBox RichTextBoxDirect;
```

When the VB compiler sees an alias type such as those generated by OCXDirect, it resolves the typedef and then forgets that it had a typedef to begin with. This is fortunate because you can use the RichTextBoxDirect name as a parameter or return type in a publicly exposed function. When VB compiles the component, the intermediate type is removed and the generated type library is built with an external dependency on RichTx32.Ocx, not on *ProjectName*DirectOcxTypes.Olb. The Direct type acts as a perfect catalyst: it triggers the reaction and leaves no trace of itself to compromise the resulting compound.

With a reference to a type that is defined in a real, distributable OCX instead of in a locally defined OCA, you can create deployable components that accept references to running controls. Take the following steps to create a helper DLL that does some standard manipulation of a RichTextBox control.

In the helper DLL, choose Project | References | Browse and open RichTx32.Ocx. Control libraries are not shown as normal references, so you have to find them. Bug alert: you can add these hidden references, but they don't appear in the list of current references when you reopen the dialog. You'll have to edit the VBP file by hand and reload the project to get rid of the reference.

A method in the helper DLL should accept the control reference as a ByVal RichTextBox. Here the RichTextBox is resolved as the native type in the OCX control.

To pass an item from your UI project to the method in the helper DLL, use RichTextBox1.Object.

If you want to include a publicly exposed method in your UI project (assuming you have a DLL that displays a form with a RichTextBox control on it), generate direct types and define the parameter or return type as Rich-TextBoxDirect. This is seen externally as the same RichTextBox exposed by the helper DLL.

You can now pass the control's native interface back and forth between components, but what happens if you want to look at the entire control, not just its native methods, properties, and events? To do this, use the IOleObject interface supported by the control to get back to the extended control from the native object. The following example is taken from a form that contains a single Rich-TextBox. The project's Direct types library has been generated, and the project references the OleTypes (VBoost: Ole Type Definitions) type library provided with the book.

```
Private WithEvents SyncRT As RichTextBoxDirect
Private WithEvents SyncRTExt As VBControlExtender


Private Sub Form_Load()
Dim pOleObject As IOleObject
Dim pOleControlSite As IOleControlSite
    'Get the native object and sync its events
    Set SyncRT = RichTextBox1.object

    'Get the IOleObject interface from the
    'native object. IOleObject gets us back
    'to the client site, which can then give
    'us the original extended object.
    Set pOleObject = SyncRT
    Set pOleControlSite = pOleObject.GetClientSite
    'Sync the extender events.
    Set SyncRTExt = pOleControlSite.GetExtendedControl
```

```
        'Demonstrate that we are back to the original
        'control. This prints the same value twice.
        Debug.Print ObjPtr(SyncRTExt), ObjPtr(RichTextBox1)
    End Sub
    Private Sub RichTextBox1_Change()
        Stop
    End Sub
    Private Sub SyncRT_Change()
        Stop
    End Sub
    Private Sub SyncRTExt_ObjectEvent(Info As EventInfo)
        If Info = "Change" Then Stop
    End Sub
```

By the time Form_Load ends, there are three objects: The original Rich-TextBox1 control reference, a direct reference to the underlying native object (SyncRT), and a reference to the extender object. In a normal project, you would now proceed to listen directly to the native events with the WithEvents SyncRT object and listen to the extender events with SyncRTExt. However, the VBControlExtender object has a special event called ObjectEvent that fires when a native event fires. Normally, you wouldn't need to use ObjectEvent because you can access the native functions event prototypes directly; I include it here to demonstrate that there are three live views on the control. All three events fire when you make a change to RichTextBox1.

The important thing to learn from this sample is that you have access to the native and extended methods, properties, and events even without using the OCA-defined RichTextBox type. You can write a helper DLL that handles not only the native portion of the control, but the extended part as well. Even better, you can get your helper DLL off your development machine and into production.

Bogus Record Types in OCA Files

There is one subtle—but deadly—bug with OCA files that I must mention. This bug essentially prevents you from using public user-defined types in VB-generated OCXs. When VB generates the OCA file, it includes a full copy of all public record types within the OCA. Despite the fact that these types have the same GUID and layout as the original types in the native OCX, the compiler considers them different types.

You can easily see a manifestation of this problem by generating an OCX with a public record type. The control should include a method that uses the type. Build the control, drop into another project, and generate direct types. The compiler now gives you a perpetual type mismatch when you try to pass the OCA-defined UDT to the OCX-defined method.

The other manifestation of this bug, which is arguably more severe, occurs when you distribute your control. Public UDTs require a type library to describe themselves. Unfortunately, the type library the UDTs are contained is the OCA back on the developer's machine, *not* the OCX on the customer's machine. Unless you ship and register the OCA with the OCX, you get type mismatch errors all over the place.

The only fix for this bug I know of is a utility called OCARecordFix.exe, included with this book. To use this utility, use the Object Browser to locate the troubled OCA file. Now exit VB and run OCARecordFix <Oca path>. This utility replaces the record redefinitions in the OCA with typedefs directly to the OCX. OCARecordFix also changes the types of all parameters and the function return values of the suspect type or types. The compiler considers the typedef and its target type to be equivalent, so when you reload VB, you'll be back in business. OCARecordFix requires resource APIs that are not supported on Windows 95 or 98, so you cannot use it on these platforms. This bug is also fixed in Visual Studio service pack 4.

Chapter 5

Object Design Constructs

Code architecture and design are fundamental to the success of any software project. If you design poorly, you end up writing a great deal of code near the end of the product cycle to stabilize an inherently unstable system. The architectural challenge lies in your inability to verify the architecture until the code is written and you start stressing the project. Although very little in life is guaranteed, you can minimize the chances that the system will fall apart under its own weight by basing the architecture on design principles that have worked in the past.

The goal of this book is not to explore design constructs in depth. Instead, I'll concentrate on a few time-tested principles and introduce technology that makes them more accessible in VB. This chapter concentrates on intra-project design. Reuse and compatibility of binary EXE, DLL, and OCX components built by different projects is covered later in the book (see "Binary Compatibility" in Chapter 15).

- **Pluggable Components** The ability to replace or update one part of a project without modifying code in the rest of the project is very important. We've all experienced the ripple effect in which an apparently minor tweak to one part of the code led to modifications in almost the entire project. In addition to reducing the headaches associated with the ripple effect, designing components to be pluggable makes new pieces easier to test. If replacing a component also makes it necessary to modify the code that calls the component, you don't know whether to point fingers at the caller or callee when a problem arises. But if you can modify a single variable in the equation, you know exactly where to place responsibility in the failure case. It's also easy to extract pluggable components from the current project for reuse in future projects.

- **Abstraction** Abstraction is fundamental to "pluggability" because it enables multiple implementations of the same abstraction without changing the abstract definition. Calling code relies only on the abstraction, not on the code behind the abstraction. Two implementations of the same abstraction become completely interchangeable from the perspective of the calling code. In the world of COM, the abstract description of an object is known as an *interface,* where an interface is an ordered list of functions. Functions in the interface map one-to-one with the vtable functions of the object that implement the interface. All COM objects are concrete implementations of an abstract interface, and the interface acts as the only protocol through which external code acts on the COM object.

- **Code Reuse** Code stability is inversely proportional to the number of lines of code you have to write. If you have code that is working and tested, you should use it again whenever possible. I'm not referring to the cut-and-paste mechanism of code reuse (also known as the "rapid-proliferation-of-bugs mechanism"). I'm describing the use of the same implementation from a number of places. Code reuse constantly plays tug-of-war with pluggability and abstraction. Pluggability suffers because the existing code often takes on new requirements, adding extra parameters to existing functions. (Optional parameters can make this much less painful.) Abstraction tugs against code reuse because abstract objects have only a description and no code, so supporting the interface on a number of objects requires an implementation of the same interface definition in multiple places. Much of this chapter will be devoted to reconciling the conflicting demands of abstraction and code reuse.

Abstraction with Implements

COM provides for multiple-interface support via the QueryInterface function, which I discussed in the "Set and IUnknown" section of Chapter 3. VB allows you to use the Implements keyword to extend the set of interfaces to which QI responds. The Implements keyword allows your object to provide an implementation of an abstract interface.

Using Implements is as easy as adding an event procedure to a Form. Simply type "Implements <*interface*>" at the top of a class module and commit the line. The left dropdown list now has an entry with the name of the interface. Select the entry in the left dropdown list and select each name in the right dropdown to insert the function prototypes for each item in the interface. You must insert a procedure skeleton for each item in the interface before you can compile successfully.

As you select items, you'll see that VB inserts Private procedures with the name "Interface_Function." The format of the name gives you separate entries if you implement two interfaces with a common function name. This is very important as it allows you to support an arbitrary number of interfaces in your class without name conflicts. (C++ and Java bind on a name basis only, causing name collisions as you add interfaces and making it impossible to tell if the *Name* function was called through the IFoo or the IBar interface.)

Marking implements functions as Private means that they are not exposed on the primary interface. You can change the functions to Public if you like, but I don't recommend it. By keeping the functions private, you are forced to call the function only via the interface on which it is defined. All three of the design principles I'm focusing on benefit greatly from letting each interface represent a unique view on the object. If you want to operate on a different view, just switch interfaces (see "Pluggability of Calling Code" below).

In order to Implement an interface, you must first define it in your project. You can use either an interface defined in a type library or the primary interface of another class in your module. The primary interface of a VB class is defined automatically to match the public methods and properties in a class module. In general, I recommend using a type library definition, but this is not a cut-and-dried issue. There are a number of things to consider when deciding where to define your interfaces.

- VB doesn't distinguish between a class created as an interface definition and a class created as a real class. Although a class module used to define an interface generally contains nothing but empty procedures, VB must provide an implementation of that class nonetheless. In other words, you end up with dead code in your project.

- VB classes are all derived from IDispatch. If you're communicating via interfaces, you're not using IDispatch. Forcing VB to provide an IDispatch implementation that is never called is a waste of code and resources. If you expose implemented interfaces to scripting languages, you need to support IDispatch. Otherwise, it's just baggage.

- If you implement an interface in a Public class, you must also set the Instancing property of the VB class whose primary interface you're implementing to PublicNotCreatable or higher. VB should provide a Private Implements to keep project-specific interface implementations from being exposed in the project's type library, but it doesn't.

- If you want to use Implements but don't want to allow external access to the interface, put the definition in a type library, and don't redistribute the external library. As long as you don't use the interface across thread boundaries, you have effectively "privatized" your interface. The type library VB generates has an unresolvable reference to your private type library, but that doesn't compromise the integrity of the library in any way. If this problem really bothers you, see "Post-Build Type Library Modifications" in Chapter 15 for a discussion of removing the interface entry altogether. Bug alert: In VB5, an unresolvable interface reference in a custom control causes the generation of an invalid OCA file. In particular, any interfaces that follow the dangling one—including the interface describing your events—are also lost. The only work-around in VB5 is to ship and register the private type libraries to the developers who use your control or modify the type library. Or you can upgrade to VB6.

- If you need to use an interface across process boundaries, the type library for that interface must be registered on the target machine, and that means deploying and registering the type library with your finished product. If you use a PublicNotCreatable class in your project to define the interface, you don't need the external library. Alternately, you can use the PowerVB Post-Build Type Library Modifier add-in to import an external type library into your executable's type library. This allows you to ship a single binary.

Although VB classes inherit from provided implementations of the IDispatch interface (which in turn inherits from IUnknown), VB does not support inheritance in code that you write. Inheritance is a common OOP design construct that allows a class to surface the implementation of an interface from another class. The class that provides the implementation is known as a *base class*. Inheritance also allows you to override specific functions in the base class's implementation. Function overriding lets you provide a custom implementation of the interface on a function-by-function basis rather than being forced to provide an implementation for every function in the interface. Some languages, such as C++, allow for multiple inheritance, which lets you derive implementation for multiple interfaces. Other languages, such as Java, allow only for single inheritance. VB doesn't support inheritance, so you have to be a little more creative to reuse an implementation.

Although it would be nice to have inheritance in VB for many situations, inheritance-based systems are not necessarily all they're cracked up to be. To show you that the grass is not always greener, I'll take a minute to discuss some of the weaknesses of inheritance.

The first problem is known as a fragile base class. When you use inheritance, you often get into a situation in which multiple classes inherit from a single base class. Then you find that you need to change the base class, but a base class change modifies the behavior of other classes as well. Your development manager won't let you destabilize the whole system by modifying the base class two weeks before the ship date, so you end up overriding many—if not all of—the base class's functions. This introduces additional problems, especially if you have several base classes between your class and the base class that's causing problems. Java's final keyword doesn't solve such problems; it just forces you to define an interface that must be implemented by the base class and your class. In this case, "final" makes things more difficult.

The second problem with inheritance is unpredictability of the function-call target and the interactions caused by mixing different implementations. Since every function in the interface definition may actually be implemented in a different class, the calling code gives you no indication of which class you'll end up in when you step into a function. With an interface-based model, the same object implements all of the functions. This makes the code more predictable and eliminates subtle bugs that occur when a derived class overrides some functions but leaves others untouched. The alternative, which we'll look at later, is to let a single object provide multiple distinct implementations. A single class that provides multiple behaviors is more centralized and predictable than multiple classes.

The final problem with inheritance (at least the final one I'll discuss) is versioning. As you move to the second version of a product, you'll often add features and capabilities to your base classes. As you do so, you'll invariably get name conflicts with existing classes that derive from the base. After all, the most compelling reason to add a *Validate* method to the base class is that several of the derived classes already had a *Validate,* and you want to formalize the concept of validation. By modifying the base class, you've just turned the *Validate* methods in derived classes into overrides, which they weren't intended to be.

You run into more problems with inheritance and versioning when you use a single component to provide two versions of the same interface. If you want to support an enhanced version of the base interface while still supporting the old version, the new base class must derive from the old base class. But if you want to change the base class, you're in trouble (especially in single-inheritance systems) because the class must derive from Base1 to participate in the old system and from Base to participate in the new one. This is not an issue with interfaces; you just Implement Base1 and Base.

Pluggability of Calling Code

As programmers, we devote a great deal of time and effort to writing classes. If we write our classes carefully, we can reuse them many times simply by writing new calling code. After all, we spend at least as much time writing code against the classes we've created as we do writing the classes. Programming tomes often refer to reusing classes, but don't say much about the calling code. I'd like to suggest that designing your classes in a way that lets you reuse the calling code is just as important and saves just as much time.

You can find a great example of calling-code reuse in the PropertyBag object that comes with VB6. You can use the following code to save the current state for any public class whose Persistable property is set to 1—Persistable. The Persistable property tells VB to provide an implementation of the IPersistStream interface for a VB class. The PropertyBag object uses IPersistStream to generate a byte array that is a snapshot of the object's current state, along with the information needed to create a new instance of the object.

```vb
'Generate a Byte array that contains the current
'state of the passed class.
Function GetClassBytes(ByVal AnyClass As Object) As Byte()
Dim PB As New PropertyBag
Dim bArr() As Byte
    With PB
        .WriteProperty "Dummy", AnyClass
        bArr = .Contents
    End With
    GetClassBytes = bArr
End Function


'Create a new instance of the class with the state
'written to the ClassBytes array by a previous instance.
Private Function RestoreClass(ClassBytes() As Byte) As Object
Dim PB As New PropertyBag
    With PB
        .Contents = ClassBytes
        Set RestoreClass = .ReadProperty("Dummy")
    End With
End Function
```

This PropertyBag code is reusable because the classes it operates against all support the IPersistStream interface. By using Implements and by following a few simple conventions in your calling code, you can also create calling code that runs unmodified against two or more different classes. Just as important, you can replace the implementation of an entire class without rewriting any calling code. The ability to plug-and-play class implementations without touching the calling code is extremely important for code maintenance. In addition to the obvious advantage of having to rewrite only one side of the code, you also get a built-in test case for the new code implementation.

The best convention to provide for the reuse of code that operates against a particular interface is to operate against only a single interface from each object in a particular procedure. By breaking code into autonomous units, each of which works with a specific interface, you can greatly increase code reuse. For example, suppose you have defined an IReport interface and an IOutput interface. You have several classes that implement IReport and several that implement IOutput. You *could* write nonreusable code as follows.

```vb
'clsOrders implements IReport
'clsRecordToFile implements IOutput
Sub OutputOrders(Orders As clsOrders, strOutFile As String)
Dim FileRecord As clsRecordToFile
Dim IReport As IReport
Dim IOutput As IOutput
    'Initialize output class
    Set FileRecord = New clsRecordToFile
    FileRecord.File = strOutFile

    'Bring orders up to date
    Orders.Freeze
    Orders.Reconcile

    'Output orders
    Set IReport = Orders
    Set IOutput = FileRecord

    'Output processing goes here

    'Clean up
    FileRecord.Close
    Orders.Unfreeze
End Sub
```

Any code in this procedure that runs against the IReport and IOutput interfaces is not directly reusable. The only code reuse comes from cut and paste, and that leads to a maintenance nightmare as you paste bugs along with code.

By breaking this procedure in two, suddenly the code becomes reusable. The OutputReport procedure knows about only the IReport and IOutput interfaces, which are retrieved on the parameter pass instead of with a Set statement. Note that the input parameters are ByVal to eliminate two additional QI calls when the procedure returns (see "Parameters and IUnknown" in Chapter 3).

```
Sub OutputOrders(Orders As clsOrders, strOutFile As String)
Dim FileRecord As clsRecordToFile
    'Initialize output class
    Set FileRecord = New clsRecordToFile
    FileRecord.File = strOutFile

    'Bring orders up to date
    Orders.Freeze
    Orders.Reconcile

    'Output orders
    OutputReport Orders, FileRecord

    'Clean up
    FileRecord.Close
    Orders.Unfreeze
End Sub
Sub OutputReport(ByVal IRep As IReport, _
                 ByVal IOut As IOutput)
    'Output processing here
End Sub
```

Implements and Implementation Reuse

The Implements keyword is very useful for creating reusable calling code. It is also a wonderful design tool because it provides a stable framework for building a complex application in which modular code communicates via abstract interface definitions. The major shortcoming of Implements is that it provides absolutely no inherent code implementation, so although the calling code is reusable, the class module code is not. Of course, this is also one of the major features of COM interfaces—you are free to use any implementation you like as long as all the procedures in the interface behave as the interface consumer expects.

There is only one way to reuse an implementation of a given interface: delegation. With delegation, a class contains a reference to another implementation of the interface. You then simply forward all the calls to the corresponding functions in the referenced implementation. The most obvious, most common, and most work-intensive way to delegate is to use the Implements keyword in a class, put in all the stub functions, and add one line of code to each function. The single line of code calls the corresponding function in the interface implementation.

```
Private Function IFoo_DoBar _
   ByVal BarData As String) As String
      IFoo_DoBar = m_IFoo.DoBar(BarData)
End Function
```

There are several obvious drawbacks to this technique, and some that aren't so obvious. Writing this code in the first place is a hassle: VB doesn't provide any sort of wizard to do it for you. Regenerating the code when the interface changes is even worse. You also take a significant performance hit from all the parameter passing. Although there are no QueryInterface calls because the object types all match exactly, AddRef/Release is present around ByVal object-type calls. There is also an extra String copy for ByVal As String and ByVal As Variant parameters. Other ByVal parameters need to be evaluated before the inner function call.

If you're not moving huge amounts of data in Strings and Variants, the extra overhead of passing parameters during delegation isn't large, but it is definitely there. The initial coding and maintenance costs are also quite real. Unfortunately, this brute force delegation model is the only alternative available in straight VB. Although the aggregation techniques discussed later eliminate the code-maintenance costs and minimize the delegation costs, I'll first look at ways to avoid delegation by using some design tweaks in straight VB.

Indirect Interface Implementation
The biggest problem with the Implements keyword is that you are forced to provide an implementation for every member function. This is little more than a point-and-click hassle when you first implement the interface; annoying, but

certainly not bad enough to stop you from using the feature. However, if you make an addition or modification to the implemented interface and you've used the interface in multiple classes, you have a legitimate code-maintenance problem that can be bad enough to prevent you from ever using Implements again.

By adding a level of indirection to the calling and implementation code, you can avoid this code maintenance problem entirely and substantially reduce the delegation code you need to write. Indirecting an interface involves moving the implementation of a commonly used interface into a separate class. The main class now implements a simple interface with a single property used to retrieve an implementation of the interface.

```
'clsExposed
Implements GetIStuff
Private m_Stuff As IStuffImpl
Private Sub Class_Initialize()
    Set m_Stuff = New IStuffImpl
    'See multiple behaviors section
    m_Stuff.Type = ForClsExposed
End Sub
Private Property Get GetIStuff_GetStuff() As IStuff
    Set GetIStuff_GetStuff = m_Stuff
End Property
```

```
'Calling code
Dim clsX As clsExposed

. . .
'Call helper
DoStuff clsX

'Helpers
Sub DoStuff(ByVal Indirect As GetIStuff)
Dim Stuff As IStuff
    Set Stuff = Indirect.GetStuff
    'IStuff code here
End Sub
```

The extra level of indirection allows you to make modifications to the IStuff interface without affecting the clsExposed implementation at all. For example, if you add a method to IStuff to support a new behavior in class clsOverExposed, only IStuffImpl and the code that actually calls the new method need to be changed. The change has no effect on clsExposed or the hypothetical myriad other classes that also use IStuff indirectly. Without the additional level of indirection, you would need to change every one of these classes.

Sharing Data with Base Classes

When you call a procedure on an object, the procedure's behavior is generally determined by three interacting sets of data: The code in the procedure, the passed parameters, and the current value of the member variables all act together to determine the action taken. A fourth set of data (which I'll ignore in this discussion) is the global state of the project. (You don't need an advanced book to tell you that you should keep instance interaction with globals to a minimum.) Let's apply this observation to the IStuffImpl class in the previous discussion.

IStuffImpl Implements IStuff, so its external behavior is defined by the definition of the IStuff interface. clsExposed must make IStuffImpl behave as if it had been implemented directly, not indirectly. This means that clsExposed must set all the member variables of the IStuffImpl class. If clsExposed has full control over the member variable state in IStuffImpl, it essentially has full control of its runtime behavior as well.

The easiest way to share all of a class's member variables is to have only one member variable. The single member variable can have a user-defined type. Class modules don't support a public variable with a UDT type, so you have to place the Type definition in a standard module. Then clsExposed can fill the structure and assign it to IStuffImpl through a Friend function.

```
'In a module
Public Type StuffImplData
    Name As String
End Type
```

```
'In IStuffImpl
Private m_Data As StuffImplData
Friend Property Get Data() As StuffImplData
    Data = m_Data
End Property
Friend Property Let Data(RHS As StuffImplData)
```

```
    m_Data = RHS
End Property
```

```
'In clsExposed
Private m_Stuff As IStuffImpl
Private Sub Class_Initialize()
Dim Data As StuffImplData
    Data.Name = "clsExposed"
    Set m_Stuff = New IStuffImpl
    m_Stuff.Data = Data
End Sub
```

Although this code works well for accessing all the data at once, it makes it necessary to make a copy of the data to initialize it and another deep copy whenever you set it. A deep data copy duplicates all the data in the structure, whereas a shallow copy duplicates only pointer values to the original data. If there are no variable-length strings or variable-size arrays in the UDT, the copy operation works reasonably well for small structures. However, if the structure includes these pointer types, the structure copy becomes much more expensive.

If you want to avoid the copy or let clsExposed have more direct access to the data in IStuffImpl, you'll have to use the array descriptor techniques, described in "Writing to Array Variables" in Chapter 2, to give the clsExposed class direct access to the m_Data structure in the IStuffImpl instance that it owns. By simply pointing a variable in each class to the same data, we eliminate the notification and copy code required to synchronize two copies of the structure.

```
'IStuffImpl class
Implements IStuff
Private m_Data As StuffImplData
Friend Property Get DataPtr() As Long
    DataPtr = VarPtr(m_Data)
End Property
Public Property Get IStuff_Name() As String
    IStuff_Name = m_Data.Name
End Property
```

```
'clsExposed class
Implements GetIStuff
```

```
Private m_Stuff As IStuffImpl
Private m_SAStuffData As SafeArray1d
Private m_StuffData() As StuffImplData
Private Sub Class_Initialize()
    Set m_Stuff = New IStuffImpl
    ShareMemoryViaArray VarPtrArray(m_StuffData), _
      m_SAStuffData, m_Stuff.DataPtr, LenB(m_StuffData(0))
    m_StuffData(0).Name = "clsExposed"
End Sub
Private Sub Class_Terminate()
    'Clean the array variable
    UnshareMemory VarPtrArray(m_StuffData)
End Sub
Private Property Get GetIStuff_GetStuff () As IStuff
    Set GetIStuff_GetStuff = m_Stuff
End Property
```

```
'Reusable helper function to process IStuff
Function GetName(ByVal Indirect As IGetStuff) As String
    GetName = Indirect.GetStuff.Name
End Function
```

```
'Calling code snippet
Dim clsExposed As New clsExposed
Debug.Print GetName(clsExposed)
```

When you use this code, you should always be sure to unshare the array
memory in the derived class's Class_Terminate. This prevents the derived class
from cleaning up the memory in the base class's data structure before the base
class's Class_Terminate can look at it. Also note that you don't have to expose all
the variables in the base class. If you want some truly private variables, move
them outside the shared structure.

Multiple Behaviors in One Class

In an inheritance model of code reuse, you often override functions to provide
different implementations. When a derived class overrides a function in the base
class's interface, the calling code jumps directly to the function on the derived
class. In many cases, the override provides modified behavior, but requires no
more data than the corresponding function in the base class.

Although VB doesn't support inheritance, you can emulate the function override in the "same data/different algorithm" override scenario by using a simple Select Case statement and a BehaviorType field in your shared data structure. By changing the BehaviorType field, you can effectively swap different algorithms into your class. Select Case blocks whose Case statements include constant expressions are very fast, so the performance overhead of this technique is minimal. For example, you may have a drawing class that can draw lines, circles, or rectangles. In an inheritance model, you would use three classes derived from an abstract base class (an abstract base class requires that you override a given function).

```vb
'In a standard module
Public Enum DrawType
    dtLine = 0
    dtRectangle = 1
    dtCircle = 2
End Enum
Public Type DrawImplData
    x1 As Single
    y1 As Single
    x2 As Single
    y2 As Single
    DrawType As DrawType
End Type


'The implementation of the DrawImpl class. For simplicity,
'IDraw simply draws to a Form. I'll let you deduce the IDraw
'interface.
Implements IDraw
Private m_Data As DrawImplData
Friend Property Get DataPtr() As Long
    DataPtr = VarPtr(m_Data)
End Property
Private Sub IDraw_Draw(ByVal Target As Form)
Dim Width As Single
Dim Height As Single
    With m_Data
        Select Case .DrawType
            Case dtLine
```

```
                    Target.Line (.x1, .y1)-(.x2, .y2)
            Case dtRectangle
                    Target.Line (.x1, .y1)-(.x2, .y2), , B
            Case dtCircle
                Width = .x2 - .x1
                Height = .y2 - .y1
                If Width > Height Then
                    Target.Circle _
                      ((.x2 + .x1) / 2, (.y2 + .y1) / 2), _
                        Height, , , , Height / Width
                Else
                    Target.Circle _
                      ((.x2 + .x1) / 2, (.y2 + .y1) / 2), _
                        Width, , , , Height / Width
                End If
            End Select
        End With
    End Sub
    Private Property Get IDraw_x1() As Single
        IDraw_x1 = m_Data.x1
    End Property
    Private Property Let IDraw_x1(ByVal RHS As Single)
        m_Data.x1 = RHS
    End Property
    Private Property Get IDraw_y1() As Single
        IDraw_y1 = m_Data.x1
    End Property
    Private Property Let IDraw_y1(ByVal RHS As Single)
        m_Data.y1 = RHS
    End Property
    Private Property Get IDraw_x2() As Single
        IDraw_x2 = m_Data.x2
    End Property
    Private Property Let IDraw_x2(ByVal RHS As Single)
        m_Data.x2 = RHS
    End Property
    Private Property Get IDraw_y2() As Single
        IDraw_y2 = m_Data.x2
    End Property
    Private Property Let IDraw_y2(ByVal RHS As Single)
        m_Data.y2 = RHS
    End Property
```

In practice, there is rarely more than a handful of variations on the base class in a particular project. By moving all the implementations into one class and setting a type property on the class, you can share a lot of code and jump quickly to the correct code, based on the class's type. The result is predictable code with a centralized implementation. If the behavioral variations become extreme, or if the data required for the implementations is substantially different, just use Implements and code another version of the base class with the same interface.

Aggregation

The term *aggregation,* as generally used in COM programming, refers to an identity trick initiated when an object is created. The identity of a COM object is determined by its controlling IUnknown pointer (as described in Chapter 3). When an object is created as an aggregate, it is handed a controlling IUnknown pointer, and it defers all external IUnknown operations to that controlling pointer. The outer object is given a second IUnknown implementation used to communicate with the inner object. In this fashion, a COM object can expose an interface by creating a second, inner object as an aggregate on the controlling IUnknown of the outer object.

The underlying concept of aggregation is much less stringent than the aggregation described by the COM specification. In general, an aggregate refers to the combination of two or more objects into a single object. The composite object is then used as if it were a single object, with some parts of the object coming from each of the aggregates. The concept behind aggregation is that it enables objects to expose complete interface implementations with very little work. You can use a single implementation of an interface to provide equivalent capabilities to several classes.

VB objects cannot be created as COM aggregates, and there is no built-in mechanism that allows a VB object to create another object as an aggregate. This lack of support shuts VB programmers out of an entire mechanism of code reuse: The implementation of any interface must be done function by function in the class module rather than using COM aggregation to defer control of an entire interface to a previously implemented object.

Because VB can't aggregate at object-creation time, and gaining control over an object before it is created is difficult (if not impossible), I won't try to show you how to support classic aggregation. However, I *can* show you how to combine one or more previously created objects and aggregate them into an existing object. Making two objects appear the same requires control of the IUnknown calls that come into the object. By hooking the IUnknown functions of an existing object and wrapping a COM object with a super-lightweight delegation layer (known as a blind vtable delegator) you can create composite objects that provide all the code-reuse advantages of aggregation. If you're interested only in creating aggregates and don't care how it's done, jump to the "Aggregating Existing Objects" section of this chapter and refer to the "Aggregation Functions" section in the Appendix.

Blind VTable Delegation

VTable delegation is a very low-level technique (implemented in assembly code) for wrapping objects so that the wrapped object behaves exactly like the unwrapped object. VTable delegation is useful for modifying the behavior of certain functions in a vtable while leaving the rest of the functions alone. In the vtable delegator used for aggregation, I provide an implementation for the three IUnknown functions and let the rest pass through.

In order to understand how vtable delegation works, you first have to know how a vtable works. The COM binary standard specifies that every COM object has a pointer to an IUnknown derived virtual function table (vtable) as its first element. So if pObj is a pointer to a COM object, *pObj (the value at the memory location pObj) is the vtable. The vtable is an ordered array of function pointers in which the functions' order corresponds to the order defined in the interface that describes the COM object. Therefore, (*pObj)[0] is the first function in the function pointer array and it is an implementation of the IUnknown.QueryInterface function. All outside calls to a COM object come through the vtable, so the external behavior of an object is the same if all functions in its vtable have the same behavior.

To see how a blind delegator works, let's consider the case of a fully blind delegator; that is, one in which all functions simply defer to the real implementation of the function. I do this for illustration only: There is no point in creating a fully blind delegator. A blind delegator object has two required elements: a vtable pointer (m_pVTable) and a pointer to the real object (m_punkInner). The m_pVTable pointer points to an array of functions, all of which move the function's offset to a CPU register, then jump to a central routine. The central routine replaces the *this* pointer on the stack with the m_punkInner pointer, looks up the real function pointer in the m_punkInner vtable (based on the passed register value), then jumps to the real function. To see this in action, let's look at the CPU registers for the blind delegation of function number 40. Because this is shown in Intel assembly, ESP is the current stack pointer, and ECX passes the function offset.

The stack looks like:

```
ESP                ;Return address (jump back here upon
                               completion))
ESP+4              ;The this pointer (points to the blind delegator
                               structure)
ESP+8              ;The first parameter
ESP+12             ;The second parameter
etc
```

Pseudocode:

```
ECX = 40
Jump to main function
ESP+4 = m_punkInner from blind delegator structure
Jump to the correct function in the real vtable, calculated
  with
(*m_punkInner)[ECX]
```

Note here that the parameters are completely untouched. Only the *this* pointer is touched on the stack, so the delegation code can run against an arbitrary function. With delegation code that runs against any vtable entry, we can use the same vtable as a blind delegator for arbitrary objects. Although this code has a small amount of overhead, it is clearly much faster than writing a delegation function in VB, where all of the parameters are touched. Calling through a blind delegator does not have a significant performance impact.

To move from a fully blind delegator to one that is useful for aggregation, you have to add a couple of member variables and override the IUnknown functions. The first new member is m_punkOuter, a pointer to a controlling IUnknown. This

IUnknown establishes the object's identity. An m_cRefs member is also added to maintain a reference count. The replaced QueryInterface function simply forwards the QueryInterface call to m_punkOuter, so the wrapped object has the same COM identity as the controlling IUnknown. The delegation structure is shown in Figure 5.1.

IUnknown Hooking

Visual Basic provides an implementation of the IUnknown functions for you. However, aggregation makes it necessary to gain control over the QueryInterface function to make the object respond to a request for an interface that the compiled object doesn't know it supports. All QI calls go back to the controlling IUnknown, so any manipulation needs to be applied to the controlling IUnknown. The goal of hooking the IUnknown implementation is to receive a callback when QueryInterface is called on an object (and to make this easy to implement in VB).

An IUnknown hook is very similar to a blind delegator, but an IUknown hook modifies an object directly instead of wrapping the object. Hooking an interface is surprisingly simple. The value of the pointer to an object is also a pointer to its vtable. To hook the functions in the vtable, simply record the current vtable

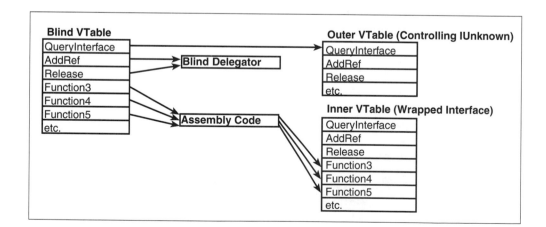

Figure 5.1.   Redirecting vtable functions in the blind delegator.

pointer and overwrite it with a pointer to a replacement vtable. The vtable call now arrives at the alternate function, which restores the object's vtable to its starting value and forwards the call. Before returning, the hooked state of the object is restored, as shown in Figure 5.2.

The VBoost objects included with this book provide IUnknown hooking capability. The fastest implementation of the hooking functions is in the C++ VBoost6.Dll implementation, but the functions are also available (using many of the techniques from this book) in the compiled in version of the VBoost objects found in VBoost.Bas. This implementation provides callbacks through the IQIHook interface before and/or after the internal QueryInterface call has completed. It also provides an opportunity to block the requested IID or to map it to a different value. You can use the IQIARHook interface to watch the AddRef and Release calls as well.

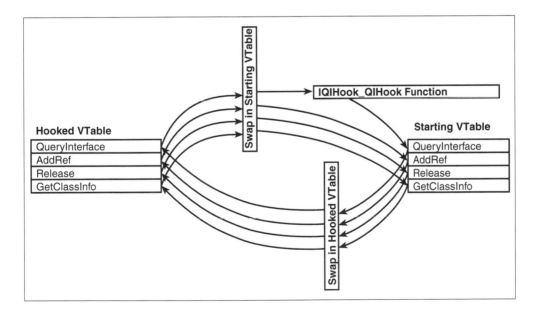

Figure 5.2. The IUnknown hook provides a complete replacement vtable for the controlling IUnknown of a VB object, allowing you to customize the QueryInterface call.

You often find that the implementation of a COM object supports an additional interface that has the same ObjPtr as the controlling IUnknown. Any vtable that replaces the QI call must also support all the additional functions. All VB objects happen to support IProvideClassInfo on the controlling IUnknown vtable, adding another function to the hooking code. The IUnknown hook in VBoost provides a vtable that modifies QueryInterface, AddRef, and Release. It also performs a simple passthrough operation on the ProvideClassInfo function.

You can use VBoost to hook other objects only if a QueryInterface request for something other than IID_IUnknown and IID_IProvideClassInfo does not return the same pointer as the controlling IUnknown. Even if the internal QI succeeds, VBoost releases the data and returns the E_NOINTERFACE error. If you want to try hooking objects created with C++, you have to modify the source code contained with the book for each type of interface.

As a simple example of hooking a QI call, here's a class that you can use to watch QI calls as they happen. In this case, the last IID is tracked. If you're working in the VB IDE, you must run this code all at once rather than stepping through it: The debugger actually makes several QI calls on the object after each step instruction.

```vb
'clsLastIID
Implements VBoostTypes.IQIHook
Private m_Hook As VBoostTypes.UnknownHook
Private m_LastIID As VBoostTypes.VBGUID
Private Sub Class_Initialize()
    'The first parameter is the controlling
    'IUnknown. The second parameter is the IQIHook callback.
    'The third is the initial flags that indicate
    'a mapiid and/or before notification and/or
    'after call notification. The fourth
    'parameter is the variable that owns the hook.
    VBoost.HookQI Me, Me, uhBeforeQI, m_Hook
End Sub

Private Sub IQIHook_MapIID(IID As VBoostTypes.VBGUID)
End Sub
Private Sub IQIHook_QIHook(IID As VBoostTypes.VBGUID, _
```

```
    ByVal uhFlags As VBoostTypes.UnkHookFlags, _
    pResult As stdole.IUnknown, _
    ByVal HookedUnknown As stdole.IUnknown)
      m_LastIID = IID
End Sub
Friend Property Get LastIID() As VBoostTypes.VBGUID
      LastIID = m_LastIID
End Property
```

```
'Calling code that determines the IID of Class1
Dim clsLastIID As New clsLastIID
Dim cls1 As Class1
Dim IID_Class1 As VBoostTypes.VBGUID
On Error Resume Next
'This will fail, but try it to see the IID
Set cls1 = clsLastIID
On Error GoTo 0
IID_Class1 = clsLastIID.LastIID
```

If you use hooked objects for very long, you might notice that the locals and watch windows don't work quite the way you expect them to. If your project contains a reference to a class that is implemented in the project, you can usually expand the object variable and look at the member variables as if you were within the class. Once you hook an object, the debugger no longer views the object as a VB object (technically it isn't: an object is identified by its vtable), so you can't look inside it the way you usually can. However, from within the object, the Me entry in the locals window is always valid.

A word of caution is required here: if you hook using the VB-implemented UnknownHook, VB will crash when you try to expand a reference to the object (but not Me); with the C++ implementation, you will simply see <no variables>. Interactions with the debugger are complex, and I can't say why this crash happens with the VB implementation but not the C++ implementation (at least, not without burning my moonlighting agreement and devoting precious hours to tracking it through the debugger). You may want to toggle the C++ version of the DLL during debugging by setting the conditional compilation flag VBOOST_INTERNAL = 0.

The VBoost aggregation objects are discussed extensively in Appendix A. I'll look at usage samples here.

Use the following code to make Class2 support a QueryInterface for Class1. This code uses the clsLastIID class shown earlier to determine the IID of Class1.

```vb
'Class2 implementation
Implements VBoostTypes.IQIHook
Private m_Hook As VBoostTypes.UnknownHook
Private IID_Class1 As VBoostTypes.VBGUID
Private m_Class1 As Class1

Private Sub Class_Initialize()
Dim clsLastIID As New clsLastIID
    On Error Resume Next
    Set m_Class1 = clsLastIID
    On Error GoTo 0
    IID_Class1 = clsLastIID.LastIID
    Set m_Class1 = New Class1
    VBoost.HookQI Me, Me, uhBeforeQI, m_Hook
End Sub

Private Sub IQIHook_MapIID(IID As VBoostTypes.VBGUID)
End Sub
Private Sub IQIHook_QIHook(IID As VBoostTypes.VBGUID, _
  ByVal uhFlags As VBoostTypes.UnkHookFlags, _
  pResult As stdole.IUnknown, _
  ByVal HookedUnknown As stdole.IUnknown)
    If IsEqualIID(IID, IID_Class1) Then
        'Create a delegator around m_Class1 using
        'HookedUnknown as the controlling IUnknown.
        Set pResult = VBoost.CreateDelegator _
          (HookedUnknown, m_Class1)
    End If
End Sub
```

```vb
'Calling code
Dim cls1 As Class1
Dim cls2 As New Class2
Set cls1 = cls2
Debug.Print cls1 Is cls2
```

```
'Output
True
```

Aggregating Existing Objects

Implementing your own IQIHook and blind-delegation code is nontrivial, so the VBoost objects provide two functions for creating aggregate objects based on passed data. One function, AggregateUnknown, uses an IUnknown hook to build an aggregate on top of an existing controlling IUnknown. The second function, CreateAggregate, creates a new controlling IUnknown that aggregates multiple objects. You must use AggregateUnknown to add interface support to MultiUse objects because these objects are created externally, so the earliest you can aggregate the object is in the Class_Initialize. If an object is PublicNotCreatable or internal, you can use the alternate CreateAggregate function because you have full control of the object's creation, and you can determine the controlling IUnknown returned to the caller. The advantage of AggregateUnknown is that any interfaces the object supports natively are not wrapped with a blind delegator, and therefore, don't take any performance hit. The disadvantage is that an IUnknown hook is required.

The AggregateUnknown and CreateAggregate functions both take an array of AggregateData structures. AggregateData is defined in VBoostTypes6.Tlb and has four members. pObject is a reference to the controlling IUnknown of the object to be aggregated, Flags is an enum to be discussed later, and FirstIID and LastIID are indices into an array of VBGUID structures that are passed to the VBoost aggregation functions alongside the AggregateData array. If FirstIID is not filled, this object is treated as a blind aggregate; a QI call is forwarded to the object regardless of the incoming IID. Blind aggregates are very easy to program because you don't have to know the expected set of interface identifiers. The VBoost aggregator objects process all specified IIDs before any of the blindly aggregated objects are given a chance to return the requested interface. Blind QI calls are processed in the order specified by the AggregateData array.

Using the AggregateUnknown function, Class2 above is much easier to write. By leaving an IID for the passed AggregateData structure unspecified, we tell VBoost to give m_Class1 a shot at any interface request that the controlling IUnknown doesn't handle. In other words, we are blindly aggregating m_Class1. The resulting interface interactions are shown in Figure 5.3.

```
'Class2 Implementation. Aggregates Class1
Private m_Hook As UnknownHook
Private m_Class1 As Class1
Private Sub Class_Initialize()
Dim AggData(0) As AggregateData
Dim IIDs() As VBGUID
    Set m_Class1 = New Class1
    Set AggData(0).pObject = m_Class1
    AggregateUnknown Me, pAggData, IIDs, m_Hook
End Sub
```

The code-reuse advantages of aggregating an existing object are obvious from this code snippet. With a small amount of code, you can take full advantage of a completed class implementation to enhance other classes. The aggregated code is also trivial to maintain. If the aggregated class or interface changes, you don't need to make any changes to the code unless a specified IID changes.

Code reuse becomes straightforward when you share memory directly with a base class and aggregate the base class into an existing IUnknown. Let's go

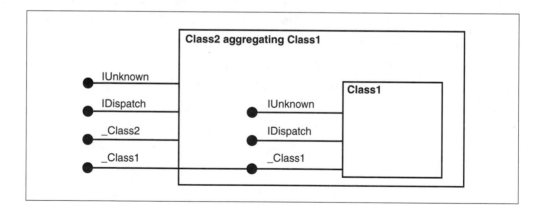

Figure 5.3.   Class2 aggregates Class1 using VBoost.AggregateUnknown. The native interfaces supported by Class2 are not wrapped, and the _Class1 interface supported by _Class1 is wrapped with a blind delegator that makes it act like a native part of Class1. There is no way for an external consumer to tell the difference between the aggregated and the natively implemented interfaces.

back to the IDraw interface shown earlier and create a DrawCircle object based on it. The object shares data with the DrawImpl class and adds a native method, or Area, that calculates the area based on the current bounding rectangle.

```
'Class DrawCircle
Private m_SADrawData As SafeArray1d
Private m_DrawData() As DrawImplData
Private m_Hook As UnknownHook
Private Sub Class_Initialize()
Dim DrawImpl As DrawImpl
Dim AggData(0) As AggregateData
Dim IIDs() As VBGUID
    Set DrawImpl = New DrawImpl
    ShareMemoryViaArray VarPtrArray(m_DrawData), _
        m_SADrawData, DrawImpl.DataPtr, LenB(m_DrawData(0))
    m_DrawData(0).DrawType = dtCircle
    Set AggData(0).pObject = DrawImpl
    'adIgnoreIIDs is the default Flags setting.
    'Since no IIDs are referenced from the AggData array,
    'there is no need to dimension the IIDs array.
    VBoost.AggregateUnknown Me, AggData, IIDs, m_Hook
End Sub
Public Property Get Area() As Single
'Area = Width/2 * Height/2 * pi
'pi = Atn(1) * 4
'The area of ellipse/circle is Width * Height * Atn(1)
    With m_DrawData(0)
        Area = (.x2 - .x1) * (.y2 - .y1) * Atn(1)
    End With
End Property
Private Sub Class_Terminate()
    UnshareMemory VarPtrArray(m_DrawData)
End Sub
```

This is a simple object, but the same principles are easily applied to much larger objects that require several aggregated interfaces. The indirect interface implementation code shown earlier is also no longer necessary: You get the same maintenance-free code when an interface changes because the aggregating class doesn't need to be modified when the aggregated object changes. The calling code is also much cleaner. The DrawCircle listing shown here doesn't implement IDraw or even have a member variable of that type, but it has full support for the interface.

There is nothing to stop you from wrapping an aggregated object within a second aggregator. After all, an aggregated object has the external characteristics of the native object. However, you do need to be sure to release the hook objects in the reverse order in which you created them if you have two or more active UnknownHook variables in the same class. For example, if you want to implement the IQIHook interface to debug an aggregated object, you need one UnknownHook variable (m_Hook) for the AggregateUnknown call and a second (m_HookDbg) for QIHook. If you called AggregateUnknown and then QIHook in Class_Initialize, your terminate event should release the hook objects in reverse order.

```
Private Sub Class_Terminate()
    Set m_HookDbg = Nothing 'Last hook established
    Set m_Hook = Nothing    'First hook established
End Sub
```

The only missing feature of inheritance is redirecting a function to an implementation in the derived class. The ability to call function pointers (which I'll show you in Chapter 11) make this possible by exposing a function pointer in the shared data structure and then calling it from the real entry point. For example, to extend IDraw to support more-complex objects and drawing options, you could let the draw method defer to a function pointer specified by the base class. This is discussed more in the "Cooperative Redirection" section of Chapter 12.

Chapter 6

Circular References

Reference counts control the lifetime of every COM object. When you use a Set statement to assign an object expression to an object variable, the variable owns a reference to the object. But owning a reference to the object does not mean that the variable owns the object itself. If the same instance of an object is assigned to two variables at the same time, then each variable owns a reference count on the object. No distinction is made between the variables—every reference has the same weight.

If variables don't own a COM object, what *does*? The answer is: the object itself. COM objects are self-destructive. They destroy themselves when the last reference is released. Releasing a reference to a COM object with a Set <variable> = Nothing statement simply decrements the reference count. Although this may appear to be a purely semantic difference, releasing a reference should never be considered the same as destroying an object in the world of COM. Owning a reference is simply a way of saying, "I'm using you," and releasing the reference says "I'm done with you." The object is responsible for its own destruction when the last reference is released.

The reference system for controlling object lifetime works well most of the time. Reference counting is lightweight: there is no extra overhead for multiple references on a single object. It also provides excellent encapsulation and consistency in that code that uses an object does not need to know anything special about terminating the object. VB simply releases the reference for an object variable and lets the object manage its own destruction.

Cyclical references are the main problem inherent in using reference counting to control object lifetime. Suppose object A holds a reference to object B, and the reference to B is released when A is destroyed. Similarly, B holds a reference to object A, and the reference to A is released when B is destroyed. This system will never destroy itself because the objects are playing a perpetual waiting game—they are waiting for the other object to tear down first, as shown in Figure 6.1.

The feature that all references are given the same consideration in keeping the object alive is the root cause of the circular-referencing problem. In order to make a circular system tear down, you need a referencing system in which A can reference B in the normal fashion while B holds a special reference to A that does not keep A alive. I'll call a reference that keeps an object alive a *strong reference* and a reference that doesn't keep an object alive a *weak reference*. Strong references are the default referencing behavior of object variables and the Set statement.

A VB object variable consists of a reference on the object and a pointer to the object. When you Set = Nothing, the reference is released, and the object pointer is set to 0. To get a usable weak reference, you need a pointer to the object without the reference count. Use the ObjPtr function, which returns a Long with the same value as the pointer to the object.

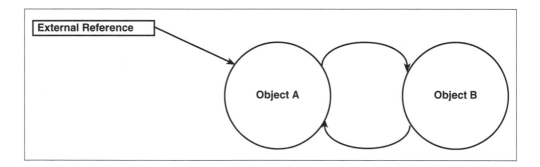

Figure 6.1.   A circularly referenced system

```
Dim StrongRef As SomeObject
Dim WeakRef As Long
Set StrongRef = MyObj
WeakRef = ObjPtr(MyObj)
```

The first problem with a weak reference is that VB makes no provision for calling a method from a Long variable. A weak reference is occasionally referred to as "freeze-dried," and the act of turning it into a strong reference is called "rehydration." As the more-colorful names imply, you can't consume a weak reference without first adding a little "water" to make it a strong reference. A strong reference allows you to consume the object's methods and properties. You can use the following function in straight VB code to achieve rehydration. The CopyMemory API function is defined in the VBoostTypes type library.

```
Function ObjFromPtr(ByVal Ptr As Long) As Object
Dim tmp As Object
    'Copy the pointer into an object variable.
    'VB now thinks that tmp contains a proper strong
    'reference; it will release the reference
    'when tmp goes out of scope or is otherwise
    'Set to Nothing.
    CopyMemory tmp, Ptr, 4
    'Use a normal Set statement to place a
    'strong reference in the function name
    Set ObjFromPtr = tmp
    'Clear the temporary variable. The Set
    'statement can't be used here because this
    'would release a reference count that was
    'never actually added.
    CopyMemory tmp, 0&, 4
End Function
```

ObjFromPtr does quite a bit of work considering that all you want is to assign a pointer value and AddRef it. ObjFromPtr is not universal; you should use a different version of this function for each type on which you hold a weak reference. The VBoost object makes this much more efficient by using the AssignAddRef function. This function uses the As Any type to turn a long value into a reference for any object type without a QueryInterface call. To use AssignAddRef to make a type-specific function, just wrap AssignAddRef within a typed function. You can use this as a prototype for any type-specific conversion function.

```
Function MyTypeFromPtr(ByVal Ptr As Long) As MyType
    VBoost.AssignAddRef MyTypeFromPtr, Ptr
End Function
```

You can now efficiently assign the return value of MyTypeFromPtr to a MyType variable or just use the function in a With statement.

```
With MyTypeFromPtr(WeakMyTypeRef)
    .MyMethod
End With
```

Safety is also a concern with weak references. If you get the ObjPtr of an object, then you don't hold a reference on the object, so you don't keep it alive. VB uses the reference-counting mechanism to guarantee that you can't use an object that points to memory that has already been freed. Weak references bypass this safety mechanism, so you must be 100 percent sure that the weak reference actually refers to a living object before you use AssignAddRef to retrieve a strong reference from the weak reference.

With weak references, you are responsible for ensuring that the weak references are valid. The easiest way to do this is to let the target object set and clear the weak reference. Since weak references are used in a circular-reference situation, the weak-referenced object (class A) already has a strong reference to the object that holds the corresponding weak reference (class B). You should use Friend functions to establish weak references. Unlike Public functions, Friend functions allow you to maintain full internal control over your weak references.

```
'Class A
Private m_B As B
Private Sub Class_Initialize()
    Set m_B = New B
    m_B.SetAPtr ObjPtr(Me)
End Sub
Private Sub Class_Terminate()
    m_B.SetAPtr 0
End Sub
```

```
'Class B
Private m_APtr As Long
Friend Sub SetAPtr(ByVal pA As Long)
    m_APtr = pA
End Sub
Public Property Get A() As A
    'AssignAddRef handles a 0 in m_APtr set the same way
    'a Set statement handles the Nothing value: it checks
    'the pointer value before calling AddRef.
    VBoost.AssignAddRef A, m_APtr
End Property
```

Intermediate Object Solutions

Since weak references are inherently unsafe, you might want to consider using alternate solutions to circular-reference problems. Although I'll discuss ways of avoiding nonterminating circular references, I hope this section shows you that the number of hoops you have to jump through to avoid the weak-reference mechanism is simply not worth the trouble or the overhead. In the initial illustration, I'll examine a system that tears down correctly using only reference counting.

If A references B and B relies on functionality from A, then you can use an intermediate helper object A' to act as a go-between. In such a scenario, A references B, and both A and B reference A'. There are no references—strong or weak—to A from A' or B. By moving the code that B relies on from A to A', you give B the support it needs without having a reference on A. If you get very far into this exercise, you'll find that you end up moving most of the functionality of A into A'. A becomes little more than a wrapper that forwards methods to A'. This system in shown in Figure 6.2.

There are no circular references in this system, there are a couple big limitations. Although B can effectively call A by calling the corresponding methods on A', B cannot return a reference to A itself. If A and B are public objects in an object model, and A is the parent object, B does not support a public Parent property.

Another limitation of this system is that A' does not have access to B because A owns B. I'm temporarily avoiding weak references, so A' can't reference A or B. This limitation is actually much more severe because A', which is the actual implementation of A, can't access its child objects. Unlike the first

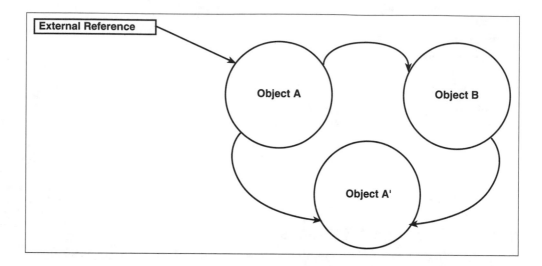

Figure 6.2. An intermediate object eliminates the circular reference between objects A and B.

limitation, this problem can be solved by removing the requirement that teardown rely solely on reference counting. The extra step beyond the reference-counting mechanism occurs in the A object's Class_Terminate, which must call a Terminate function on the A' object. Terminate on A' releases all references to B, and the system can tear down. This system is shown in Figure 6.3.

Of course, this system is actually circular in nature, but the use of an intermediate object guarantees that a Class_Terminate event fires on the system's noncircular object, allowing the circular reference between A' and B to be explicitly broken. You have to be very careful to actually write the teardown code, or your system will leak objects (and their associated memory) like a sieve.

```
'Class A
Private m_Helper As AHelper
Private Sub Class_Initialize()
    Set m_Helper = New AHelper
End Sub
Private Sub Class_Terminate()
    m_Helper.Terminate
End Sub
Public Property Get Child() As B
```

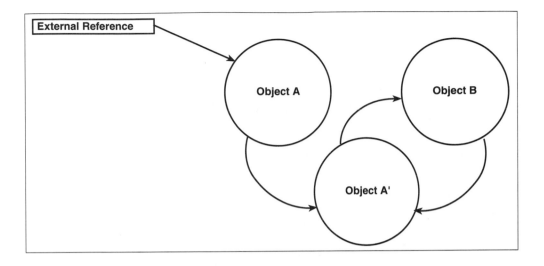

Figure 6.3. An explicit Terminate method, called by Class_Terminate in A, is exposed by the intermediate object (A') to tell it to let go of any B references.

```
        Set Child = m_Helper.Child
End Property
```

```
'Class AHelper
Private m_Child As B
Friend Property Get Child() As B
    If m_Child Is Nothing Then
        InitChild
    End If
    Set Child = m_Child
End Property
Friend Sub Terminate()
    Set m_Child = Nothing
End Sub
Private Sub InitChild()
    Set m_Child = New B
    m_Child.SetParent Me
End Sub
```

```
'Class B
Private m_Parent As AHelper
```

```
Friend Sub SetParent(Parent As AHelper)
    Set m_Parent = Parent
End Sub
```

Although this system is a little on the messy side, it is reasonably manage-able. I'm going to make it much more complicated by adding a Parent property to the child class. Since weak references are ignored as an available tool, you can't return the original A. However you *can* return an object that is functionally equivalent by creating a new A and pointing it to the same AHelper object. This complicates things because A should call Terminate only if it's the last A that references AHelper, but that isn't accessible information. The result is that AHelper now needs to keep an explicit count of the A instances that use it, and A has to notify AHelper when it starts to use it as well as when it's done. As you review this new system, remember that you could be writing all of this code simply to avoid using a weak reference.

```
'Class A
Private m_Helper As AHelper
Private Sub InitHelper()
    Set m_Helper = New AHelper
    AHelper.Advise
End Sub
Friend Sub SetHelper(Helper As AHelper)
    If Not m_Helper Is Nothing Then m_Helper.UnAdvise
    Set m_Helper = Helper
    Helper.Advise
End Sub
Private Sub Class_Terminate()
    If Not m_Helper Is Nothing Then m_Helper.UnAdvise
End Sub
Public Property Get Child() As B
    If m_Helper Is Nothing Then InitHelper
    Set Child = m_Helper.Child
End Property
```

```
'Class AHelper
Private m_Child As B
Private m_cAdvised As Long
Friend Property Get Child() As B
```

```
    If m_Child Is Nothing Then
        InitChild
    End If
    Set Child = m_Child
End Property
Friend Sub Advise()
    m_cAdvised = m_cAdvised + 1
End Sub
Friend Sub UnAdvise()
    m_cAdvised = m_cAdvised - 1
    If m_cAdvised = 0 Then
        Set m_Child = Nothing
    End If
End Sub
Private Sub InitChild()
    Set m_Child = New B
    m_Child.SetParent Me
End Sub
```

```
'Class B
Private m_Parent As AHelper
Friend Sub SetParent(Parent As AHelper)
    Set m_Parent = Parent
End Sub
Public Property Get Parent() As A
    Set Parent = New A
    Parent.SetHelper m_Parent
End Property
```

It is reasonable to use an explicit teardown function to ensure correct termination within the same project, but you should always avoid the practice across components. If you keep the rules for object-model teardown as simple as possible for the client (meaning releasing all references in a random order is sufficient), the consumers of the object always know how to use the object model. Microsoft has botched these simple guidelines several times over the years.

The first example of poor object model design is the Excel.Application.Quit method, designed to be called by the client when Excel was no longer needed. The problem was that Quit also stopped Excel for all other clients, not just for yours. Quit was eventually modified to not actually shut the program down, thereby avoiding this very unneighborly behavior. Data objects, such as DAO, provide another example of poor teardown behavior. DAO has Close methods that must often be called in the correct order, and the objects must be released in the correct order as well (Recordset before Database, for example). This single poor object model behavior has led to the misconception that VB leaks memory unless you explicitly set all the local variables to Nothing at the end of a function. This is a completely false notion in a well-designed object model. VB can clear the variables faster at the End Sub line than you can from code, and it checks the variables even if you explicitly release your references. Any effort you make is duplicated.

Weak References and Collections

ObjPtr is very useful when you store objects in a VBA Collection. ObjPtr provides not only a means of weak referencing, but also a string identifier for the object. Even if you're not using weak references, you will frequently find yourself using ObjPtr to generate a unique key for an object. Since ObjPtr is the pointer to an object and remains the same over the object's lifetime, the number returned by ObjPtr, when converted to a string, provides a unique key. The Collection object won't accept a numeric key, but it is quite happy with a String, even if the String contains a number. Let's look at the code that tracks all outstanding instances of a class within a collection. Such a tracking system requires weak references because the tracker should track existing objects, but not keep them alive. The code is surprisingly easy.

```
'In a bas module
Public g_CollMyClass As New VBA.Collection
Public Sub DumpMyClass()
Dim Inst As MyClass
Dim Iter As Variant
    For Each Iter In g_CollMyClass
        'MyClassFromPtr as above
        Set Inst = MyClassFromPtr(Iter)
        'Debug.Print Inst.Data
    Next
End Sub
```

```
'MyClass class module
Private Sub Class_Initialize()
Dim pMe As Long
    pMe = ObjPtr(Me)
    g_CollMyClass.Add pMe, CStr(pMe)
End Sub
Private Sub Class_Terminate()
    g_CollMyClass.Remove CStr(ObjPtr(Me))
End Sub
```

Transferring Object Ownership

There are times when you can greatly simplify algorithms and reduce code by storing object references in something other than an object variable. For example, you can associate an item in a ListBox with an underlying object. The non-ObjPtr solution to this problem involves making each string in the ListBox a key in a collection that stores the objects. However, selecting an item then requires a corresponding collection lookup to access the item, and you have to worry about duplicate strings in the ListBox.

To simplify this approach, a ListBox has an ItemData property that lets you associate a Long value with each item. If you just want to solve the unique key problem, you can key your collection of objects with CStr(ObjPtr(object)) and store the ObjPtr in the ItemData. But you must still perform a collection-lookup to retrieve the object. Rather than storing the object somewhere else, you can just as easily store the ObjPtr in ItemData and also let the ItemData own the object.

```
Private Sub AddListObject( _
   Name As String, ByVal Obj As Object)
Dim pObj As Long
    With lstObjects
        .AddItem Name
        'Transfer ownership of the reference to a
        long value
        VBoost.AssignSwap pObj, Obj
        .ItemData(.NewIndex) = pObj
End With
End Sub
Private Sub RemoveListObject(ByVal Index As Long)
```

```
     Dim tmp As Object
     With lstObjects
          'Transfer ownership to a local variable
          'that will be released when this procedure
          'goes out of scope.
          VBoost.Assign tmp, .ItemData(Index)
          .RemoveItem Index
     End With
End Sub
```

You now have a simple object-ownership mechanism that uses no storage object other than the ListBox. You can use AssignAddRef in the lstObjects_Click event to get a strong reference to the underlying object. Of course, the disadvantage if this method is that you have to write explicit clean-up code before the ListBox is cleared. The ListBox is oblivious to the fact that it is now the proud owner of a set of objects—you are responsible for clearing it explicitly on teardown.

Hierarchical Object Models

Almost all object models are hierarchical, meaning that there is some kind of parent/child relationship among the different objects in the object model. For example, a Word Document object has a Paragraphs property that returns a Paragraphs object. Document is the parent of the Paragraphs collection object and the associated Paragraph objects, and, as expected, Paragraphs.Parent or Paragraphs(1).Parent both return the Parent document. Similarly, a Paragraph object is the parent of the ParagraphFormat object, so Paragraph acts as both a parent and a child.

Hierarchical object models are highly cyclical. Parent properties, whether they are called Parent, Container, Owner, or something similar, are almost always required for programming flexibility. Hierarchical object models are a common design construct that you will use many times. If you use them well, your components will have a professional programming model and feel.

When creating hierarchical object models in VB, you must first determine the parent/child relationships in the system. If the parent object holds a strong reference to its children and the child object receives a weak reference to its parent object via a Friend function called by the parent, you have a solid model on which to build an object model. You may think that the material shown so far is sufficient for you to create great hierarchical object models. After all, you can support weak references to parent objects and rehydrate parent pointers when you need to call the parent or pass a parent reference to the outside world. What more is there to do?

The remaining issues of using an object model fall under the category of creating robust objects. In the context of object models, one of the requirements for robustness is that an object is fully functional even when it is the only external reference held against an object in the object model. For example, this code should run correctly:

```
Dim P As Parent
Dim C As Child
    Set P = New Parent
    Set C = P.Children(1)
    Set P = Nothing
    Set P = C.Parent
```

This code may seem diabolical when you view it sequentially. But to be robust, objects must be prepared to handle such a situation. Note that in the model shown above, Set P = Nothing releases the Parent object, which calls the SetParentPtr Friend function on the Child object with a 0 pointer. Therefore, C.Parent returns Nothing.

Generally, Child objects are well-defined only in the context of their Parents, so this Child object is no longer fully functional. An object in a less-than-functional state is said to be "zombied"—its methods and properties do nothing or return errors because the context under which the object was created no longer exists. A fully robust object should only "zombie" when absolutely necessary. For example, it is valid for the Visual Basic IDE's extensibility model to be partially zombied during teardown (meaning not all methods work) because extensibility is simply a view of a set of objects, as opposed to an owner of a strong reference to those objects.

You need two versions of the child object to stop a Child object from reaching a zombied state. The first version is internal. This is the version of the object referenced by the Parent. To ensure proper teardown, the internal version has a weak reference to the parent object. You also need an external version of the child object. The external version is returned from a Public procedure to an external client. To keep the object robust, the external version of the object must have a strong reference to the parent but behave like the internal child object in all other aspects.

The goal is to reconcile these requirements while using the least amount of code. It may seem easier to just zombie the object, but zombieing often requires error-checking code in most member functions, adding overhead and code complexity to the class and error-trapping code to all the consumers. By proactively keeping any publicly exposed object in a fully valid state, you can eliminate validation code from the public procedures. A little extra code to make the object robust can save you and your consumers a lot of grief down the road.

The requirements for an external version of the child object are twofold. First, the external object must support all the interfaces supported by the internal child. Second, the external object must hold a strong reference on all objects that are held as weak references internally. If you try to do this in straight VB, you end up with an object that implements multiple interfaces (including Child) and forwards all calls to an m_RealChild member variable. This approach has some obvious problems: No one wants to write it in the first place, code maintenance is a hassle, and there is a runtime performance hit as all those calls are forwarded to the internal member variable. There is also a less-obvious problem in that the external object doesn't support late binding on its primary interface unless you can exactly duplicate all the public procedures in the Child class in addition to implementing the Child interface. Exact duplication is very difficult, as the target object layout is a function of both the project's compatibility settings, the function order in the class module, and any special procedure attributes. Based on this never-ending paragraph, I assume you don't want to code this.

In order to make a workable hierarchical system, you need to aggregate the external object on top of the child object using the VBoost objects (see "Aggregating Existing Objects" in Chapter 5). This is easy to do with the VBoost.CreateAggregate function. You can do this with minimal code using a GetExternalChild Friend function in the child class. The new system is shown in Figure 6.4.

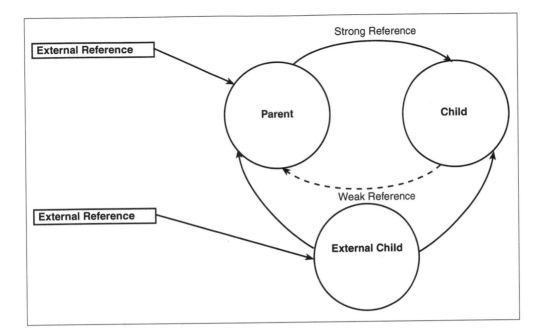

Figure 6.4. An external to a child object also holds an implicit strong reference to the parent object.

```
'In Child.cls
Private m_ParentPtr As Long
Private m_ExternalPtr As Long
Friend Sub SetParentPtr(ByVal ParentPtr As Long)
    m_ParentPtr = ParentPtr
End Sub
Public Property Get Parent() As Parent
    VBoost.AssignAddRef Parent, m_ParentPtr
End Property
Friend Function GetExternalChild() As Child
Dim AggData(1) As AggregateData
Dim IIDs () As VBGUID
Dim pUnk As IUnknown
    If m_ExternalPtr Then
        'Something is already holding a reference to an
        'external object. Just rehydrate its IUnknown
        'pointer and return.
        VBoost.AssignAddRef pUnk, m_ExternalPtr
```

```
        Set GetExternalChild = pUnk
    Else
        'Defer all QueryInterface calls to the child
        With AggData(0)
            Set .pObject = Me
            .Flags = adIgnoreIIDs
        End With


        'Let the aggregator hold the parent reference for us.
        With AggData(1)
            'Rehydrate the parent into the AggData structure
            VBoost.AssignAddRef .pObject, m_ParentPtr

            'Tell the aggregator to own this object, but
            'not to publicly expose it via a QueryInterface
            .Flags = adDontQuery
        End With


        'Create the aggregate object and write the pointer of
        'its controlling IUnknown to the given memory
        'location. This memory is cleared when the external
        'object is destroyed and rehydrated in the mean time.
        Set GetExternalChild = VBoost.CreateAggregate( _
            AggData, IIDs, VarPtr(m_ExternalPtr))
    End If
End Function
```

```
'In Parent.cls
Private m_Children As Collection
Friend Property Get ChildInternal(ByVal Index As Long) As
                                    Child
    Set ChildInternal = m_Children(Index)
End Property
Public Property Get Child(ByVal Index As Long) As Child
    Set Child = InternalChild(Index).GetExternalChild
End Property
```

If you use this code in all of your child objects, the child object always has a valid reference to its Parent. This code is also shown in a generalized format in the "CreateAggregate" section of Appendix A. In fact, if you can be sure that your project's internal child references also have a valid parent reference, you don't even have to call SetParentPtr 0 on each child when the parent object is destroyed. You know the parent can't be destroyed when an external child reference is still outstanding, so the very fact that the parent *is* being destroyed means that none of the child object's public functions will be called again. This makes it unnecessary to clean up the weak references. Clearly, this requires discipline in your internal code: You have to make sure that the parent holds the only remaining child references. But such discipline can significantly simplify your teardown code and provide a performance boost as well.

With the code above, the only external evidence that you're using a wrapper object is that the child object's ObjPtr may change over time. Also note that the aggregator uses blind vtable-delegation internally. There is a very small performance impact, but the overhead is negligible, particularly when compared to the Implements and forwarding code you would have to write to achieve the same effect.

Chapter 7

External Object Creation

Publicly exposed objects are plentiful in the COM land-scape. One of your jobs as a VB programmer is to add to the set of public objects that you and other members of your organization can leverage to build applications. Understanding how to create external objects is an impor-tant step in using them. This chapter looks at how VB creates external objects using New, CreateObject, and GetObject; and API-based alternatives to object creation.

Before it can create an external COM object, VB must first be able to locate the object in the system. The HKEY_CLASSES_ROOT\CLSID registry section maps a CLSID (class identifier) to a physical location on the local system or a remote system. A CLSID is just one way COM uses a GUID (globally unique identifier), a 128-bit structure guaranteed to be unique across all systems. In order to support external object creation, an ActiveX server registers a CLSID for each supported object and publishes a list of the supported classes in the server's typelib. The typelib, which is generally built into the server's executable file as a resource, is a description of the supported classes in a library and the interfaces supported by those classes.

VB uses two mechanisms for providing a CLSID to COM, allowing COM to create an external object. In the first, VB adds a project reference to the typelib that contains the CLSID. This is the preferred mechanism for object creation; the compiled VB code knows which CLSID it must create and does not need to search for it. In the second mechanism, VB looks up the CLSID at runtime based on a friendly name for the object (called a ProgID). A ProgID generally takes the form of *ServerName.ClassName*. This string is also stored in the system registry and simply points to the CLSID key. Unfortunately, the ProgID string value is not entirely trustworthy because there is no guarantee that the string is unique. If the consumers of a particular ActiveX server rely on the ProgID, the external objects are effectively removed from the system if another ActiveX server happens to register the same ProgID. The key's potential duplication and the extra registry lookup required makes it best to use a CLSID directly whenever possible.

If you use VB's New keyword, the compiled code always knows the CLSID at runtime. If you use CreateObject, VB finds the CLSID by using the ProgID stored in the registry. This generates an extra system call for each object you create. Using CreateObject also makes you vulnerable to naming conflicts because a ProgID is not a unique identifier.

New and CreateObject also return different initial interfaces. In the case of New, the first interface requested is the default interface of the class, as described in the typelib. If you create an object on another machine, process, or thread, you want to request only the interfaces you need because requesting additional interfaces is expensive. However, CreateObject returns the IDispatch (As Object) interface or the IUnknown interface if IDispatch is not available. Any request for an additional interface—including the object's primary interface—must be made with a subsequent Set statement.

In most uses, New and CreateObject are adequate for external COM-object creation. With VB6's introduction of a second machine-name parameter to CreateObject, you can specify the DCOM server you would like the objects to be created on. Although this new feature eliminates a common need for API work to create an object, the API still offers a great deal more flexibility than VB's built-in creation functions. I'll look at how you can use VB's GetObject function and the CoGetClassObject API to locate a class factory for any CLSID. This allows you to eliminate the bulk of the object-creation machinations from all but the first instance in which you create a specific class of object. All the API and interface definitions you will need for this chapter's code are declared in

ObjCreate.Olb (VBoost: Object Creation and Security). I'm also assuming that your project includes a reference to VBoostTypes6.Olb and an instantiated VBoost variable.

Object Creation with Class Factories

The COM specification does not include a mechanism for direct object-creation against a DLL or EXE server. Instead, COM uses an intermediate interface, called IClassFactory, that is a system standard for creating objects. When you call CreateObject or New, which map to the CoCreateInstance and CoCreateInstanceEx APIs, you tell COM to locate an IClassFactory instance for the CLSID. COM then calls the IClassFactory.CreateInstance method to create the requested object.

If you need to create multiple objects of the same type, you waste a lot of processing cycles by constantly releasing and relocating the class factory. It is much more efficient to get a class factory once and then call CreateInstance a number of times. For example, in the discussion of multiple threads in Chapter 13, you'll see that you must use CreateObject against objects in your own project in order to create objects on different threads. It is more efficient for the main thread to retrieve a class factory once, and then call CreateInstance to launch each worker thread.

Using the built-in system clsid moniker and GetObject is the easiest way to get a class-factory interface. The following code does the same work as CreateObject, but it doesn't call the object-initialization interfaces (see "Initializing Persistable Objects" later in this chapter). However, the function returns a class factory and leaves the last step of calling CreateInstance to the caller.

```
Public Function CreateClassFactory( _
  CLSID As CLSID) As IClassFactory
Dim GuidString As String * 38
    StringFromGUID2 CLSID, GuidString
    Set CreateClassFactory = GetObject("clsid:" & GuidString)
End Function

'Calling Code, roughly equivalent to CreateObject
Dim MyObj As MyObject
```

```
Dim MyObjCF As IClassFactory
Dim IID_IUnknown As IID
    IID_IUnknown = IIDFromString(strIID_IUnknown)
    Set MyObjCF = CreateClassFactory( _
      CLSIDFromProgID("MyProj.MyObj"))
    Set MyObj = MyObjCF.CreateInstance(Nothing, IID_IUnknown)
```

By referencing the class factory explicitly, you can choose whether to use a CLSID or a ProgID as the primary means of identifying the target object. All Win32 platforms up to Windows 2000 required that you go through the class factory to skip the ProgID-resolution code. Windows 2000 lets you replace "clsid:" with "new:" in the GetObject argument to create a single instance directly instead of retrieving the class factory.

Class Factory Retrieval

The standard mechanism for retrieving a class factory varies according to whether you get the object from a DLL, a local EXE, or from DCOM. I'll look closely at the architechure of DLL and local EXE cases so that you can gain even finer control of object creation.

The CoGetClassObject API call manages all class-factory retrieval processes. CoGetClassObject takes four parameters. The first is the CLSID of the object you need to create, and the last is the IID of the interface you want to call the object with (generally IID_IClassFactory). The remaining parameters, dwClsContext and pServerInfo, provide information about the context (DLL, EXE, or DCOM) to create the object in, and information about the DCOM server in the case of a remote object.

The context values are listed in the CLSCTX enum, with all but the three most-common values hidden in VBoostTypes. The three values that you'll generally use in VB are CLSCTX_INPROC_SERVER, CLSCTX_LOCAL_SERVER, and CLSCTX_REMOTE_SERVER. These context values load an object from a DLL, an EXE, or a DCOM server, respectively. A class factory in the same thread as the caller is considered INPROC even if the EXE supplies it rather than a DLL. If more than one value is specified and the same CLSID is supported at multiple context levels, COM resolves to the closest possible context (DLL over EXE over DCOM).

Context resolution can be ambiguous when multiple running servers support the same CLSID. You can easily see this problem by launching multiple instances of the same ActiveX EXE when the EXE is used as a stand-alone appliation. A VB-created ActiveX EXE registers class factories only on the primary thread. This means that a CLSCTX_INPROC_SERVER request for a MultiUse object exposed in the same EXE succeeds in the primary thread but not in a secondary thread. However, if a secondary thread uses CLSCTX_LOCAL_SERVER to retrieve a class factory, there is no guarantee that the class factory comes from the primary thread of the same process. In fact, the returned class factory always comes from the first EXE instance that registered its class factory. The solution is to specify CLSCTX_INPROC_SERVER Or CLSCTX_LOCAL_SERVER as the context parameter. CoGetClassObject handles this request specially and always returns a class factory from the same process if one is available.

Set the pServerInfo parameter to 0 if you don't want to create a DCOM object or if you want to use the currently registered server to create the object. The COSERVERINFO structure identifies a remote machine and provides user authentication and authorization information. Although I have defined all the COM security structures and APIs in the ObjCreate typelib, I won't address the topic of security. Refer to Keith Brown's *Programming Windows Security* for a full discussion of security. In order to get a class factory from a machine with default security, use the following code as an outline. CreateRemoteFromCLSID is functionally equivalent to CreateObject with a server name.

```
Public Function CreateRemoteFromCLSID( _
    ServerName As String, CLSID As CLSID) As IUnknown
Dim ServerInfo As COSERVERINFO
Dim pCF As IClassFactory
    ServerInfo.pwszServerPrincName = StrPtr(ServerName)
    Set pCF = CoGetClassObject(CLSID, CLSCTX_REMOTE_SERVER, _
        VarPtr(ServerInfo), IIDFromString(strIID_IClassFactory))
    Set CreateRemoteFromCLSID = pCF.CreateInstance( _
        Nothing, IIDFromString(strIID_IUnknown)
End Function
```

DLLs and EXEs are fundamentally different. An EXE controls its lifetime, and a DLL does not. The DLL is always at the mercy of the EXE process that loaded it. Unlike an EXE, a DLL can export functions. These differences lead to fundamentally different mechanisms for exposing class factories.

COM retrieves a class factory from a DLL by using the exported DllGetClassObject function. COM loads the DLL specified by the InprocServer32 entry in the registry's CLSID section, uses GetProcAddress to locate the DllGetClassObject entry point, and calls the function pointer to get a class factory for the requested CLSID. Once the in-process class factory makes it back to the requesting object, COM is completely out of the object-interaction picture. COM's only remaining responsibility is to unload the DLL. You can call the CoFreeUnusedLibraries API, which calls the DllCanUnloadNow entrypoint for all DLLs loaded by CoGetClassObject, to see if all the objects and class factories in a given DLL have been released by the current thread. When DllCanUnloadNow returns a success code, the DLL is removed from memory with the FreeLibrary API. VB calls CoFreeUnusedLibraries occasionally if a form is showing. However, you can call it yourself anytime if you have reason to believe that one or more COM DLLs are no longer in use.

In the case of an EXE, COM reads the LocalServer32 key in the CLSID section to locate the server EXE, then launches the process. The EXE registers all its supported class factories with COM by using the CoRegisterClassObject API call. Once the object is fully registered, COM looks up the requested CLSID in an internal table and returns the class-factory reference to the caller. If COM already has an IClassFactory reference, it uses the existing factory rather than relaunching the EXE. On process termination, the EXE unregisters the class factory with CoRevokeClassObject.

Initializing Persistable Objects

If you create an external object with a class factory instead of with New or CreateObject, you've done almost everything that VB does to initialize a new object. However, VB takes an extra step to ensure that all the objects it creates are fully initialized. Immediately after it creates an object, VB attempts to retrieve the IPersistStreamInit interface so that it can call InitNew. If the external class was built with VB and has the Persistable attribute set to 1 - Persistable, this code runs the Class_InitProperties event (if you have it defined). If VB can't

get an IPersistStreamInit interface, it tries to get an IPersistPropertyBag interface. IPersistPropertyBag also has an InitNew method.

ObjCreate.Olb includes interface definitions that allow you to initialize
objects by using these standard interfaces. If you know the object you're creating
does nothing in InitNew, you can skip the initialization code. The following snippet uses the CreateClassFactory function I showed you earlier, but this time it
also attempts to initialize the object.

```
'Calling Code, even closer to CreateObject
Dim MyObj As MyObject
Dim MyObjCF As IClassFactory
Dim IID_IUnknown As IID
Dim pInit As IPersistStreamInit
    IID_IUnknown = IIDFromString(strIID_IUnknown)
    Set MyObjCF = CreateClassFactory(CLSIDFromProgID( _
      "MyProj.MyObj"))
    Set MyObj = MyObjCF.CreateInstance(Nothing, IID_IUnknown)
    On Error Resume Next
    Set pInit = MyObj
    On Error GoTo 0
    If Not pInit Is Nothing Then pInit.InitNew
```

Loading DLL Objects Directly

Although you can duplicate all the steps that CoGetClassObject goes through to
retrieve a class factory from a DLL, there is no inherent reason for you to rely on
a registry entry to locate and load a DLL. There are two big advantages to loading a COM object based on the path of the executable rather than on a path in
the system registry.

The first advantage is that you can use the DLL in the same thread without
registering it with COM. The distribution and versioning advantages of this
approach are numerous. You can distribute multiple versions of the same DLL
and isolate each version to completely eliminate any chance of compromising a
previously installed application that uses the same DLL. You must register the
type library if you plan to pass an object between threads or processes, but even
in this case you don't need to use the registry to locate and load the DLL.

The second advantage is that you can load multiple equivalent DLLs and use the same code to control their objects. You can easily give multiple DLLs the same set of CLSIDs and IIDs by using the same binary-compatible file for multiple DLL projects. This allows you to define a standard set of interfaces for adding capabilities to the main application, and then add pieces to the application dynamically by adding or removing DLLs from a directory or data file in the application's directory. By loading the DLLs directly, you can also unload and upgrade them directly, allowing you to update pieces of the application without shutting it down. Just be sure to use nonconflicting base addresses for each DLL.

The MSDN documentation says that CoLoadLibrary function uses the bAutoFree parameter to specify that the DLL is unloaded automatically if it is no longer in use when the CoFreeUnusedLibraries API is called. Don't believe the documentation (except for the part that says you shouldn't call CoLoadLibrary directly). If you step through the API call with system symbols in place, you'll see that the bAutoFree parameter is ignored. CoLoadLibrary is nothing more than a thin wrapper on LoadLibraryEx. CoGetClassObject maintains the list of loaded libraries for CoFreeUnusedLibraries without using CoLoadLibrary. Since direct loading doesn't use CoGetClassObject, this means that you can't use CoFreeUnusedLibraries to implicitly free the DLL.

The one special thing that CoLoadLibrary does is to call LoadLibraryEx with the LOAD_WITH_ALTERED_SEARCH_PATH flag. When you specify a full path for the DLL, this flag tells Windows to search for dependent DLLs starting with the DLLs directory *not* in the directory of the application that is using it. Using the DLL search path can be especially important if you call LoadLibraryEx from another DLL rather than from an EXE.

You can use LoadLibrary[Ex] indirectly to specify a DLL path for Declare calls. This can be especially useful in DLL projects, which attempt to resolve the library names relative to the path of the EXE that loaded them. A Declare statement in a DLL doesn't even pick up another DLL in the same directory unless the directory is also part of the application path. If you are not sure that a DLL will be located on the path but you know the path relative to the EXE or DLL, you can set up an error trap for the API call. If a file error occurs, call Load-Library with a full path to the DLL, then the VB-declared API, and then Free-Library. The API call succeeds on subsequent calls because VB doesn't let go of a library once it loads it with a Declare call. You don't have this luxury with typelib-defined function declarations, all of which are resolved when the process is loaded. You should also avoid locking yourself into a specific installation directory by not hard-coding any paths into your Declare statements.

These functions load a DLL and retrieve a class factory, and then test to see if the DLL can be unloaded. This code (which you'll find in COMDllLoader.Bas) uses FunctionDelegator.Bas (discussed in Chapter 11) to call the DllGetClassObject and DllCanUnloadNow function pointers.

```
'Requires a reference to ObjCreate.olb and VBoostTypes6.olb
'FunctionDelegator.Bas must also be loaded in the project.
Private m_fInit As Boolean
Public IID_IClassFactory As IID
Public IID_IUnknown As IID
Private m_FDDllGetClassObject As FunctionDelegator
Private m_pCallDllGetClassObject As ICallDllGetClassObject
Private m_FDDllCanUnloadNow As FunctionDelegator
Private m_pCallDllCanUnloadNow As ICallDllCanUnloadNow

Private Sub Init()
    IID_IClassFactory = IIDFromString(strIID_IClassFactory)
    IID_IUnknown = IIDFromString(strIID_IUnknown)
    Set m_pCallDllGetClassObject = _
      InitDelegator(m_FDDllGetClassObject)
    Set m_pCallDllCanUnloadNow = _
      InitDelegator(m_FDDllCanUnloadNow)
    m_fInit = True
End Sub

Public Function GetDllClassObject(ByVal DllPath As String, _
  CLSID As CLSID, hModDll As HINSTANCE) As IClassFactory
    If Not m_fInit Then Init
    If hModDll = 0 Then
        hModDll = LoadLibraryEx( _
```

```vb
        DllPath, 0, LOAD_WITH_ALTERED_SEARCH_PATH)
    If hModDll = 0 Then
        Err.Raise &H80070000 + Err.LastDllError
    End If
    End If
    m_FDDllGetClassObject.pfn = GetProcAddress( _
        hModDLL, "DllGetClassObject")
    If m_FDDLLGetClassObject.pfn = 0 Then
        Err.Raise &H80070000 + Err.LastDllError
    End If
    'The function declaration specifies an HRESULT return
    'value, so this can raise a standard error.
    Set GetDllClassObject = m_pCallDllGetClassObject.Call( _
        CLSID, IID_IClassFactory)
End Function


Public Sub TestUnloadDll(hModDll As HINSTANCE)
    If Not m_fInit Then Init
    If hModDll Then
        m_FDDllCanUnloadNow.pfn = GetProcAddress( _
            hModDll, "DllCanUnloadNow")
        If m_FDDllCanUnloadNow.pfn = 0 Then
            Err.Raise &H80070000 + Err.LastDllError
        End If
        If m_pCallDllCanUnloadNow.Call = 0 Then
            FreeLibrary hModDll
            hModDll = 0
        End If
    End If
End Sub
```

To load and unload DLLs, you must determine a CLSID of an object in the DLL, the DLL's location, and keep track of its module handle after you load it. The CLSID is a moving target if you don't set the DLL's compatibility level to the project or binary level. There are several ways to determine the CLSID. You can use a low-level type library browser (such as OleView.Exe), the TLI (TypeLib Information) objects included with VB, or a utility called DumpClassData.Exe included with the book. DumpClassData generates a CLSID constant for each creatable class in a type library and a runtime license key for licensed objects in a DLL or OCX. Run DumpClassData by specifying a file on the command line or by selecting one in a dialog. In either case, the utility generates clipboard data that looks something like this.

```
'Target control
Private Const strCLSID_Target As String = _
  "{C33A1760-A296-11D3-BBF5-D41203C10000}"
Private Const RTLic_Target As String = "mkjmmmrlhmknmo"
```

Once you have obtained the CLSID, you can use this calling code to load and unload the DLL. This code loads from a single DLL, and doesn't cache the class factory. You can modify the code to track multiple DLLs or cache the class factory.

```
Const strDllObjectCLSID As String = _
  "{C33A1760-A296-11D3-BBF5-D41203C10000}"
Dim CLSID_DllObject As CLSID
Dim m_hModMyDll As Long


Sub CreateMyDllObject(RelPath As String) As MyDllObject
Dim pCF As IClassFactory
    If m_hModMyDll = 0 Then
        'Load or reload the DLL
        CLSID_DllObject = GUIDFromString(strDllObjectCLSID)
        Set pCF = GetDLLClassObject(App.Path & "\" & _
          RelPath, CLSID_DllObject, m_hModMyDll)
    Else
        Set pCF = GetDllClassObject(vbNullString, _
          CLSID_DllObject, m_hModMyDll)
    End If
    'Create the instance. IID_IUnknown is declared in
    'COMDllLoader.Bas.
    Set CreateMyDllObject = _
      pCF.CreateInstance(Nothing, IID_IUnknown)
End Sub


Sub UnloadDll()
    TestUnloadDll m_hModMyDll
End Sub
```

You should control the DLL loading only if the application's single-threaded or if the DLL supports apartment threading. Do not use the "load-it-yourself" code to violate COM's apartment rules. If the target DLL is single-threaded, COM creates all objects on a single thread and provides a proxy object instead of a directly created object. Fortunately, it is trivially easy to change a project property and make VB-created DLLs apartment threaded.

Custom Loading Custom Controls

An OCX is just an ActiveX DLL with a fancy file extension. An OCX and a DLL expose the same four DLL entrypoints. However, the OCX presents itself to the outside world differently by changing some typelib flags and registration settings. The library attributes of an OCX typelib are marked with the control attribute, which prevents VB from listing the library as an available choice in the Project|References dialog. The coclass definition in the typelib for each of an OCX's controls is also marked with the control and noncreatable attributes, which block object-creation with the New keyword. A registered control also registers a Control key in its CLSID section, which tells VB to show the control on the Controls tab of the Project|Components dialog.

The tweaks that turn a DLL into an OCX involve only a superficial handful of typelib attributes and registry settings. There are no fundamental differences between an OCX and a DLL once you get inside the DLL itself. COM loads controls from the OCX by calling DllGetClassObject for an IClassFactory and then calling CreateInstance on the class factory, just as it does with a normal DLL. When you use objects from an OCX in VB, you use a different dialog to add them to your project, and VB handles all the object creation for you.

When you custom-load an object from an OCX, you have to consider licensing. You don't have to consider this when you use objects in a DLL. In order to create a licensed control, you need a special entry in the registry's HKEY_CLASSES_ROOT\Licenses section, or you need to use the CreateInstanceLic method on the IClassFactory2 interface instead of the CreateInstance on IClassFactory. If the regular license key is not present, CreateInstanceLic takes a string parameter that is required to create an instance of the control. On a machine where the control has a design-time license, this runtime license string is also available from the IClassFactory2 interface. You can generate runtime license keys along with the CLSID values using the DumpClassData utility mentioned earlier in this chapter. The license strings are available only for controls that have a design-time license on the current machine.

Since you don't use New or CreateObject to load a custom control, you can't use the functions from COMDllLoader.bas functions to directly load a COM control the way you would an object from a DLL. You need to let VB create a control for you, and then redirect all requests to the VB-created control to a control object you've custom loaded from an OCX. Making an object appear to be another object is easy with the VBoost objects, but there are some drawbacks to this technique that I need to mention before I show you the code. You have to decide if it is worth trading these limitations for the DLL heaven and code-reuse advantages that custom DLL-loading provides.

- Custom OCX loading doesn't let you use the property sheet to set native control properties. However, all the extender properties and property pages are fully accessible. Also, any properties you set at design time are written correctly to the containing .Frm, .Ctl (UserControl), or .Dob (UserDocument) files and are reflected when the control is instantiated at runtime. See "VTable Binding Custom Control Interfaces" in Chapter 4 for more information on native and extender properties of custom controls.

- Custom OCX loading doesn't allow you to receive native control events directly through the control variable. Instead, you must receive extender events (GotFocus, and so on) through the normal mechanism and use a separate WithEvents variable to get the native events.

- You must block support for the IQuickActivate interface, which increases the performance of loading custom controls. IQuickActivate fails to reconcile the event interface it expects with the one that the custom-loaded control actually supports.

If you can accept these limitations, you can custom load OCX files just like DLLs. You simply need to know the OCX's location (relative to the application path) and the CLSID of the control. To dynamically load the control, add a new UserControl to your project and run the following code for every control you want to load. The only property you have to set is the WindowLess property, which should match the control you're trying to load. Your project must have a VBoost object available, a reference to ObjCreate.olb, and the OcxLoader.Bas, COMDllLoader.Bas, and FunctionDelegator.Bas.

```vb
'wrap
Private Const strCLSID_Target As String = _
    "{662AE532-AFF5-11D3-BC07-D41203C10000}"
Private Const strTargetOCX As String = "Target.ocx"
Private m_OcxLoadData As OcxLoadData

Private Sub UserControl_Initialize()
    LoadWrappedOcx m_OcxLoadData, Me, _
        strTargetOcx, GUIDFromString(strCLSID_Target)
End Sub

Private Sub UserControl_Terminate()
    UnloadWrappedOcx m_OcxLoadData
End Sub
```

```vb
'OcxLoader.Bas
'External dependencies:
'COMDllLoader.Bas
'FunctionDelegator.Bas

Public Type OcxLoadData
    hInstDll As Long
    Hook As UnknownHook
End Type

Public Type OcxTargetData
    TargetOcx As String
    CLSID As CLSID
    RTLicenseKey As String
    fTargetAbsolute As Boolean
End Type
Public g_OcxTargetData As OcxTargetData

Private Type OcxHookAggData
    AggData(1) As AggregateData
```

```vb
    pIIDs(0) As IID
End Type

'Load an OCX into the Wrapper object based on a relative
'path. This should be called from the UserControl_Initialize
'event of the wrapper UserControl class.
'
'TargetOcx:        Path to the OCX relative to the application,
'                  unless fTargetAbsolute is true, in which
'                  case this is an absolute path.
'CLSID_Target:     CLSID supported by the wrapped OCX.
'RTLicenseKey:     The key to create a control that doesn't
'                  have a registered license key. Can be
'                  obtained from IClassFactory2.RequestLicKey
'                  using the GetRTLicKey utility on a machine
'                  where the control is fully licensed.
'fTargetAbsolute:  An optional flag indicating that the
'                  TargetOCX argument is an absolute, not a
'                  relative, path.
Public Sub LoadWrappedOcx( _
  LoadData As OcxLoadData, _
  ByVal Wrapper As IUnknown, _
  TargetOcx As String, _
  CLSID_Target As CLSID, _
  Optional RTLicenseKey As String, _
  Optional ByVal fTargetAbsolute As Boolean = False)
Dim HookData As OcxHookAggData
Dim pCF As IClassFactory
Dim pCF2 As IClassFactory2

    'If this is used at design time, then Sub Main may
    'not have run, so the VBoost object has not been
    'created.
    If VBoost Is Nothing Then InitVBoost

    'Use the helper function to load the OCX.
    If fTargetAbsolute Then
        Set pCF = GetDllClassObject(TargetOcx, _
          CLSID_Target, LoadData.hInstDll)
    Else
        Set pCF = GetDllClassObject(App.Path & "\" & _
                                    TargetOcx, _
```

```vb
                CLSID_Target, LoadData.hInstDll)
    End If


    'See about licensing.
    If Len(RTLicenseKey) Then
        Set pCF2 = pCF
        With pCF2.GetLicInfo
            If .fLicVerified Then
                'pCF.CreateInstance will succeed
                Set pCF2 = Nothing
            Else
                If 0 = .fRuntimeKeyAvail Then
                    'Can load only a licensed control
                    TestUnloadDll LoadData.hInstDll
                    Exit Sub
                End If
            End If
        End With
    End If


    'Aggregate the created object with priority before the
    'wrapping object. The adNoDelegator removes the
    'per-interface overhead of the aggregator, but breaks COM
    'identity with the wrapping object. In practice, we don't
    'really care much about the wrapping object, and there are
    'a substantial amount of interfaces that need to be
    'wrapped with a custom control, so we use adNoDelegator.
    With HookData.AggData(0)
        .Flags = adIgnoreIIDs Or adBeforeHookedUnknown _
            Or adNoDelegator
        If pCF2 Is Nothing Then
            Set .pObject = pCF.CreateInstance( _
                Nothing, IID_IUnknown)
        Else
            Set .pObject = pCF2.CreateInstanceLic( _
                Nothing, Nothing, IID_IUnknown, RTLicenseKey)
        End If
    End With


    'Block IQuickActivate
    With HookData.AggData(1)
```

```
        HookData.pIIDs(0) = IIDFromString( _
          strIIDI_QuickActivate)
        .FirstIID = 0
        .Flags = adBlockIIDs
    End With


    VBoost.AggregateUnknown _
      Wrapper, HookData.AggData, HookData.pIIDs, _
        LoadData.Hook
End Sub


'Call LoadWrappedOcx using the global data
Public Sub LoadWrappedOcxFromGlobalTargetData( _
  LoadData As OcxLoadData, ByVal Wrapper As IUnknown)
    With g_OcxTargetData
        LoadWrappedOcx LoadData, Wrapper, _
            .TargetOcx, .CLSID, .RTLicenseKey, .fTargetAbsolute
    End With
End Sub


'Unload the OCX file. This should be called from the
'UserControl_Terminate event of the wrapper control.
Public Sub UnloadWrappedOcx(LoadData As OcxLoadData)
    'Unhook to release all references on the wrapped object.
    Set LoadData.Hook = Nothing
    'Let go of the OCX file if no one else is using it.
    TestUnloadDll LoadData.hInstDll
End Sub
```

Controls.Add and Dynamic Controls

The sample code shown above uses one UserControl file per wrapped control
and hard coded class information. However, this is not a requirement for using
the OCX wrapping code. The only requirement is that the information for loading the class factory be available in the UserControl_Initialize. Since VB doesn't
let you pass parameters to the Initialize event, you need to either hard code
the values or read them from global variables. If you load controls onto your
form at design-time, you want to use the private values. If you want to go
totally dynamic and add your controls with Controls.Add, you can use a single

UserControl wrapper that assumes the g_OcxTargetData variable in OcxLoader.Bas has all the load information. Your code will look something like this.

```
'DynamicLoad UserControl class
Private m_OcxLoadData As OcxLoadData

Private Sub UserControl_Initialize()
    If Len(g_OcxTargetData.TargetOcx) = 0 Then Exit Sub
    LoadWrappedOcxFromGlobalTargetData _
      m_OcxLoadData, Me
End Sub
Private Sub UserControl_Terminate()
    UnloadWrappedOcx m_OcxLoadData
End Sub
```

```
'Snippet to load the control
Dim ctl As VBControlExtender
    With g_OCXTargetData
        .CLSID = GUIDFromString( _
          "{662AE532-AFF5-11D3-BC07-D41203C10000}")
        .RTLicenseKey = "mkjmmmrlhmknmo"
        .TargetOcx = "Target.Ocx"
        .fTargetAbsolute = False
    End With
    Set ctl = Controls.Add("MyProject.DynamicLoad", "ctl1")
```

There are a couple of issues you must deal with in this situation. First, if you load both windowed and windowless controls, you need one DynamicLoad-style UserControl for each type of control. Second, if you have the Remove information about unused ActiveX Controls option selected on the bottom of the Make tab of the Project|Properties dialog, then you can't successfully call Controls.Add on a control that isn't already on a form. This option is designed to eliminate the overhead of supporting controls that aren't currently in use in your project and disables Controls.Add for controls in the project and any toolbox control that isn't actually on a form. You can either clear the option (it is on by default), or you can simply drop a DynamicLoad control on at least one form and set the control's Visible property to False.

The ability to dynamically load entire forms into an MDI app is a very power-ful example of dynamic control loading. You get the same effect as using Controls.Add by placing a single DynamicLoad control on an MDIChild Form and filling the g_OcxTargetData structure before you create a new form. One line of code in the Form_Resize gives the dynamically loaded OCX full control of your form. If you have the form to support menus, simply add menus to the UserControl with the NegotiatePosition set to a nonzero value, and leave the form's NegotiateMenus property set to True. You now have a lightweight framework with minimal code that lets you dynamically add forms to an MDI application—and you don't even have to use the registry.

The DynamicMDI sample included with the book demonstrates the use of a data file with application-relative OCX files to populate MDI menus and load individual forms. The DynamicMDI also has sample code (contained in Lookup-CLSID.Bas) that registers a public context object (discussed in "Custom Class Objects" in this chapter) and determines a CLSID from an OCX or DLL based on a class name. The result is an easily customizable data-driven MDI framework with child forms provided by dynamically loaded, unregistered OCXs. There are no special interface requirements on the individual OCXs.

Using Properties, Methods, and Events

Creating a control is all very nice, but it doesn't do you much good if you can't set its properties, call its methods, or respond to events it raises. In short, you end up with a pretty piece of UI but no way to interact with it. VB knows only about the interfaces and events of the thin wrapper control—not the control that you dynamically load. You must let the VB compiler know about the interfaces and events in your wrapped control if you want to interact with the control itself. Any direct interaction with native interfaces in VB requires a type-library reference.

Adding a custom control reference is not as straightforward as adding a reference to a normal DLL. VB explicitly eliminates all type libraries that have a control attribute from the list of available references. To add a reference to a control with the Project|References dialog, you must click the Browse button and find the file yourself. Note that there is a bug in VB6 such that you can add these hidden references, but they don't appear in the list of current references when you reopen the Project|References dialog. You'll have to hand edit the VBP file and reload the project to get rid of the reference.

Once your project includes have a direct type-library reference, you simply declare a variable of the correct type (using WithEvents if needed) and use the Set statement to get the native object from the control's object property. You can use this variable to manipulate the native portions of the control and the VBControlExtender object to manipulate the extender portions. You can't use the ObjectEvent event on the VBControlExtender object to listen to the native events because, like the IQuickActivate interface, VB expects support for a specific event set.

Custom Class Objects

When the first thread is launched in a VB ActiveX EXE server, VB registers all of its public-creatable objects with COM using the CoRegisterClassObject API call. The class object is most commonly used as a class factory that supports the IClassFactory interface. However, there is absolutely nothing stopping you from registering your own class object with COM. The only caveat is that you must call CoRevokeClassObject before the public objects that VB knows about have terminated (causing the server to shut down).

You should recognize the CoRegisterClassObject's first three parameters from your experience with CoGetClassObject: rclsid is a CLSID, pUnk is a reference to the object to be returned by CoGetClassObject, and dwClsContext specifies the scope in which the object is visible. CLSCTX_INPROC_SERVER indicates that the object is visible only to other objects in the current thread, and CLSCTX_LOCAL_SERVER means that other threads can retrieve the object as well. The fourth parameter, Flags, takes a value from the REGCLS enumeration. Generally, you will specify REGCLS_MULTIPLEUSE for this value. This corresponds to the MulitUse value of a VB class's Instancing property and means that the class object remains visible until it is revoked.

If you register a class object correctly, then you can retrieve it from any code within the registered scope. A class object is for all intents and purposes a singleton object, meaning that you can retrieve the same instance of the object from multiple pieces of code, and all calls return the same instance of the class. If you've programmed with ATL, you know that you can create a singleton object by always returning the same object from the class factory's CreateInstance method. However, this extra CreateInstance call isn't really necessary because all registered class objects are also singletons.

A registered class object can provide global data for your application that spans thread and executable boundaries. For example, if you wish to provide context information for your components without passing an object to every call, you can register a class object and publish the CLSID with which you registered instead. Note that the CLSID doesn't have to be a registered CLSID. You can use any unique GUID, including the interface identifier of the context object. The following code shows a form registering a class object, and a DLL retrieving the class object using CoGetClassObject.

```vb
'AppContext class
'Instancing = PublicNotCreatable
Implements IAppContext
Public Property Get IAppContext_AppPath() As String
    IAppContext_AppPath = App.Path
End Property
'etc.
```

```vb
'frmMain.frm
'Constant pulled from the type library for this executable.
Private Const cstrIID_IAppContext As String = _
  "{C33A1761-A296-11D3-BBF5-D41203C10000}"
Private m_dwRegisterCustomCF As DWORD
Private Sub Form_Initialize()
    m_dwRegisterCustomCF = CoRegisterClassObject( _
      IIDFromString(cstrIID_IAppContext), _
      New AppContext, _
      CLSCTX_INPROC_SERVER Or CLSCTX_LOCAL_SERVER, _
      REGCLS_MULTIPLEUSE)
End Sub
Private Sub Form_Terminate()
    If m_dwRegisterCustomCF Then
        CoRevokeClassObject m_dwRegisterCustomCF
        m_dwRegisterCustomCF = 0
    End If
End Sub
```

```
'Class in a DLL loaded by main app.
Private Const cstrIID_IAppContext As String = _
   "{C33A1761-A296-11D3-BBF5-D41203C10000}"
Private IID_IAppContext As IID


Private Function Get AppPath() As String
Dim pContext As AppContext
    If IID_IAppContext.Data1 = 0 Then
        IID_IAppContext = IIDFromString( _
           cstrIID_IAppContext)
    End If
    Set pContext = CoGetClassObject( _
      IID_IAppContext, _
      CLSCTX_INPROC_SERVER Or CLSCTX_LOCAL_SERVER, _
      0, _
      IID_IAppContext)
    AppPath = pContext.AppPath
End Sub
```

Win32 operating systems before Windows 2000 allowed you to use GetObject("CLSID: C33A1761-A296-11D3-BBF5-D41203C10000") to retrieve any registered object. The GetObject code is less direct than CoGetClassObject because it goes through an extra layer or two, but it is easier to use. The CLSID resolution on Windows 2000 gained additional smarts: it actually requires the CLSID to be registered on the system for resolution to succeed. If you want to use the GetObject syntax, you must use a MultiUse class in an ActiveX EXE and the class must be properly registered. However, the singleton design is violated if you create the object directly. If you don't care about cross-thread support, you can register any class in a Standard EXE with the CLSCTX_INPROC_SERVER flag and eliminate all registration requirements; just don't try to retrieve the reference with GetObject on Windows 2000.

With the code shown above, you can use the registered AppContext object from any thread or from any DLL loaded in the application. The PublicNotCreatable attribute on AppContext, combined with the inclusion of the CLSCTX_LOCAL_SERVER flag, enables you to safely retrieve and marshal the object across thread boundaries. If you don't need cross-thread support, you can make the class private and use the CLSCTX_INPROC_SERVER context. The *Custom ROT Monikers* section of Chapter 10 shows you how to use custom monikers to register and retrieve a process-private object in the running object table, yielding a result similar to that of a cross-component singleton. Class-object registration is generally a much cleaner approach.

Chapter 8

Lightweight COM Objects

The lifetime of a COM object is controlled with a reference-counting mechanism. This lets you maintain multiple references to the same object at the same time. As you saw in "Sharing Data with Base Classes" in Chapter 5, VB does not have a built-in mechanism for referencing structures (also called "user-defined types") because there is no inherent mechanism for reference-counting a structure's memory. In this chapter, I'll show you how to create "lightweight objects," which I'll define as structures that are also COM objects.

The question you may be asking now is one of relevancy: Why would you want to create a COM object from a VB structure when COM objects materialize automatically from every class module? I'll give you a list of the uses for lightweight objects presented in this and subsequent chapters and let you decide if they are relevant to you.

- Lightweight objects improve memory usage for systems with large numbers of small objects. Lightweight objects use significantly less memory (4 to 12 bytes per instance) than a class instance (96 bytes per instance). You can also create an arbitrary number of lightweight objects with a single memory allocation and free all the objects with a single call. Lightweight objects let you design systems that scale painlessly to handle thousands of objects.

- Lightweight objects don't require separate heap allocation. An instance of a class module is always allocated on the heap, but you can allocate lightweight objects directly on the stack or as an embedded member of a class. Note that a stack-allocated lightweight object is not a normal COM object because a reference to the object doesn't keep the object's memory valid. However, it is enough of a COM object for VB to call its methods.

- You can implement arbitrary interfaces. Some interfaces simply cannot be implemented in class modules, even with a "VB-ized" typelib. However, lightweight objects don't have this restriction. You can then use the aggregation techniques described earlier to attach your lightweight implementation to a class module.

- You can override interfaces. Lightweights make it much easier to wrap an existing interface implementation. When you wrap an interface, you generally care only about modifying the behavior of a handful of functions. Lightweights let you write code for only those functions.

- You can add termination code to structures. Lightweight objects allow you to give structures the equivalent of a terminate event. Just initialize the structures and let VB's scoping rules do the rest. Termination code on a structure lets you use stack-allocated structures where you would normally use heap-allocated objects, reducing memory usage and greatly improving performance.

This is just a sampling of the uses of lightweight objects. As with normal structures and classes, lightweight objects are user-extensible: You can do whatever you want with them. Lightweights provide flexibility by acting as both a structure and a COM object simultaneously.

Lightweight Basics

There is only a small difference between a structure and a COM object. Simply put, a COM object is a structure whose first element points to an IUnknown-derived vtable. To turn a structure into a COM object, you must lay out an array of function pointers and point the first element of the structure to the beginning of the function pointer array. Once the first element of the structure points to a valid vtable, a simple VBoost.Assign (or CopyMemory) call into an object-type variable turns the structure into a VB-usable COM object.

The list of functions in a vtable, combined with the interface that describes the vtable, determine a class's behavior. Since each instance of a class should behave the same way, you generally want to share a single vtable with all instances of the class. You have to fill the vtable array only when the object is first created. A COM object has at least three functions in its vtable: QueryInterface, AddRef, and Release. These functions are the minimum set of functions required for the vtable of a lightweight or any other COM object.

All objects, whether they are structures or class modules, start life as a block of uninitialized memory. This uninitialized block of memory is then given character by populating the memory as a given type. There are essentially three ways to get a block of memory.

- Push it on the stack. Stack memory is temporary space limited to the scope of a function call. For reasonably small amounts of memory, stack memory is by far the cheapest way to get memory. However, stack memory is limited, so pushing massive amounts of data onto the stack can produce an out-of-stack-space error. In practice, VB has a large stack and you have to work very hard to hit this limit. Nonpointer-type local variables are always allocated on the stack.

- Allocate it from heap memory. A "heap" is a general term for all memory-management objects that support *allocate* and *free* functions. Every heap object uses slightly different names for these functions, but they all have the same purpose. When you need a block of memory to create the object, you call the heap's allocate function. When you are done with the memory, call the free function to tell the heap that it can give the memory out as part of another allocation request. VB classes, variable-size arrays, and variable-length strings are examples of heap-type allocations.

- Embed it in a heap or stack allocation. In practice, using embedded memory is very similar to using stack memory. You don't free the memory directly. Instead, you are allowed to use the memory only while the memory is in scope. In the stack allocation case, the scope is determined by the function. In this case, the scope of the embedded memory is determined by the lifetime of the containing memory block. A structure-type member variable in a class module is a form of embedded memory.

To make the best use of memory, limit first the number and then the size of heap allocations by using stack memory and embedded objects. If you have to use heap memory, it is always cheaper to create one heap object with two embedded objects than it is to create two separate heap objects. Although the price of RAM has dropped dramatically, the performance cost of managing all that heap memory has remained relatively flat. Abusing memory is the easiest way to slow down your application.

Heap-Allocated Lightweight Objects

You're now ready to create a lightweight object. This first example isn't very useful because it doesn't actually *do* anything, but it provides a starting point for other objects. I'll use the COM allocator functions CoTaskMemAlloc and CoTaskMemFree (defined in VBoostTypes) as the heap allocator and create a traditional reference-counted COM object.

```
Private Type LightEmptyVTable
    VTable(2) As Long
End Type
Private m_VTable As LightEmptyVTable
Private m_pVTable As Long

Private Type LightEmpty
    pVTable As Long
    cRefs As Long
End Type

Public Function CreateLightEmpty() As IUnknown
Dim Struct As LightEmpty
Dim ThisPtr As Long
    'Make sure we have a vtable
    If m_pVTable = 0 Then
        With m_VTable
            .VTable(0) = FuncAddr(AddressOf QueryInterface)
```

```
          .VTable(1) = FuncAddr(AddressOf AddRef)
          .VTable(2) = FuncAddr(AddressOf Release)
          m_pVTable = VarPtr(.VTable(0))
      End With
   End If

   'Allocate the memory.
   ThisPtr = CoTaskMemAlloc(LenB(Struct))
   If ThisPtr = 0 Then Err.Raise 7 'Out of memory

   'Initialize the structure.
   With Struct
       .pVTable = m_pVTable
       .cRefs = 1
   End With

   'Move the bytes in the initialized structure
   'into the allocated memory.
   'Note that the VarPtr(Struct) and ZeroMemory calls are
   'overkill for this structure, but are often required.
   CopyMemory ByVal ThisPtr, Struct.pVTable, LenB(Struct)
   ZeroMemory Struct.pVTable, LenB(Struct)

   'Assign the ThisPtr into the function name variable
   'to officially vest it as a COM object. Use Assign
   'instead of AssignAddRef since the cRefs field is
   'already set to 1.
   VBoost.Assign CreateLightEmpty, ThisPtr
End Function

Private Function QueryInterface(This As LightEmpty, _
   riid As Long, pvObj As Long) As Long
   'Just fail for now. (I'll discuss QI later in the chapter)
   pvObj = 0
   QueryInterface = E_NOINTERFACE
End Function
Private Function AddRef(This As LightEmpty) As Long
   With This
       .cRefs = .cRefs + 1
       AddRef = .cRefs
   End With
```

```
End Function
Private Function Release(This As LightEmpty) As Long
    With This
        .cRefs = .cRefs - 1
        Release = .cRefs
        If .cRefs = 0 Then
            'Add object specific cleanup here

            'Free the memory. Don't step over CoTaskMemFree
            'in the debugger because the memory associated
            'with the This parameter is being freed. Now is
            'a good time to hit F5 or Ctrl-Shift-F8.
            CoTaskMemFree VarPtr(This)
        End If
    End With
End Function


'Helper function
Private Function FuncAddr(ByVal pfn As Long) As Long
    FuncAddr = pfn
End Function
```

There are several things you should notice in this baseline code. The first strange thing is that the vtable is declared as a structure rather than as a fixed-size array. As mentioned in Chapter 2, the data for a fixed-size array is actually heap allocated, so it must be freed during the teardown. If you happen to have a lightweight object at module level that still points to the vtable, your application is very, very dead if it happens to teardown after its vtable. By declaring the vtables as shown above, you have guaranteed that the vtables will be around longer than any object in the project.

Another thing you should notice in the code is that you deal with allocated memory as a raw pointer only when the object is first created and when it is being freed. At all points in between, you can look at the LightEmpty structure directly. The three IUnknown vtable functions, and all other vtable functions shown in the chapter, have a first parameter typed "This As <Struct>". As the parameter name indicates, the This parameter is the typed memory associated with the current object. In VB and C++ classes, the this/Me parameter is implied as part of the language. Although you don't see it as a parameter, it is always passed nevertheless. To get the memory address of the object (which you need only when it is time to free the memory), simply call VarPtr(This) or the equivalent VarPtr(This.pVTable).

In the CreateLightEmpty function, a LightEmpty structure is filled and then copied into an allocated memory location. The point of transfer seems pretty complicated. Your first attempt might involve just coding the copy with a simple CopyMemory call.

```
CopyMemory ByVal ThisPtr, Struct, LenB(Struct)
```

There are two problems with this code when you apply it to an arbitrary structure. These problems don't exist with the LightEmpty structure because it isn't complex enough, but you must watch out for them in general. The first problem occurs if Struct contains string parameters. If you use a CopyMemory API call declared in VB, any string parameters undergo UNICODE/ANSI translation during the API call. You can prevent string translation by replacing Struct with ByVal VarPtr(Struct). In the case of a lightweight object, however, the first element of the structure is a Long, which doesn't undergo translation during an API call. Combine the lack of translation on a Long with the fact that VarPtr(Struct) and VarPtr(Struct.<FirstMember>) are always equivalent, and you see that ByVal VarPtr(Struct) is equivalent to ByRef Struct.pVTable. Of course, if the CopyMemory is typelib declared, such as the VBoostTypes-declared CopyMemory function, you won't have this potential problem, but the code shown in the listing is always safe.

The second problem with the single CopyMemory call is that VB thinks the data in Struct needs to be freed when the function goes out of scope. VB has no way of knowing that ownership of the structure has moved elsewhere. If the structure contains object or variable-size String or array types, VB will kindly free them for you when the object goes out of scope. But you are still using the structure, so this is an unwanted favor. To prevent VB from freeing referenced memory in the stack object, simply ZeroMemory the structure. When you apply the CopyMemory call's ANSI/UNICODE precautions to ZeroMemory, you get the transfer code seen in the listing.

There is an additional memory problem to watch out for. In this situation, you are responsible for explicitly freeing pointer-type members in the structure before you delete its memory. The CopyMemory call transfers ownership to the heap allocation, so you take ownership of the object's scope. This makes you responsible for freeing contained pointer references before the structure goes out of scope at the CoTaskMemFree call. There are two ways to do this. The first is to use brute force in-line code. This code assigns all strings to vbNullString (not ""), sets all objects to Nothing, and erases all arrays. This is a hassle for a complex object and a potential source of memory leak bugs. The alternative is to write a helper sub that makes VB clean the structure for you. This procedure is used in place of the CoTaskMemFree call in the Release function.

```
Private Sub DeleteThis(This As AnyStruct)
Dim tmp As AnyStruct
Dim pThis As Long
    pThis = VarPtr(This)
    CopyMemory ByVal VarPtr(tmp), ByVal pThis, LenB(This)
    CoTaskMemFree pThis
End Sub
```

DeleteThis uses the temporary structure variable to do the work you prevented VB from doing way back in the creation function. DeleteThis transfers ownership of the This structure back to a VB local variable, making VB free the structure members when the procedure exits. Note that a ZeroMemory call after the CopyMemory is redundant because the This memory is about to be freed. Of course, if you like to clean your garbage before throwing it out, you're welcome to make the ZeroMemory call.

Stack-Allocated Lightweight Objects

The memory-allocation and data-transfer work forms the majority of the code in the heap-based LightEmpty example. This code is greatly simplified when the lightweight object gets stack or embedded memory on which to build the object. The nonheap lightweight case actually splits into two cases. In the first case, the COM object needs to run code when the object is destroyed. In the second case, no termination code is required. In either case, the memory on which the COM object is built is cleaned and freed automatically when the structure it is built on goes out of scope. Let's look at LightEmpty code for these two cases.

```vbnet
Private Type LightEmptyVTable
    VTable(2) As Long
End Type
Private m_VTable As LightEmptyVTable
Private m_pVTable As Long


Public Type LightEmpty
    pVTable As Long
    cRefs As Long
End Type


Public Function InitializeLightEmpty(Struct As LightEmpty) _
  As IUnknown
    'Make sure we have a vtable.
    If m_pVTable = 0 Then
        With m_VTable
            .VTable(0) = FuncAddr(AddressOf QueryInterface)
            .VTable(1) = FuncAddr(AddressOf AddRef)
            .VTable(2) = FuncAddr(AddressOf Release)
            m_pVTable = VarPtr(.VTable(0))
        End With
    End If

    'Initialize the structure.
    With Struct
        .pVTable = m_pVTable
        .cRefs = 1
    End With

    'Assign the pointer to the structure to
    'the function name.
    VBoost.Assign InitializeLightEmpty, VarPtr(Struct)
End Function


Private Function QueryInterface(This As LightEmpty, _
  riid As Long, pvObj As Long) As Long
    'Just fail. (I'll discuss QI later in the chapter).
    pvObj = 0
    QueryInterface = E_NOINTERFACE
End Function
```

```
Private Function AddRef(This As LightEmpty) As Long
    With This
        .cRefs = .cRefs + 1
        AddRef = .cRefs
    End With
End Function
Private Function Release(This As LightEmpty) As Long
    With This
        .cRefs = .cRefs - 1
        Release = .cRefs
        If .cRefs = 0 Then
            'Run termination code here.
        End If
    End With
End Function
```

This code is much simpler. All of the memory-management code is gone. LightEmpty is now declared as Public, so it can be used outside the module. This style of object requires that the final release on the COM object must happen before the memory goes out of scope, so you need to be sure you don't use stack-allocated lightweight objects outside the scope of the stack memory. The code gets even easier when termination code is not required. In this case, there is no need for a reference count because the reference count only determines when the termination code should run, not when to release the memory.

```
Private Type LightEmptyVTable
    VTable(2) As Long
End Type
Private m_VTable As LightEmptyVTable
Private m_pVTable As Long


Public Type LightEmpty
    pVTable As Long
End Type


Public Function InitializeLightEmpty(Struct As LightEmpty) _
    As IUnknown
    'Make sure we have a vtable.
    If m_pVTable = 0 Then
```

```
        With m_VTable
            .VTable(0) = FuncAddr(AddressOf QueryInterface)
            .VTable(1) = FuncAddr(AddressOf AddRefRelease)
            .VTable(2) = .VTable(1)
            m_pVTable = VarPtr(m_VTable(0))
        End With
    End If


    'Initialize the structure.
    With Struct
        .pVTable = m_pVTable
        'More stuff in a non-empty example.
    End With


    'Copy the pointer to the structure into the
    'the function name.
    VBoost.Assign InitializeLightEmpty, VarPtr(Struct)
End Function

Private Function QueryInterface(This As LightEmpty, _
   riid As Long, pvObj As Long) As Long
    'Just fail. (I'll discuss QI later in the chapter).
    pvObj = 0
    QueryInterface = E_NOINTERFACE
End Function
Private Function AddRefRelease(This As LightEmpty) As Long
    'Nothing to do.
End Function
```

With the reference count gone, AddRef and Release have no responsibilities, and they point to the same empty function. I've found that this is the type of lightweight object I use the most.

Termination Code on Structures

As my first concrete example of using lightweights, I'll create a lightweight object to show and hide an hourglass cursor. This is first shown as a normal VB class.

```
'HourGlass class
Private m_PrevCursor As Long
```

```
Public Sub ShowHourGlass()
    With Screen
        m_PrevCursor = .MousePointer
        If m_PrevCursor <> vbHourGlass Then
            .MousePointer = vbHourClass
        End If
    End With
End Sub
Private Sub Class_Terminate()
    'Only change back if we set it
    If m_PrevCursor  vbHourGlass Then
        With Screen
            'Don't touch if someone else changed it.
            If .MousePointer = vbHourGlass Then
                .MousePointer = m_PrevCursor
            End If
        End With
    End If
End Sub

'Class usage
Sub DoLotsOfStuff()
Dim HG As New HourGlass
    HG.ShowHourGlass
End Sub
```

The HourGlass class is a great candidate for a stack-allocated lightweight object because its scope is limited to a single function. Creating a heap-allocated VB class here is pretty extreme when you balance the class overhead against the amount of code and data being run. The advantage of the class is that you call only one function on the object to show the hourglass. The hourglass hides automatically when the class goes out of scope.

I'll use a simple trick to duplicate the single function call and automatic termination code that the lightweight object provides the class. I'll make the structure for the lightweight object own the lightweight object created on it. This way, when the structure goes out of scope, it releases itself and runs its own termination code. There are no additional AddRef calls against the generated lightweight object, so the only Release call occurs at the scope boundary. There is no need for a cRefs variable. Here is the lightweight version of the HourGlass code.

```vb
Public Type HourGlass
    pVTable As Long
    pThisObject As IUnknown
    PrevCursor As Long
End Type

Private Type HourGlassVTable
    VTable(2) As Long
End Type
Private m_VTable As HourGlassVTable
Private m_pVTable As Long

Public Sub ShowHourGlass(HG As HourGlass)
Dim PrevCursor As Long
    If m_pVTable = 0 Then
        With m_VTable
            .VTable(0) = FuncAddr(AddressOf QueryInterface)
            .VTable(1) = FuncAddr(AddressOf AddRef)
            .VTable(2) = FuncAddr(AddressOf Release)
            m_pVTable = VarPtr(.VTable(0))
        End With
    End If

    With Screen
        PrevCursor = .MousePointer
        If PrevCursor <> vbHourglass Then
            .MousePointer = vbHourglass
            With HG
                .PrevCursor = PrevCursor
                .pVTable = m_pVTable
                VBoost.Assign .pThisObject, VarPtr(.pVTable)
            End With
        End If
    End With
End Sub

Private Function QueryInterface(This As HourGlass, _
  riid As Long, pvObj As Long) As Long
    Debug.Assert False 'QI not expected
    pvObj = 0
    QueryInterface = E_NOINTERFACE
End Function
```

```
Private Function AddRef(This As HourGlass) As Long
    Debug.Assert False 'AddRef not expected
End Function
Private Function Release(This As HourGlass) As Long
    With Screen
        If .MousePointer = vbHourglass Then
            .MousePointer = This.PrevCursor
        End If
    End With
End Function
```

```
'Calling code
Sub DoLotsOfStuff()
Dim HG As HourGlass
    ShowHourGlass HG
End Sub
```

In addition to the big performance boosts gained by eliminating the overhead of class-module creation, the lightweight version of the HourGlass object also has the advantage of not running any termination code if it didn't actually turn on the hourglass cursor. You now have a way to run termination code against a structure without turning the structure into full-blown VB class. Yes, you have to write a little more code, but most of it is cut and paste, plus a search-and-replace to update the type of the This parameter.

LastIID Lightweight

As another example of lightweight objects that don't require a typelib-provided interface definition, I'll make a lightweight version of the LastIID class shown in the aggregation discussion in Chapter 5. In the original sample, I used a QIHook in a class module to watch the QueryInterface requests. I used this class as a local variable, so I was creating two heap objects (the class and the UnknownHook) to watch a single call. The class is an ideal candidate to be tossed in favor of a lightweight object: it is small, and is used only as a locally scoped object. As with the HourGlass code, the crux of the code is the same for the class module and the lightweight; you just have to generate a little more surrounding code.

In the LastIID sample, the QIThis member variable of the LastIID structure is equivalent to the pThisObject in the HourGlass example in that it points back to the structure that owns it. The VBGUID definition is supplied by a VBoost reference. A GuidString helper function for printing the string representation of a GUID is also shown.

```
Public Type LastIID
    pVTable As Long
    QIThis As IUnknown
    IID As VBGUID
End Type


Private Type LastIIDVTable
    VTable(2) As Long
End Type
Private m_VTable As LastIIDVTable
Private m_pVTable As Long


Public Sub InitLastIID(LastIID As LastIID)
    If m_pVTable = 0 Then
        With m_VTable
            .VTable(0) = FuncAddr(AddressOf QueryInterface)
            .VTable(1) = FuncAddr(AddressOf AddRefRelease)
            .VTable(2) = .VTable(1)
            .pVTable = VarPtr(.VTable(0))
        End With
    End If
    With LastIID
        .pVTable = m_pVTable
        CopyMemory .QIThis, VarPtr(.pVTable), 4
    End With
End Sub


Private Function QueryInterface(This As LastIID, _
  riid As VBGUID, pvObj As Long) As Long
    'Cache the IID, then fail.
    This.IID = riid
    pvObj = 0
    QueryInterface = E_NOINTERFACE
End Function
Private Function AddRefRelease(This As LastIID) As Long
    'Nothing to do.
End Function
```

```
'Helper function to get string version of a guid.
Public Function GuidString(pguid As VBGUID) As String
    GuidString = String$(38, 0)
    StringFromGUID2 pguid, StrPtr(GuidString)
End Function
```

```
'Snippet to use LastIID to get the IID of Class1.
Dim LastIID As LastIID
Dim Dummy As Class1
    InitLastIID LastIID
    On Error Resume Next
    Set Dummy = LastIID.QIThis
    On Error GoTo 0
    Debug.Print "The IID for Class1 is: " & _
        GuidString(LastIID.IID)
```

The only thing to bear in mind as you use the LastIID lightweight is that you can't step through the code without corrupting the IID value. The debugger itself uses QueryInterface to determine how much information it can place in the locals and watch windows. Place the cursor on a line after you read the IID and use Ctrl-F8 (step to cursor) instead of F8 (step into) or Shift-F8 (step over) if you need to debug this function.

ArrayOwner Lightweight

The ArrayOwner lightweight object runs termination code during module teardown to clear a module-level array that references a custom array descriptor. Usage for this class is shown in the "Module Level Arrays" section in Chapter 2. ArrayOwner has pVTable and pThisObject entries for trapping the teardown and a third SafeArray1d field called SA. I assume that the ArrayOwner structure is embedded in another structure which has a typed array member immediately following the ArrayOwner (refer to the usage sample).

ArrayOwner uses VBoost when it is initialized but not during teardown. VBoost is unreliable at this time because it is a module-level variable, and it may actually have been released before the ArrayOwner code runs. ArrayOwner has two vtable options. The first vtable, DestroyData, destroys the data in the array. The second, IgnoreData, ignores the SA.pvData field. Ignore is the default, allowing you to leave invalid data in any of the SafeArray structure's fields with impunity. You can find this code in ArrayOwner.Bas. Also included is an ArrayOwnerIgnoreOnly.Bas, which does not support the fDestroyData parameter.

```vb
'ArrayOwner Implementation
Private Type ArrayOwnerVTables
    DestroyData(2) As Long
    IgnoreData(2) As Long
End Type
Private m_VTables As ArrayOwnerVTables
Private m_pVTableDestroy As Long
Private m_pVTableIgnore As Long


Public Type ArrayOwner
    pVTable As Long
    pThisObject As IUnknown
    SA As SafeArray1d
    'pSA() As <any type> assumed in this position
End Type


Public Sub InitArrayOwner(ArrayOwner As ArrayOwner, _
  ByVal cbElements As Long, ByVal fFeatures As Integer, _
  Optional ByVal fDestroyData As Boolean = False)
    If m_pVTableDestroy = 0 Then
      With m_VTables
        .DestroyData(0) = FuncAddr(AddressOf QueryInterface)
        .IgnoreData(0) = .DestroyData(0)
        .DestroyData(1) = FuncAddr(AddressOf AddRef)
        .IgnoreData(1) = .DestroyData(1)
        .DestroyData(2) = _
           FuncAddr(AddressOf ReleaseDestroyData)
        .IgnoreData(2) = FuncAddr(AddressOf ReleaseIgnoreData)
        m_pVTableDestroy = VarPtr(.DestroyData(0))
        m_pVTableIgnore = VarPtr(.IgnoreData(0))
      End With
    End If
    With ArrayOwner.SA
        If .cDims = 0 Then
            .cDims = 1
            .fFeatures = fFeatures
            .cElements = 1
            .cbElements = cbElements
```

```vb
                With ArrayOwner
                    If fDestroyData Then
                        .pVTable = m_pVTableDestroy
                    Else
                        .pVTable = m_pVTableIgnore
                    End If
                    VBoost.Assign .pThisObject, VarPtr(.pVTable)
                    VBoost. ByVal VBoost.UAdd( _
                      VarPtr(ArrayOwner), LenB(ArrayOwner)), _
                      VarPtr(.SA)
                End With
            End If
        End With
End Sub


Private Function QueryInterface( _
  ByVal This As Long, riid As Long, pvObj As Long) As Long
    Debug.Assert False 'QI not expected
    pvObj = 0
    QueryInterface = E_NOINTERFACE
End Function
Private Function AddRef(ByVal This As Long) As Long
    Debug.Assert False 'No need to addref.
End Function
Private Function ReleaseDestroyData( _
  This As ArrayOwner) As Long
    With This
        If .SA.pvData Then
            On Error Resume Next
            SafeArrayDestroyData VarPtr(.SA)
            On Error GoTo 0
        End If
        'Zero the descriptor and array.
        ZeroMemory This.SA, LenB(This) - 4
    End With
End Function
Private Function ReleaseIgnoreData(This As ArrayOwner) As Long
    'Zero the descriptor and array.
    ZeroMemory This.SA, LenB(This) - 4
End Function
```

```
Private Function FuncAddr(ByVal pfn As Long) As Long
    FuncAddr = pfn
End Function
```

Where's the Interface?

A VB class module provides more than a class implementation; it also provides an interface definition. In most programming languages, the interface definition and an implementation of a COM object's interface are separate entities.
A COM class provides an implementation for an interface defined in a typelib
or header file, but the class does not define the interface. If you could disable
Public procedures in VB class modules, allowing external calls only through
Implements-defined interfaces, you would have a good approximation of coding
a COM class when the interface definition and implementation are completely
uncoupled.

Lightweight objects don't generate an interface definition, so the definition
must come from some other source. Interfaces can be categorized in two
groups: those that VB code needs to call directly, and standard COM-defined
interfaces, such as IUnknown (all COM objects), IDispatch (late binding support), and IEnumVARIANT (For Each support). When implementing standard
interfaces with lightweight objects, you need to know the vtable layout and the
IID to provide an implementation of a given interface. However, if you want lightweight objects to act as replacements for VB project-private class modules, you
must be able to call the interface from VB. VB's compiler knows about only
those interfaces defined in a referenced type library or project and interfaces
defined in the same project in class-type modules (Class, Form, UserControl,
and so on). In order to make a lightweight object callable from VB code, you
must give VB's compiler an interface definition and match the function order
specified in the interface definition in the lightweight object's vtable.

You might think that the easiest way to define an interface is by writing
the class as a VB class and then matching the interface in the lightweight
object. There are several difficulties you might face when using this approach.
First, the actual vtable layout of a VB class's primary interface is not obvious.
The class's IID is even less obvious. The only way to fix the layout and IID is to

set Instancing on the class to PublicNotCreatable or higher and enable binary compatibility for the project. If you use lightweights for internal optimization (the normal usage because publicly exposing lightweights directly is difficult), adding public information to your executable in order to support an internal implementation detail is an extreme measure. And because VB classes are always derived from IDispatch, the base vtable is much more difficult to implement than the simple IUnknown vtable you've seen so far. Also, if the objects are for internal use only, you should never have a reason to do anything other than vtable bind, so an IDispatch implementation is baggage that you'll carry but never open.

Using VB classes to define the interface for a lightweight object is problematic, so I recommend using a typelib to define the interface for your lightweight objects. Chapter 15 looks at creating typelibs for use with VB, so I won't duplicate it here. However, there is one issue that needs to be addressed before you can build a custom lightweight object.

To Err or Not to Err

Publicly exposed functions in a VB class module always return an HRESULT, which is a 32-bit (Long) value indicating standard COM error information. This begs a question: All functions exposed from a VB class module as Public or via Implements return an HRESULT, so how do VB functions actually return values? Return values from VB's vtable functions always come back as output parameters, not in the return value. The return value is reserved for error information and can be managed only with the Err object.

A simple function in a VB class may look like this.

```
Public Property Get Value() As Long
```

But it actually looks like this to everything outside the class.

```
HRESULT get_Value(long* retVal);
```

After putting this function in a lightweight object's vtable, it looks like this:

```
Private Function get_Value(This As SomeStruct, _
  retVal As Long) As Long
```

There are three costs associated with the use of a vtable entry that returns an HRESULT. First, the calling function must push an extra variable so it can provide that variable's address to the return-value parameter. Second, the calling code must handle two output values instead of one. Third, the calling code must always be prepared for an error return. The sad thing about this entire mechanism is that the vast majority of functions never actually raise an error, so all this effort is wasted.

Although the OLE Automation standards that VB follows in all of its classes prohibit return types other than HRESULT (or void, which VB doesn't leverage), VB can call almost any nonautomation-compatible interface. In particular, VB can call functions that don't return an HRESULT and functions that return data directly in the return value. This built-in support provides some alternatives when you define the interface for a lightweight structure. Let's look at the two alternatives for publicly exposing the Value member of this lightweight structure.

```
Private Type ValueStruct
    pVTable As Long
    cRefs As Long
    Value As Long
End Type


// ODL snippet for first possibility.
interface IValue : IUnknown
{
    [propget]
    HRESULT Value([out,retval] long* retVal);
    [propput]
    HRESULT Value([in] long RHS);
}


'VB functions for first possibility.
Private Function get_Value( _
  This As ValueStruct, retVal As Long) As Long
    retVal = This.Value
End Function
Private Function put_Value( _
  This As ValueStruct, ByVal RHS As Long) As Long
```

```
        This.Value = RHS
End Function


// ODL snippet for second possibility.
interface IValue : IUnknown
{
    long Value();
    void SetValue([in] long NewValue);
}


'VB functions for second possibility.
Private Function Value(This As ValueStruct) As Long
    Value = This.Value
End Function
Private Sub SetValue(This As ValueStruct, _
  ByVal NewValue As Long)
    This.Value = NewValue
End Sub
```

Clearly, it is easier to code an implementation of the second mechanism. If you're not validating the incoming values, there is no reason to add the HRESULT overhead. Unfortunately, Value is not a true property of the light-weight object, so you have to call SetValue as a method rather than as a property. The propget/propput attributes require functions that have HRESULT return codes. There are a couple of advantages to omitting the HRESULT that make the loss of built-in property support well worth the tradeoff.

- The code is slightly faster. The tests I've performed indicate an eight to 15 percent performance gain, depending on the return type. Although this sounds like a huge gain, consider that you have to make several million calls to get readings in tenths of a second for either of these calling methods. Although this gain certainly doesn't hurt, there are other places to look if you need to tune your application's performance.

- The generated code for each call is significantly smaller. The code for the function itself is somewhat smaller, but the code in the calling function is approximately one-third the size of code for the non-HRESULT functions. Most of the extra code runs only in error conditions. The extra code doesn't create a big performance hit, but it does bloat the executable. If you keep your executable small, your application has fewer page exceptions on startup and performs better in low-memory conditions.

If you use lightweight objects, you have full control of your object. You might as well take advantage of this control by telling VB not to expect an error return from a given function. The code is more efficient, and it's easier to write.

Returning Errors from Lightweights

COM methods indicate error values by returning HRESULT error codes. VB functions use structured exception handling to return errors across functions. COM specifies that methods must not raise exceptions across a vtable boundary. VB raises errors by throwing exceptions across function boundaries. Lightweight objects are in a precarious position between these two error-handling approaches.

VB functions are easily divided into two categories: those in a standard module and those in a class module. All functions in standard modules (except the Sub Main entrypoint) assume that there is another VB function above them to catch any errors they might throw. After all, the only valid entrypoints into a VB process are Sub Main and vtable entries on public COM objects. All VB class module functions are equipped to catch errors, so procedures in standard modules assume that they are never in danger of throwing an error that can't be caught. This is one of the main reasons why hacking a DLL to expose direct entrypoints is very dangerous: if an error gets by you, you can easily take the calling EXE down (the second reason is thread initialization, which I'll discuss in Chapter 13).

A Public function in a class module cannot assume that the caller can catch a thrown exception. For this reason, class module functions actually catch their own errors and translate them into HRESULT return values before the function completes. The class module function always returns control to the caller the same way, regardless of the error state. VB deals with exceptions better than HRESULTs, so any error HRESULT returned by a method on a COM object is translated immediately into an exception and thrown.

Vtable functions in a lightweight object are actually COM methods, so they should never let an untrapped error escape from the function. You should be religious about following this rule if the lightweight is aggregated as part of a publicly exposed object. But if you break this rule when the object is used only from internal code, you won't actually break anything because VB is ready to catch any error you throw at it. In fact, you beat VB at its own game because it's about to throw an exception derived from the HRESULT return anyway.

Raising untrapped errors directly is easy, but returning the correct HRESULT from the function is not quite as straightforward. By the time the error trap sees an error, VB has already adulterated the information by mapping some standard errors to VB error numbers, and stripping the top 16 bytes off all VB error numbers to turn them into the friendly numbers you are used to seeing. All VB error numbers are in the range &H800A0001 to &H800AFFFF (called the FACILITY_CONTROL range), but the VB Err object shows this range as &H00000001 to &H0000FFFF.

The VB error numbers are nice to work with because of their compressed size. However, the rest of the COM world, including VB in the role of caller, does not consider these values error numbers because the SEVERITY_ERROR bit (&H80000000) is not set. You need to put the high bits back into the error number before returning it from a lightweight method in order to convince any callers that it is indeed an error value. The following function is good enough for almost all purposes, although it doesn't contain an advanced reverse-map for performing transformations such as mapping Error 7 (Out of memory) to the system standard &H8007000E (E_OUTOFMEMORY). In addition to being poorly defined (VB maps multiple system errors to a single VB error), the complete reverse error map is large and undocumented. This won't affect most applications, but you can easily add a Select Case statement to the provided MapError function if you need special handling for specific error values.

```vb
Public Function MapError() As Long
Dim Number As Long
    Number = Err.Number
    If Number Then
        If Number > 0 Then Number = &H800A0000 Or Number
        MapError = Number
```

```
        End If
End Function
```

```
'Calling code.
Private Function MyVTableEntry() As Long
    On Error GoTo Error
    'Perform processing here.
    Exit Function
Error:
    MyVTableEntry = MapError
End Function
```

You must error-trap and call MapError on publicly exposed vtable functions that might throw an error, but you do not need to trap if you can guarantee that an error will never be thrown. If you call COM methods, you can actually redefine a version of the COM interface with methods that return Long instead of HRESULT. VB doesn't consider the return value an error without the HRESULT in the function definition. The ROTHook sample shown in Chapter 10 makes all COM calls using this mechanism to catch errors. I originally designed the ROTHook code to live as a DLL object, and the continued reliance on HRESULTs rather than raising exceptions makes this code easy to move into a helper DLL.

There are several disadvantages to doing away with the HRESULTs. First, you have to create the type library. You can't put two interfaces with the same IID in the same library, but you can put multiple definitions of the same interface in separate referenced type libraries. Multiple definitions allow you to have one version of the interface for use inside a lightweight and another that is called from normal code. Once you have the type defined, you have to write extra code to check the error-return codes. You also lose the benefits of return values and property statements.

Rich Error Information

HRESULT values are only part of the picture when it comes to error information. The error number is easily understood by code that calls the object, but a raw error number is of very little use to an end user. Users prefer text, so COM allows you to return a set of rich error information to display to the user. You can set the Description, Source, HelpFile, and HelpContext appropriate for the error.

Calling code should never programmatically rely on the strings in the rich information; it should just display the information to the user. If your program relies on the string information, it is subject to localization dependencies and the whims of your documentation team. If you forward error information to another caller, you can change the error number so that it falls within the range of errors returned by the program, but you should not wholly replace the description field. The source of the error is best qualified to provide high-quality feedback for the user. You may add text to the beginning of the description to provide an error chain, but you should keep the original information intact whenever possible.

You set VB's rich error information by using the properties of the Err object. Err lets you set the rich error properties before calling the Err.Raise method. You can also use the optional parameters in the Raise method itself. Populating the Err object is only the start of the rich error information's journey from the error's source back to the calling code. COM must now negotiate with the object to ensure that rich error information is available and that the information is current.

Error negotiation relies on the IErrorInfo interface and the SetErrorInfo and GetErrorInfo API calls. IErrorInfo has methods that look a lot like the properties on the Err object; Err.Description maps to IErrorInfo.GetDescription, and so on. SetErrorInfo sets the thread's current IErrorInfo reference to a specified IErrorInfo implementation, and GetErrorInfo retrieves the reference. GetErrorInfo clears the thread's current reference, so you should call it only once for each SetErrorInfo call.

Not every caller cares about error information, so it is possible that the thread's rich error information has nothing to do with the currently running code. A secondary support interface, ISupportErrorInfo, is needed to verify that the error information is current. ISupportErrorInfo has one method, InterfaceSupportsErrorInfo, which takes an IID parameter that corresponds to the owning interface of the method that just returned a failing HRESULT error code.

Rich Error Negotiation Steps

1. The object generating the error creates an IErrorInfo implementation and calls SetErrorInfo.

2. A method returns a failing HRESULT.

3. The caller sees the failing HRESULT and queries the object for the ISupportErrorInfo interface.

4. If ISupportErrorInfo.InterfaceSupportsErrorInfo succeeds, the caller uses GetErrorInfo to retrieve the error information.

An implementation of ISupportErrorInfo can simply return NOERROR without checking the IID parameter. If you don't want to bother with tracking the current IID, you just have to make sure that the error information is set correctly before returning an error. If rich error information is not available, clear the thread's current error by sending the SetErrorInfo API a Nothing reference.

The book provides a simple implementation of IErrorInfo and ISupportErrorInfo to help you add rich error support to lightweight object implementations. RichError.Bas provides a constant and four public functions that make integration of the Err object and rich error information straightforward. MapError is shown above, MapErrorKeepRich populates the rich error information from the Err object and calls SetErrorInfo, ClearErrorInfo calls SetErrorInfo to clear stale error information, and CheckErrorInfo is a helper function for your QueryInterface implementation.

```vb
'QueryInterface implementation using RichError.Bas.
Private Function QueryInterface( _
    This As LightStruct, riid As VBGUID, pvObj As Long) As Long
    'Check your own IIDs here, Exit Function on success.
    If riid.Data1 = ISupportErrorInfo_Data1 Then
        If Not CheckErrorInfo( _
          QueryInterface, riid, pvObj) Then
            pvObj = 0
            QueryInterface = E_NOINTERFACE
        End If
    End If
End Function
Private Function MyVTableEntry() As Long
    On Error GoTo Error
    'Normal VB code goes here.
    Exit Function
```

```
Error:
    MyVTableEntry = MapErrorKeepRich
End Function
```

The implementation of the error objects recycles the same two objects. This implementation relies on standard practices being followed with error objects: The IErrorInfo reference is released immediately after the rich error information is retrieved, and each member function is called only once per error. Error information is supported only if the IErrorInfo object is currently being referenced.

```
'Selections from RichError.Bas
Private Declare Function SetErrorInfo Lib "oleaut32.Dll" _
    (ByVal dwReserved As Long, perrinfo As Long) As Long
Private Type RichErrorVTables
    SEI(3) As Long  'ISupportErrorInfo
    EI(7) As Long   'IErrorInfo
End Type
Private m_VTables As RichErrorVTables

'Structure and singleton for IErrorInfo implementation.
Private Type ErrorInfo
    pVTable As Long
    cRefs As Long
    Source As String
    Description As String
    HelpFile As String
    HelpContext As Long
End Type
Private m_ErrorInfo As ErrorInfo

'VTable and singleton for ISupportErrorInfo.
'The vtable is the only required element, so there
'is no reason to bother with a structure.
Private m_pSEIVTable As Long
Private m_pSupportErrorInfo As Long

'Provides a quick check to determine if a call
'to CheckErrorInfo is indicated.
Public Const ISupportErrorInfo_Data1 As Long = &HDF0B3D60
```

```vbnet
Public Function MapErrorKeepRich() As Long
Dim Number As Long
    With Err
        Number = .Number
        If Number Then
            If Number > 0 Then _
                Number = &H800A0000 Or Number
            If m_pSupportErrorInfo = 0 Then Init
            m_ErrorInfo.Source = .Source
            m_ErrorInfo.Description = .Description
            m_ErrorInfo.HelpFile = .HelpFile
            m_ErrorInfo.HelpContext = .HelpContext
            .Clear
            SetErrorInfo 0, m_ErrorInfo.pVTable
            MapErrorKeepRich = Number
        End If
    End With
End Function
Public Sub ClearErrorInfo()
    If m_ErrorInfo.cRefs Then SetErrorInfo 0, ByVal 0&
End Sub
Public Function CheckErrorInfo(hr As Long, _
  riid As VBoostTypes.VBGUID, pvObj As Long) As Boolean
    If m_ErrorInfo.cRefs = 0 Then Exit Function
    If IsEqualGUID(riid, IID_ISupportErrorInfo) Then
        pvObj = m_pSupportErrorInfo
        hr = 0
        CheckErrorInfo = True
    End If
End Function
Private Function InterfaceSupportsErrorInfo( _
  This As Long, riid As VBoostTypes.VBGUID) As Long
    If m_ErrorInfo.cRefs = 0 Then _
        InterfaceSupportsErrorInfo = E_FAIL
End Function
Private Function IEIGetSource( _
  This As ErrorInfo, pBstrSource As Long) As Long
    pBstrSource = 0
    VBoost.AssignSwap pBstrSource, This.Source
End Function
```

Most of the lightweight object code shown here is of the cookie-cutter variety. The IEIGetSource implementation is the only one that includes special handling. pBstrSource is actually a String, but it is declared as a Long and initialized to 0. You should take this precaution for all String, object, and array parameters that are flagged as out only in the defining interface. There is no guarantee that an out-only parameter is initialized with valid data when it is passed to a function. VBoost.AssignZero is the function of choice for performing this operation against a pointer type parameter. Lightweight objects should always explicitly zero out-only parameters before using them.

Since the memory referenced by the out parameter is not initialized, VB could free invalid data and crash if pBstrSource were declared As String and then assigned a new value using normal String assignment. In this implementation, however, I lied about the type of pBstrSource so that I could use a simple numeric assignment to clear it. The code then steals the current Source value with VBoost.AssignSwap. In practice, GetSource is called only once, so there is no reason to hang onto m_ErrorInfo.Source beyond the GetSource call.

Not Supporting Rich Error Information

Although you normally don't have to worry when a lightweight object doesn't support rich error information, there is one case in which you do. If you return a failing HRESULT from a vtable call and don't support the ISupportErrorInfo interface, VB holds a reference to the object until the next time an error is raised. I consider this a bug in VB6. The dangling reference is released during teardown after all the memory for all modules has been freed. Since all module memory is gone, all lightweight vtables are gone, and any call to the lightweight object's vtable will cause a crash.

The easiest way to fix this problem is to ignore it during the lifetime of your project and raise a trapped error during module teardown. I've included ResetError.Bas with the book to make this process painless. ResetError is a simple lightweight object with termination code in the Release entry, much like the HourGlass lightweight. The Release function and a calling code snippet are shown below. You may want to include this code if you use lightweights and you find that the built executable crashes sometime during teardown.

```
'Release function.
Private Function Release(This As ResetError) As Long
    On Error Resume Next
    Err.Raise 5
    On Error GoTo 0
End Function
```

```
'Calling code.
Private m_ResetError As ResetError
Sub Main()
    InitResetError m_ResetError
    'The rest of the program.
End Sub
```

Aggregating Lightweight Objects

A lightweight object is simply the custom implementation of a specified interface. You often define this interface yourself, but you will also find that external objects require you to implement specific, defined interfaces. It is not always possible to implement these interfaces in a VB class module. If you hit this limitation, then you can simply implement the stubborn interface as a lightweight object and use the aggregation techniques discussed in the "Aggregating Existing Objects" section of Chapter 5 to merge it into your object.

The IObjectSafety interface is a good example of the type of interface you can implement with a lightweight object. You can use this code as a template for other implementations. With a bit of typelib tweaking, you can come extremely close to correctly implementing IObjectSafety in VB. The only shortcoming is that the documentation for IObjectSafety explicitly requires the implementation to return an E_NOINTERFACE (&H80004002) HRESULT value if the requested interface is not supported. VB always maps this error code to a standard *Type mismatch* error (&H800A000D) before the caller sees it, so you end up violating the interface specification. Other interfaces that require success codes as HRESULT return values (IEnumVARIANT, for example) cannot be implemented in normal VB code.

The easiest way to create a custom interface implementation is to build a lightweight object on memory embedded in the instance of the main object.

When you embed the structure, you don't have to worry about memory allocation or reference counting, so you can concentrate on implementing the interface functions that you care about. Embedded memory eliminates the need for explicit reference counting in AddRef and Release, and you don't have to work much harder to eliminate the need for code in the QueryInterface function as well. This type of lightweight object is designed for explicit use as part of an aggregate, so it already includes code that manages the QueryInterface call for you. If you specify adUseIIDs as one of AggregateData flags, VBoost doesn't query you for anything other than the specified IID. You can eliminate the possibility of the QueryInterface request for the specified IID as well by specifying adFullyResolved.

To be sure that the aggregation flags are set in a fashion consistent with your lightweight implementation, you should populate the AggregateData and associated IID entry as part of the lightweight initialization function. This helps minimize the amount of code in the object that consumes the lightweight implementation, and it makes the code easier to maintain.

The ObjectSafety lightweight implements the simple IObjectSafety interface, which tells controls and objects created in a safe host what the control is allowed to do. For example, if the control says it is safe for an untrusted caller by returning a success code from the SetInterfaceSafetyOptions function, the control knows it should fail operations that require the control to write to the system registry or perform other diabolical actions. The lightweight implementation is shown first, followed by a sample usage.

```
'ObjectSafety lightweight object implementation.
'Contained in ObjectSafety.Bas.
'Requires VBoost.Bas.
Private Const strIID_IObjectSafety As String = _
  "{CB5BDC81-93C1-11CF-8F20-00805F2CD064}"

Private Type IObjectSafetyVTable
    VTable(4) As Long
End Type

Private m_VTable As IObjectSafetyVTable
Private m_pVTable As Long

Private IID_IObjectSafety As VBGUID
```

```vb
Public Enum SafetyOptions
    INTERFACESAFE_FOR_UNTRUSTED_CALLER = 1
    INTERFACESAFE_FOR_UNTRUSTED_DATA = 2
    INTERFACESAFE_USES_DISPEX = 4
    INTERFACE_USES_SECURITY_MANAGER = 8
End Enum


Public Type ObjectSafety
    pVTable As Long
    CurrentSafety As SafetyOptions
    SupportedSafety As SafetyOptions
    pUnkOuter As Long
End Type


Public Sub InitObjectSafety(ObjSafe As ObjectSafety, _
  AggData As AggregateData, IID As IID, _
    ByVal IIDNumber As Long, _
  ByVal punkControllingIUnknown As IUnknown, _
  ByVal Supported As SafetyOptions)
    If m_pVTable = 0 Then
        'VBoost may not be initialized in a UserControl
        'at design time, so make sure it's alive.
        If VBoost Is Nothing Then InitVBoost
        IID_IObjectSafety = IIDFromString( _
          strIID_IObjectSafety)
        With m_VTable
            .VTable(0) = FuncAddr(AddressOf QueryInterface)
            .VTable(1) = FuncAddr(AddressOf AddRefRelease)
            .VTable(2) = .VTable(1)
            .VTable(3) = FuncAddr( _
              AddressOf GetInterfaceSafetyOptions)
            .VTable(4) = FuncAddr( _
              AddressOf SetInterfaceSafetyOptions)
            m_pVTable = VarPtr(.VTable(0))
        End With
    End If

    'Create the lightweight object.
    With ObjSafe
        .pVTable = m_pVTable
        .CurrentSafety = 0
```

```vb
            .SupportedSafety = Supported
            'ObjPtr without the AddRef/Release
            VBoost.Assign .pUnkOuter, punkControllingIUnknown
            IID = IID_IObjectSafety
        End With


        'Populate the AggregateData structure.
        With AggData
            VBoost.Assign .pObject, VarPtr(ObjSafe)
            .FirstIID = IIDNumber
            .Flags = adUseIIDs Or adFullyResolved
            IID = IID_IObjectSafety
        End With
    End Sub


    Private Function QueryInterface( _
        ByVal This As Long, riid As VBGUID, pvObj As Long) As Long
            'This structure is used as an aggregate with both the
            'adUseIIDs and adFullyResolved flags set, which means
            'that it will never actually receive a QueryInterface
            'call.
        Debug.Assert False
        pvObj = 0
        QueryInterface = E_NOINTERFACE
    End Function
    Private Function AddRefRelease(ByVal This As Long) As Long
            'No need to AddRef or Release. This is used inside a
            'blind delegator, which holds the necessary reference
            'on the controlling IUnknown, and the memory is owned
            'by the controlling IUnknown.
    End Function


    Private Function GetInterfaceSafetyOptions( _
        This As ObjectSafety, riid As VBGUID, _
        pdwSupportedOptions As SafetyOptions, _
        pdwEnabledOptions As SafetyOptions) As Long
            With This
                If CheckInterface(.pUnkOuter, riid) Then
                    'Set the options.
                    pdwSupportedOptions = .SupportedSafety
                    pdwEnabledOptions = .CurrentSafety
```

```vb
        Else
            'Failure case.
            GetInterfaceSafetyOptions = E_NOINTERFACE
            pdwSupportedOptions = 0
            pdwEnabledOptions = 0
        End If
    End With
End Function
Private Function SetInterfaceSafetyOptions( _
    This As ObjectSafety, riid As VBGUID, _
    ByVal dwOptionSetMask As SafetyOptions, _
    ByVal dwEnabledOptions As SafetyOptions) As Long
    With This
        If CheckInterface(.pUnkOuter, riid) Then
            If dwOptionSetMask And Not .SupportedSafety Then
                SetInterfaceSafetyOptions = E_FAIL
            Else
                'Toggle only the specified safety bits.
                .CurrentSafety = _
                    (.CurrentSafety And Not dwEnabledOptions) _
                    Or dwOptionSetMask
            End If
        Else
            SetInterfaceSafetyOptions = E_NOINTERFACE
        End If
    End With
End Function


'Helper function to verify if an interface is supported.
Private Function CheckInterface( _
    ByVal pWeakUnk As Long, riid As VBGUID) As Boolean
Dim pUnk As IUnknownUnrestricted
Dim pvObj As Long
    If pWeakUnk = 0 Then Exit Function
    With VBoost
        .Assign pUnk, pWeakUnk
        'Test for the interface.
        If 0 = pUnk.QueryInterface(riid, pvObj) Then
            'Clear the reference.
            .Assign pUnk, pvObj
            pUnk.Release
```

```
              CheckInterface = True
        End If
        .AssignZero pUnk
    End With
End Function
```

```
'Sample usage of ObjectSafety.
'Place this code in a UserControl to enable IObjectSafety.
'You can also use this lightweight interface implementation
'with normal classes designed for consumption by the Windows
'Scripting Host. m_ObjSafe.CurrentSafety contains the current
'safety setting.
Private m_ObjSafe As ObjectSafety
Private m_Hook As UnknownHook
Private Sub UserControl_Initialize()
Dim AggData(0) As AggregateData
Dim IIDs(0) As IID
    InitObjectSafety m_ObjSafe, AggData(0), IIDs(0), 0, _
      Me, _
        INTERFACESAFE_FOR_UNTRUSTED_CALLER Or _
        INTERFACESAFE_FOR_UNTRUSTED_DATA
    VBoost.AggregateUnknown Me, AggData, IIDs, m_Hook
End Sub
```

Coding the QueryInterface Function

I've ignored the need to code the QueryInterface entry of your lightweight vtables for about as long as I can. Just as the AddRef and Release functions don't have much to do, the requirements for QueryInterface are also minimal in the lightweight objects you've seen so far. In fact, the function is never even called in most cases because the VB compiler doesn't generate QueryInterface calls when it assigns references between equivalently typed variables.

The QueryInterface function provides a generic casting mechanism. In any programming language, a cast takes place when you instruct the compiler to view a particular piece of memory as a different type. In the interface-based COM model, in which all communication with a given object takes place through its vtable, a cast becomes a request for a different interface. QueryInterface is designed to provide references to recognized interfaces and to not return interfaces that it doesn't support. Since QI is the only casting means available to

COM objects, not returning a given interface blocks unwanted casts. This level of safety is a good thing from a robustness perspective because arbitrary casting is very dangerous and a large source of crashing bugs in languages that allow it, such as C and C++.

Unfortunately, QueryInterface often supports a lot of Query, but not a lot of Interface. There is an incredible proliferation of interfaces that COM and other components can request. Your object will generally say "no" to most and "yes" to only a select handful. It is a good idea to optimize the QueryInterface implementation as much as possible. You need to look only as far as the OLE control interfaces to see an example of QI gone haywire. The IQuickActivate interface was added to the control specification in 1996 because it was found that 60 percent of an average ActiveX control's startup time was spent in the QueryInterface function. Clearly, some of this is a result of the architecture, but brain-dead QI implementations were also partly to blame.

Lets look at the IObjectSafety sample's QueryInterface function and examine several implementations that support both the IUnknown and IObjectSafety interfaces. Of course, this is just for show because QueryInterface is never actually called in this function. All the implementations assume that IID_IObjectSafety and IID_IUnknown are defined and initialized.

```
'Implementation 1
Private Function QueryInterface( _
  This As ObjectSafety, riid As VBGUID, pvObj As Long) As Long
    If IsEqualIID(riid, IID_IUnknown) Then
    ElseIf IsEqualIID(riid, IID_IObjectSafety) Then
    Else
        pvObj = 0
        QueryInterface = E_NOINTERFACE
        Exit Function
    End If
    pvObj = VarPtr(This)
End Function


'Implementation 2
Private Const Data1_IID_IUnknown As Long = 0&
Private Const Data1_IID_IObjectSafety As Long = &HCB5BDC81
Private Function QueryInterface( _
```

```
        This As ObjectSafety, riid As VBGUID, pvObj As Long) As Long
Dim fOK As BOOL 'IsEqualIID returns a BOOL, not a Boolean.
    If riid.Data1 = Data1_IID_IUnknown Then
        fOK = IsEqualIID(riid, IID_IUnknown)
    ElseIf riid.Data1 = Data1_IID_IObjectSafety Then
        fOK = IsEqualIID(riid, IID_IObjectSafety)
    End If
    If fOK Then
        pvObj = VarPtr(This)
    Else
        pvObj = 0
        QueryInterface = E_NOINTERFACE
    End If
End Function


'Implementation 3
Private Const Data1_IID_IUnknown As Long = 0&
Private Const Data1_IID_IObjectSafety As Long = &HCB5BDC81
Private Function QueryInterface( _
 This As ObjectSafety, riid As VBGUID, pvObj As Long) As Long
Dim fOK As BOOL
    Select Case riid.Data1
        Case Data1_IID_IUnknown
            fOK = IsEqualIID(riid, IID_IUnknown)
        Case Data1_IID_IObjectSafety
            fOK = IsEqualIID(riid, IID_IObjectSafety)
    End Select
    If fOK Then
        pvObj = VarPtr(This)
    Else
        pvObj = 0
        QueryInterface = E_NOINTERFACE
    End If
End Function
```

Although these functions do the same thing, the code generated for each is
quite different. The first implementation calls the API function IsEqualIID multiple times; the second and third implementations call it only once. In the last
two samples, the first four bytes of the IID have been extracted and defined as
constants, allowing a check without a function call. The final example is the

most efficient because a Select Case statement with constant Case statements generates code equivalent to a C switch statement. This is much better than the code generated by a series of ElseIf statements. The use of constants and Select Case makes all the failing calls to the QueryInterface function run very quickly. There are no external function calls to check the full IID in the failure case.

Now that the basic architecture of lightweight objects is in place, the next three chapters will look at different uses of this technology. I'll use lightweights to create a system with a large number of small objects, create a lightweight object to help place VB in the running object table, then look at lightweights that allow you to call function pointers.

Chapter 9

Large Systems of Objects

When you program complex algorithms, you often need many instances of the same type of object. In systems with a large number of interacting objects, you may be discouraged from using VB classes because the overhead is too high. At this point, you might turn to an array of structures instead of class modules. To reference one structure array element from another, you simple store the index into the array. So whenever you want to look at a particular item, you need the array and the index. Such a system resembles the following example. Note that the stored index is always one higher than the actual position in the array; a NextIndex of 0 indicates that you've reached the end of the list.

```
Public Type LinkedPoint
    x As Single
    y As Single
    PrevIndex As Long
    NextIndex As Long
End Type
```

```
Public Sub WalkPoints( _
    Points() As LinkedPoint, ByVal StartIndex As Long)
Dim CurIndex As Long
    CurIndex = StartIndex
    Do
        With Points(CurIndex - 1)
            Debug.Print .x, .y
            CurIndex = .NextIndex
        End With
    Loop While CurIndex
End Sub
```

At first glance, this example doesn't seem so bad. The fact that the array must be passed and dereferenced to get at an item is annoying, but workable. However, the situation starts getting out of hand quickly if you hit the limits of the array. Suppose you anticipate needing 100 items up front, but you find half-way through the algorithm that you suddenly need space for number 101. The first reaction is a call to ReDim Preserve to simply make the array larger. However, this call gets more and more painful from a performance standpoint as the system grows. You request more and more memory and possibly touch all the memory you've previously filled. Even if you ReDim Preserve in chunks instead of one element at a time, you'll find that the ReDim call is the slowest part of the system.

The alternative to using ReDim on your entire array is to create a second array when the first fills up. Although this is a much more efficient algorithm from a memory thrashing perspective, the system is much more difficult to index. VB can't reference arrays, so you have to store the arrays in an object. An array of these objects is small enough that ReDim Preserve is cheap, so making the array larger is acceptable. In this more dynamic system, NextIndex grows to become a double index: NextArray and NextIndex. NextArray is set one too high, so 0 indicates that there is no next item. The indices also get an Integer type instead of a Long because the overflow chance has been eliminated for all practical purposes by making several small buffers instead of one huge one.

```
'clsLinkedPoints buffer class
Private m_Buffer(cChunkSize - 1) As LinkedPoint
Friend Property Get Item( _
    ByVal Index As Integer) As Linked Point
```

```
        Item = m_Buffer(Index)
End Property


'modLinkedPoint
Public Const cChunkSize As Long = 100
Public Type LinkedPoint
    x As Single
    y As Single
    PrevArray As Integer
    PrevIndex As Integer
    NextArray As Integer
    NextIndex As Integer
End Type


Public Sub WalkPoints(Points() As clsLinkedPoints, _
    ByVal StartArray As Integer, ByVal StartIndex As Long)
Dim CurArray As Integer
Dim CurIndex As Integer
    CurArray = CurIndex
    CurIndex = StartIndex
    Do
        With Points(CurArray).Item(CurIndex)
            Debug.Print .x, .y
            CurArray = .NextArray
            CurIndex = .NextIndex
        End With
        If CurArray = StartArray Then
            If CurIndex = StartIndex Then Exit Do
        End If
    Loop While CurArray
End Sub
```

This code is significantly more cumbersome. You not only have to pass three items to reference the correct structure, you also end up making a full copy of each structure whenever you use it. This is a painful piece of code for VB programmers used to working with object references. You really want LinkedPoints to be an object and WalkPoints to look like this.

```
Public Sub WalkPoints(StartingPoint As LinkedPoint)
Dim CurPoint As LinkedPoint
```

```
    Set CurPoint = StartingPoint
    Do Until CurPoint Is Nothing
        With CurPoint
            Debug.Print .x, .y
            Set CurPoint = .NextPoint
        End With
    Loop
End Sub
```

Lightweight objects enable you to write normal object-oriented VB code against structures. By adding a vtable to your structure, you can establish references into a dynamic group of arrays of structures. However, the code that operates on the objects doesn't have to deal with the intricacies of locating the structure. By moving the array allocation and management into a separate object (which I'll call a "memory manager") and turning the structure into a lightweight object, you can create a system for a large number objects that allows you to create both VB- and memory-friendly code.

Using a Fixed-Size Memory Manager

In the lightweights you've seen so far, the memory for the lightweight objects has been allocated on the heap or the stack a single item at a time. However, if you want a large number of small objects, then allocating them on the heap one at a time is painfully inefficient, and allocating them as an array of structures leads to the reallocation problems I just discussed. What you really need is a versatile and efficient mechanism for allocating multiple objects with a single heap allocation. Each lightweight object can then be built on a piece of memory embedded in the larger allocation.

If you look back at the LightEmpty sample, you'll see that the CoTaskMemAlloc functioned returns a pointer, not a specific type. To use an embedded memory pointer instead of one allocated directly off the heap, you need to call a type-agnostic allocation function to get an embedded pointer into a heap allocation. Since the return value is typed only as a pointer, the memory manager can be type-agnostic. The same memory-management object works for all types of lightweight objects.

Allocating memory from system-heap objects is slow for three reasons. First, the heap object must make sure that the requested memory is available. If it isn't, the heap object must retrieve it from the system, which is the slowest step in the whole allocation process. Second, the heap must support requests for allocations with different sizes. The size of a given allocation must be stored so that the heap knows how much memory is involved when the Free function is called. The size (and possibly other information) is generally stored in a header that precedes the memory pointer. This header must be present for every pointer returned by Alloc, and it can easily be as large as the requested object itself. The header allocation accounts for a large percentage of the memory use when you request a large number of small allocations. Third, the system heaps support compaction: When you free enough memory from the heap, the heap gives it back to the system.

Although the system requirements can never be eliminated from memory allocation, there is no hard-and-fast rule that a memory-management object must support variable size allocations and compaction. In fact, removing the variable-size requirement allows you to make a very fast allocator, and removing the compaction requirement makes it even faster. A fixed-size allocation algorithm is also easy to write without the use of headers on each allocation, so more of the allocated memory is used for your objects instead of memory-management overhead. Since each instance of a specific lightweight object requires the same amount of memory, you can greatly increase the memory efficiency when creating multiple lightweight objects by using a fixed-size allocation object.

The general technique employed to create a fixed-size memory manager uses a system-provided heap allocator to allocate large blocks of memory. This memory is subdivided into smaller blocks, and the pointers to these subdivisions are handed out from the Alloc function. When one large block of memory has been completely used, the memory manager goes back to the system for a new block. The memory manager provides the same effect as allocating multiple arrays and managing the indexes into those arrays. However, all the details are hidden from you: You just call Alloc. You also get to use a single pointer-value instead of the double index required to keep track of both the array and the element index in that array.

VBoost implements two fixed-size memory managers: FixedSizeMemory-Manager and CompactibleFixedSizeMemoryManager. Use the VBoost.Create-FixedSizeMemoryManager function to retrieve an instance of either of these allocators. CreateFixedSizeMemoryManager takes ElementSize and Elements-PerBlock parameters and an fCompactible flag that indicates whether you want to support compaction. You can view the implementation of these objects in either C++ or VB in the book's source code, but the implementation details would just be a distraction at this point. The methods and properties of these objects are described in the "Memory-Allocation Objects" section of Appendix A.

Scribble Sample

Scribble is a simple program that lets you use the mouse to scribble on the surface of a window. The beginnings of a scribble implementation are trivially easy to write in VB. When the following code is added to a new form, you get a line for every mouse movement when the left mouse button is down, and no lines when the button is up. You should Set ClipControls to False on your form to minimize the surface area that needs to be redrawn.

```vb
Private Sub Form_MouseDown( _
  Button As Integer, Shift As Integer, _
    X As Single, Y As Single)
    If Button = vbLeftButton Then
        CurrentX = X
        CurrentY = Y
    End If
End Sub
Private Sub Form_MouseMove( _
  Button As Integer, Shift As Integer, _
    X As Single, Y As Single)
    If Button = vbLeftButton Then
        Line -(X, Y)
    End If
End Sub
Private Sub Form_MouseUp( _
  Button As Integer, Shift As Integer, _
    X As Single, Y As Single)
    If Button = vbLeftButton Then
        PSet (X, Y)
    End If
End Sub
```

The problem with this scribble code is that it doesn't maintain the picture. If you cover the form and force it to repaint, all of the scribbles are gone. If you turn AutoRedraw on, the lines are maintained, but using AutoRedraw on a Form is expensive from a memory perspective (and the AutoRedraw solution doesn't go very far towards demonstrating lightweight objects.) In order to enable redrawing in the Form_Paint event, you need a history of all of the visited points. The history mechanism is a classic example of an object system that has a large number of small objects.

Our object system has two types of objects: ILinkedPoint and IStartingPoint (shown here). Note that these interface definitions use ByRef semantics (ILinkedPoint**) whenever possible to cut down on AddRef/Release cycles. There are no error-return codes. The only possible error in the object system comes during allocation. Once the memory is allocated successfully, there will be no errors, so there is no reason to use HRESULT returns in the vtable functions.

```
interface ILinkedPoint : IUnknown
{
    long X();
    long Y();
    ILinkedPoint* Next();
    void SetNext([in] ILinkedPoint** pNext);
}
interface IStartingPoint : IUnknown
{
    IStartingPoint* Next();
    ILinkedPoint* First();
    void AddPoint([in] ILinkedPoint** pNew);
}
```

I've associated two creation functions with these objects: NewPoint, which takes X and Y parameters and returns an ILinkedPoint implementation; and NewStartingPoint, which takes an existing point and the current starting point. The current starting point becomes the Next of the new starting point, allowing the owning object to hold only a single IStartingPoint reference to keep the whole system alive. AddPoint is called to add a new point to an existing chain of objects. The point-tracking system adds only two lines of code to the initial implementation. MouseDown calls NewStartingPoint, and MouseMove calls AddPoint. With these point tracking calls in place, the Scribble form code is longer, but still very manageable. It is also completely object-oriented, although the point objects are actually lightweight. The underlying memory-manager and structures are fully encapsulated, so the form code doesn't have to worry about them. You may also notice in Form_DblClick how easy it is to release the entire system of points.

```vb
Private m_StartingPoint As IStartingPoint
Private Sub Form_MouseDown( _
  Button As Integer, Shift As Integer, _
    X As Single, Y As Single)
    If Button = vbLeftButton Then
        CurrentX = X
        CurrentY = Y
        Set m_StartingPoint = NewStartingPoint( _
          NewPoint(X, Y), m_StartingPoint)
    End If
End Sub


Private Sub Form_MouseMove( _
  Button As Integer, Shift As Integer, _
    X As Single, Y As Single)
    If Button = vbLeftButton Then
        If Not m_StartingPoint Is Nothing Then
            Line -(X, Y)
            m_StartingPoint.AddPoint NewPoint(X, Y)
        End If
    End If
End Sub


Private Sub Form_MouseUp( _
  Button As Integer, Shift As Integer, _
    X As Single, Y As Single)
    If Button = vbLeftButton Then
        If Not m_StartingPoint Is Nothing Then
            PSet (X, Y)
        End If
    End If
End Sub
```

```
Private Sub Form_DblClick()
    Set m_StartingPoint = Nothing
    Refresh
End Sub


Private Sub Form_Paint()
Dim pCurStart As IStartingPoint
Dim pCur As ILinkedPoint
Dim pCurNext As ILinkedPoint
    Set pCurStart = m_StartingPoint
    Do Until pCurStart Is Nothing
        Set pCur = pCurStart.First
        CurrentX = pCur.X
        CurrentY = pCur.Y
        Set pCurNext = pCur.Next
        Do Until pCurNext Is Nothing
            Set pCur = pCurNext
            Line -(pCur.X, pCur.Y)
            Set pCurNext = pCur.Next
        Loop
        PSet (pCur.X, pCur.Y)
        Set pCurStart = pCurStart.Next
    Loop
End Sub
```

The BAS code that implements the two types of point objects uses a CompactibleFixedSizeMemoryManager to transparently handle the memory requirements. When CompactOnFree is set to True, the code that uses these objects needn't worry about heap compaction when all the items are freed. As long as all references in the memory block are set to Nothing before the memory manager is released, the system is safe. Since module-level variables in BAS modules are torn down after all the exposed or visible class instances (including forms) are released, all the points owned by the form are released automatically before the memory manager tears down. Here's the code from the BAS module. With the exception of the different memory-allocation changes, the lightweight code should look familiar by now. The three IUnknown functions are omitted for the sake of brevity—they are the same as the refcounted LightEmpty functions shown earlier.

```vb
Private m_MM As CompactibleFixedSizeMemoryManager
Private Type PointVTable
    VTable(6) As Long
End Type
Private m_VTable As PointVTable
Private m_pVTable As Long


Private Type StartVTable
    VTable(5) As Long
End Type
Private m_StartVTable As StartVTable
Private m_pStartVTable As Long


Private Type LinkedPoint
    pVTable As Long
    X As Long
    Y As Long
    Next As ILinkedPoint
    cRefs As Long
End Type


Private Type StartingPoint
    pVTable As Long
    Next As IStartingPoint
    First As ILinkedPoint
    Last As ILinkedPoint
    cRefs As Long
End Type


'The structures are the same size, so we use the same
'memory manager to allocate them.
Private Const cPointMemMgrSize As Long = 20
Private Const cPointsPerBlock As Long = 128


Public Function NewPoint( _
   ByVal X As Long, ByVal Y As Long) As ILinkedPoint
Dim Struct As LinkedPoint
Dim ThisPtr As Long
    If m_pVTable = 0 Then
        If m_MM Is Nothing Then
            Set m_MM = VBoost.CreateFixedSizeMemoryManager( _
```

```
                cPointMemMgrSize, cPointsPerBlock, True)
            m_MM.CompactOnFree = True
        End If
        With m_VTable
            .VTable(0) = FuncAddr(AddressOf QueryInterface)
            .VTable(1) = FuncAddr(AddressOf AddRef)
            .VTable(2) = FuncAddr(AddressOf Release)
            .VTable(3) = FuncAddr(AddressOf GetX)
            .VTable(4) = FuncAddr(AddressOf GetY)
            .VTable(5) = FuncAddr(AddressOf GetNext)
            .VTable(6) = FuncAddr(AddressOf SetNext)
            m_pVTable = VarPtr(.VTable(0))
        End With
    End If
    ThisPtr = m_MM.Alloc
    With Struct
        .pVTable = m_pVTable
        .X = X
        .Y = Y
        .cRefs = 1
        CopyMemory ByVal ThisPtr, .pVTable, LenB(Struct)
        ZeroMemory .pVTable, LenB(Struct)
        VBoost.Assign NewPoint, ThisPtr
    End With
End Function
Public Function NewStartingPoint( _
  FirstPoint As ILinkedPoint, _
  PrevStart As IStartingPoint) As IStartingPoint
Dim Struct As StartingPoint
Dim ThisPtr As Long
    If m_pStartVTable = 0 Then
        If m_MM Is Nothing Then
            Set m_MM = VBoost.CreateFixedSizeMemoryManager( _
                cPointMemMgrSize, cPointsPerBlock, True)
            m_MM.CompactOnFree = True
        End If
        With m_StartVTable
            .VTable(0) = FuncAddr( _
                AddressOf StartQueryInterface)
            .VTable(1) = FuncAddr(AddressOf StartAddRef)
            .VTable(2) = FuncAddr(AddressOf StartRelease)
```

```
                    .VTable(3) = FuncAddr(AddressOf StartGetNext)
                    .VTable(4) = FuncAddr(AddressOf StartGetFirst)
                    .VTable(5) = FuncAddr(AddressOf StartAddPoint)
                m_pStartVTable = VarPtr(.VTable(0))
            End With
        End If
        ThisPtr = m_MM.Alloc
        With Struct
            .pVTable = m_pStartVTable
            Set .Next = PrevStart
            Set .Last = FirstPoint
            Set .First = .Last
            .cRefs = 1
            CopyMemory ByVal ThisPtr, .pVTable, LenB(Struct)
            ZeroMemory .pVTable, LenB(Struct)
            VBoost.Assign NewStartingPoint, ThisPtr
        End With
    End Function


    'VTable functions for the ILinkedPoint
    'IUnknown functions are omitted.


    'Called by Release to do the dirty work.
    Private Sub DeleteThis(This As LinkedPoint)
    Dim tmp As LinkedPoint
        This = tmp
        m_MM.Free VarPtr(pThis)
    End Sub
    Private Function GetX(This As LinkedPoint) As Long
        GetX = This.X
    End Function
    Private Function GetY(This As LinkedPoint) As Long
        GetY = This.Y
    End Function
    Private Function GetNext(This As LinkedPoint) As ILinkedPoint
        Set GetNext = This.Next
    End Function
    Private Sub SetNext( _
      This As LinkedPoint, pNext As ILinkedPoint)
        Set This.Next = pNext
    End Sub
```

```
'VTable functions for the IStartingPoint
'IUnknown functions are omitted.

'Called by Release to do the dirty work.
Private Sub StartDeleteThis(This As StartingPoint)
Dim tmp As StartingPoint
    This = tmp
    m_MM.Free VarPtr(this)
End Sub
Private Function StartGetNext( _
   This As StartingPoint) As IStartingPoint
    Set StartGetNext = This.Next
End Function
Private Function StartGetFirst( _
   This As StartingPoint) As ILinkedPoint
    Set StartGetFirst = This.First
End Function
Private Sub StartAddPoint( _
   This As StartingPoint, pNew As ILinkedPoint)
    With This
        .Last.SetNext pNew
        Set .Last = pNew
    End With
End Sub
```

Now you have a complete system for maintaining a set of points. However, if you start stepping through this code, you will find that all is not rosy. You spend most of the time in the AddRef and Release functions while you're establishing points. Since the functions are fast, this really isn't that bad. However, if you step through the teardown code, you see just how much work is required to free all those little objects back into the allocator. You'll also see that the stack depth is excessive. In particular, LinkedPoint's Release function recurses to the depth of the number of items in a list of points. (You can usually step over the Free call with the VBoost allocators; pVTable is the only member that changes. The only time you'll get into trouble is if you are unlucky enough to trigger a memory compaction.)

The scary thing about the complications you encounter when this system is torn down is that the system is actually very simple. By adding a Previous function to the Next function, you could end up with a doubly-linked system instead of the current singly-linked system. This addition would make you deal with circular references, so releasing the top object would not have actually repopulated the allocator. Of course, you can use the circular reference techniques described in Chapter 6 to get around this, but you still have to visit all the objects in the system during teardown to massage the reference counts. Otherwise, the objects won't free themselves back to the allocator.

One of the frustrations of circularly referenced object systems is that they are significantly harder to tear down than they are to build up. By taking explicit control of the memory management, you can actually tear the system down without bothering with reference counts at all. The teardown then involves three steps.

1. Visit all the nodes in the system to release references to objects, strings, and arrays that are not controlled by a memory manager you own. (Optional depending on object.)

2. Release all the references VB may be holding on objects in the system.

3. Release the memory manager itself.

With this in mind, let's make a few changes to the points code.

- NewPoint and NewStartingPoint take a FixedSizeMemoryManager reference to provide an allocator.

- The cRefs members are eliminated from both structures, and the IUnknown functions no longer count references.

- LinkedPoint.Next, StartingPoint.Next, and StartingPoint.First are given type Long instead of an object type. The access functions change accordingly to return and take Long values. This change is an optimization so that the values don't have to be assigned with a Set statement. Set would generate an AddRef that is meaningless in a nonrefcounted system. StartingPoint.Last retains its ILinkedPoint type so the StartAddPoint function can easily call Last.SetNext.

```
'Code changes for non-refcounted objects.
Private Type LinkedPoint
    pVTable As Long
```

```vb
        X As Long
        Y As Long
        Next As Long 'ILinkedPoint
End Type


Private Type StartingPoint
    pVTable As Long
    Next As Long 'IStartingPoint
    First As Long 'ILinkedPoint
    Last As ILinkedPoint
End Type


'Make the constant public for external allocators.
Public Const cPointMemMgrSize As Long = 16


Public Function NewPoint( _
  MM As FixedSizeMemoryManager, _
  ByVal X As Long, ByVal Y As Long) As ILinkedPoint
Dim Struct As LinkedPoint
Dim ThisPtr As Long
    If m_pVTable = 0 Then
        'etc.
    End If
    ThisPtr = MM.Alloc
    With Struct
        .pVTable = m_pVTable
        .X = X
        .Y = Y
        CopyMemory ByVal ThisPtr, Struct, LenB(Struct)
        VBoost.Assign NewPoint, ThisPtr
    End With
End Function


Public Function NewStartingPoint( _
  MM As FixedSizeMemoryManager, _
  FirstPoint As ILinkedPoint, _
  PrevStart As IStartingPoint) As IStartingPoint
Dim Struct As StartingPoint
Dim ThisPtr As Long
    If m_pStartVTable = 0 Then
        'etc.
```

```vb
        End If
        ThisPtr = MM.Alloc
        With Struct
            .pVTable = m_pStartVTable
            .Next = ObjPtr(PrevStart)
            Set .Last = FirstPoint
            .First = ObjPtr(.Last)
            CopyMemory ByVal ThisPtr, Struct, LenB(Struct)
            'We don't care about ZeroMemory because a Release
            'doesn't matter.
            VBoost.Assign NewStartingPoint, ThisPtr
        End With
    End Function


    'Use these IUnknown functions for both types.
    Private Function QueryInterface( _
      ByVal This As Long, riid As Long, pvObj As Long) As Long
        'This actually never fires because we use only strong
        'types. Assert and fail just in case.
        Debug.Assert False
        pvObj = 0
        QueryInterface = E_NOINTERFACE
    End Function
    Private Function AddRefRelease(ByVal This As Long) As Long
        'Nothing to do.
    End Function


    'VTable functions for ILinkedPoint.
    'GetX, GetY unchanged.
    Private Function GetNext(This As LinkedPoint) As Long
        GetNext = This.Next
    End Function
    Private Sub SetNext(This As LinkedPoint, pNext As Long)
        This.Next = pNext
    End Sub


    Private Function StartGetNext( _
      This As StartingPoint) As Long 'IStartingPoint.
        StartGetNext = This.Next
    End Function
    Private Function StartGetFirst( _
```

```
   This As StartingPoint) As Long    'ILinkedPoint
        StartGetFirst = This.First
End Function
'StartAddPoint unchanged.
```

With these changes in place, the form that uses the Points objects is now responsible for providing the memory manager and for tearing down the system in the correct order. The Form now needs Load and Unload code and some changes to the DoubleClick event that refresh the points and screen. The only changes in the Mouse* routines is that m_PointMM is now passed to the NewPoint and NewStartingPoint functions.

```
Private m_PointMM As FixedSizeMemoryManager
Private m_StartingPoint As IStartingPoint
Private Const cPointsPerBlock As Long = 128


Private Sub Form_DblClick()
    'Release all of VB's references to objects
    'owned by the memory manager.
    Set m_StartingPoint = Nothing

    'Release the memory manager to free all memory.
    'The placement of this statement is discussed below.
    Set m_PointMM = Nothing

    'Recreate the memory manager.
    Set m_PointMM = VBoost.CreateFixedSizeMemoryManager( _
      cPointMemMgrSize, cPointsPerBlock)
    Refresh
End Sub


Private Sub Form_Load()
    Set m_PointMM = VBoost.CreateFixedSizeMemoryManager( _
      cPointMemMgrSize, cPointsPerBlock)
End Sub


Private Sub Form_Unload(Cancel As Integer)
    'Release the starting point before m_PointMM
    'because m_PointMM owns the memory for the object.
    Set m_StartingPoint = Nothing
```

```
    Set m_PointMM = Nothing
End Sub
```

The only unusual code here is the explicit Set = Nothing call that releases the memory manager. I rarely perform an explicit Set = Nothing because VB checks all object variables and Releases them for us at the end of a function, so the extra code doesn't make a difference. I release the reference explicitly here because of the order in which VB executes the Set statement. VB first evaluates the expression on the right, and releases the reference to the pointer currently in the object variable only if the evaluation of the right expression is successful.

The order of the QI and Release calls made during the Set statement creates a situation in which two memory managers are alive at the same time unless the explicit Set = Nothing call is made. When you explicitly release the old reference before you create the new manager, an absolutely beautiful thing happens. Most of the time, ObjPtr(m_PointMM) is the same for both the old and new functions. The noncompactible memory manager is optimized to allocate its first block from the heap along with its own memory. On teardown, any additional buffers are freed to the heap, and then the double-duty object/first buffer allocation is freed.

In the code above, the next request to the heap comes as the new object is created; the new object is exactly the same size as the memory just freed. Unless heap compaction occurred as the result of the Free call, the heap gives back the same block of memory. Essentially, you end up placing a washed-up player on waivers only to retrieve him a few minutes later as a star rookie. The resulting state is exactly the same as if you had used the compactible allocator—one free block with no items allocated. The only difference is that there was no need to execute all the refcount-driven teardown code to get back to ground zero. What a deal!

In this example, I've created something that VB thinks is a set of COM objects. All the calling code interacts with the objects through fully object-oriented COM method and property calls. I used only as much COM as I needed to add OOP constructs to the system and no more. The IUnknown vtable is there, but no reference-counting takes place in AddRef/Release, and no interface validation takes place in QueryInterface. I've also reduced error checking by using a nonOLE Automation-compatible interface and eliminated many AddRef and Release calls with a simple modification to the parameter types in the vtable functions. The result is a very efficient system that tears down extremely easily and uses only 16 bytes of memory per object.

Chapter 10

VB Objects and the Running Object Table

The Running Object Table ("ROT" for short) is a global system table that associates a name with a currently running object. The ROT is a central store that allows objects to be located across process boundaries without requiring the processes to define custom communication-protocols. When a process registers an object it owns in the ROT, the process states that it is ready to share that object with any other process that knows the object's name. If another process doesn't know the name, it can't get the object. If two objects are registered with the same name, the ROT does not define which of the objects you get.

VB's only built-in interactions with the ROT occur with some variations of the GetObject function and when it attempts to automatically instantiate application objects. GetObject has four syntaxes, two of which interact with the ROT.

1. GetObject("", "Server.Class") is equivalent to CreateObject("Server.Class").

2. GetObject(, "Server.Class") searches the ROT for an object with the given class.

3. GetObject("PickAName") uses a complex name-resolution process to resolve the name to an object. The process may involve the running object table. (I won't discuss this mechanism, but you can find more information by searching for GetObject in MSDN.)

4. GetObject("FileName", "Server.Class") creates the "Server.Class" object and tries to load its contents from FileName using the IPersistFile interface.

An application object is any type library-defined createable class flagged with the appobject attribute. You can define an appobject class in VB by setting a class's Instancing property to GlobalMultiUse or GlobalSingleUse. When VB tries to instantiate an application object, it first looks for an object of the specified type in the ROT. It creates a new instance only if no object was registered.

An active object is any object in the ROT that can be found with the second GetObject syntax. There are three standard APIs that simplify the process of moving objects into and out of the ROT. RegisterActiveObject registers the object and returns a cookie value to the caller. RevokeActiveObject is called against the cookie to remove it from the table, and GetActiveObject is called to retrieve the item from the ROT. VB's GetObject function with syntax two maps directly to the GetActiveObject API, which in turn calls the GetObject method on the IRunningObjectTable interface.

The following API calls translate VB's ProgID request into a method call on the running object table.

1. VB.GetObject calls CLSIDFromProgID to get a CLSID.

2. VB.GetObject calls GetActiveObject with the CLSID.

3. GetActiveObject calls StringFromGUID2 to convert the CLSID to a string.

4. GetActiveObject calls CreateItemMoniker to create an IMoniker object that represents the CLSID string. (Think of a moniker as an object that represents a parseable string).

5. GetActiveObject calls GetRunningObjectTable to get an IRunningObject-Table reference.

6. GetActiveObject calls IRunningObjectTable.GetObject with the generated moniker.

There are several things to bear in mind when you look at this API sequence. First, you can skip steps one through three if you already have a string representation of the CLSID. Second, the moniker is completely CLSID-based, so there is no distinction made between processes in the running object table. If the process puts an item in the ROT and requests it again based solely on the CLSID, you can only guarantee that you got the same item back if no other processes have registered an item with the same name.

Although the process ambiguity of ROT entries is in keeping with the intent of the ROT as a system-wide object bulletin board, ambiguous entries mean that you can't use RegisterActiveObject or GetActiveObject directly to register ROT entries for process-specific objects. However, by creating your own process-specific monikers, you can guarantee that you get back the expected item. You just have to create your own monikers and manipulate the ROT directly. For example, if you use strCLSID & Hex$(App.hInstance) as the base string for the moniker, you can regenerate the moniker from anywhere within the current process and guarantee that you get back an item that was implemented by your project.

Registering VB Objects with the ROT

Registering a Multiuse VB object in the ROT is easy. First, determine the CLSID. At runtime the CLSID can be found with the CLSIDFromProgID API function or stored as a string constant if you're sure it's not going to change. You can turn the string into a CLSID using the CLSIDFromString function defined in VBoostTypes. The CLSID is static if binary compatibility is enabled. You can also determine the CLSID at runtime by using the CLSIDFromFileAndClassName function in the LookupCLSID.Bas file on the book's CD.

With the CLSID in hand you may think that you are now ready to finish registering your object in the ROT with a simple call to RegisterActiveObject. However, life becomes difficult when you do that. RegisterActiveObject adds one or more references to the object, so the act of adding the object to the ROT keeps the object from being in the ROT and hitting its Class_Terminate event at the same time. If you intend to terminate an ActiveX server gracefully, it is completely unacceptable to have outstanding references on an object. You are stuck in the ROT until someone happens to explicitly remove you. Even if the process ends (without running the termination code), the entry you placed in the ROT remains there until you reboot the machine. The ROT has no way to clean up after itself.

To be a good COM citizen, you must be able to put the object in the ROT and run termination code when the only thing keeping the object alive is the references held by the ROT. You can't do this with a normal VB object. However, a highly specialized lightweight object, called ROTHook, allows the object to be in the ROT *and* terminate correctly. I'll first look at how to use the ROTHook object and then delve into its implementation.

Using the ROTHook Object

The ROTHook object is very easy to use in spite of its complexity under the covers. The ROTHook structure has two members: Hook and Struct. Hook points to the lightweight object implementation in Struct and has type IROTHook. The IROTHook interface has two methods, ExposeObject and HideObject, and one property, Locked. ExposeObject's first parameter is the object to place in the ROT, usually Me. The second parameter is the object's ProgID. The following steps are sufficient to place the first object in the ROT—and to get it out again.

1. Create an ActiveX EXE project.

2. Establish a global VBoost variable by adding VBoost.Bas and the appropriate project references (see "VBoost Objects" in Chapter 1 or Appendix A).

3. Add a project reference to VBoost: ROT Hook Types. You'll find this library in ROTHookTypes.Olb.

4. Add the ROTHook.Bas file to your project.

5. Add the following code to a class with the Instancing property set to MultiUse or GlobalMultiUse class.

```
'Class DemoClass.
Private m_ROTHook As ROTHook
Private Sub Class_Initialize()
    InitROTHook m_ROTHook
    m_ROTHook.Hook.ExposeObject Me, "ROTDemo.DemoClass"
End Sub
Private Sub Class_Terminate()
    m_ROTHook.Hook.HideObject
End Sub
```

Creating a DemoClass instance from inside or outside the project now places the object in the ROT, and GetObject(, "ROTDemo.DemoClass") successfully retrieves the registered instance of the class. The object stays in the ROT until the last object retrieved via an external CreateObject or GetObject is released or until you make an explicit call to HideObject. If you never create an object from within the same project, such as when you have a server that has no UI, the object is always created and released externally. The HideObject call in Class_Terminate is not needed to remove the ROT entry in the no-UI case.

Debugging with ROTHook

You have to be aware of ROT implications when you debug projects that include registered objects from inside the IDE. The ROTHook object works well in the IDE, except for the debugging limitations that result from an IUnknown hook (see "IUnknown hooking" in Chapter 5). If you stop the program with the End statement or the End button, you don't run normal termination code, and you can leave garbage in the ROT. The system can generally work around the orphaned entries, but it does not clean them up until you reboot. To help you end a debugging session cleanly, ROTHook.Bas includes a debug function, ClearROT, that you can call from the immediate pane by calling HideObject on all the currently registered objects. To enable this capability, you must add the conditional compilation constant DEBUGROT and set it to a nonzero value. You should turn the debugging code off before making an executable.

There are a couple of tools that can help you debug the ROT. The first tool, IROTView.Exe, ships in the Tools\OLETools directory on the VB CD. IROTView lets you look at the names of all objects currently in the ROT. You can see this list change as you add and remove objects from the ROT. There is one other tool publicly available from Microsoft, ROTClean.Exe. ROTClean removes orphaned entries from the ROT, but is offered without source code or promises of future compatibility—search for ROTCLEAN on http://msdn.microsoft.com.

Locking an Entry in the ROT

If you have an ActiveX object that presents no UI, you know the object is always created externally and that ROTHook removes the entry from the ROT on shutdown. However, there are many cases in which an active object is associated with a visible UI element in the process that owns the object. For example, a central tracking system used by multiple objects may have a status form. Applications that report to your tracking system call GetObject(, "Tracker.Report"), and then use the returned object to report a set of results. In this scenario, the application provides an object through the running object table, but the ROTHook removes the object as soon as every report is finished—a totally unacceptable situation.

You need to add an artificial external connection to an object to keep the object in the ROT while the UI is still alive. The Locked property on the IROTHook interface provides this capability for you via the handy CoLockObjectExternal API call, designed specifically for the purpose of adding an external connection to an object in the same process. Since the Locked property must be set from outside the hooked object, and should only be set from a UI element inside the project, you can add a Friend function to the hooked object to enable locking and unlocking the object. Simply add this code to the base ROTHook usage code shown earlier.

```
Friend Property Let Locked(ByVal RHS As Boolean)
    m_ROTHook.Hook.Locked = RHS
End Property
```

If a UI element is associated with an ROT-registered object, you typically create the object and set the Locked property to True as you create the UI, (such as in the Form_Load event). You must set the Locked property to False before the UI releases its reference on the object (such as in Form_Unload). Locking is generally used only with visible applications because a user action is required to remove the item from the ROT. If you lock an ActiveX server in place without providing a means to unlock the server object, you've effectively locked the server in memory even though it is not used.

Custom ROT Monikers

The initial ROTHook usage instructions specify that only an ActiveX EXE should use the hook. This limitation is valid if you register the object based solely on its ProgID. The ProgID becomes a CLSID, which is then entered into the ROT with no process information. If you register an object based solely on a CLSID in an ActiveX DLL with the intent of sharing the object within your process, you may actually end up sharing an object with another instance of the same application. In order to guarantee that you use only objects in the process, you must register and retrieve the objects with a process-specific name.

If you wish to register your object with a nonstandard name, simply pass the name into the ProgID parameter of the Expose object and set the third parameter (fProgIDIsMoniker) to True. ExposeObject then skips the ProgID registry-lookup and jumps straight to the ROT registration code. This feature also enables you to pass the string version of your CLSID, bypassing the nonunique ProgID altogether.

```
'Register this object with a custom moniker.
Private m_ROTHook As ROTHook
Private Sub Class_Initialize()
Dim strGuid As String
    StringFormGUID2 _
      CLSIDFromProgID("ROTDemo.DemoClass"), strGuid
    InitROTHook ROTHook
    ROTHook.Hook.ExposeObject _
      Me, strGuid & Hex$(App.hInstance), True
End Sub
```

Of course, getting the custom object into the ROT is only half the problem. Getting the object *out* of the ROT just became more difficult. You can no longer use GetObject to retrieve the item. The GetMonikeredObject function shown here is included in ROTHook.Bas. Simply pass the same string with which you registered the object to get the object back.

```
'Public function to get an object by a non-progid moniker.
'All API calls are also declared in ROTHook.Bas
'or ROTHookTypes.olb.
Public Function GetMonikeredObject( _
    strMoniker As String) As IUnknown
Dim hr As Long
Dim pmk As IMonikerStub
Dim pROT As IRunningObjectTableStub
    hr = CreateItemMoniker("!", strMoniker, pmk)
    If hr = 0 Then
        hr = GetRunningObjectTable(0, pROT)
        If hr = 0 Then
            hr = pROT.GetObject(pmk, GetMonikeredObject)
        End If
    End If
    If hr Then Err.Raise hr
End Function
```

Other ROTHook Usage Issues

This book does not cover the use of VB objects as NT services, but service support is built into the ROTHook object. IRunningObjectTable.Register supports a ROTFLAGS_ALLOWANYCLIENT flag that tells the ROT to allow this item to be retrieved from clients other than the client that created it. The fourth parameter of IROTHook.ExposeObject, ServiceSupport, lets you specify no service support, required service support, or attempted service support. In the case of attempted service support, an attempt is made to register with ROTFLAGS ALLOWANYCLIENT, but the object is registered without this flag in the case of failure. Registering with this flag always fails without additional work in the AppID and other registry sections. See IRunningObjectTable::Register in MSDN for more information.

Many people ask me how to get a ROTHook object to work with DCOM. Unfortunately, there is no GetActiveObject equivalent to the CoCreateInstanceEx API, which is used for object creation. CoCreateInstanceEx (and the corresponding CreateObject function in VB) have parameters that specify the machine on which to create the object. Without this extra parameter in the system-provided GetRunningObjectTable or GetActiveObject API calls, there is no simple way to pull objects directly from the ROT of a remote machine. However, with aggregation support, you can create a remote object that uses VBoost to aggre-gate an object retrieved from the local ROT. The only place you'll need code is in Class_Initialize.

ROTHook Implementation Details

The strategy used with the ROTHook lightweight is straightforward: call Register-ActiveObject with the CLSID, but pass a helper object instead of the real object. The ROTHook object receives all the reference-counting hits requested by the sys-tem during the RegisterActiveObject API call and defers IUnknown requests to the main object after registration is complete. The post registration pass-through mode makes additional interface requests go directly to the main object. See Figure 10.1 for the referencing relationships between ROTHook and the main object.

IExternalConnection is one of the interfaces requested during Register-ActiveObject. IExternalConnection is important because it allows COM servers to distinguish between references held by internal objects and those held by external objects. The two IExternalConnection methods, AddConnection and ReleaseConnection, form a secondary reference-counting mechanism for track-ing the number of external object references. VB automatically cleans up all

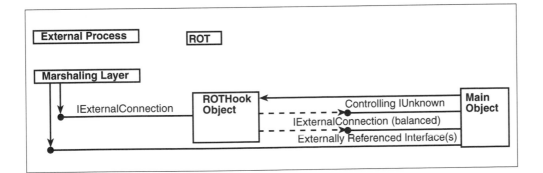

Figure 10.1. Both the main object and the Running Object Table hold strong refer-ences to the ROTHook objects, but the only strong references on the main object are held by external objects. Registering an ROTHook object in the ROT does not affect the lifetime of the main object itself. In the diagram, solid lines represent strong references; dotted lines represent weak references.

internal objects and shuts down the process when all visible and external objects have been released, so it is crucial to maintain an accurate external reference count to avoid premature shutdowns and leaked processes.

The ROT requests a reference to IExternalConnection during registration, and then calls AddConnection when an object is retrieved from the ROT. ReleaseConnection is called when the external reference is released. By monitoring the AddConnection and ReleaseConnection calls, the ROTHook object is able to determine when the final external connection has been released. When there are no more connections, the ROTHook object revokes the ROT registration.

Multiple VTables on a Lightweight

So far, I've discussed two interfaces—IROTHook and IExternalConnection—supported by the ROTHook lightweight object. As you'll see later, ROTHook must also support IQIHook, which is a third vtable. Since this lightweight object is the first I've discussed that requires support for multiple interfaces and, hence, vtables, let's take a look at how this is best done.

To support multiple vtables, you need a data member in the structure for each vtable. Establish your primary vtable as you always do by returning VarPtr(.pVTable) from the creation routine. However, in the QueryInterface implementation, you can return either VarPtr(.pVTable) for the main interface or VarPtr(.pVTableSecondary) for a secondary interface. Just remember that the *This* parameter being passed to the vtable functions for the secondary routine does not have the same type as the *This* parameter passed into the vtable functions that fill the primary vtable array.

In order to code against the *This* object in the secondary interface functions, you first place all the vtable members at the top of the structure, and then make a copy of the main structure for each additional vtable. The only difference among the copies is that one vtable entry is eliminated per copy, and each copy has a different name. See the IROTHookImpl, IExtConImpl, and IQIHookImpl structure definitions in Listing 10.1 for an example of how this is done.

The only problem with cutting members off a structure is that then you can't reference them. The interface listed last can't directly look at the interfaces before it. All is not lost, however. Since all of the discarded members are vtable pointers, you can still get to the helper objects via the interface that corresponds to the vtable. You just have to know how far back the vtable is. For example, the ROTHook function ReleaseConnection is part of the IExternalConnection interface, but it needs to run the code in HideObject on the IROTHook interface. IExternalConnection is based on the pVTableExtCon field, located eight bytes after the pVTableMain item in the IROTHookImpl structure. The following code is required to call HideObject.

```
Dim tmpROTHook As IROTHook
    VBoost.Assign tmpROTHook, _
        VBoost.UDif(VarPtr(.pVTableExternal), 8)
    tmpROTHook.HideObject
    VBoost.AssignZero tmpROTHook
```

Safe Weak Referencing of Secondary Interfaces

In order to prevent the VB server from destroying itself while external objects are still using it, the ROTHook object holds a reference to the native object's IExternalConnection interface and forwards all AddConnection and Release-Connection calls to the VB object. However, the ROTHook can't keep a strong reference to an interface that belongs to the native object because the strong reference would stop the Class_Terminate from firing.

Until now, you've maintained weak references by holding a Long variable that contains the pointer to an object. However, the ROTHook uses two alternate mechanisms. ROTHook keeps a weak reference to the native object's controlling IUnknown in an IUnknownUnrestricted variable called pOuter. To prevent an extra release call, this variable is zeroed before the ROTHook object is destroyed. The second weak reference (to the IExternalConnection interface of the native object) is a very interesting case that deserves further explanation.

In general, it is safe to keep a weak reference to an object if you are sure that the object will be alive when you call it. A weak reference to the controlling IUnknown of an object is always safe because the controlling IUnknown lives at least as long as any other interface on the object. However, keeping a weak reference to a noncontrolling interface can be very dangerous when you apply it to arbitrary objects. There is no COM rule that says that references for all of an object's supported interfaces must be alive for the full lifetime of the object itself.

A COM object is free to dynamically create companion objects to support different interface requests. These objects are known as *tearoffs,* and help reduce the size and initial cost of creating an object. When an object creates a tearoff in response to an interface request, it can cache the tearoff for later use or simply let it die when the last reference to the tearoff object is released. The VBoost aggregators support cached tearoffs with the adDelayCreation flag and uncached tearoffs with the adDelayDontCacheResolved flag. You can't keep a weak reference on a tearoff just by holding its pointer; if you release the last reference on the specific interface, the interface is dead even though the main object is still alive.

Since an external consumer has no idea if a returned interface is a tearoff, the consumer should never hold a weak reference on a secondary interface. The one thing you can count on, however, is that the tearoff itself holds a strong reference to the controlling IUnknown. You can balance the strong reference you're forced to hold on the secondary interface by releasing a reference on the controlling IUnknown. Since weak references are used only in circular reference situations, you can rest assured that the reference you release on the controlling IUnknown is not the final reference. If this *were* the final controlling IUnknown reference, the code we're discussing now couldn't even be running because the main object would already have terminated.

When ROTHook receives the first request for an IExternalConnection interface, it requests the same interface on the main object. ROTHook keeps this strong reference but balances the reference count by calling Release on the controlling IUnknown and setting the fAddRefOuter flag to True so it knows to call AddRef before zeroing the weak reference to the controlling IUnknown. ROTHook then returns a reference to its own IExternalConnection implementation, which defers to the wrapper implementation after performing its own reference-count tracking.

Counting All External Requests

The ROTHook architecture I've looked at up to this point was released with the August 1997 issue of *Visual Basic Programmer's Journal.* The issue discussed how to use the object but not how to implement it. The article is also included in the Visual Studio 6.0 version of the MSDN library (a cruel trick, because they didn't include code). However, it turns out that there is a major hole in the original algorithm that can't be fixed without the VBoost technologies. You can see it with the following sequence of calls.

1. The object is created with a CreateObject or New request from an external client.

2. During Class_Initialize, the ROTHook object registers itself in the ROT. The ROT now has a reference to the IExternalConnection implementation provided by the ROTHook.

3. An IExternalConnection object is retrieved from the newly created object, and AddConnection is called.

4. A second client calls GetObject, which calls AddConnection on the ROTHook IExternalConnection interface.

5. The second client releases the reference. ROTHook thinks that this is the last external reference and removes the object from the ROT.

Although the object is still alive and has an external reference to it, it no longer has an entry in the ROT. The problem is that the ROTHook object must monitor all AddConnection and ReleaseConnection calls, not just the ones that come from the running object table. The only way to solve this problem is to use an UnknownHook. With a uhBeforeQI hook that redirects all IExternalConnection requests to the ROTHook implementation, the ROTHook code is complete.

Listing 10.1. The ROTHook lightweight object.

```
'Use private version of CLSIDFromProgID instead of the
'declare in VBoostTypes to return long instead of HRESULT.
Private Declare Function CLSIDFromProgID Lib "ole32.Dll" _
  (ByVal ProgID As Long, rclsid As VBGUID) As Long
Private Declare Function CoLockObjectExternal _
  Lib "ole32.Dll" _
  (ByVal pUnk As Long, ByVal fLock As Long, _
  ByVal fLastUnlockReleases As Long) As Long
Private Declare Function RegisterActiveObject _
  Lib "oleaut32.Dll" _
```

```vb
        (ByVal pUnk As Long, rclsid As VBGUID, _
          ByVal dwFlags As Long, pdwRegister As Long) As Long
    Private Declare Function RevokeActiveObject
      Lib "oleaut32.Dll" _
      (ByVal dwRegister As Long, _
        Optional ByVal pvReserved As Long = 0) As Long
    Private Const ACTIVEOBJECT_WEAK As Long = 1
    Private Const MK_S_MONIKERALREADYREGISTERED As Long = &H401E7

    Private IID_IUnknown As VBGUID
    Private IID_IExternalConnection As VBGUID
    Private IID_IROTHook As VBGUID
    Private IID_IQIHook As VBGUID

    Public Type IROTHookImpl
        pVTableMain As Long
        pVTableQIHook As Long
        pVTableExternal As Long
        pExternal As IExternalConnection
        cRefsExternal As Long
        cConnections As Long
        UnkHook As UnknownHook
        pOuter As IUnknownUnrestricted
        cRefs As Long
        dwRegister As Long
        fLocked As Boolean
        fPassThrough As Boolean
        fAddRefOuter As Boolean
    End Type
    Public Type ROTHook
        Hook As IROTHook
        Struct As IROTHookImpl
    End Type

    'These are just copies of IROTHookImpl that start
    'at different vtable levels.
    Private Type IQIHookImpl
        pVTableQIHook As Long
        pVTableExternal As Long
        pExternal As IExternalConnection
        cRefsExternal As Long
        cConnections As Long
```

```vb
        UnkHook As UnknownHook
        pOuter As IUnknownUnrestricted
        cRefs As Long
        dwRegister As Long
        fLocked As Boolean
        fPassThrough As Boolean
        fAddRefOuter As Boolean
End Type
Private Type IExtConImpl
        pVTableExternal As Long
        pExternal As IExternalConnection
        cRefsExternal As Long
        cConnections As Long
        UnkHook As UnknownHook
        pOuter As IUnknownUnrestricted
        cRefs As Long
        dwRegister As Long
        fLocked As Boolean
        fPassThrough As Boolean
        fAddRefOuter As Boolean
End Type


Private Type ROTHookVTables
        Main(6) As Long
        'Don't bother with MapIID entry. It's never called.
        QIHook(3) As Long
        ExtCon(4) As Long
End Type
Private m_VTables As ROTHookVTables
Private m_pVTableMain As Long
Private m_pVTableExtCon As Long
Private m_pVTableQIHook As Long

#If DEBUGROT Then
'Debugging object collection. See ClearROT procedure
'for an explanation.
Private m_ObjColl As New Collection
#End If

Public Sub InitROTHook(ROTHook As ROTHook)
    If m_pVTableMain = 0 Then
        If VBoost Is Nothing Then InitVBoost
```

```
                  'Fill in our interface identifiers
                  IID_IUnknown = IIDFromString(strIID_IUnknown)
                  IID_IExternalConnection = _
                    IIDFromString(strIID_IExternalConnection)
                  IID_IROTHook = IIDFromString(strIID_IROTHook)
                  IID_IQIHook = IIDFromString(strIID_IQIHook)


              With m_VTables
                    .Main(0) = FuncAddr(AddressOf QueryInterface)
                    .Main(1) = FuncAddr(AddressOf AddRef)
                    .Main(2) = FuncAddr(AddressOf Release)
                    .Main(3) = FuncAddr(AddressOf ExposeObject)
                    .Main(4) = FuncAddr(AddressOf HideObject)
                    .Main(5) = FuncAddr(AddressOf get_Locked)
                    .Main(6) = FuncAddr(AddressOf put_Locked)
                    .ExtCon(0) = FuncAddr( _
                      AddressOf QueryInterfaceExtCon)
                    .ExtCon(1) = FuncAddr(AddressOf AddRefExtCon)
                    .ExtCon(2) = FuncAddr(AddressOf ReleaseExtCon)
                    .ExtCon(3) = FuncAddr(AddressOf AddConnection)
                    .ExtCon(4) = FuncAddr(AddressOf ReleaseConnection)
                    .QIHook(0) = FuncAddr( _
                      AddressOf QueryInterfaceQIHook)
                    .QIHook(1) = FuncAddr( _
                      AddressOf AddRefReleaseQIHook)
                    .QIHook(2) = .QIHook(1)
                    .QIHook(3) = FuncAddr(AddressOf QIHook)
                    'MapIID not used, don't bother
                    '.QIHook(4) = FuncAddr(AddressOf MapIID)
                    m_pVTableMain = VarPtr(.Main(0))
                    m_pVTableExtCon = VarPtr(.ExtCon(0))
                    m_pVTableQIHook = VarPtr(.QIHook(0))
              End With
          End If
          With ROTHook.Struct
                .cRefs = 1
                .pVTableMain = m_pVTableMain
                .pVTableQIHook = m_pVTableQIHook
                .pVTableExternal = m_pVTableExtCon
              VBoost.Assign ROTHook.Hook, VarPtr(.pVTableMain)
```

```
        End With
End Function


'QueryInterface for the main vtable. If we're already
'registered, this just defers to the main object.
Private Function QueryInterface( _
   This As IROTHookImpl, riid As VBGUID, pvObj As Long) As Long
With This
If .fPassThrough Then
    QueryInterface = .pOuter.QueryInterface(riid, pvObj)
Else
    Select Case riid.Data1
        Case 0&
            fOK = IsEqualGUID(riid, IID_IUnknown)
        Case &H995811
            fOK = IsEqualGUID(riid, IID_IROTHook)
        Case &H19
            If IsEqualGUID(riid, IID_IExternalConnection) Then
                If .pExternal Is Nothing Then
                    QueryInterface = _
                       .pOuter.QueryInterface(riid, pvObj)
                    If QueryInterface = 0 Then
                        .pOuter.Release
                        .fAddRefOuter = True
                        VBoost.Assign .pExternal, pvObj
                    End If
                End If
                If QueryInterface = 0 Then
                    .cRefsExternal = .cRefsExternal + 1
                    pvObj = VarPtr(.pVTableExternal)
                    Exit Function
                End If
            End If
    End Select
    If fOK Then
        pvObj = VarPtr(.pVTableMain)
        .cRefs = .cRefs + 1
    Else
        pvObj = 0
        QueryInterface = E_NOINTERFACE
```

```vb
            End If
        End If
    End With
End Function
Private Function AddRef(This As IROTHookImpl) As Long
    With This
        .cRefs = .cRefs + 1
        AddRef = .cRefs
    End With
End Function
Private Function Release(This As IROTHookImpl) As Long
    With This
        .cRefs = .cRefs - 1
        Release = .cRefs
        If .cRefs = 0 Then
            If .fAddRefOuter Then
                .pOuter.AddRef
                .fAddRefOuter = False
            End If
            VBoost.AssignZero .pOuter
            Set .UnkHook = Nothing
            'Remove this object from our debug only
            'collection.
            #If DEBUGROT Then
            On Error Resume Next
            m_ObjColl.Remove CStr(VarPtr(.pVTableMain))
            On Error GoTo 0 'Clear the error just in case.
            #End If
        End If
    End With
End Function
Private Function ExposeObject( _
    This As IROTHookImpl, ByVal pUnk As IUnknown, _
    ByVal ProgID As String, ByVal fProgIDIsMoniker As Boolean, _
    ByVal ServiceSupport As ROTServiceSupport) As Long
Dim CLSID As VBGUID
Dim pmk As IMonikerStub
Dim pROT As IRunningObjectTableStub
Dim pQIHook As IQIHook
    If This.dwRegister Then HideObject This
    If pUnk Is Nothing Then
```

```vb
    Debug.Assert False
    'If this happens, then we're being called incorrectly.
    'Let's return an error instead of GPF'ing.
    ExposeObject = &H800A005B 'Error 91
End If
If fProgIDIsMoniker Then
    ExposeObject = CreateItemMoniker("!", ProgID, pmk)
Else
    ExposeObject = CLSIDFromProgID(StrPtr(ProgID), CLSID)
    If ExposeObject = 0 And ServiceSupport Then
        'We need a moniker, get one now
        ProgID = String$(38, 0)
        StringFromGUID2 CLSID, ProgID
        ExposeObject = CreateItemMoniker("!", ProgID, pmk)
        fProgIDIsMoniker = True
    End If
End If
If ExposeObject Then Exit Function
'Register object
'Assign outer pointer without calling AddRef.
VBoost.Assign This.pOuter, pUnk
If fProgIDIsMoniker Then
    'Use IRunningObjectTable.Register directly.
    ExposeObject = GetRunningObjectTable(0, pROT)
    If ExposeObject = 0 Then
        If ServiceSupport Then
            ExposeObject = _
              pROT.Register(ROTFLAGS_ALLOWANYCLIENT, _
              VarPtr(This), pmk, This.dwRegister)
            'Put in a failover case
            If ExposeObject And _
              ServiceSupport = ssAttemptServiceSupport _
                Then
                ExposeObject = _
                  pROT.Register(ROTFLAGS_DEFAULT, _
                  VarPtr(This), pmk, This.dwRegister)
            End If
        Else
            ExposeObject = _
              pROT.Register(ROTFLAGS_DEFAULT, _
              VarPtr(This), pmk, This.dwRegister)
```

```vb
                End If
            End If
        Else
            ExposeObject = RegisterActiveObject(VarPtr(This), _
                CLSID, ACTIVEOBJECT_WEAK, This.dwRegister)
        End If
        'Check for harmless success code.
        If ExposeObject = MK_S_MONIKERALREADYREGISTERED Then _
            ExposeObject = 0
        If ExposeObject = 0 Then
            This.fPassThrough = True
            'Attempt to hook the unknown.
            With VBoost
                .Assign pQIHook, VarPtr(This.pVTableQIHook)
                On Error Resume Next
                .HookQI pUnk, pQIHook, uhBeforeQI, This.UnkHook
                .AssignZero pQIHook
                If Err Then
                    HideObject This
                    ExposeObject = Err
                End If
                On Error GoTo 0
            End With
        Else
            If This.fAddRefOuter Then
                This.pOuter.AddRef
                This.fAddRefOuter = False
            End If
            VBoost.AssignZero This.pOuter
        End If
        'Debug only code: allows call to ClearROT to
        'enable normal shutdown. See comments in ClearROT routine.
        #If DEBUGROT Then
        If ExposeObject = 0 Then
            On Error Resume Next
            m_ObjColl.Add VarPtr(This), CStr(VarPtr(This))
            On Error GoTo 0 'Clear the error just in case.
        End If
        #End If
    End Function
    Private Function HideObject(This As IROTHookImpl) As Long
```

```vb
Dim tmpRegister As Long
    With This
        If .dwRegister Then
            'Guarantee that this isn't reentered.
            tmpRegister = .dwRegister
            .dwRegister = 0
            If .fLocked Then put_Locked This, False
            .fPassThrough = False
            HideObject = RevokeActiveObject(tmpRegister)
            Set .UnkHook = Nothing
        End If
    End With
End Function
Private Function get_Locked( _
  This As IROTHookImpl, retVal As Boolean) As Long
    retVal = This.fLocked
End Function
Private Function put_Locked( _
  This As IROTHookImpl, ByVal RHS As Boolean) As Long
    With This
        If .fLocked <> RHS Then
            If .dwRegister Or .fLocked Then
                .fLocked = RHS
                .fPassThrough = False
                put_Locked = CoLockObjectExternal( _
                  VarPtr(This), -RHS, 1)
                .fPassThrough = True
            Else
                'Object variable not set.
                put_Locked = &H800A005B
            End If
        End If
    End With
End Function


'IQIHook implementation.
Private Function QueryInterfaceQIHook( _
  ByVal This As Long, riid As VBGUID, pvObj As Long) As Long
Dim fOK As BOOL
    Select Case riid.Data1
        Case 0&
```

```vb
            fOK = IsEqualGUID(riid, IID_IUnknown)
        Case &H20708EE4
            fOK = IsEqualGUID(riid, IID_IQIHook)
        Case Else
            fOK = BOOL_FALSE
    End Select
    If fOK Then
        pvObj = This
    Else
        pvObj = 0
        QueryInterfaceQIHook = E_NOINTERFACE
    End If
End Function
Private Function AddRefReleaseQIHook( _
  ByVal This As Long) As Long
    'Nothing to do.
End Function
Private Function QIHook(This As IQIHookImpl, riid As VBGUID, _
  ByVal uhFlags As UnkHookFlags, pResult As stdole.IUnknown, _
  ByVal HookedUnknown As stdole.IUnknown) As Long
    If riid.Data1 = &H19 Then
        If IsEqualGUID(riid, IID_IExternalConnection) Then
            With This
                If Not .pExternal Is Nothing Then
                    .cRefsExternal = .cRefsExternal + 1
                    VBoost.Assign pResult, _
                      VarPtr(.pVTableExternal)
                End If
            End With
        End If
    End If
End Function


'IExternalConnection implementation.
Private Function QueryInterfaceExtCon( _
  This As IExtConImpl, riid As VBGUID, pvObj As Long) As Long
    QueryInterfaceExtCon = This.pExternal.QueryInterface
      (riid, pvObj)
End Function
Private Function AddRefExtCon(This As IExtConImpl) As Long
    'No need to AddRef the main object. It's already kept alive
```

```
        'by the single reference we have on it.
    With This
        .cRefsExternal = .cRefsExternal + 1
        AddRefExtCon = .cRefsExternal
    End With
End Function
Private Function ReleaseExtCon(This As IExtConImpl) As Long
    With This
        .cRefsExternal = .cRefsExternal - 1
        ReleaseExtCon = .cRefsExternal
        If .cRefsExternal = 0 Then
            If .fAddRefOuter Then
                .pOuter.AddRef
                .fAddRefOuter = False
            End If
            Set .pExternal = Nothing
            'Nothing left to hook.
            Set .UnkHook = Nothing
        End If
    End With
End Function
Private Function AddConnection(This As IExtConImpl, _
  ByVal extconn As Long, ByVal reserved As Long) As Long
    With This
        AddConnection = .pExternal.AddConnection( _
            extconn, reserved)
        .cConnections = .cConnections + 1
    End With
End Function
Private Function ReleaseConnection(This As IExtConImpl, _
  ByVal extconn As Long, ByVal reserved As Long, _
  ByVal fLastReleaseCloses As Long) As Long
Dim tmpROTHook As IROTHook
    With This
        ReleaseConnection = .pExternal.ReleaseConnection( _
            extconn, reserved, fLastReleaseCloses)
        .cConnections = .cConnections - 1
        If .cConnections = 0 Then
            If .fAddRefOuter Then
                .pOuter.AddRef
                .fAddRefOuter = False
```

```vb
        End If
        'Back up two vtable entries (8 bytes)
        'to get at the ROTHook object.
        VBoost.Assign tmpROTHook, _
          VBoost.UDif(VarPtr(.pVTableExternal), 8)
        tmpROTHook.HideObject
        VBoost.AssignZero tmpROTHook
      End If
    End With
End Function
Private Function FuncAddr(ByVal pfn As Long) As Long
    FuncAddr = pfn
End Function
```

Chapter 11

Calling Function Pointers

Although Visual Basic's AddressOf operator lets you specify a function pointer as a callback for external operations, VB provides no native means of actually calling a function pointer. However, with the combination of lightweight objects, and a few bytes of assembly code, you can easily construct an object that helps you call an arbitrary standard call function pointer.

The standard call calling convention (_stdcall in C++) is just one of several calling conventions, but it is the only one that VB supports. All VB functions use the _stdcall calling convention, as do all COM method calls and all Win32 API calls. A calling convention is a means of specifying how parameters are passed to a function, how the function returns a value, and how the stack is cleared. With _stdcall, parameters are passed right to left on the stack, and the called function is responsible for clearing the stack; all the parameters the caller pushed onto the stack are off of the stack when the called function returns. The return value comes back in the eax register, at least for four-byte integer types. In _stdcall, the *this* pointer is passed as the leftmost parameter.

Since VB can call any method on a typelib-defined interface but not an arbitrary function pointer, you must create a COM object with a method that does nothing more than forward all its parameters (except the *this* pointer) to a function pointer. Let's assume that the COM object stores the value of this function pointer at offset four, the first slot available after the vtable pointer. To see how to forward the call, let's look at the stack at the beginning of a COM call. The stack pointer is at the top of this list (smaller addresses are listed first).

```
return address
this
parameter 1
. . .
parameter n
```

To call a function pointer with the same parameters, the stack must look like this at the beginning of the function.

```
return address
parameter 1
. . .
parameter n
```

To forward a call to a function pointer, our COM method simply squeezes the *this* pointer out of the picture and turns control over to the function pointer. The assembly code that does this is shown below. It is important to note that this code is parameter- and return-value invariant, so you can use it to forward any standard vtable call with a *this* pointer (which includes all COM calls) to a function pointer with the same parameters.

```
// Retrieve the return address and
// remove it from the stack (59).
pop ecx
// Retrieve the this pointer and
// remove it from the stack (58).
pop eax
// Put the return address back on the stack (51).
push ecx
// Jump to the function pointer at this + 4 (FF 60 04).
jmp DWORD PTR [eax + 4]
```

The bytes generated by this assembly code are 59 58 51 FF 60 04 (in hexadecimal). Now comes the lightweight-object connection. In order to make VB call the assembly code, you must construct a COM object that has this byte stream in one of its vtable functions. I'll use a lightweight COM object with the standard IUnknown functions in the first three vtable slots, and the magic byte stream in the fourth. The QueryInterface function will be very trusting on the first call: it assumes that you are requesting an interface that matches the parameters supported by the function pointer. All subsequent QueryInterface calls fail.

Since the actual asm code is only six bytes, I'll pad it with two int 3 instructions (CC CC) to make eight bytes. It can now be stored in a Currency constant. int 3 corresponds to a break statement, so you'll see a system error dialog if something goes wrong. int 3 is a standard padding instruction; nop (no operation, byte code 90) is the other. Since a constant isn't in executable memory—running the code at VarPtr(asmconst) causes a crash—the data is copied from the constant to a module-level Currency variable. The VarPtr of the Currency variable becomes the fourth vtable entry. The code below shows the InitDelegator function, which initializes the stack-allocated version of the FunctionDelegator lightweight. Code for the heap-allocated lightweight, created with NewDelegator, is included on the book's CD in the FunctionDelegator.bas file. You can compile out either version using the FUNCTIONDELEGATOR_NOHEAP or FUNCTIONDELEGATOR_NOSTACK conditional compilation values.

```
'The magic number
Private Const cDelegateASM As Currency = _
  -368956918007638.6215@
```

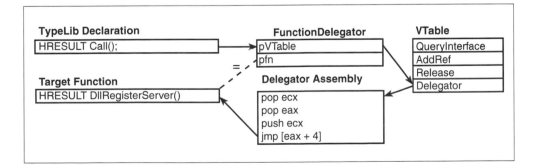

Figure 11.1.   The FunctionDelegator redirection architecture

```vb
'Module-level variables
'The variable to hold the asm bytes
Private m_DelegateASM As Currency


Private Type DelegatorVTables
    'OKQI vtable in 0 to 3, FailQI vtable in 4 to 7
    VTable(7) As Long
End Type


'Structure and vtables for a stack allocated Delegator
Private m_VTables As DelegatorVTables


'Pointer to success vtable, stack allocation version
Private m_pVTableOKQI As Long


'Pointer to failing vtable, stack allocation version
Private m_pVTableFailQI As Long


'Type declaration.
Public Type FunctionDelegator
    pVTable As Long    'This has to stay at offset 0.
    pfn As Long        'This has to stay at offset 4.
End Type


'Initialize an existing FunctionDelegator structure
'as a delegator object.
Public Function InitDelegator( _
  Delegator As FunctionDelegator, _
  Optional ByVal pfn As Long) As IUnknown
    If m_pVTableOKQI = 0 Then InitVTables
    With Delegator
        .pVTable = m_pVTableOKQI
        .pfn = pfn
    End With
    CopyMemory InitDelegator, VarPtr(Delegator), 4
End Function
Private Sub InitVTables()
Dim pAddRefRelease As Long
    With m_VTables
        .VTable(0) = FuncAddr(AddressOf QueryInterfaceOK)
        .VTable(4) = FuncAddr(AddressOf QueryInterfaceFail)
```

```
        pAddRefRelease = FuncAddr(AddressOf AddRefRelease)
        .VTable(1) = pAddRefRelease
        .VTable(5) = pAddRefRelease
        .VTable(2) = pAddRefRelease
        .VTable(6) = pAddRefRelease
        m_DelegateASM = cDelegateASM
        .VTable(3) = VarPtr(m_DelegateASM)
        .VTable(7) = .VTable(3)
        m_pVTableOKQI = VarPtr(.VTable(0))
        m_pVTableFailQI = VarPtr(.VTable(4))
    End With
End Sub


'VTable functions for the stack-allocated delegator.
Private Function QueryInterfaceOK(This As FunctionDelegator, _
    riid As Long, pvObj As Long) As Long
    'Return this object.
    pvObj = VarPtr(This)
    'Block all future QI calls.
    This.pVTable = m_pVTableFailQI
End Function
Private Function QueryInterfaceFail _
    (ByVal This As Long, riid As Long, pvObj As Long) As Long
    pvObj = 0
    QueryInterfaceFail = E_NOINTERFACE
End Function
Private Function AddRefRelease(ByVal This As Long) As Long
    'Nothing to do; memory not refcounted.
End Function
'Helper function
Private Function FuncAddr(ByVal pfn As Long) As Long
    FuncAddr = pfn
End Function
```

Sample: Calling DLLRegisterServer

Now that the InitDelegator function gives you a COM object that defers to a function pointer, you simply have to persuade the VB compiler to call the correct function in the vtable. VB knows how to make COM calls against any typelib-defined interface, so you have to turn to typelib generation to define an interface that VB can call. Once the interface is defined and referenced, the FunctionDelegator object happily agrees to a QI request for this interface (or for any other interface), and VB has a reference against which it can make a call. Because the function prototype used here returns an HRESULT, VB requests an ISupportErrorInfo interface in the case of failure, so it's imperative that all subsequent QI calls to the Function Delegator lightweight fail. Let's look at the process for calling the DllRegisterServer entry point in a COM DLL. The DllRegisterServer function takes no parameters and returns an HRESULT.

First, you have to step outside VB to define the interface. Although the interface shown here is already defined in VBoostTypes, these steps are required for a general function pointer. Here's a suitable ODL definition. (See Chapter 15 for a discussion of MIDL/IDL versus mktyplib/ODL.) Save this as FuncDeclLib.Odl and call mktyplib FuncDeclLib.Odl. Add a project reference to the resulting FuncDeclLib.Olb. Note that the interface definition is IUnknown-derived, and it has a single function. This matches the manufactured vtable. The interface's IID is required to build the typelib, but is not used elsewhere.

```
[
    uuid(8F633500-459A-11d3-AB5C-D41203C10000),
    helpstring("Function pointer definitions"),
    lcid(0x0),
    version(1.0)
]

library FuncDeclLib
{
    importlib("stdole2.tlb");
     [uuid(8F633501-459A-11d3-AB5C-D41203C10000), odl]
    interface ICallVoidReturnHRESULT : IUnknown
    {
        HRESULT Call();
    }
}
```

Now that you have a callable interface defined, you have to get a function pointer for DllRegisterServer with the LoadLibrary and GetProcAddress API calls. Once you have a function pointer—pfnDllRegisterServer—you can call InitDelegator (pfnDllRegisterServer) and assign the object to an ICallVoidReturnHRESULT-typed variable. A simple call to the typelib-defined Call method calls the asm code in the lightweight object, which defers to the function pointer.

```
'modDLLRegister
'API declares are in the VBoostTypes type library.

Public Sub DllRegisterServer(DllName As String)
    CallDllRegEntry DllName, "DllRegisterServer"
End Sub
Public Sub DllUnregisterServer(DllName As String)
    CallDllRegEntry DllName, "DllUnregisterServer"
End Sub
Private Sub CallDllRegEntry (DllName As String, _
  EntryPoint As String)
Dim pCall As ICallVoidReturnHRESULT
Dim Delegator As FunctionDelegator
Dim hMod As Long
Dim pfn As Long
    'Load the DLL.
    hMod = LoadLibrary(DllName)
    If hMod = 0 Then Err.Raise 5

    'Error trap to make sure we free the library.
    On Error GoTo Error

    'Find the entry pointer.
    pfn = GetProcAddress(hMod, EntryPoint)
    If pfn = 0 Then Err.Raise 5

    'Create and assign the delegator object.
    Set pCall = InitDelegator(Delegator, pfn)

    'Call the function pointer.
    pCall.Call
Error:
    'Free the library handle.
    FreeLibrary hMod
    'Propagate any error.
    With Err
        If .Number Then .Raise .Number
    End With
End Sub
```

With the delegator assembly code in place, a call to a function pointer is completely straightforward. Obtaining the function pointer is significantly more work than initializing the delegator object and making the call. If the Function-Delegator and its structure are declared at the same scope (local, in a standard module, or as member variables of a class module), they leave scope at the same time. This means that the object variable referencing the Function-Delegator structure still has a valid vtable because VB calls Release on all references before it releases other memory in the class or module. The bottom line is that the heap-allocated NewDelegator version of the FunctionDelegator is needed only if you don't declare the object variable with the same scope as the FunctionDelegator structure that it points to.

In the DllRegisterServer sample, you saw a call directed to an arbitrary DLL. You can't make such calls with a VB Declare statement. However, you are not limited to using FunctionDelegator calls for DLLs that are undefined at design time. FunctionDelegator calls offer you dynamic loading and dynamic unloading. You can load a DLL with the LoadLibrary or LoadLibraryEx API calls, and then unload it with FreeLibrary when you are done. If you use the DLL infrequently as part of a long process, this approach allows you to free memory and system resources when you are no longer using them.

VBoostTypes contains several simple interfaces that allow you to call typical function pointers without actually generating your own type library. The supported function prototypes are shown in Table 11.1.

Table 11.1   FunctionDelegator interface declarations in VBoostTypes6.Olb

Interface Name	C++ Function Prototype
ICallVoidReturnVoid	void Call(void);
ICallLongReturnVoid	void Call(long);
ICallLongReturnLong	long Call(long);
ICallVoidReturnLong	long Call(void);
ICallVoidReturnHRESULT	HRESULT Call(void);
ICallLongReturnHRESULT	HRESULT Call(long);

Sample: QuickSort, Once and for All

I have rarely seen a sort routine written in straight VB that didn't make me cringe. Sort routines, regardless of the algorithm used, compare and swap the elements in an array. Comparing elements in VB is straightforward, but it requires a new sort routine for each type of array to be sorted. Having a new routine for each data type wasn't quite enough to evoke a shudder; the shudder generally requires an examination of the swapping code. Although swapping elements may seem straightforward, it is extremely expensive for pointer types because VB always performs a deep copy. Consider the code required to swap two strings.

```
Dim tmp As String
tmp = StrArray(i)
StrArray(i) = StrArray(j)
StrArray(j) = tmp
```

This code makes two new copies of the string originally contained in the i position, and one copy of the string originally contained at position j. Since items are swapped multiple times during a sort, routines such as these can end up fully duplicating all the data in the array multiple times. The data duplication ends up being significantly slower than the sort itself.

The immediate workaround to the deep copy problem is to use a companion Long array, which is initialized 0, 1,..., n–1. By swapping elements in the Index array (which is cheap because there is no pointer allocation), you can save the deep String copies. The downside is that you have to keep the Index array around after the sort. StrArray(Index(0)) is the first sorted item. The one advantage of this mechanism is that you can maintain multiple sort orders on the same array. Even when using an Index array, you still have to write different sort routines for each data type.

When sorting in C/C++ land, you don't have to worry about the deep copy problem or about sorting multiple data-types. C and C++ use a callback function for the item comparisons, and pointer arithmetic to perform the array manipulation. The actual sort routine doesn't know or care about the data type it is sorting; it just needs the size of the data type in memory, the number of elements in the array, and a function pointer it can call to compare two array elements.

Now that VB can call function pointers, you can use the C++-style sorting techniques. First, you have to establish a definition for the function pointer. Because the sort routine will handle pointer values exclusively, and pointers in VB are best stored in a Long value, the typelib definition for the Compare function will take two ByVal As Long parameters. It is standard practice for a Compare function to return −1 if the two elements compare less than, 0 if they are equal, and 1 if they compare greater than. You can follow this convention by defining a Compare function that returns a Long value. The ODL for the function pointer description is shown below. It may look unusual to you to see an interface function returning a long instead of an HRESULT, but VB is quite capable of calling this type of interface, and it greatly simplifies the function-pointer definition.

```
[uuid(C9750741-4659-11d3-AB5C-D41203C10000), odl]
interface ICallCompare : IUnknown
{
    long Compare([in] long Elem1, [in] long Elem2);
}
```

Now you have to write a corresponding function in VB. A function for comparing two strings is a good example. Note that this function's parameters are not ByVal As Long. To keep the compare callback routine data-type agnostic, the sort routine tells VB that it is passing two Long values to the function, but you know that these values are pointers to elements in an array. The array elements have a type known to the callback function, so the callback parameters in the CompareStrings function are defined ByRef As String. Of course, if you want to use lots of CopyMemory calls to dereference ByVal As Long parameters into a known type, you are welcome to. But it is so much easier to tell VB a white lie and plug in a function pointer with the correct parameter type. The correct input type makes CompareStrings trivially simple.

```
Public Function CompareStrings( _
  Elem1 As String, Elem2 As String) As Long
    CompareStrings = Sgn(StrComp(Elem1, Elem2))
End Function
```

With the callback function pointer definition established, you can now use the standard QuickSort algorithm. The implementation shown here contains three functions: QuickSort, which establishes the FunctionDelegator object and allocates a buffer for use when swapping elements; QuickSortInternal, which performs the actual recursions of the sorting algorithm; and SwapBytes, a helper function used to swap elements in the sorted array.

```vb
'Pass a structure to the recursive QuickSortInternal
'function to minimize stack usage.
Private Type QuickSortData
    Size As Long
    Compare As ICallCompare
    ByteSwapper() As Byte
End Type

Public Sub QuickSort( _
  ByVal pBase As Long, _
  ByVal Number As Long, _
  ByVal Size As Long, _
  ByVal pfCompare As Long)
Dim Data As QuickSortData
Dim Delegator As FunctionDelegator
    With Data
        .Size = Size
        Set .Compare = InitDelegator(Delegator, pfCompare)
        ReDim .ByteSwapper(0 To Size - 1)
        QuickSortInternal _
          pBase, pBase + (Number - 1) * Size, Data
        Set .Compare = Nothing
    End With
End Sub

Private Sub QuickSortInternal(ByVal Low As Long, _
  ByVal High As Long, Data As QuickSortData)
Dim PivotIndex As Long
Dim i As Long, j As Long
If Low < High Then
    'Only two elements in this subdivision; swap them
    'if they are out of order, then end recursive calls.
    If High - Low = Data.Size Then
        If Data.Compare.Compare(Low, High) > 0 Then
            SwapBytes Low, High, Data
        End If
```

```vb
Else
    'Pick a pivot element in the middle, then move
    'it to the end.
    'Don't use (Low + High) \ 2: it can overflow.
    PivotIndex = Low \ 2 + High \ 2

    'Align on m_Size boundary
    PivotIndex = _
      PivotIndex - ((PivotIndex - Low) Mod Data.Size)
    SwapBytes High, PivotIndex, Data

    'Move in from both sides toward the
    'pivot element.
    i = Low: j = High
    Do
        Do While (i < j) And _
          (Data.Compare.Compare(i, High) <= 0)
            i = i + Data.Size
        Loop
        Do While (j > i) And _
          (Data.Compare.Compare(j, High) >= 0)
            j = j - Data.Size
        Loop

        'If we haven't reached the pivot element, it
        'means that two elements on either side are
        'out of order, so swap them.
        If i < j Then
            SwapBytes i, j, Data
        End If
    Loop While i < j

    'Move the pivot element back to its proper
    'place in the array.
    SwapBytes i, High, Data

    'Recursively call the QuickSortInternal procedure.
    'Pass the smaller subdivision first to use less
    'stack space.
    If (i - Low) < (High - i) Then
        QuickSortInternal Low, i - Data.Size, Data
```

```
                    QuickSortInternal i + Data.Size, High, Data
            Else
                    QuickSortInternal i + Data.Size, High, Data
                    QuickSortInternal Low, i - Data.Size, Data
            End If
        End If
    End If
End Sub


Private Sub SwapBytes( _
    ByVal pElem1 As Long, ByVal pElem2 As Long, _
    Data As QuickSortData)
        With Data
            CopyMemory .ByteSwapper(0), ByVal pElem1, .Size
            CopyMemory ByVal pElem1, ByVal pElem2, .Size
            CopyMemory ByVal pElem2, .ByteSwapper(0), .Size
        End With
End Sub
```

```
'Calling QuickSort, string sorting routine.
Public Sub SortStrings(Strings() As String)
    'Assume one-dimensional array.
    QuickSort VarPtr((LBound(Strings)), _
        UBound(Strings) - LBound(Strings) + 1, _
        4, AddressOf CompareStrings
End Sub
```

This sort routine can be used with any data type. All you have to do is provide a Compare function for the particular data type and figure out the size of the data element. Note that determining the size of an element in a UDT array can be nontrivial. If you guess, you could easily be wrong, and LenB does not always yield the correct element size. See the "Determining Element Size" section of Chapter 2 for more information about reading an array's element size at runtime.

Function Pointers in VB for Alpha

The standard Alpha function-call mechanism is much different from the _stdcall calling convention. _stdcall uses the stack to pass the *this* pointer and all the parameters. On the Alpha, the first six parameters, including *this,* are passed directly in registers; subsequent parameters are passed on the stack. The *this* pointer is not easily squeezed out of the picture with stack manipulations, so an Intel-style function pointer technique does not work. However, there is still a mostly functional—albeit less elegant—solution.

As an alternative to a function that turns around and calls a function pointer, the alternate mechanism provides a function pointer that plugs directly into the vtable. I'll call this a DirectFunctionDelegator object instead of a Function-Delegator because the vtable makes a direct call. In this mechanism, every DirectFunctionDelegator instance owns its own vtable because every vtable is different. In many ways, this is much easier to code. Here are the changed functions and structures for the DirectFunctionDelegator lightweight object. There are no longer module-level variables because the vtable is not shared. You can find this code in the DirectFunctionDelegator.Bas file.

```
Private Type DirectFunctionDelegator
    pVTable As Long
    VTable(3) As Long
End Type

Public Function InitDirectDelegator( _
  Delegator As DirectFunctionDelegator, _
  ByVal pfn As Long) As IUnknown
    With Delegator
        .VTable(0) = FuncAddr( _
          AddressOf QueryInterface-NoAlloc)
        .VTable(1) = FuncAddr(AddressOf AddRefReleaseNoAlloc)
        .VTable(2) = .VTable(1)
        .VTable(3) = pfn
        .pVTable = VarPtr(.VTable(0))
        CopyMemory InitDirectDelegator, VarPtr(.pVTable), 4
    End With
End Function
Private Function QueryInterfaceOKQI( _
  This As DirectFunctionDelegator, _
  riid As Long, pvObj As Long) As Long
    pvObj = VarPtr(This)
    This.VTable(0) = FuncAddr(AddressOf QueryInterfaceFail)
End Function
Private Function QueryInterfaceFail( _
  ByVal This As Long, riid As Long, pvObj As Long) As Long
```

```
      pvObj = 0
      QueryInterfaceFail = E_NOINTERFACE
End Function
Private Function AddRefRelease(ByVal This As Long) As Long
      'Nothing to do, memory not refcounted.
End Function
```

Of course, because the provided code is no longer capable of squeezing the *this* pointer, the function pointer you provide must include an extra slot in its parameter list. However, the type-library declaration that allows you to call the function does not change. The first parameter in the provided function pointer should be declared ByVal This As Long and should not be used. Here is the modified CompareStrings function from the QuickSort sample.

```
Public Function CompareStrings( _
   ByVal This As Long, _
   Elem1 As String, Elem2 As String) As Long
      CompareStrings = Sgn(StrComp(Elem1, Elem2))
End Function
```

The function signature of function pointers retrieved via GetProcAddress rarely includes a dummy long value as the first parameter, so you can't use a DirectFunctionDelegator to call arbitrary function pointers. However, if the function pointer has no parameters, the *this* pointer is simply ignored on the Alpha platform. Therefore, because the DLL registration functions shown above take no parameters, you can still call them on the Alpha. You're out of luck on most other functions, however.

Stack Allocation

On the Intel platform something curious happens with the DirectFunction-Delegator. If you use a DirectFunctionDelegator instead of a FunctionDelegator in the CallDllRegEntry function shown earlier, the function appears to work correctly. This is a little scary because the function prototypes don't match. However, the prototypes don't match after the stack position that the DllRegisterServer function looks for. The compiler pushes four bytes onto the stack, and the Dll-RegisterServer function pops off 0, essentially leaking four bytes of stack. The leak is reclaimed when the function returns, so it isn't a huge or permanent loss.

To monitor stack usage before and after the call, I threw together a few more bytes of asm code and plugged them into a function delegator. The function takes no parameters and returns a long value, so you can call it with the ICallVoid-ReturnLong interface provided in VBoostTypes.

```
'Assembly code we're using to make a stack pointer.
'mov eax, esp   ;Get the current stack pointer, 8B C4
'add eax, 4     ;Account for return address, 83 C0 04
'ret            ;Return, C3

Private Const cCheckESPCode As Currency = _
    -368935956954613.2341@
Private CheckESPCode As Currency
Private pCallObj As ICallVoidReturnLong
Private FD As FunctionDelegator
Public Property Get GetESP() As ICallVoidReturnLong
    If pCallObj Is Nothing Then Init
    Set GetESP = pCallObj
End Property
Private Sub Init()
    CheckESPCode = cCheckESPCode
    Set pCallObj = InitDelegator(FD, VarPtr(CheckESPCode))
End Sub
```

```
'Calling code.
Debug.Print Hex$(GetESP.Call)
```

If you run the DirectFunctionDelegator version of CallDllRegEntry and check the current stack position immediately after the delegated call to DllRegister-Server, you'll see that the stack value has dropped by four bytes. There are two things to point out here. First, VB doesn't complain about the stack discrepancy, even in the IDE. But if you make an API call that messes up the stack in this fashion, VB tells you about it loud and clear. This check takes place in the IDE as a favor to let you debug API declarations. No stack checking takes place at run-time, but the IDE stack-checks make it prohibitively difficult to use API calls that leak stack.

The second thing to point out is that, in general programming terms, there is nothing wrong with calling a function that modifies the stack. DllRegisterServer leaked unintentionally because it was called incorrectly, but there are also good leaks. In fact, the _alloca function in C++ is designed specifically to push extra stack. In C++, I use stack allocation whenever I can because it greatly reduces the number of heap allocations during the program. Since VB doesn't care about stack pushed during a vtable call, you can write a stack allocation routine for use in VB code without being punished immediately, as you would be with an API call.

Before looking at the StackAlloc code, a short discussion of how the stack is used might make you more comfortable with moving the stack pointer during a function call. You will also see that unmanaged stack leaks can wreak havoc with calling functions. There are two CPU registers that are used to control stack: esp (**s**tack **p**ointer) and ebp (**b**ase **p**ointer). esp is the current position of the stack. Pushing stack (that is, adding new data to the stack) decreases the value of esp. Popping stack increases the value in this register. ebp is called the stack frame and is used to give every function a base reference point in the stack. The first instructions to run in a function are known as *prolog code*. The standard prolog code looks something like the following.

```
push ebp              ;push the current stack frame
mov ebp,esp           ;ebp=esp, use the stack position as the
                      ;new frame
sub esp, localsize    ;esp=esp-localsize, push stack for local
                      ;variables
push ebx              ;save the ebx register on the stack
push esi              ;save the esi register on the stack
push edi              ;save the edi register on the stack
```

The standard prolog code saves the current stack frame by pushing it on the stack, moves the frame up to the current stack position, and pushes enough stack to handle its local variables. Then the registers that must be maintained across function calls are pushed on the stack. After the prolog code, the stack looks like this, with the current stack pointer at the top of this list.

```
previous value of edi (stack pointer after prolog)
previous value of esi
previous value of ebx
. . .
local variable 2
```

```
local variable 1
stack pointer before prolog (ebp points here)
return address
parameter 1
 . . .
parameter n
```

With the prolog code completed, the function can now run code. With ebp established, parameters are accessed via positive offsets from ebp, so parameter 1 is ebp + 8. Locals are negative offsets, with local 1 at ebp − 4. When the function completes, it runs code something like the following. This is known as *epilog code*.

```
pop edi                ;restore edi register
pop esi                ;restore esi register
pop ebx                ;restore ebx register
mov esp, ebp           ;undo the second statement
                       ;in the prolog code
pop ebp                ;undo the first statement
                       ;in the prolog code
ret n                  ;return, taking an additional n bytes of
                       ;stack. n is the number of bytes
                       ;pushed as parameters.
```

The key to leaving a function successfully is getting to the epilog code with the stack in the same place as it was at the end of the prolog code. After each line of VB code has executed successfully, the stack is always in the correct position to exit the function gracefully. VB pushes as much stack as it needs for the duration of a function when it pushes the space required for local variables.

Since all local variables are accessed as offsets from the stack frame, VB (and Win32 code in general) doesn't care where the stack pointer is during the body of the function. The pointer just needs to be back at the correct location by the time the epilog code runs. If the stack pointer is not returned to its home position correctly, the edi, esi, and ebx registers are restored incorrectly. This register corruption causes miscellaneous and unpredictable problems for the calling functions. For example, esi and edi are used as loop counters, so corrupting these registers can badly throw off a loop currently running in a calling function.

Corrupted registers are very deceptive: The stack frame itself is not corrupted, so the function returns correctly and there may be no indication that anything went wrong.

Since you must have esp at the original position by the time the prolog code runs, any stack allocation routine you use must also be balanced by a call that pops the corresponding amount of stack. During the body of the function, the home stack position (just above the cached register values) is the current stack pointer at the beginning of every line of VB code. VB doesn't proactively restore the stack to this position after every call; it just pushes and pops values as needed. The reason that esp is the same at the beginning of every line of code is simple: VB does not leak stack. Since esp is used to push and pop values onto the stack, extra stack is unnoticed and benign until something goes wrong and VB tries to restore the stack pointer. Something going wrong in VB means that an error has occurred.

Errors are thrown at any time during the execution of a line of VB code—not necessarily at the beginning—so the stack position cannot be trusted when an error occurs. The error-handler itself also needs stack to do its work, and it starts at the home position. The good news is that if you hit an error, VB automatically cleans up the stack and restores the registers correctly. The bad news is that any extra stack you may have pushed is history once you hit a local error-handler or raise an error during On Error Resume Next mode. The stack is moved back to its comfortable home position in both the error handler and in the body of the function after a Resume or Resume Next statement.

At the conclusion of this discussion, I'll leave you with a simple rule: In order to maintain the stack, you must pop as many extra bytes as you've pushed, unless there has been an error, in which case any extra bytes you've pushed are overwritten and immediately lost. If you follow these guidelines, stack allocation from within VB is perfectly safe. If you don't follow the rules, you'll corrupt your registers when you fail to restore the stack pointer. Your program will crash immediately if you pop stack that an error handler has already popped for you.

The book includes code for three stack-allocation functions: StackAlloc, StackAllocZero, and StackFree. StackAlloc pushes the requested number of bytes onto the stack and returns the pointer to the block it just pushed. StackAllocZero pushes the bytes and zeroes the memory, and StackFree pops the requested number of bytes from the stack. The code for these functions looks almost exactly like the GetESP code shown above, except they require a lot more assembly code. For performance and stability reasons, the number of bytes you request must be a multiple of four. If the request is not on a four-byte boundary, any functions called after you've pushed stack will use misaligned data. VB cannot handle the misaligned stack and Y crashes. Usually an AlignedSize Function is included in StackFree.Bas.

I know I said you'd seen your last QuickSort, but here is a modification that uses stack allocation instead of a ReDim. With this change, the entire QuickSort routine runs without a single heap allocation!

```vb
Private Type QuickSortData
    Size As Long
    Compare As ICallCompare
    pBytes As Long
End Type

Public Sub QuickSort( _
  ByVal pBase As Long, _
  ByVal Number As Long, _
  ByVal Size As Long, _
  ByVal pfCompare As Long)
Dim Data As QuickSortData
Dim FDCompare As FunctionDelegator
Dim cBytes As Long
    With Data
        .Size = Size
        Set .Compare = InitDelegator(FDCompare, pfCompare)
        cBytes = AlignedSize(Size)
        .pBytes = StackAlloc.Call(cBytes)
        On Error GoTo Error
        QuickSortInternal pBase, _
            pBase + (Number - 1) * Size, Data
    End With
    If cBytes Then StackFree.Call cBytes
    Exit Sub
Error:
    With Err
        .Raise .Number, .Source, .Description, _
```

```
            .HelpFile, .HelpContext
        End With
End Sub


'QuickSortInternal does not change.

Private Sub SwapBytes( _
    ByVal pElem1 As Long, ByVal pElem2 As Long, _
    Data As QuickSortData)
    With Data
        CopyMemory ByVal .pBytes, ByVal pElem1, .Size
        CopyMemory ByVal pElem1, ByVal pElem2, .Size
        CopyMemory ByVal pElem2, ByVal .pBytes, .Size
    End With
End Sub
```

Generating Your Own In-Line Assembly

Visual Basic has never provided a way to write in-line assembly code. However, with the FunctionDelegator object, you can now come very close. Although I can't make VB compile assembly code for you, you can now make it call an arbitrary function, which can just be a stream of bytes. If you want to write inline assembly code, you need to use a tool that can compile assembly code and then let you read the compiled bytes. Note that you can also use this technique to get the bytes for optimized C functions as well as assembly code, so you can often get away with writing C code and let the C compiler generate assembly.

As an example, I'll write assembly code that reads data at offsets from the current base pointer. The function I'm generating takes one parameter, adds it to the base pointer, then dereferences that pointer to read a value from the stack. The value is returned in the eax register (the x86 assembly standard). The assembly code for the function is minimal.

```
mov ecx, [esp + 4]
mov eax, [ebp + ecx]
ret 4
```

You can follow these steps in Microsoft Visual C++ 6.0 to generate a byte stream for this code.

1. In the MSVC development environment, open the Projects tab of the File | New dialog.

2. Select Win32 Application and call the project GenASM. Click on OK.

3. Select a simple Win32 application and click Finish to generate the project.

4. Open GenASM.cpp.

```cpp
#include "stdafx.h"

int APIENTRY WinMain(HINSTANCE hInstance,
                     HINSTANCE hPrevInstance,
                     LPSTR     lpCmdLine,
                     int       nCmdShow)
{
    // TODO: Place code here.

    return 0;
}
```

5. Edit the function to add assembly code.

```cpp
int APIENTRY WinMain(HINSTANCE hInstance,
                     HINSTANCE hPrevInstance,
                     LPSTR     lpCmdLine,
                     int       nCmdShow)
{
    _asm
    {
        mov ecx, [esp + 4]
        mov eax, [ebp + ecx]
        ret 4
    }
    return 0;
}
```

6. Press F9 to place a breakpoint on the first mov statement.

7. Press F5 to build and run the project.

8. At the breakpoint, choose View | Debug Windows | Disassembly to see the decompiled assembly code, which will look something like this.

```
11:            _asm
12:            {
13:                mov ecx, [esp + 4]
00401028    mov             ecx,dword ptr [esp+4]
14:                mov eax, [ebp + ecx]
0040102C    mov             eax,dword ptr [ebp+ecx]
15:                ret 4
00401030    ret             4
16:            }
```

9. To see the actual byte values, open the context menu in the dis-
    assembly window and select the Code Bytes menu option to get:

```
11:            _asm
12:            {
13:                mov ecx, [esp + 4]
00401028 8B 4C 24 04              mov       ecx,dword ptr [esp+4]
14:                mov eax, [ebp + ecx]
0040102C 8B 44 0D 00              mov       eax,dword ptr [ebp+ecx]
15:                ret 4
00401030 C2 04 00                 ret       4
16:            }
```

10. You can now read the bytes for the function. However, the Intel byte
    ordering can make the bytes difficult to interpret if you want to store
    the bytes in a Long variable. To get help with the byte ordering, you
    have a little more work to do.

11. Select View|Debug Windows|Memory.

12. Open the context menu in the Memory window and select Long Hex
    Format.

13. Back in the disassembly window, use a double-click to select the
    address to the far left of the first line of disassembly (00401028).

14. Drag and drop this value onto the first line of the memory window to
    see the bytes in Long format. You can compare this with the earlier
    code bytes to see the different byte ordering.

```
00401028    04244C8B
0040102C    000D448B
```

```
00401030   330004C2
00401034   5B5E5FC0
00401038   3B40C483
0040103C   001EE8EC
```

15. You can determine the last relevant byte by comparing the long bytes with the code bytes in the disassembly window and looking at the address of the statement immediately following the relevant one. Count bytes top to bottom, right to left. In this case, the line after the inline assembly displays an address of 0040133, which is the fourth (leftmost) byte in the third line.

16. Select and copy the three lines of relevant code and replace the irrelevant bytes with 90 (nop, the no operation instruct).

17. Stop debugging.

18. Copy the relevant bytes generated into a Long array. Remember to place the array declaration in a structure so VB won't free it during teardown while other modules are still using it.

19. Be sure to save the asm code listing with the file so that you can edit and regenerate it later.

It is easy to access the code generated by this exercise through a FunctionDelegator, producing the following code (minus the assembly code comments). This is DerefEBP.Bas, included on the CD.

```
Private Type DerefEBPCode
    Code(2) As Long
End Type
Private FD As FunctionDelegator
Private DerefEBPCode As DerefEBPCode
Private pCallObj As ICallLongReturnLong
Public Function DerefEBP() As ICallLongReturnLong
    If pCallObj Is Nothing Then Init
    Set DerefEBP = pCallObj
End Function
Private Sub Init()
    With DerefEBPCode
        .Code(0) = &H4244C8B
```

```
        .Code(1) = &HD448B
        .Code(2) = &H900004C2
    End With
    Set pCallObj = InitDelegator(FD, VarPtr(DerefEBPCode))
End Sub
```

Walk the Stack

You can use the DerefEBP function to investigate the stack yourself and verify everything I've mentioned about stack layout. For example, after the prolog runs in a class module function, the previous ebp value has been pushed on the stack just above the return address. Now the stack at the ebp value looks like this.

```
previous ebp value
return address
this pointer
first parameter
```

The first parameter is always 12 bytes away from ebp. This is quite useful if the last parameter is a ParamArray: It lets you get the array pointer. VB generates the "Invalid ParamArray use" compile error when you try to pass a ParamArray to a normal VB array parameter in a helper function, and you can't even pass a ParamArray to the VarPtrArray function. Using DerefEBP and VBoost.AssignSwap, you can easily steal the ParamArray and put it in a normal array variable.

```
Public Sub TestParamArray(ParamArray Values() As Variant)
Dim StealValues() As Variant
    VBoost.AssignSwap ByVal VarPtrArray(StealValues), _
      ByVal DerefEBP.Call(12)
    'Values is now an empty array and StealValues contains
    'the ParamArray data.
End Sub
```

There are a number of disadvantages to using DerefEBP in a BAS module, where the stack is much harder to calculate. The parameter locations in a BAS module depend on the type of the return value. The return value in a class module is always an HRESULT, which is a fixed 4-byte value. But BAS-module functions don't return HRESULTs, so the size of the returned type is variable, affecting the stack layout. A function returns one to four bytes of data in the eax register. Five to eight bytes come back in eax and edx. To return a larger number of bytes, the calling function provides a pointer to the memory address to which the called function should write the returned data. The address for the return-value location is passed as the first parameter on the stack. Therefore, the first visible parameter is offset by an extra four bytes if the size of the return type is larger than eight bytes.

Another problem with using DerefEBP with BAS modules is that VB pushes four extra bytes of stack in the IDE and with pcode executables. The stack size is different in the IDE than it is in an EXE, making it impossible to enter a constant value that works in both the IDE and in a native EXE. There are several ways to determine whether a program is running in the IDE, but it's much harder to determine whether an executable is pcode or a native EXE.

```
'Check if we're in the IDE.
Public Function InIDE() As Boolean
    On Error Resume Next
    Debug.Assert 1 \ 0
    InIDE = Err
    On Error GoTo 0
End Function
```

Here are a few examples of stack offsets for the final parameter in some standard module functions.

```
'Start with 8 + 4 byte return value + 8 byte ByVal Double
'Total: 20 in native, 24 in IDE
Function First( ByVal Value As Double,_
    ParamArray PA() As Variant) As Variant
```

```
'Start with 8 + 4 byte ByRef Variant
'Total: 12 in native, 16 in IDE
Sub Second( _
    Value As Variant, ParamArray PA() As Variant)
```

```
'Start with 8 + 0 byte return value + 16 byte ByVal Variant
'Total: 24 in native, 28 in IDE
```

```
Function Third( _
    ByVal Value As Variant, ParamArray PA() As Variant) As Long
```

```
'Start with 8 + 0 byte return value + 4 byte ByVal Byte
'Total: 12 in native, 16 in IDE
'Note that each parameter takes a minimum of four bytes.
Function Fourth( ByVal OneByte As Byte, _
    ParamArray PA() As Variant) As Currency
```

Locating the Current Function

Visual Basic has no built-in mechanism for determining which function is currently running. However, you can determine this information in a native executable at runtime by using a small amount of assembly code that determines the next instruction in the calling function. We've already seen that the next statement value is pushed on the stack whenever you call a function, so the next instruction is not difficult to get. There are two pieces of assembly code that are useful for this. The first returns the next instruction of the calling function. The second looks back one function level and gets the next instruction in the function that called the current function, allowing you to get an instruction address from an error-logging routine. You can use the ICallVoidReturnLong definition to call both of these.

```
'Selections from GetIP.Bas
'// Code to get the next instruction in the current function.
'// long GetIP()
'// Get the return address from the current stack location.
'mov eax, [esp]
'// 8B 04 24
'ret              // Return
'// C3


Private Const cGetIPCode As Long = &HC324048B


'As in DerefEBP.Bas
Public Property Get GetIP() As ICallVoidReturnLong


'As in DerefEBP.Bas
```

```
'Selections from GetCallingIP.Bas.
'// Code to get the next instruction in the calling function.
'// Note that this only works if the compiler generated enough
'// code to warrant pushing a base pointer in the calling
'// function, but calling GetCallingIP.Call is sufficient, so
'// this isn't a problem in practice.
'// long GetCallingIP()
'mov eax, [ebp + 4] // Get the return address off the stack.
'// 8B 45 04
'ret                 // Return
'// C3


Private Const cGetCallingIPCode As Long = &HC304458B
'As in DerefEBP.Bas
Public Property Get GetCallingIP() As ICallVoidReturnLong
'As in DerefEBP.Bas.
```

```
'Calling code. The second number shown will be a few bytes
'higher than the first.
'This requires a VBoostTypes reference,
'FunctionDelegator.Bas, GetIP.Bas, and GetCallingIP.Bas.
Sub Main()
    MsgBox Hex$(GetIP.Call)
    TestCallingIP
End Sub
```

```
Sub TestCallingIP()
    MsgBox Hex$(GetCallingIP.Call)
End Sub
```

Of course, reading the current instruction pointer is only half the story. You also need a mechanism of interpreting the number. This is generally done with a MAP file output from Link.Exe. The fact that VB doesn't provide an IDE option for generating this file is only a small hindrance. You can easily modify the environment variable settings and make VB generate a MAP file.

1. Close the VB IDE.

2. Set the LINK environment variable to /MAP

3. Restart VB.

4. Compile your project.

This generates a MAP file that you can use to pin the IP number down to a specific function. If you're tracing in a DLL, you may want to record the App.hInstance value along with the IP so that you can account for the rebasing of the DLL. For more information on MAP files and all things debuggable, refer to books and articles by John Robbins.[1]

Pointers to Class Functions

Although the compiler generates code that calls a Friend function directly (as opposed to being called through a vtable) you can't use AddressOf against a Friend function like you can with a function in a BAS module. There are two very good reasons for VB to make this restriction. First, Friend functions have an implicit Me parameter, meaning that you must provide a reference to the object with the function pointer. Second, Friend functions all return hidden HRESULT values, so they don't have the same function signature as a function in a standard module. The modified function signature would prohibit a Friend function from participating in the API functions for which AddressOf was originally added.

Regardless of the reasons for the limitation, it can often get in the way when you want to direct a callback function directly to a class module. For example, when you're catching Windows messages by subclassing a Form, you want to run code in the Form module, not in a standard module. The redirection from the standard module to the code in your Form is easy once you have a Form reference, but this reference is not generally supplied with the function pointer.

To solve this problem, I've created some assembly code called a PushParamThunk. This code dynamically generates a function that has the reference to the target object and the address of a standard module function built-in. You can't code this function at design-time because both of these values are available only at runtime. I'll show a sample usage of the thunk, then I'll look at

---

[1] John's latest book is *Debugging Applications* from *Microsoft Press*. See http://www.jprobbins.com for other article references.

the code that makes it work. This snippet looks a lot like standard Windows sub-classing code. The difference is that the window handle (hWnd) is not used to store the pointer to the class associated with the window. The initialized Push-ParamThunk structure is a function with the pointer to a class instance coded into the function and a pointer to that function.

```vb
'Code in Form1
Private m_WndProcThunk As PushParamThunk
Private m_WndProcNext As Long
Private Sub Form_Load()
    InitPushParamThunk _
        m_WndProcThunk, ObjPtr(Me), AddressOf ForwardWndProc
    m_WndProcNext = _
        SetWindowLong(hWnd, GWL_WNDPROC, m_WndProcThunk.pfn)
End Sub
Friend Function WndProc( _
    ByVal hWnd As Long, ByVal uMsg As Long, _
    ByVal wParam As Long, ByVal lParam As Long) As Long
    'Processing
    WndProc = CallWindowProc( _
        m_WndProcNext, hWnd, uMsg, wParam, lParam)
End Function
'More code
```

```vb
'Code in a standard module
Public Function ForwardWndProc(ByVal This As Form1, _
    ByVal hWnd As Long, ByVal uMsg As Long, _
    ByVal wParam As Long, ByVal lParam As Long) As Long
    ForwardWndProc = This.WndProc(hWnd, uMsg, wParam, lParam)
End Function
```

As you can see in the listing, PushParamThunk is simple to use. If your function prototype has four parameters, the target callback function is called with the real parameters shifted right and a new first parameter, which will be the value you specified in the InitPushParam call. The translation between ObjPtr(Me) and ByVal This As Form1 is clearly only one possibility; you can use PushParamThunk to add a custom parameter to any function. In general, you should always make the first parameter ByVal.

```
Private Type ThunkBytes
    Thunk(5) As Long
End Type
Public Type PushParamThunk
    pfn As Long
    Code As ThunkBytes
End Type
Public Sub InitPushParamThunk(Thunk As PushParamThunk, _
  ByVal ParamValue As Long, ByVal pfnDest As Long)
    With Thunk.Code
        .Thunk(0) = &HB82434FF
        .Thunk(1) = ParamValue
        .Thunk(2) = &H4244489
        .Thunk(3) = &HB8909090
        .Thunk(4) = pfnDest
        .Thunk(5) = &H9090E0FF
    End With
    Thunk.pfn = VarPtr(Thunk.Code)
End Sub
'asm code
'push [esp]
'mov eax, 1234h // Dummy value, pushed parameter
'mov [esp + 4], eax
'nop            // nop Adjustment so the next long is aligned
'nop
'nop
'mov eax, 5678h // Dummy value, destination function
'jmp eax
'nop
'nop
```

The PushParamThunk code shown here works for functions with sufficiently small return types, but it fails with large return types because of the extra stack parameter used for return types larger than eight bytes. If you want to use a PushParamThunk with a function that returns a Variant (16 bytes) or other large type, you need to use a modified version of the assembly code. To accommodate this requirement, the PushParamThunkStackReturn code included in PushParamThunk.bas inserts the parameter value as the second parameter rather than the first. You can simply use the alternate structure and initialization function if you require this capability. You can use the conditional compilation values PUSHPARAM_NONORMAL or PUSHPARAM_NOSTACKRETURN to eliminate capabilities you aren't using in your project.

Using CDECL Functions

Visual Basic functions defined with the Declare statement are always assumed to be _stdcall. All functions you code are also generated using this calling convention. However, there are many exported functions in various DLLs that use the alternate _cdecl calling convention. The code provided with the book provides a CDECLFunctionDelegator.bas file that is similar to the FunctionDelegator.bas file, but which calls CDECL functions. This section looks at the provided functions, but not the assembly code implementation.

Before you get overly excited about the prospects of calling _cdecl functions, please consider the amount of assembly code required to make these calls. You must run significantly more than the six bytes of assembly code required to squeeze the *this* pointer. In fact, for a small function, the call overhead could be more than the cost of the call itself. You should call _cdecl functions with discretion.

In addition to the function pointer, the cdecl delegator functions also require a StackSize value. In a cdecl function call, the called function does not pop the parameters from the stack. Parameter popping is left to the calling function. In the case of a cdecl delegator, the calling function is provided by the asm code in the delegator, so the delegator must know the stack size. The two cdecl delegator functions are called InitCDECLDelegator and NewCDECLDelegator. They act like the corresponding InitDelegator and NewDelegator functions, except they have an extra StackSize parameter. The CDECLFunctionDelegator passed into InitCDECLDelegator is also the same as the FunctionDelegator, except it has a StackSize member.

Using these two functions, you can call a GetProcAddress-retrieved cdecl function pointer. However, this is only half the story because you can't use AddressOf directly to provide a cdecl callback function. The InitCDECLThunk function solves the second half of the cdecl problem. InitCDECLThunk takes a CDECLThunk structure, a function pointer, and a stack size. After the function returns, the pfn field of the CDECLThunk variables contains the function pointer. If you want to reuse the CDECLThunk structure with a different function pointer and stacksize, you can update the code with the UpdateCDECLThunk function. With these functions at your disposal, you are ready to call a cdecl function and provide a cdecl callback function. You can use the same callback functions you used with the VB-defined QuickSort earlier in the chapter, but this time let the qsort function in msvcrt.Dll do all the work.

Since qsort is now a function pointer, you need a typelib definition to enable the compiler to call the cdecl delegator. Here's the ODL for the sort function, described as stdcall, not cdecl. CRTQuickSort function uses InitCDECLDelegator and InitCDECLThunk, so this function works without using heap-allocated memory.

```
[uuid(C9750742-4659-11d3-AB5C-D41203C10000), odl]
interface ICallQSort : IUnknown
{
    void QSort([in] long pBase, [in] long Number,
               [in] long Size, [in] long pfCompare);
}


Public Sub CRTQuickSort( _
  ByVal pBase As Long, _
  ByVal Number As Long, _
  ByVal Size As Long, _
  ByVal pfCompare As Long)
Dim pQSort As ICallQSort
Dim CompareThunk As CDECLThunk
Dim Delegator As CDECLFunctionDelegator
Dim pCRT As Long
Dim pfnQSort As Long
    pCRT = LoadLibrary("msvcrt.Dll")
    pfnQSort = GetProcAddress(pCRT, "qsort")

    '4 long parameters = 16 byte stack size
    Set pQSort = InitCDECLDelegator( _
      Delegator, pfnQSort, 16)

    '2 long parameters = 8 byte stack size
    InitCDECLThunk CompareThunk, pfCompare, 8
```

```
        pQSort.QSort pBase, Number, Size, CompareThunk.pfn

        FreeLibrary pCRT
End Sub
```

If you were to use this function in real code, you would most likely encapsulate it in a class to cache the module handle for msvcrt.Dll and the address of qsort. Note that if you compile VB to fast code with array bounds checking disabled, the VB QuickSort performs about 35 percent faster than the CRTQuickSort version because of the cdecl thunking overhead. Of course, if the CRTQuickSort—or the next cdecl function you want to use—is fast enough for your needs, then you can skip coding a replacement function in VB altogether. printf, anyone?

Chapter 12

Overriding Functions

Visual Basic's Implements keyword natively supports the interface-based approach to programming. I've emphasized designing with interfaces throughout the book because it is an excellent model for abstraction and calling-code reuse. The VBoost aggregator objects give you reuse of complete interface implementations as well.

I discussed some of the pitfalls inherent in inheritance-based systems in "Abstraction with Implements" in Chapter 5, but that doesn't mean that inheritance has no value as a programming model. Interface implementation can solve most problems, but occasionally you just want to override specific functions instead of either picking up the entire implementation with aggregation or having no implementation at all with Implements.

A function that renders a certain type of graphic is a good example of a function that needs inheritance. The "Multiple Behaviors in One Class" section of Chapter 5 showed a simple implementation of an IDraw interface that used a member property to decide whether to draw a line, rectangle, or ellipse. The shared property was appropriate and fast for this scenario because all three cases required the same data. But what happens if you want to use the same interface to inscribe a more complex object into the rectangle? The calling code should still be able to call IDraw.Draw, but the Draw function should map to a different implementation of the function in an object that has more data.

There are two main benefits to the inheritance model. First, you can share data seamlessly with a base class. Second, you can override virtual functions to modify the base class's behavior. You've already seen how to share data by using arrays to share memory. In this chapter, you'll see three ways to redirect a function call to code in a derived class. Function redirection relies heavily on technologies you've already seen. This chapter uses function-pointer delegation, redirection to class functions, blind vtable wrappers, aggregation objects, lightweight objects, and direct memory sharing.

All three samples in this chapter address the same problem of redirecting a public function on a base class that returns a string. Each technique is implemented in the same classes—called Base and Derived—and both use a helper module called modDerived. You can weigh the benefits of each of these techniques against the cost of implementation and decide which you will use. You can use the following code to test all three samples.

```
Dim Derived As New Derived
Dim Base As Base
    Set Base = Derived
    MsgBox Base.OverrideMe
```

Cooperative Redirection

The first technique is called "cooperative redirection" because the base-class function is the key player. The original function is called and then redirects to a function pointer provided by the derived function. Clearly, this technique relies on the base class's cooperation in the redirection. Although this is the safest and easiest technique to get right, it is nowhere near as elegant as the last two solutions.

The strategy for cooperative redirection is simple. The base and derived classes share a structure that exposes a function pointer. The derived class sets the function pointer and a second field with user-defined data (generally the ObjPtr of the derived class). The cooperating function then calls the agreed-upon function pointer, which generally looks like the overridden function with an extra data parameter.

Listing 12.1. Use shared memory and a function pointer to redirect a function call on the base. This sample can be found in Samples\FunctionOverrides\CooperativeRedirection.

```
'modDerived.bas, type definitions and a callback function.
'Requires: ArrayOwner.Bas or ArrayOwnerIgnoreOnly.Bas,
'          PushParamThunk.Bas
Public Type BaseData
    OverrideMeThunk As PushParamThunk
End Type
Public Type OwnedBaseData
    Owner As ArrayOwner
    Data() As BaseData
End Type
Public Function Override(ByVal This As Derived) As String
    Override = This.Base_OverrideMe
End Function
```

```
'Base.cls
Private m_Data As BaseData
Friend Function DataPtr() As Long
    DataPtr = VarPtr(m_Data)
End Function
Public Function OverrideMe() As String
Dim FD As FunctionDelegator
Dim pCall As ICallVoidReturnString
    With m_Data.OverrideMeThunk
        Set pCall = InitDelegator(FD, .pfn)
        OverrideMe = pCall.Call()
    End With
End Function
```

```
'Derived.cls
Private Type InitData
    AggData(0) As AggregateData
    IIDs() As VBGUID
End Type

Private m_Data As modDerived.OwnedBaseData
Private m_Hook As UnknownHook
Private m_Base As Base
```

```
Private Sub Class_Initialize()
Dim InitData As InitData
    Set m_Base = New Base
    InitArrayOwner m_Data.Owner, LenB(m_Data.Data(0)), 0, False
    m_Data.Owner.SA.pvData = m_Base.DataPtr
    With m_Data.Data(0)
        InitPushParamThunk .OverrideMeThunk, _
            ObjPtr(Me), AddressOf modDerived.Override
    End With

    With InitData
        With .AggData(0)
            Set .pObject = m_Base
            .Flags = adIgnoreIIDs
        End With
        VBoost.AggregateUnknown Me, .AggData, .IIDs, m_Hook
    End With
End Sub


Friend Function Base_OverrideMe() As String
    Base_OverrideMe = "Base.OverrideMe redirected to Derived"
End Function
```

```
'ODL interface prototype for ICallVoidReturnString
[
    uuid(795984A1-928C-11d3-BBDD-D41203C10000),
    odl
]
interface ICallVoidReturnString : IUnknown
{
    BSTR Call();
}
```

Cooperative redirection is a relatively safe system for redirecting a function, but it doesn't have many of the features you'd expect to see in an inheritance model. For example, the fact that the base class has to participate at all is a disadvantage. The base class's decision to return after calling the redirected function instead of running its own code is also a branch that should be left to the discretion of the derived class. In short, this technique works, but it requires a lot of extra code and data in the base class.

Interface Wrapping

The cooperative redirection technique places the bulk of responsibility on the base class. By using an additional wrapper around Base, you can completely eliminate all base class requirements. This provides the advantage of less base-class code and leaves the Base class's implementation of the overridden function intact. You can call the original function from the override because, unlike the cooperative redirection method, the original function hasn't changed to support the override.

The steps for wrapping an object's interface are straightforward, but you must be sure to get each step correct. The basic idea is to hand out a blind vtable wrapper around an instance of the wrapped interface, and then hand the wrapped object to any external requests for the overridden interface. To override a function, simply copy as many functions as you need from the VBoost-provided blind delegator vtable into another vtable array, and then replace the functions you want to override with the AddressOf operator. See Figure 12.1.

You must be aware of two issues to successfully override the interface and replace the function. First, the blind delegator wrapper is very thin, and the wrapped object has no idea that it is wrapped. If you let a QueryInterface call for the wrapped interface reach the wrapped object, you'll get the original vtable instead of the override. In order to aggregate a wrapped interface into your object, you need to specify an IID for the interface and set the adFullyResolved flag to prevent the VBoost aggregators from querying the wrapped object for the

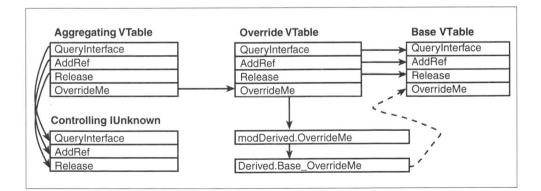

Figure 12.1. Override functions in an interface provided by an aggregated object

overridden interface. If the Base class implements additional interfaces that you would like to expose on the derived object, then add an additional blindly aggregated AggregateData entry to the Base object after the wrapped interface.

The second issue is that any object passed to AggregateUnknown must not hold a reference to an interface on the main object (an IDelayCreation reference is the exception). In the BaseOverride structure shown below, pDerived is a Long member, and it holds a weak reference on the controlling IUnknown. A strong reference would be circular because the main object owns the UnknownHook, which in turn owns the object built on the BaseOverride structure, which in turn references an interface on the controlling IUnknown.

Listing 12.2. **Wrap an interface with no base class cooperation. See the Samples\FunctionOverrides\DoubleWrap directory.**

```vb
'modDerived.Bas
Private Const cVTableSize As Long = 8
Private Type WrapVTable
    VTable(cVTableSize - 1) As Long
End Type
Private m_VTable As WrapVTable
Private m_pVTable As Long


Public Type BaseOverride
    BD As BlindDelegator
    pDerived As Long
End Type


'Construct a vtable using VBoost's BlindDelegator vtable.
Public Sub HookVTable(pBDVTable As Long)
    If m_pVTable = 0 Then
        With m_VTable
            CopyMemory .VTable(0), ByVal pBDVTable, _
              4 * cVTableSize
            .VTable(7) = FuncAddr(AddressOf OverrideMe)
            m_pVTable = VarPtr(.VTable(0))
        End With
    End If
    pBDVTable = m_pVTable
End Sub
```

```vb
Private Function OverrideMe( _
    This As BaseOverride, retVal As String) As Long
Dim Derived As Derived
    'Make sure [out] param is 0.
    VBoost.AssignZero retVal

    On Error GoTo Error
    'Jump to friend function in derived class.
    VBoost.AssignAddRef Derived, This.pDerived
    retVal = Derived.Base_OverrideMe
    Exit Function
Error:
    OverrideMe = MapError
End Function
```

```vb
'Base.cls
Public Function OverrideMe() As String
    OverrideMe = "Base.OverrideMe"
End Function
```

```vb
'Derived.cls
Private Type InitData
    AggData(0) As AggregateData
    IIDs(0) As VBGUID
End Type

Private m_Hook As UnknownHook
Private m_BaseOverride As BaseOverride
Private m_Base As Base

Private Sub Class_Initialize()
Dim InitData As InitData
Dim pBaseWrapped As IUnknown
Dim LastIID As LastIID

    'Get the IID for the base class.
    'This is required so that we can
    'set adFullyResolved on this IID.
    InitLastIID LastIID
    On Error Resume Next
```

```
        Set m_Base = LastIID.QIThis
        On Error GoTo 0

        Set m_Base = New Base

        With m_BaseOverride
            Set pBaseWrapped = VBoost.CreateDelegator( _
              m_Base, m_Base, , VarPtr(.BD))
            modDerived.HookVTable .BD.pVTable
            .pDerived = ObjPtr(Me)
        End With

        With InitData
            With .AggData(0)
                .Flags = adUseIIDs Or adFullyResolved
                .FirstIID = 0
                Set .pObject = pBaseWrapped
            End With
            .IIDs(0) = LastIID.IID
            VBoost.AggregateUnknown Me, .AggData, .IIDs, m_Hook
        End With
    End Sub

    Friend Function Base_OverrideMe() As String
        Base_OverrideMe = m_Base.OverrideMe & _
          " overridden by Derived"
    End Function
```

Wrapping Your Own Interface

Using CreateDelegator up front to populate the aggregator has no side-effects if
you wrap references from another class. However, if you want to wrap an interface that you implement directly on the class, you can't use this function
because the CreateDelegator function holds strong references on both the punk-
Outer and punkDelegatee objects. You can still use a BlindDelegator structure,
but you can't use CreateDelegator to initialize it for you.

There are two things you must do to put weak references in a BlindDelegator
structure. You must find the vtable, which you can get by passing the special
value −1 to the VBoost.BlindFunctionPointer function. You must also pay atten-

tion to the destructor callback. If the pfnDestroy field is set, the BlindDelegator vtable's Release function knows that it did not allocate the BlindDelegator structure. A pfnDestroy value of –1 indicates that there is nothing to do, but any other nonzero value indicates that the destructor function should be called to clean up and free the structure.

The destructor function is passed the BlindDelegator structure, which may or may not have other items after it. The one guarantee is that the punkOuter and punkInner fields are zero. These values are transferred to local variables and passed as ByRef parameters to the pfnDestroy function. These references are both released after pfnDestroy has completed—unless you free them or zero them yourself. If you zero the pOuter parameter, the function should return the value returned from the Release call. No matter how you choose to handle the weak reference, the destructor function gives you the chance to either zero your weak references or turn them into strong references. The modified code for wrapping an interface native to the controlling object looks like this.

Listing 12.3. **Use a custom BlindDelegator structure to override an interface that is implemented directly on the controlling IUnknown. You can find this code in the Samples\FunctionOverrides\ DoubleWrapSelf directory.**

```
'Code in a BAS module to override an interface on the
'controlling object.
Public Type SelfOverride
    BD As BlindDelegator
End Type


Public Function InitSelfOverride( _
  Struct As SelfOverride, ByVal pSelf As Long) As IUnknown
Dim pUnk As IUnknownUnrestricted
    If m_pVTable = 0 Then
        With m_VTable
            CopyMemory .VTable(0), _
              ByVal VBoost.BlindFunctionPointer(-1), _
              4 * cVTableSize
            .VTable(7) = FuncAddr(AddressOf OverrideMe)
            m_pVTable = VarPtr(.VTable(0))
        End With
```

```vb
        End If
        With Struct.BD
            VBoost.Assign .pInner, pSelf
            'pUnk is IUnknownUnrestricted so that this code
            'generates a QueryInterface.
            Set pUnk = .pInner
            VBoost.Assign .pOuter, pUnk
            .cRefs = 1
            .pfnDestroy = FuncAddr(AddressOf DestructSelfOverride)
            .pVTable = m_pVTable
            VBoost.Assign InitOverride, VarPtr(.pVTable)
        End With
End Function
Private Function DestructSelfOverride( _
    This As SelfOverride, pInner As IUnknown, _
    pOuter As IUnknownUnrestricted) As Long
        VBoost.AssignZero pInner
        'Leave a reference in pOuter so that VBoost can
        'read the return value from the Release call.
        pOuter.AddRef
End Function
Private Function OverrideMe( _
    This As SelfOverride, retVal As String) As Long
Dim pSelf As SelfOverride
        'Make sure [out] param is NULL.
        VBoost.AssignZero retVal


    On Error GoTo Error
        'Jump to a Friend function in this class.
        VBoost.AssignAddRef pSelf, This.BD.pInner
        retVal = pSelf.Derived_OverrideMe
    Exit Function
Error:
        OverrideMe = MapError
End Function
```

```vb
'Calling code snippet; callback functions remain as before.
Private Sub Class_Initialize()
Dim InitData As InitData
Dim LastIID As LastIID
```

```
Dim pObjImpl As IImplemented

    'Get the IID for the base class.
    InitLastIID LastIID
    On Error Resume Next
    Set pObjImpl = LastIID.QIThis
    On Error GoTo 0

    With InitData
        Set pObjImpl = Me
        With .AggData(0)
            .Flags = adUseIIDs Or adFullyResolved Or _
                     adBeforeHookedUnknown
            .FirstIID = 0
            Set .pObject = modSelfOverride.InitSelfOverride( _
                m_SelfOverride, ObjPtr(pObjImpl))
        End With
        .IIDs(0) = LastIID.IID
        VBoost.AggregateUnknown Me, .AggData, .IIDs, m_Hook
    End With
End Sub
```

The main difference in the calling code is that the Flags now include the adBeforeHookedUnknown flag. If you let the QueryInterface sequence read the primary object with this IID, you will never see the override because the aggregator always goes with the first object that can resolve the requested interface. You'll see later that this mechanism is much easier to use if you simply wait to fill the BlindDelegator fields until they are absolutely needed.

Thinner Interface Wrapping

The first wrapped version of this code actually ends up with two vtable delegators around the target interface implementation. The CreateDelegator call in the last section specified m_Base for both the punkOuter and punkDelegatee parameters, so the Base object is both the controlling IUnknown and the delegator for the wrapped object. In this case you may be tempted to simply specify Derived as the controlling IUnknown. However, this creates a circular reference, so the aggregator can't own the object. If you want to eliminate a wrapper, you need to return the wrapped interface during an incoming QI call. But you can't store the wrapped object with the aggregator objects. See Figure 12.2.

The AggregateData structure provides enough options to make it possible to return the wrapped interface without storing it indefinitely. The extra flags you need to set are adDelayDontCacheResolved and adNoDelegator. You can then defer filling in the BlindDelegator structure until IDelayCreation_Create. In the code listing, you should also pay close attention to the existing instance checking code in IDelayCreation_Create and the DestructBaseOverride function. You can avoid the weak reference to Derived that was required when the aggregator owned the wrapped interface reference by specifying a destructor function in CreateDelegator. This time, the destructor function is used for cleaning up custom data rather than for enabling weak references in the pOuter and pInner fields, as you saw in the last example.

The code shown in Listing 12.4 shows an IDelayCreation in the derived class itself. You can also implement the IDelayCreation interface using a lightweight object if you want to reduce the amount of code in the derived class. See the Code\InitInPlaceObjectWindowlessHook.Bas, used in "Windowless Controls" section of Chapter 16, for an example using this technique.

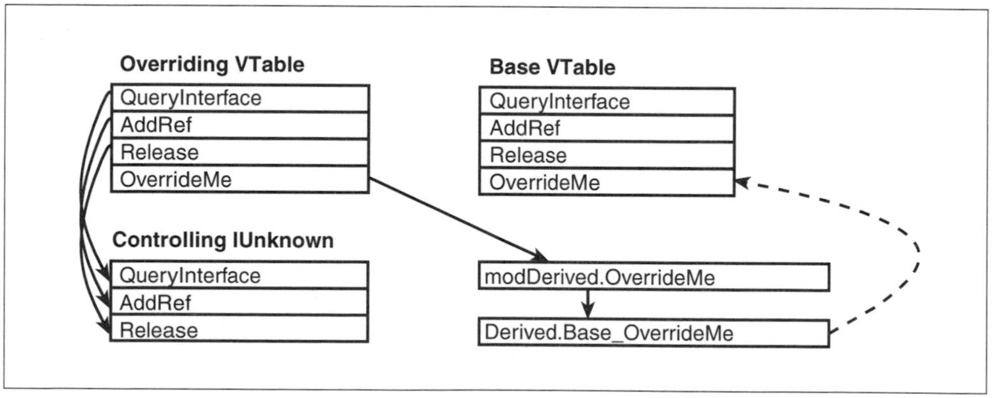

Figure 12.2.   Wrap an interface with a single blind vtable delegator by using a BlindDelegator structure and delayed creation.

Listing 12.4. Wrap an interface with a single blind delegator. See the Samples\FunctionOverrides\SingleWrap directory.

```
'modDerived.Bas
Private Const cVTableSize As Long = 8
Private Type WrapVTable
    VTable(cVTableSize - 1) As Long
End Type
Private m_VTable As WrapVTable
Private m_pVTable As Long


Public Type BaseOverride
    BD As BlindDelegator
    Derived As Derived
End Type


'Construct a vtable using VBoost's BlindDelegator vtable.
Public Sub HookVTable(pBDVTable As Long)
    If m_pVTable = 0 Then
        With m_VTable
            CopyMemory .VTable(0), ByVal pBDVTable, _
              4 * cVTableSize
            .VTable(7) = FuncAddr(AddressOf OverrideMe)
            m_pVTable = VarPtr(.VTable(0))
        End With
    End If
    pBDVTable = m_pVTable
End Sub
Public Function DestructBaseOverride(This As BaseOverride, _
  pInner As IUnknown, pOuter As IUnknown) As Long
    'Clear Derived so that we don't leak.
    Set This.Derived = Nothing
End Sub
Private Function OverrideMe(This As BaseOverride, _
  retVal As String) As Long
    'Make sure [out] param is 0.
    VBoost.AssignZero retVal

    On Error GoTo Error
    'Jump to Friend function in derived class.
    retVal = This.Derived.Base_OverrideMe
```

```vb
        Exit Function
Error:
    OverrideMe = MapError
End Function
```

```vb
'Base.cls
Public Function OverrideMe() As String
    OverrideMe = "Base.OverrideMe"
End Function
```

```vb
'Derived.cls
Implements IDelayCreation

Private Type InitData
    AggData(0) As AggregateData
    IIDs(0) As VBGUID
End Type

Private m_Hook As UnknownHook
Private m_BaseOverride As BaseOverride
Private m_Base As Base

Private Sub Class_Initialize()
Dim InitData As InitData
Dim LastIID As LastIID

    'Get the IID for the base class.
    InitLastIID LastIID
    On Error Resume Next
    Set m_Base = LastIID.QIThis
    On Error GoTo 0

    Set m_Base = New Base

    With InitData
        With .AggData(0)
            .Flags = adUseIIDs Or adNoDelegator Or _
                adDelayDontCacheResolved Or adFullyResolved
            .FirstIID = 0
            Set .pObject = Me
        End With
```

```
                .IIDs(0) = LastIID.IID
            VBoost.AggregateUnknown Me, .AggData, .IIDs, m_Hook
        End With
    End Sub


    Private Function IDelayCreation_Create _
        (IID As VBoostTypes.VBGUID) As stdole.IUnknown
        'We have specified only one IID, so we don't
        'have to check if we got the right one.
        'If there is more than one delayed IID,
        'store the IIDs at module level.
        With m_BaseOverride
            If .BD.cRefs Then
                'Return the current item.
                VBoost.AssignAddRef _
                    IDelayCreation_Create, VarPtr(.BD)
            Else
                Set IDelayCreation_Create = _
                    VBoost.CreateDelegator( _
                    Me, m_Base, , VarPtr(.BD), _
                    AddressOf modDerived.DestructBaseOverride)
                Set .Derived = Me
                modDerived.HookVTable .BD.pVTable
            End If
        End With
    End Function


    Friend Function Base_OverrideMe() As String
        Base_OverrideMe = m_Base.OverrideMe & _
            " overridden by Derived"
    End Function
```

Wrapping Your Own Interface

It is much easier to place a wrapper on your own interface using delayed creation than it is to use custom creation and destruction code for the blind delegator structure. In fact, to wrap your own interface using the delayed creation code, you only have to add an adBeforeHookedUnknown flag to the four other flags (adUseIIDs, adNoDelegator, adDelayDontCacheResolved, adFullyResolved). Because the wrapper releases all references during teardown and is not cached, you don't have to worry about the circular-referencing issues that you encountered with the non-delayed wrapper. See the Samples\FunctionOverrides\SingleWrapSelf directory.

Wrapping Issues

There are several challenges associated with overriding functions. Although the code is mostly cut-and-paste, there *is* quite a bit. You also have to get the vtable entries correct or your application will die miserably. VB uses three vtable entries for each Public object or Variant-type module variable, plus one for each Public procedure, counted from the top of the file down. If you have binary compatibility in place, however, all bets on the vtable order are off. The easiest way to find the vtable layout is to ask the object about its vtable using TLI (TypeLib Information). Add a reference to TLI, then run the following in the Immediate Window while you're at a breakpoint within the class to list the vtable offsets.

```
for each mem in _
  TLI.InterfaceInfoFromObject(me).VTableInterface.Members: _
? mem.Name, mem.InvokeKind, mem.VTableOffset\4: next
```

With true inheritance, calling an overridden function from within the Base class calls the override. With an interface wrapper in place, the Base class itself is completely unaffected by the wrapper. If you want Base to call the current override, you'll need to let Derived pass a pointer to the controlling IUnknown for the Derived object. You must store a weak reference to the controlling IUnknown to avoid a circular dependency. The Base code now looks like this.

```
Private m_pOuter As Long
Public Function OverrideMe() As String
    OverrideMe = "Base.OverrideMe"
End Function
Friend Function SetOuter(ByVal pOuter As IUnknown)
    m_pOuter = ObjPtr(pOuter)
End Function
Private Function GetOuter() As IUnknown
    VBoost.AssignAddRef GetOuter, m_pOuter
End Function
```

```
'Code in Base to call wrapped OverrideMe.
Dim pWrapped As Base
    Set pWrapped = GetOuter
    Debug.Print pWrapped.OverrideMe

'Code in Derived, called before or after aggregation.
m_Base.SetOuter Me
```

When wrapping, you will almost always want to use Base with multiple Derived versions. If the vtable override points to a single type of derived class, you need a completely separate vtable for every class that Derives from the base. If you want to interact with a Friend function, a separate BAS module function is required for each derived class, but completely redoing the vtable is extreme. In order to avoid this, combine the wrapper technique with the redirection technique shown earlier. You can use a PushParamThunk as part of the BaseOverride structure and a FunctionDelegator object to redirect to the function specified in the PushParamThunk.pfn field. The DoubleWrapRedirect and SingleWrapRedirect directories in Samples\FunctionOverrides on the CD demonstrate this approach for both singly and doubly wrapped interfaces.

Chapter 13

Threads in VB

Visual Basic supports the creation of multithreaded EXEs, DLLs, and OCXs. You can interpret this deceptively simple statement several ways. Support for multiple threads means several things: the ability to concurrently execute multiple threads of code in the same process, the ability to call code running in a different thread, or the ability to run multiple threads concurrently against the same set of data. VB supports multiple threads of code execution, but it does not natively support free threading, which is the ability to run multiple threads against the same set of data. VB can call another component if it supports free threading.

Visual Basic threads are built upon what COM calls *apartments*. In the Project | Properties dialog for an ActiveX DLL or OCX, you can set the threading model to either Single Threaded or Apartment Threaded. The naming of the options provided here is unfortunate because the single-threaded case also uses apartment threading. The options are more accurately named "One Single-Threaded Apartment" and "Multiple Single-Threaded Apartments."

The term apartment is very descriptive of the underlying concept. Think of an apartment as the room in which code runs. In a single-threaded apartment (STA), you can access anything you like in the room, and the walls prevent anyone else from accessing anything in the room without going through the front door. In addition to the front-door restriction, the apartment also has very limited seating: it can hold only one guest at a time. All other guests from other apartments must line up outside the door until the current honoree leaves. You'll see a coordinated gate crashing mechanism later, but even in that case, every guest must come through the front door.

The apartment metaphor is weaker in the case of a multithreaded apartment (MTA). An MTA has no door, and the walls are just dotted lines that allow guests to enter the apartment from any direction. The guests come and go as they please, and you are expected to provide reasonable service to all of them at the same time. Clearly, avoiding chaos in an MTA requires a lot of planning. To maintain some semblance of order, you must make sure your guests take turns using the items in your apartment. Essentially, you tell your guests to line up in short lines within the apartment instead of making them line up outside the door. In an MTA, you have to provide the synchronization code that the door would provide in an STA. Each process has at most one MTA.

I'll get back to a more concrete definition. For an object in an STA, COM allows a method call to be made only from the same thread that the object was created on. Code inside an STA always runs on the same thread. COM provides a *marshaler* that translates all calls from a foreign thread into a call on the native thread. The marshaler also provides synchronization by blocking incoming method calls until a running call is completed. You code for an STA the same as you would for a single-threaded application: No explicit synchronization code is required. From the perspective of the threads waiting for a chance to enter, the queue at the marshaler can be a long ordeal.

In an MTA, methods can be called from any thread, and COM provides no inherent synchronization. You must provide customized synchronization, generally via kernel synchronization objects such as events, mutexes, and critical sections. The performance benefits are obvious, however. A calling thread with a small amount of work to do isn't left outside the door waiting until a thread with a lot of work to do leaves the apartment.

Visual Basic supports calling both MTAs and STAs, but it can create only STAs. In a single-threaded DLL, VB creates all objects on a single thread, and all calls from outside threads must be marshaled into the single STA. In a multi-threaded DLL (called "Apartment Threaded" in the Project | Properties dialog), VB simply joins an existing STA. All VB DLLs use the STA model; a multi-threaded VB DLL supports the creation of objects in more than one STA. You should never confuse support for multiple STA threads with support for creating objects in the MTA.

Thread Local Storage

Visual Basic's runtime is apartment thread safe, but it is not safe for use in a free threaded (MTA) environment. Apartment thread safety is actually very easy to achieve. VB gives every apartment its own set of global data. Since no data is shared across apartments, there is no chance that different threads will wreak havoc by accessing the same data at the same time. In an STA environment, using thread-global data instead of process-global data is sufficient to ensure data integrity because, by definition, an object in an STA runs code only in the thread on which it was created. The thread-global data also makes cross-thread interaction almost nonexistent. Each thread has its own set of data, so there is no need for threads to wait in line (or *synchronize*) reads and writes of global data.

To create separate blocks of global data for each thread, VB leverages the Win32-provided Thread Local Storage (TLS) APIs: TlsAlloc, TlsGetValue, TlsSetValue, and TlsFree. With TLS, each thread allocates memory for its own thread-specific data and uses TLS indices to store and retrieve the memory for individual threads. TlsAlloc is called once to retrieve a process-global index, which is a slot for placing thread-specific data. Each thread uses TlsSetValue and TlsGetValue against global TLS slots to set and retrieve thread-specific data. Obviously, TlsSetValue must be set for each thread before TlsGetValue can return valid data.

The VB runtime relies heavily on TLS to support apartment threading. TLS slots are used to store both thread-global and project-specific data. Without TLS, the only things the runtime does well are Beep and crash. With the diminished runtime capacity comes the inability to use error trapping, file I/O, the Set statement, method calls, Declare functions, fixed-size arrays, and so on. In fact, the only thing you *can* do without TLS is to make type library defined API calls. You'll see how hard it is to run even limited code without TLS in the "Creating Worker Threads in DLLs" section of this chapter. Running extensive VB code without TLS should be called "The Losing Struggle" and left alone.

Since TLS-less VB is severely hobbled, it's important to know when VB calls TlsSetValue to initialize its thread and project data. TLS data is allocated and initialized when the first object is created on a given thread, and it is released when the last object is destroyed. The good news is that for everyday VB code, you don't even have to worry about this at all because the only entry points into VB are through ActiveX object-creation (and Sub Main, which is a special entry point). In general, VB code never runs on a thread without an object present on the same thread, meaning that the TLS slots always have valid data.

So how would you ever get in a situation where VB tried to run code without TLS? There is one easy answer to this question: AddressOf. The AddressOf operator can be used to hand out an arbitrary function pointer. Several API calls tell Windows to use a function pointer as a callback point for an arbitrary thread. For example, this happens while creating new threads, system or process-wide keyboard hooks, and NT services. Note that DLL modification techniques that expose entry points leave VB in exactly this situation. Let's take a quick look at what needs to happen to get a VB DLL to a state in which it can run VB code when entered from an arbitrary function.

If a function is called in a VB DLL on a thread without TLS, the code is limited to simple arithmetic and type library defined API calls. The API call support allows you to use COM API functions to create a VB object. The first call is CoInitialize, which establishes or joins a COM STA and enables subsequent Co* API calls. You can then use CoCreateInstance against a CLSID in the same VB DLL to create a VB object and, hence, initialize all TLS slots. At this point, almost everything in the runtime turns back on. I've found that MsgBox, InputBox, the App object, and possibly other language features don't work in the immediate function, but everything works perfectly in a called function. This means that you should call a helper function immediately after CoCreateInstance. The thread state remains valid until you release the initial object. After the processing is done, just release your explicitly created object (and any COM allocated locals you may be using), and then call CoUninitialize to balance the CoInitialize call.

The problem with this series of steps is that the overhead makes it prohibitively slow for many callback functions. If the exposed function is called often, as it is with a keyboard hook, you end up constantly reinitializing an STA on the thread. STA initialization creates a background window for the synchronized STA message queue, and it allocates and initializes runtime data and the global data that goes in VB's TLS slots. Doing this for every keystroke is simply too slow, especially if the VB thread is really uninitialized (the CoInitialize/CoCreate-Instance/CoUninitialize sequence is very fast if COM and/or VB are already initialized on the thread). In general, you'll want to do this only in cases where the thread has enough longevity to justify the expense, such as with an NT service, or with the explicit DLL thread creation techniques I'll show later.

Can You Avoid the Marshaling Overhead?

It's really easy in the world of STAs to break the rules. After all, the objects you're dealing with are all in the same process, so the pointers are all directly accessible without fear of a GPF. You can just use ObjPtr to pass the pointer disguised as a Long to an object in another thread. With a couple of CopyMemory or VBoost calls, you have a direct pointer back to the object. Since both threads have initialized TLS, you can now call methods directly on the object without any marshaling overhead . . . Did you bite? Sorry, the hook is barbed.

This is a direct violation of STA rules. By bypassing the marshaling layer, you're running code in an object from a thread other than the thread in which it was created. In addition to breaking COM rules, this is also incredibly dangerous from a synchronization standpoint because you can access class members from two threads simultaneously without synchronization. You also end up using both project and runtime global variables from the wrong thread, which can lead to myriad problems. Just walk away from this approach. As tempting as it may be from a performance perspective, it simply isn't worth the trouble. Cheating the threading model in this fashion also goes against a fundamental principle of this book, which is to work *with* VB and COM, not against them.

To Thread or Not to Thread

To those who haven't visited, the Land of Threads sounds like a performance paradise. The glossy travel brochure promises great performance at bargain fares, but threading is not cheap, and many of the performance gains are an illusion. The brochure never mentions the prodigious local insect life. Threads keep an application responsive with the goal of giving the impression of great performance. In a single-user app, responsiveness means that the user can keep typing and clicking. With a component that services multiple users from a server, responsiveness means that each user is serviced in approximately the same amount of time.

The performance benefit of multiple threads on a busy system leads to the illusion that the system itself is running more efficiently. Each thread is given a time slice and serviced in a round-robin fashion. When the thread's time slice is up, the OS first takes a snapshot of the state so that it can continue from the same point when the thread's turn rolls around again. The OS then turns the CPU over to another thread. Neither thread creation nor switching among threads is free. When multiple threads are running, the operating system never lets a single thread run full tilt. To keep every thread responsive, the time slices get thinner as the thread count increases.

Let's run some numbers: Assume you have 10 tasks to accomplish. Each task takes two seconds when it runs uninterrupted. If you launch all 10 tasks on the same thread at the same time, the first one completes after two seconds; the tenth is done in 20 seconds. The total time is 20 seconds, the maximum response time is 20 seconds, and the average response time is 11 seconds. If you run each task on a separate thread and assume 10 percent thread-switching overhead, the total processing time is 22 seconds.

The average and maximum response times in a multithreaded scenario are not as easy to calculate. The only thing you know for certain is that the minimum, maximum, and average values are approximately the same for multiple threads (of the same thread priority) performing the same task. The availability of the CPU and other system-level services, such as network and hard-drive access, determines the actual response time of a multithreaded system. If each thread runs at full speed with 10 percent of the CPU, the 10 threads return in approximately 2.2 seconds. In practice, you'll get this performance only if each thread is in a separate process and each process has a dedicated CPU. However, if the thread needs 100 percent of the CPU, all 10 threads return in 22 seconds. In other words, if the system is not busy, spawning multiple threads is very efficient. But the opposite is true as a system nears capacity. If the system has plenty of capacity left, the average drops from 11 to 2.2 seconds and the total response time drops from 20 to 2.2 seconds. But, if the system is extremely busy, the average response time doubles.

Balancing the amount of threading to use and the threshold levels on servers is an art. On a busy system, your goal is to sacrifice a little bit of overall processing time to increase the average response time, but this backfires if the server gets too busy. You should always be aware of where the processing requests come from and the performance required by each type of request. In a situation in which 10 objects want to run one task each, threading will help. However, if one entity waits for 10 tasks before proceeding, you may want to queue the requests in a single thread and leave more threads available for other processes.

If you try to run too many threads, the system ends up spending a great deal more than 10 percent of its time on thread management. If you create too many threads, you actually degrade system performance, and it becomes more efficient to queue operations on fewer threads. The average response time for a given action is shown with the following equation. You can see that the line for $QS<>1$ crosses the function for $QS=1$ when $QS=TO$, meaning that you need to spend three times as much time managing threads as you do running code to make a three-item queue perform better than three threads. The moral of the story is that threads are not free. Excessive threads are detrimental to system performance. You can limit the number of threads in an ActiveX EXE server by using VB's Thread Pool setting in Project|Properties.

Table 13.1   Determining the average response time of a multithreaded system

PCO = Processing cost of the operation

Slice = Amount of processor time received (0 to 1)

TO = Threading overhead (>= 0)

QS = Queue Size, then number of tasks queued per thread

ART = Average response time

*ART = QS * b(QS b+ 1) / 2 * Slice * PCO * b(1 +b TO / QSb)b*

I haven't yet addressed the cost of threads interacting with other threads and of multiple threads interacting with shared system-resources. When two threads share a common resource, they must synchronize their efforts. Synchronization between threads almost always involves one thread waiting on, or being blocked by, another thread. The blocking factor is particularly visible when using COM STAs. COM calls between STAs are automatically synchronized via message queues on hidden windows. COM calls are also synchronous; the caller cannot continue until the callee has returned from the method call. This is especially bad when there is a line at the front door of the called STA. You end up with multiple threads blocked while a single thread does all the processing. If there are four threads, and threads two through four are blocked on thread one, you incur the overhead of maintaining four threads but get the benefit of only one.

With all this in mind, some general guidelines for threading are:

- Put as many tasks on a single thread as can be accommodated by the required minimum and average response times for each task.

- Add threads only if they are required by the system's average response time.

- Always minimize interactions among threads when you design a multi-threaded application. Threads run best when left alone.

- Keep the threads busy or suspended. Use synchronization if you want to recycle a worker thread. Do not let secondary threads poll continuously for new data—it is much more efficient to let the primary thread poll for multiple conditions while the secondary threads sleep.

Creating Threads in a Client EXE

Running code on a thread is not the same as actually creating a new thread. The amount of work required to make it possible to run VB code on a thread consists of a single setting in the Project|Properties dialog. If you specify a Threading Model of Apartment Threaded for a DLL, the ThreadingModel value is set to Apartment for the CLSID\{...}\InprocServer32 key of every object in your project. COM then knows the DLL supports multiple STAs. For an EXE server, the Thread per Object and Thread Pool settings determines whether VB creates a new thread when it receives an external request for a new object.

The question of the hour is: How do you force VB to create an object for you on a new thread in the same process? The answer: Request a new object from your own server the same way an external process would request it. An internal request always creates an object on the same thread. To support external object creation, you must first create an ActiveX EXE project. Standard EXEs don't expose public objects, so external requests aren't possible. To guarantee that the external request creates a new thread, you must select the Thread per Object project property.

VB always creates an internal instance if you use the New keyword to create an object in your project. For obvious performance reasons, the normal COM creation mechanism is bypassed in this case, even for public classes. However, if you use the CreateObject keyword instead of New, then VB defers to the CoCreateInstance API call, which then calls back to VB. With CreateObject, VB can't distinguish between a request that comes from outside the ActiveX EXE and a request that comes from within. The object is always created as if the request were external. Refer to Chapter 7 for alternate external object creation techniques that don't force you to use a ProgID.

The initial steps for creating a standalone multithreaded application in VB are:

1. Create a new ActiveX EXE project.

2. Set the threading option to Thread Per Object.

3. Use CreateObject to create an instance of a MultiUse class when you need a new worker thread.

Several steps remain after you get this initial framework in place. You'll want to show a user interface in your client application and enable communication between the UI on the main thread and any worker threads you create. Because an ActiveX EXE can't have a startup form, you must set the startup option to Sub Main and explicitly create a form in that procedure. You can create the UI object directly or create another object (clsMain) that creates UI for you. The problem inherent in this approach is that Sub Main is called for every new thread, so using CreateObject to create a worker runs Sub Main a second time. You want to launch the application's UI only the first time it runs.

You might first try to handle this situation by simply setting a global flag that indicates whether you're on the first thread. The problem, of course, is that all the global variables are per thread, so the flag in the first thread isn't visible from the second. VB's App object is no help here, so you're left with using API calls to determine the first thread. The easiest and lightest mechanism I've found is to simply add an atom based on the App.hInstance value. Think of the OS-provided atom table as a valueless, keyed collection. All you can do is add or remove a string and check if it's already there. Fortunately, that is all you need to do in this case.

```vb
'ThreadCheck class
'Instancing = Private
Private Declare Function FindAtom Lib "kernel32" _
    Alias "FindAtomA" (ByVal AtomName As String) As Integer
Private Declare Function AddAtom Lib "kernel32" _
    Alias "AddAtomA" (ByVal AtomName As String) As Integer
Private Declare Function DeleteAtom Lib "kernel32" _
    (ByVal Atom As Integer) As Integer
Private m_Atom As Integer
Private Sub Class_Initialize()
Dim strAtom As String
    strAtom = AtomString
    If FindAtom(strAtom) = 0 Then
        m_Atom = AddAtom(strAtom)
    Else
    'In order to clear this setting and allow you to debug,
    'run ?DeleteAtom(FindAtom(strAtom))in the immediate window
    'until it returns 0, then set the next statement to the
    'If line above.
        Debug.Assert False
    End If
End Sub
Private Function AtomString() As String
    AtomString = "ThreadCheck" & CStr(App.hInstance)
End Function
Private Sub Class_Terminate()
    If m_Atom Then DeleteAtom m_Atom
End Sub
Public Property Get First() As Boolean
```

```
        First = m_Atom
End Property
```

```
'Using ThreadCheck with Sub Main
Private m_ThreadCheck As New ThreadCheck
Sub Main()
Dim frmMain As New frmMain
    If m_ThreadCheck.First Then
        'Launch the UI
        frmMain.Show
    Else
        'Nothing to do, and the ThreadCheck
        'instance is no longer needed.
        Set m_ThreadCheck = Nothing
    End If
End Sub
```

The next problem lies in establishing communication between the main (UI) thread and any worker threads you create. This is easier to achieve. Since VB threads are on COM STAs, calls between them are marshaled. For COM to successfully marshal an interface, the interface must be publicly registered. Within VB projects, this means you can make cross thread calls only against public classes. Communication within a project is the goal, so you don't need to enable external creation of these classes. Setting the Instancing property to PublicNotCreatable is sufficient for communication objects. Your UI form should use New to instantiate a PublicNotCreatable object to pass to the worker threads. This object also holds a reference back to the form. You can use the Form_Unload event to break the reference cycle between the form and the communication object.

```
'Main form and cross thread class layout
'Form frmMain
Private m_MainClass As clsMain
Private Sub Form_Load()
    Set m_MainClass = New clsMain
    Set m_MainClass.MainForm = Me
End Sub
Private Sub Form_Unload()
    'Break the circular reference.
```

```
        Set m_MainClass.MainForm = Nothing
        Set m_MainClass = Nothing
    End Sub
    Friend Sub Notify()
        'Stub for clsMain to call back into the form.
    End Sub
```

```
    'Class clsMain
    'Instancing = PublicNotCreatable
    Private m_frmMain As frmMain
    Friend Property Set MainForm(ByVal RHS As frmMain)
        'Note that this is a Friend, so it is callable only
        'from its own thread. Also, VB doesn't support a
        'private Form variable in a Public function on a Public
        'class. So VB is actually enforcing the desired behavior
        'in this case.
        Set m_frmMain = RHS
    End Property
    Public Sub Notify()
        'Stub callback function designed to be called by
        'worker threads when they have something to report.
        'Add parameters as needed.
        If Not m_frmMain Is Nothing Then
            m_frmMain.Notify
        End If
    End Sub
```

Now that this code is in place, you can add a CreateObject call from either frmMain or clsMain to spawn a worker thread. After you pass a clsMain instance to each worker thread, the workers can call back to the main thread across the thread boundary in a fully synchronized fashion.

Asynchronous Calls

Within COM, calls to other COM objects are synchronous. Whether you call an object directly via a method call or indirectly by raising an event, you as the caller must wait until the callee has finished processing before you continue the code. When applied to a multithreaded VB application, this means that any call to an object in another thread blocks the calling thread until all processing in the called thread has completed. The main reason for running multiple threads is to perform extensive background processing while keeping the main thread responsive, so blocking the main thread while the worker thread chews on the DoLongProcess method call is counter-productive.

Since COM methods are synchronous, using a cross-thread call to launch extensive processing directly is not an option. In fact, the only way to keep all threads busy is to have each thread call its own long methods. Any cross-thread calls should be designed to run as little code as possible. A multithreaded application should use short cross-thread calls to signal the called thread to call itself as soon as possible. If a thread calls itself and subsequently minds its own business, then it is neither blocked nor blocking any other thread. A synchronous cross-thread call that returns immediately is a good enough approximation of an asynchronous call. See Figure 13.1.

The remaining question: How do you force a thread to call itself? Use a timer. You could use a Timer control on a form, but creating a form on an otherwise nongraphical thread is a waste of resources. Instead, I recommend using an API-defined timer. The code below allows you to set a timer that fires once by calling back into the implemented FireTimer_Go function.

```
'FireTimer.cls (interface definition)
'Instancing = PublicNotCreatable
Public Sub Go()

End Sub
```

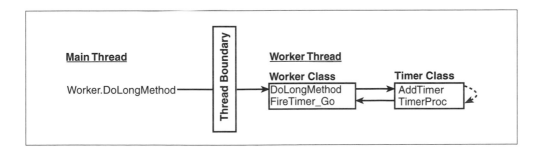

Figure 13.1. **A good approximation of an asynchronous call uses a timer in the called thread to start extensive processing in a worker thread (without blocking the main thread).**

```vb
'FireOnceTimers.Bas
Private m_FireOnceTimers As New VBA.Collection


Function AddTimer(ByVal FOT As FireTimer) As Long
    'Create a new timer object.
    AddTimer = SetTimer(0, 0, 1, AddressOf TimerProc)
    If AddTimer Then
        'If successful, add the object to a collection as
        'a weak reference.  This means that if something
        'happens that kills the class before the Timer fires,
        'then this won't artificially keep the class instance
        'alive.  The downside is that the class must call
        'ClearTimer explicitly on shutdown if FireTimer_Go has
        'not been called yet. FireTimer_Go should always clear
        'this value.
        m_FireOnceTimers.Add ObjPtr(FOT), CStr(AddTimer)
    End If
End Function
Public Sub ClearTimer(ByVal TimerID As Long)
    On Error Resume Next
    m_FireOnceTimers.Remove CStr(TimerID)
    If Err Then
        Err.Clear
    Else
        KillTimer 0, TimerID
    End If
End Sub
Private Sub TimerProc(ByVal hWnd As Long, ByVal uMsg As Long, _
    ByVal idEvent As Long, ByVal dwTime As Long)
Dim Fire As FireTimer
Dim FireRefed As FireTimer
Dim pFire As Long
Dim strKey As String
    On Error Resume Next
    strKey = CStr(idEvent)
    pFire = m_FireOnceTimers(strKey)
    If pFire Then
        'Remove the weak reference from the collection object,
        'make sure it gets a properly counted reference, clean
        'up the collection and timer, and then call Go.
        CopyMemory Fire, pFire, 4
```

```
        Set FireRefed = Fire
        CopyMemory Fire, 0&, 4
        m_FireOnceTimers.Remove strKey
        KillTimer 0, idEvent
        FireRefed.Go
    End If
End Sub
```

```
'Sample Usage
Implements FireTimer
Private m_TimerID As Long
Private m_Data As Variant

Public Sub Go(Data As Variant)
    m_Data = Data
    m_TimerID = AddTimer(Me)
End Sub
Private Sub FireTimer_Go()
    m_TimerID = 0
    'Process m_Data
End Sub
Private Sub Class_Terminate()
    If m_TimerID Then ClearTimer m_TimerID
End Sub
```

Cross-Thread Signaling

Visual Basic provides two built-in mechanisms for interacting with COM objects: methods and events. A close examination of these mechanisms for cross-thread communication reveals that both are too cumbersome for frequent use in a well-designed multithreaded system.

As I've already discussed, a multithreaded system should let each thread run unhindered by other threads, which means that cross-thread calls should be limited to creation and a nearly asynchronous call to start processing, usually followed by a callback to the controlling thread to return the results from the worker thread. Unfortunately, such a level of communication is rarely sufficient if you want to keep the program responsive. Normally, you want progress notification, the ability to cancel a long operation, and (gasp!) the option to stop the program gracefully. If you're not careful, adding support for these requirements causes so much thread interaction that your otherwise speedy threads slow to a crawl. Progress and cancel support both involve issues very similar to those of program termination, which is the ultimate cancel command. I'll look at termination first.

To support teardown, the controlling thread, which I'll assume is the only thread with a UI, must be able to tell a long operation on another thread that it is no longer needed and should go away. This is an absolute requirement if the long operation runs indefinitely: without such an ability, your EXE would never terminate. If the operation is finite, you could just orphan the operation by closing the UI and letting the object go away when it is done. ActiveX EXEs keep running until all UIs have been closed and all public objects have been released. But you'd be a bad Windows citizen if you kept an EXE running after the user can no longer interact with it. Besides wasting processing cycles, remember that many users know how to use the Task Manager. You invite users to rudely shut down the process if the shutdown sequence continues to run after a reasonable time. It's definitely better to perform teardown in a coordinated fashion.

At first glance, it seems that using a method call to tell a running thread that it's time to quit is an obvious solution. After all, a single method call is just a blip in the overall lifetime of the worker thread. Of course, this assumes that the method call is processed immediately. But because the call is made against an STA, it gets through immediately only if the STA isn't processing another method. Herein lies the problem: *if the thread weren't currently running a method, it would already have terminated.* Running an extensive method call is the whole point of the worker thread, so the StopNow method isn't called until the thread is done anyway. The controlling thread is blocked in the meantime.

In order to let the method call through, you'll need to break through the STA synchronization mechanism. Since COM uses a background window as the means of synchronizing apartments, the StopNow method actually sits in a message queue, where it waits for the running method to finish. If you call DoEvents occasionally while the worker thread processes, the StopNow method actually fires. In this case, StopNow should just set a flag and return immediately: This allows the controlling thread to call StopNow on other workers without waiting for you to finish cleaning up. Calling DoEvents often enough to keep the thread responsive is a less-than-optimal solution because you add significant overhead to the thread in addition to adding code overhead for handling reentrancy. The bottom line is that using a method for notification slows down the thread for its entire lifetime—just to enable the reception of a single method call.

A method call has problems, so lets look at using an event instead. In this scenario, the worker thread defines an Event Notify(ByVal Progress As Single, ByRef fStopNow As Boolean). The controlling thread holds a WithEvents reference to the worker. The worker calls RaiseEvent Notify occasionally to notify the controller of its progress and to see if it's time to quit. Like the method call, this technique looks like a solid design at first glance. However, events add significantly more overhead than method calls.

The first problem with repeatedly firing the event is that it's a cross-thread call, so your worker thread is blocked during the call. In addition, if multiple worker threads check in with the controlling thread, you might have multiple worker threads trying to talk to the controlling thread simultaneously. This causes the worker threads to block each other. The result is that *none* of the threads are left alone to run unhindered. Even if you replace the Invoke-bound event callback with an occasional method call from the worker to the controller, you hit the same blocking problem as multiple threads try to get through the marshaler to the main thread at the same time.

We've seen that both method calls and events are weak solutions, so it's time to look beyond COM's calling capabilities. Do you sense an API coming?

Direct Cross-Thread Memory Access

Windows doesn't let you read and write cross-process memory: you get a GPF, AV, IPF, or TLA *du jour*. Whatever you call it, you know the process is finished. If two threads run in the same process, they have legal access to memory allocated by the other thread. Since language-inherent synchronization is not possible with this level of arbitrary cross-thread memory access, VB provides no built-in mechanism for accessing memory outside of your own thread.

Let's ignore synchronization requirements for a moment and look at how to retrieve and modify memory in another thread. In order to modify memory, you need a pointer to that memory. You've already used VarPtr, CopyMemory, ZeroMemory, and array descriptors to access memory in VB. There is also a set of API calls for making less-arbitrary changes to a 32-bit long memory location:

InterlockedIncrement, InterlockedDecrement, and InterlockedExchange are examples. By using normal COM calls to pass VarPtr-generated pointers across thread boundaries, you can gain access to and modify memory in another thread. But remember that you should never call the methods on an STA COM object from another thread, so passing an ObjPtr is a very bad idea.

Passing and modifying memory is easy, but it must be done according to some simple rules. Rule one is that you must be able to guarantee that any memory you access has not been released. You can do this easily by letting VarPtr point to a member variable in a class instance. If the thread modifying the memory holds a reference to the class that allocated the memory, the memory is guaranteed to be valid. Rule two is to not let two threads modify memory at the same time. A second thread can usually read the memory while it is being modified, but letting *both* threads modify memory at the same time yields unpredictable results.

Rule three is a bit more subtle: When accessing a VarPtr-exposed variable in the thread that owns the pointed-to address, never trust VB to give you the current value. In C++, you can mark a variable as volatile: This makes the compiler go directly to memory to get the current value of the variable. If a variable is not marked as volatile, the compiler may cache its value in a CPU register so changes in its true value may not be reflected in the variable itself. Since VB has no means of marking a variable as volatile, you must access the variable either through an accessor function or by copying the data directly from the variable's VarPtr. The accessor function is easiest.

Let's take a look at the code. The controlling thread must store two values: a reference to the worker thread's object and a pointer to its signal variable. To avoid creating a helper class in the controlling thread for each worker, this object/pointer tuple is moved into a Currency for easy storage in an ObjPtr-keyed collection.

```
'Controlling thread
Private Type WorkerData
    NotifyPointer As Long
    WorkerObject As Worker
End Type
Private m_Workers As Collection
```

```vb
Private Sub Class_Initialize()
    Set m_Workers = New Collection
End Sub
Friend Sub StartNewWorker(Data As Variant)
Dim WD As WorkerData
Dim CacheWD As Currency
Dim strKey As String

    'Create the worker.
    Set WD.WorkerObject = CreateObject("MyApp.Worker")

    'Launch the task and retrieve its notify pointer.
    WD.NotifyPointer = WD.WorkerObject.DoStuff(Me, Data)

    'Transfer ownership of WD to the Currency
    'and place it in the collection.
    strKey = CStr(ObjPtr(WD.WorkerObject))
    CopyMemory CacheWD, WD, LenB(CacheWD)
    ZeroMemory WD, LenB(CacheWD)
    m_Workers.Add CacheWD, strKey
End Sub
Public Sub WorkerDone( _
  ByVal Worker As Worker, Data As Variant)
Dim WD As WorkerData
Dim CacheWD As Currency
Dim strKey As String
    'Do something with Data.
    strKey = CStr(ObjPtr(Worker))

    'If worker has been signalled, then
    'it is already out of the collection,
    'so we have to error trap this.
    On Error Resume Next
    CacheWD = m_Workers(strKey)
    On Error GoTo 0
    If CacheWD Then
        CopyMemory WD, CacheWD, LenB(CacheWD)
        CacheWD.Remove strKey
    End If
End Sub
Friend Sub SignalWorkers()
```

```
        Dim WD As WorkerData
        Dim CacheWD As Currency
        Dim Iter As Variant
            For Each Iter In m_Workers
                CacheWD = Iter
                CopyMemory WD, CacheWD, LenB(CacheWD)
                InterlockedIncrement WD.NotifyPointer
                Set WD.WorkerObject = Nothing
            Next
            Set m_Workers = New Collection
        End Sub
```

```
    'Worker class
    Implements FireTimer
    Private m_Notify As Long
    Private m_TimerID As Long
    Private m_Data As Variant
    Private m_Controller As Controller
    Private Function HaveBeenNotified() As Boolean
        HaveBeenNotified = m_Notify
    End Function
    Public Function DoStuff( _
      ByVal Controller As Controller, _
      Data As Variant) As Long
        m_Data = Data
        Set m_Controller = Controller
        m_TimerID = AddTimer(Me)
        DoStuff = VarPtr(m_Notify)
    End Sub
    Private Sub FireTimer_Go()
    Dim Data As Variant
        m_TimerID = 0
        'Process Data
        'Do
        If HaveBeenNotified Then
            'Just quit, or call WorkerDone.
        End If
        'Loop
        'WorkerDone required for teardown.
        m_Controller.WorkerDone Me, Data
    End Sub
```

```
Private Sub Class_Terminate()
    If m_TimerID Then
        ClearTimer m_TimerID
    End If
End Sub
```

You should note that the teardown order is quite lax in this example. If SignalWorkers is called and the Controller object is released by the controlling thread, a worker releases the last reference to the Controller object. There may be code running in the worker thread after the Controller has been released. But, if all worker threads have called WorkerDone before SignalWorkers is called, the last code in the process most likely runs on the controlling thread, not on the worker. In an ActiveX EXE, there is no danger in tearing down threads in a random order because each apartment can run on its own. VB coordinates teardown for you. You'll see later that being this lax about teardown order is fatal when you create worker threads in DLLs.

Bidirectional Cross-Thread Direct Memory Access

Following Rule one described above, in order to let the controlling thread signal a worker thread the controlling thread must hold a reference to the worker object that owns the signaled memory location. If you also want the worker to modify memory owned by the controlling thread, you have to use similar precautions. Let's design a worker thread that gives a continuous progress report to the controlling thread and can still be cancelled or terminated by the controller.

In this scenario, the main difference is that the Worker holds a pointer into memory that is provided by the controlling thread. To provide this memory, the controller creates a private object (let's call it ThreadData) for every worker thread, and the worker holds a pointer to an address in the ThreadData class.

```
'ThreadData class
Private m_NotifyProgress As Long
Private m_CancelPtr As Long
Private m_Worker As Worker
Friend Sub CreateWorker( _
    Parent As Controller, _
    Data As Variant, _
```

```
    Workers As Collection)
      Set m_Worker = CreateObject("MyApp.Worker")
      m_CancelPtr = m_Worker.DoStuff( _
        Parent, Data, VarPtr(m_NotifyProgress))
      Workers.Add Me, CStr(ObjPtr(m_Worker))
  End Sub
  Friend Sub CancelWorker()
      'Signal if we haven't signalled before.
      If m_CancelPtr Then
          InterlockedIncrement m_CancelPtr
          m_CancelPtr = 0
      End If
  End Sub
  Friend Property Get Progress() As Single
      'Return a percentage.
      Progress = m_NotifyProgress / 100
  End Function
```

```
  'Controlling class.
  Private m_Workers As Collection
  Friend Sub StartNewWorker(Data As Variant)
  Dim ThreadData As New ThreadData
      ThreadData.CreateWorker(Me, Data, m_Workers)
  End Sub
  Public Sub WorkerDone( _
    ByVal Worker As Worker, Data As Variant)
      'Do something with Data.

      'Remove the ThreadData object from the collection.
      'Unlike the first example, we know it is
      'there because signaling does not remove the
      'item from the collection.
      m_Workers.Remove CStr(ObjPtr(Worker))
  End Sub
  Friend Sub SignalWorkers()
  Dim TD As ThreadData
      For Each TD In m_Workers
          TD.CancelWorker
      Next
  End Sub
```

```
Private Sub Class_Initialize()
    Set m_Workers = New Collection
End Sub
```

```
'Worker class
'Same as before, except that DoStuff takes a ProgressPtr
'parameter. Worker should increment this value 100 times
'with InterlockedIncrement while performing its
'processing.
```

With this design in place, you have a very efficient threading architecture in which the worker threads can be cancelled at any time and the workers can give progress notifications to the controlling thread. You can use a timer in the controlling thread's UI to regularly display progress data. The only cross-thread COM calls occur when the worker thread is created and when it is terminated, so the controlling thread and all its workers run independently and do not block each other.

Eliminating Proxy/Stub Overhead

Further optimization is possible even after the number of COM calls has been reduced to a minimum. You can reduce the overhead by adjusting the number and longevity of the COM proxy/stub pairs created by the marshaler simply to maintain the references required to keep the signal pointers pointing to valid memory. The marshaled object returned by CreateObject is clearly required to start the worker thread and to call it, but it is not required to keep the new object running. You can also eliminate the overhead of creating a proxy/stub for the controller to pass to each worker.

In order to keep your notify pointers valid, you must be sure that there is still a reference to the object that owns the pointer. The only difference between this example and the previous example is that the thread that created the reference (not the thread that signals the pointer) now holds the reference. To keep the controlling thread alive, each ThreadData holds a reference to the public Controller. The Worker class keeps the worker thread alive simply by keeping a reference to itself.

```vb
'ThreadData class
Private m_NotifyProgress As Long
Private m_CancelPtr As Long
Private m_Worker As Worker
Private m_ReturnData As Variant
Private m_Parent As Controller
Friend Sub CreateWorker( _
    Parent As Controller, Data As Variant, _
    Workers As Collection)
    Set m_Worker = CreateObject("MyApp.Worker")
    m_CancelPtr = m_Worker.DoStuff( _
        Data, VarPtr(m_NotifyProgress), VarPtr(m_ReturnData))
    Workers.Add Me, CStr(ObjPtr(m_Worker))
    Set m_Parent = Parent
End Sub
Friend Sub CancelWorker()
    'Signal if we haven't signaled before.
    If m_CancelPtr Then
        InterlockedIncrement m_CancelPtr
        m_CancelPtr = 0
    End If
End Sub
Friend Property Get Progress() As Single
    'Return a percentage.
    Progress = m_NotifyProgress / 100
End Function
Friend Function Finished(ReturnData As Variant) As Boolean
    Finished = Not IsEmpty(m_ReturnData)
    If Finished Then
        ReturnData = m_ReturnData
    End If
End If
```

```vb
'Worker class
Implements FireTimer
Private m_Notify As Long
Private m_TimerID As Long
Private m_ReturnDataPtr As Long
Private m_ProgessPtr As Long
Private m_Me As Worker
```

```
Private Function HaveBeenNotified() As Boolean
    HaveBeenNotified = m_Notify
End Function
Public Function DoStuff( _
  Data As Variant, _
  ByVal ProgressPtr As Long, _
  ByVal ReturnDataPtr As Long)
    m_ReturnDataPtr = ReturnDataPtr
    m_ProgressPtr = ProgressPtr
    m_TimerID = AddTimer(Me)
    DoStuff = VarPtr(m_Notify)
    Set m_Me = Me
End Function
Private Sub FireTimer_Go()
Dim Data As Variant
Dim fDoIncrement As Boolean
    m_TimerID = 0
    'Process Data
    'Do
    If HaveBeenNotified Then
        Data = "Not Completed"
        GoTo Finish
    End If
    'fDoIncrement = True
    If fDoIncrement
        InterlockedIncrement m_ProgressPtr
    End If
    'Loop
Finish:
    'Transfer the memory into the DataPtr.
    CopyMemory ByVal m_ReturnDataPtr, ByVal VarPtr(Data), 16
    CopyMemory ByVal VarPtr(Data), 0, 2
    'We're done. Release ourselves and exit.
    Set m_Me = Nothing
End Sub
Private Sub Class_Terminate()
    If m_TimerID Then
        ClearTimer m_TimerID
    End If
End Sub
```

Do you see the crash-and-burn bug in this sample? This code crashes occasionally because it accesses released memory. The m_ReturnDataPtr access is safe if the ThreadData class is not released until after Finished returns True. ThreadData stays alive because it holds a reference on the Controller object, which, being public, keeps the main thread alive. The other direct memory access call involves m_CancelPtr, which is valid as long as Worker is alive. The problem is that Worker can complete and terminate at any time, so the memory might be invalid. The CancelWorker code can be improved to first check if data has been returned, indicating that m_CancelPtr is now invalid.

```
Friend Sub CancelWorker()
    'Signal if we haven't signaled before.
    If m_CancelPtr Then
        If Not IsEmpty(m_ReturnData) Then
            InterlockedIncrement m_CancelPtr
        End If
        m_CancelPtr = 0
    End If
End Sub
```

The timing problem that occurs when CancelWorker is called while the Worker class is being released is a classic case of a cross-thread synchronization bug. These bugs are very difficult to reproduce reliably because the code runs in a random order. You can best track these bugs by using the painstaking and error prone process of manually examining code from the interacting threads. Step through the program from outside the debugger, and analyze alternating blocks of code from each thread to see if there is a potential problem. The size of a block of code should range from a procedure to parts of a single statement. For example, let's look at the interaction between the concluding code in Worker's FireTimer_Go and ThreadData's CancelWorker. Lines from Worker are marked with a *W*; lines from ThreadData with a *T*.

```
T:If m_CancelPtr Then
T:If Not IsEmpty(m_ReturnData) Then
W:CopyMemory ByVal m_ReturnDataPtr, ByVal VarPtr(Data), 16
W:CopyMemory ByVal VarPtr(Data), 0, 2
T:InterlockedIncrement m_CancelPtr
```

```
T:m_CancelPtr = 0
W:Set m_Me = Nothing
W:End Sub
```

This ordering of the code runs fine because m_CancelPtr is modified before the Worker class that owns the memory is released. However, in the following ordering, there's an obvious problem.

```
T:If m_CancelPtr Then
T:If Not IsEmpty(m_ReturnData) Then
W:CopyMemory ByVal m_ReturnDataPtr, ByVal VarPtr(Data), 16
W:CopyMemory ByVal VarPtr(Data), 0, 2
W:Set m_Me = Nothing
W:End Sub
T:InterlockedIncrement m_CancelPtr
T:m_CancelPtr = 0
```

The code crashes on the InterlockedIncrement line when run in this order because the memory for the Worker instance that owns m_CancelPtr has been freed. In order to handle this type of condition, you must explicitly synchronize these blocks of code to eliminate the chance of running code from two threads in an order that might crash.

You can solve the synchronization problem with a Win32 critical section object to guarantee that m_CancelPtr is not accessed after it is released. A critical section variable adds less overhead to the system than mutexes or event objects because critical sections work only in a single process. A critical section object, once initialized, can be entered with EnterCriticalSection. The first EnterCritical-Section call establishes ownership of the synchronization object. Subsequent EnterCriticalSection requests against the same object are blocked until the first thread that entered the critical section calls LeaveCriticalSection. Critical-section synchronization, like all mechanisms that block threads, should be avoided whenever possible because blocking hurts overall performance. This is one case, however, where some sort of synchronization is required. The critical section is owned by the Controller object and used by the Worker and ThreadData objects. All the APIs used here are declared in the provided ThreadAPI.Olb. (VBoost: API declares used for threading.)

```
'Controller
Private m_CritSect As CRITICAL_SECTION
Private Sub Class_Initialize()
    InitializeCriticalSection VarPtr(m_CritSect)
End Sub
Private Sub Class_Terminate()
    DeleteCriticalSection VarPtr(m_CritSect)
End Sub
Friend Function CritSect() As Long
    CritSect = VarPtr(m_CritSect)
End Function
```

```
'Worker
Private m_pCritSect As Long
Public Function DoStuff( _
  Data As Variant, ByVal ProgressPtr As Long, _
  ByVal ReturnDataPtr As Long, ByVal CritSectPtr As Long)
    'Same as before
    m_pCritSect = CritSectPtr
End Function
Private Sub FireTimer_Go()
    'Same as before
Finish:
    'Transfer the memory to the DataPtr.
    EnterCriticalSection m_pCritSect
    CopyMemory ByVal m_ReturnDataPtr, ByVal VarPtr(Data), 16
    CopyMemory ByVal VarPtr(Data), 0, 2
    'We're done. Release ourselves and exit.
    Set m_Me = Nothing
    LeaveCriticalSection m_pCritSect
End Sub


'ThreadData class.
Friend Sub CancelWorker()
    'Signal if we haven't signalled before.
    If m_CancelPtr Then
        EnterCriticalSection m_Parent.CritSect
        If Not IsEmpty(m_ReturnData) Then
            InterlockedIncrement m_CancelPtr
        End If
        m_CancelPtr = 0
```

```
        LeaveCriticalSection m_Parent.CritSect
    End If
End Sub
```

The order-dependent code now runs in one of two orders:

```
'Order 1
T:If Not IsEmpty(m_ReturnData) Then
T:InterlockedIncrement m_CancelPtr
T:End If
T:m_CancelPtr = 0
W:CopyMemory ByVal m_ReturnDataPtr, ByVal VarPtr(Data), 16
W:CopyMemory ByVal VarPtr(Data), 0, 2
W:Set m_Me = Nothing

'Order 2
W:CopyMemory ByVal m_ReturnDataPtr, ByVal VarPtr(Data), 16
W:CopyMemory ByVal VarPtr(Data), 0, 2
W:Set m_Me = Nothing
T:If Not IsEmpty(m_ReturnData) Then
T:InterlockedIncrement m_CancelPtr
T:End If
T:m_CancelPtr = 0
```

Both of these code orderings are safe.

Coordinated Gate Crashing in STA Apartments

In the STA threading model, the COM marshaler provides synchronization by allowing only a single method call to be processed at a time. You must explicitly force COM to let extra calls into the process if you want them to run before the current method returns. The exception to this blocking mechanism occurs when you call a method on an external thread yourself and receive a method call from that thread before the initial call returns. If COM didn't let this call through, the system would deadlock while both threads waited for each other.

The COM marshaler performs its magic by using hidden windows on each thread. When you call a method from another thread, COM places the message in the called thread's synchronization window and waits for the message queue to process. (This is an oversimplification, but the details aren't relevant to this discussion). Unprocessed COM calls are simply messages in the window waiting for the current message to finish processing. To allow pending messages to be processed while the current message runs, you must process messages from the hidden window.

Visual Basic provides the DoEvents function for arbitrarily clearing pending messages in all the current thread's windows. Since pending methods masquerade as messages, calling DoEvents lets them through. The problem is that DoEvents lets everything else through as well. You get a flood instead of a trickle. If you want only the trickle, you'll have to use something other than DoEvents.

DoEvents first clears all pending keystrokes from the SendKeys function and then enters a loop that clears all messages with the PeekMessage API. Finally, DoEvents calls the Sleep API to release the remaining time slice on the current thread. The only part of DoEvents that you really want is the PeekMessage loop, and you want to run PeekMessage only against the COM synchronization window, not against all windows. By limiting the scope of the message clearing, you avoid the nasty reentrancy side-effects that are normally part of DoEvents.

There are two distinct tasks required to process pending messages. First, you find the synchronization window. Second, you use PeekMessage and its supporting API functions to clear the message loop. If you don't want to bother to find the OLE window, you can limit the scope of the messages processed to the messages in the WM_USER range; this is the range used for processing messages that correspond to method calls.

The unfortunate aspect of this process is that the steps to locate the correct window depend on the OS. For most current operating systems—Win95 OSR2, Win95 with DCOM, Win98, NT4, and Windows 2000—the target window has a window class of OleMainThreadWndClass and a name of OleMainThreadWndName. However, the original Win95 used a window class name that starts with WIN95 RPC Wmsg. In addition to the class name complications, Windows 2000 added the concept of a message-only window. This new classification makes the OLE window much harder to find on Windows 2000. You can find the window with the FindWindow or FindWindowEx API calls, but not with EnumThreadWindows or EnumChildWindow.

The bottom line is that although the OLE window has remained relatively stable across several OS releases, there is no guarantee that a future service pack won't break the location mechanism. You should always include code that addresses the possibility that you might not find the window. If you can't find the window, you should just use the second technique of spinning all windows in the WM_USER range. Although it is theoretically possible that the window location routines will lock onto the wrong window in future releases, it is much more likely that they will simply be insufficient for finding the correct window and will fall back on spinning all windows with a constrained range of messages.

The following routine, SpinOlehWnd, is a snippet from the Thread-OlePump.Bas file included with the book. SpinOlehWnd attempts to find the correct window by calling FindOLEhWnd the first time it is called on each thread. Calling SpinOlehWnd allows any pending messages to process before the current method returns.

```
Private m_fInit As Boolean
Private m_OLEhWnd As Long

Public Sub SpinOlehWnd(ByVal fYield As Boolean)
Dim PMFlags As PMOptions
Dim wMsgMin As Long
Dim wMsgMax As Long
Dim MSG As MSG
    If Not m_fInit Then FindOlehWnd
    If fYield Then
        PMFlags = PM_REMOVE
    Else
        PMFlags = PM_REMOVE Or PM_NOYIELD
    End If
    If m_OLEhWnd = 0 Then
    'Not sure which window to spin (this is very unlikely).
    'A PeekMessage loop on all windows can still beat DoEvents
    'and reduce side effects just by looking at WM_USER
    'messages and higher. Note that the current implementation
    'uses only the single WM_USER message, but this code
    'never runs in the current implementation, so I'm playing
    'it safe.
```

```
        wMsgMin = &H400  'WM_USER
        wMsgMax = &H7FFF
    End If
    Do While PeekMessage( _
      MSG, m_OLEhWnd, wMsgMin, wMsgMax, PMFlags)
        'Probably does nothing, but technically correct
        TranslateMessage MSG
        'Process the message
        DispatchMessage MSG
    Loop
End Sub
```

Creating Worker Threads in DLLs

When you write an EXE, you have full control of the threads and lifetime of your process. When you write a DLL or OCX, your threads and their lifetimes are completely at the mercy of the EXE that loaded the library. In an ActiveX EXE, you can specify that VB must create a new thread for every externally created object. In an ActiveX DLL, all external objects are created on the thread that requested the object. Since VB doesn't create threads for you in a DLL, you must explicitly create worker threads yourself.

Any threads you create must be extremely responsive to the process lifetime because a DLL has no control over its termination. An EXE always assumes that it created all the threads that run in its process. When the last known thread is finished, so is the process. The EXE knows nothing about a worker thread you launched in a DLL, so any worker threads that are still running when the owning process is terminated by the EXE are orphaned and will generally crash right away.

There are a number of issues you need to overcome if you want to create worker threads in a DLL. Some of these issues are shared with the thread-interaction case in an EXE, but the lifetime and thread initialization issues are unique to worker threads in a DLL. You must address all but the last of these issues for every worker thread you create.

- VB won't create a new thread for you, so you must create your own thread with the CreateThread API.

- You must initialize the created thread using only type library defined API functions.

- Once the thread is initialized enough to support object creation, you must create a VB object in the current DLL on that thread.

- You must terminate all worker threads created by a thread in the DLL before the EXE terminates that thread.

- You must make it easy for the main thread to signal your worker threads so that the controlling process doesn't block during teardown.

- If you need to call methods on an object in the main thread from the worker thread, then you must correctly marshal the calling object into the worker thread.

I'll show three variations of an architecture for creating worker threads in a DLL. The first variation can pass objects among the main and worker threads and gives immediate error feedback at the time of thread creation. Variation number two drops support for any cross-thread object communication and provides no immediate feedback. (A variation between one and two with no object support but with immediate feedback is included on the CD-ROM). As the features decline, so does the architecture's overhead. The final variation is a modification of the second architecture that enables you to recycle worker threads instead of creating and destroying them repeatedly.

Worker threads in a DLL are a great tool for client applications. However, you should use extreme discretion before you deploy them in the server space. Server architectures, such as COM+ and IIS, carefully balance the number of threads they create in their process space. If you create extra threads, you can disrupt the entire balance of the server. It is also inappropriate to block one of these threads while another terminates.

It is a common misconception that apartment threads are painfully inefficient in the IIS space. In fact, IIS threads are themselves apartment threaded, so they run apartment-threaded DLLs extremely well. VB5 did have some performance issues with unnecessary synchronization during object creation and teardown, but VB6 fixed this bug. VB6 object creation waits on only three critical sections, all of which are already on the heap when additional threads are created. During a test on a single-processor computer, VB6 handled about 350 ASP requests per second with no measurable performance difference compared to free-threaded ATL objects. You can also use the Retain In Memory feature of unattended ActiveX DLLs to ensure that once an ASP thread is initialized, it is never uninitialized until the thread terminates. Apartment-threaded objects have no negative performance problems unless you store them at Session scope. (IIS won't let you use apartment-threaded objects at Application scope.) If you place an apartment-threaded object at session scope, you lock the session into using a single thread. If two sessions are locked into the same thread, they must wait for each other even if there are 99 other inactive threads.

The Basic Architecture

The basic threading architecture uses three core components and two custom components. I'll describe the role of each piece and then look at three different implementations. The object interactions are shown in Figure 13.2.

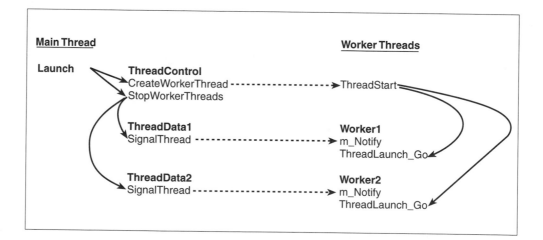

Figure 13.2. Objects with well-defined responsibilities on each side of the thread boundary make the creation of worker threads safe and efficient.

The ThreadControl Object

ThreadControl is the object responsible for creating worker threads and for blocking the main thread while the workers terminate. ThreadControl has two main functions: CreateWorkerThread and StopWorkerThreads. CreateWorkerThread gets the CLSID of the object that the worker thread creates to do all the real work. It also gets an InputData Variant that is passed to the new object. Each architecture specifies additional optional parameters for CreateWorkerThread. The second method, StopWorkerThreads, takes no parameters and doesn't return until all the worker threads have completed.

The ThreadData Object

The ThreadData object exists in the same thread as ThreadControl. One ThreadData is created for each worker thread. ThreadData has three main responsibilities. First, it owns a reference to the ThreadControl instance that created it, guaranteeing that ThreadControl outlives every worker it created. Second, it owns a handle to the calling thread. The handle allows ThreadData to determine if the worker is still running and retrieve its exit code when it completes. Third, ThreadData provides a memory location that can be modified by the worker thread when the thread is completed, providing an efficient mechanism for signaling completion. ThreadData objects are cleaned up in a lazy fashion: The Launch object, prompted by a timer or another mechanism, must call CleanCompletedThreads to explicitly free ThreadData objects and close the thread handle. CreateWorkerThread and StopWorkerThread call CleanCompletedThreads internally.

The Worker Class

The worker class is a MultiUse class that implements the ThreadLaunch interface. ThreadLaunch has a single function, Go, that is the functional entry point for the new thread. The thread terminates just after ThreadLaunch_Go is completed. The worker thread must provide a signal pointer to the ThreadControl object and regularly check the signal to see if it is time to preemptively terminate the thread.

The ThreadStart Procedure

ThreadStart is the starting point for the new thread. ThreadStart receives data via the CreateThread API, which is called by CreateWorkerThread. ThreadStart uses API calls to initialize the thread and calls the CoCreateInstance API to create the object. ThreadStart then requests the ThreadLaunch interface from the created object and calls Go to do all the work.

The Launch Object

Launch is any object that holds a reference to a ThreadControl object. Launch should be a PublicNotCreatable or MultiUse object so that an external reference to the Launch object keeps the server alive. Launch must call ThreadControl. StopWorkerThreads before it releases the ThreadControl object. StopWorkerThreads is generally called from the Launch object's Terminate event.

Workers with Cross-Thread Object Support

You can use a familiar programming model if you create a worker thread that can call the main thread with standard COM method calls. Using COM methods to pass data back and forth is easy to code, but it does come with the price of blocking the worker and the main thread during the method call. If two or more workers wait on the main thread, they are also waiting on each other. This can lead to a synchronization bottleneck.

In the first threading model, I pass the ThreadControl object to the worker thread to expose a RegisterNewThread method for the worker at the beginning of the ThreadLaunch_Go function. The Instancing property of ThreadControl is set to PublicNotCreatable and RegisterNewThread is declared as a public function. All other exposed methods on ThreadControl are Friend rather than Public, forcing every call except the registration callback to come from ThreadControl's thread.

RegisterNewThread takes four parameters that are crucial to the correct operation and teardown of the worker thread. Cross thread interactions are shown in Figure 13.3.

ThreadDataCookie   is the ObjPtr of the ThreadData object. ThreadData itself is a private object and cannot be passed among threads, but its pointer can be passed to uniquely identify the worker thread instance in RegisterNewThread.

ThreadSignalPointer   is the address of a variable in the Worker class than can be incremented to signal the thread.

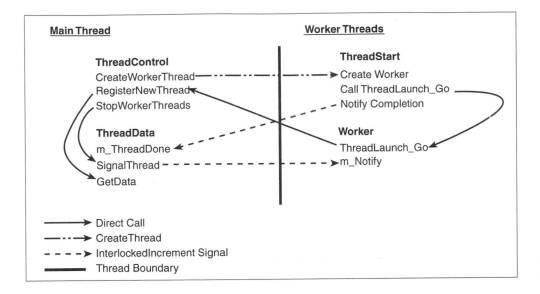

Figure 13.3. **Cross-thread interactions required to support workers threads that communicate with the controlling thread via COM method calls.**

ThreadControl is a ByRef parameter used to guarantee that the Worker doesn't hold a reference to ThreadControl after the RegisterNewThread call. If the worker holds a ThreadControl reference, it is possible that the final release of the ThreadControl object will come from the worker instead of from the Launch class. This is a crash-and-burn scenario.

InputData is the Variant that was passed to CreateWorkerThread. InputData can contain any type of data, including object types. In order to correctly marshal object types in InputData from the controlling thread to the worker thread, RegisterNewThread must be public. Since methods can be called from the worker thread at anytime and StopWorkerThreads doesn't block until all workers have completed, StopWorkerThreads must call SpinOlehWnd to allow messages to come through. Spinning the messages makes pending RegisterNewThread messages get through, as do callbacks into any objects passed to an InputData parameter. However, StopWorkerThreads can guarantee that messages will get through only to the controlling thread. This places a basic restriction on InputData objects: They must be native to the STA of the calling thread to ensure proper termination.

You must go through the COM marshaler to call methods on STA objects from different threads. Any object created in another thread or process with CoCreateInstance is automatically marshaled for you, as is any object you pass to methods or properties of a cross-thread object. Marshaling takes place for every case in VB with the exception of explicit thread creation in a DLL because both the object's native thread and the calling thread are fully COM-initialized. Thread creation is an exceptional case because the calling thread hasn't been created—not to mention initialized for COM—when you try to pass an object to it.

COM provides two API functions to correctly marshal an object between threads. You must call the first API, CoMarshalInterThreadInterfaceInStream, from the native thread to create marshaling data for the object. The marshaling data is stored in a multithreaded stream object that any thread in the process can call without marshaling. The API declarations in ThreadAPI.olb define the returned IStream object as a Long to make the object easier to use in VB. The stream pointer is passed to the ThreadStart procedure, which then calls CoGet-InterfaceAndReleaseStream to retrieve a marshaled object. You should always marshal the object's controlling IUnknown which you can then use to retrieve any properly marshalled interface.

The pivotal API function for creating a thread is CreateThread (*there's* a shocker). CreateThread takes several arguments, two of which are central to the architecture. The lpStartAddress argument receives the address of the Thread-Start function, and the lpParameter argument takes the address of data passed to ThreadStart. The data passed to lpParameter is the VarPtr of a structure that includes all the information needed to create an object on the new thread and coordinate with the controlling thread. Some of the other fields are the CLSID of the worker class, the pointer to the unmarshaling stream, and a critical section pointer used to coordinate teardown. The data received by ThreadStart is actually a reference to a local structure variable in CreateWorkerThread. Thread-Control uses a Win32 Event object to block CreateWorkerThread until the worker thread has read all the data from the local variable.

Listing 13.1. ThreadLaunch, ThreadControl, ThreadStart, and Thread Data for cross-thread object support

```
'ThreadLaunch interface definition, ThreadLaunch.cls
'Instancing = PublicNotCreatable
Public Function Go(Controller As ThreadControl, _
  ByVal ThreadDataCookie As Long) As Long
End Function
```

```
'ThreadControl class, ThreadControl.cls
'Instancing = PublicNotCreatable

'Collection that holds ThreadData objects for each thread
Private m_RunningThreads As Collection
'Currently tearing down, so don't start anything new
Private m_fStoppingWorkers As Boolean
'Synchronization handle
Private m_EventHandle As Long
'Critical section to avoid conflicts when signalling threads
Private m_CS As CRITICAL_SECTION
'Pointer to m_CS structure
Private m_pCS As Long


'Called to create a new worker thread.
'CLSID can be obtained from a ProgID via CLSIDFromProgID.
'InputData contains the data for the new thread.
'fStealInputData should be True if the data is large. If
'  this is set, InputData is Empty on return. If
'  InputData contains an object reference, the object
'  must have been created on this thread.
'fReturnThreadHandle must explicitly be set to True to
'  return the created thread handle. This handle can be
'  used for calls like SetThreadPriority and must be
'  closed with CloseHandle.
Friend Function CreateWorkerThread( _
  CLSID As CLSID, InputData As Variant, _
  Optional ByVal fStealInputData As Boolean = False, _
  Optional ByVal fReturnThreadHandle As Boolean = False) _
  As Long
Dim TPD As ThreadProcData
Dim IID_IUnknown As VBGUID
Dim ThreadID As Long
```

```vb
    Dim ThreadHandle As Long
    Dim pStream As IUnknown
    Dim ThreadData As ThreadData
    Dim fCleanUpOnFailure As Boolean
    Dim hProcess As Long
        If m_fStoppingWorkers Then Err.Raise 5, , _
            "Can't create new worker while shutting down"
        'We need to clean up sometime, this is as good a time
        'as any.
        CleanCompletedThreads
        With TPD
            Set ThreadData = New ThreadData
            .CLSID = CLSID
            .EventHandle = m_EventHandle
            With IID_IUnknown
                .Data4(0) = &HC0
                .Data4(7) = &H46
            End With
            .pMarshalStream = _
                CoMarshalInterThreadInterfaceInStream( _
                IID_IUnknown, Me)
            .ThreadDonePointer = ThreadData.ThreadDonePointer
            .ThreadDataCookie = ObjPtr(ThreadData)
            .pCritSect = m_pCS
            ThreadData.SetData InputData, fStealInputData
            Set ThreadData.Controller = Me
            m_RunningThreads.Add ThreadData, _
                CStr(.ThreadDataCookie)
        End With
        ThreadHandle = CreateThread(0, 0, _
            AddressOf ThreadProc.ThreadStart, _
            VarPtr(TPD), 0, ThreadID)
        If ThreadHandle = 0 Then
            fCleanUpOnFailure = True
        Else
            'Turn ownership of the thread handle over to
            'the ThreadData object.
            ThreadData.ThreadHandle = ThreadHandle
            'Make sure we've been notified by ThreadProc before
            'continuing to guarantee that the new thread has
            'gotten the data out of the ThreadProcData structure.
            WaitForSingleObject m_EventHandle, INFINITE
            If TPD.hr Then
```

```vb
            fCleanUpOnFailure = True
        ElseIf fReturnThreadHandle Then
            hProcess = GetCurrentProcess
            DuplicateHandle hProcess, ThreadHandle, _
              hProcess, CreateWorkerThread
        End If
    End If
    If fCleanUpOnFailure Then
        'Failure: clean up stream by making a reference
        'and releasing it.
        CopyMemory pStream, TPD.pMarshalStream, 4
        Set pStream = Nothing
        'Tell the thread it's done using the normal mechanism.
        InterlockedIncrement TPD.ThreadDonePointer
        'There's no reason to keep the new thread data.
        CleanCompletedThreads
    End If
    If TPD.hr Then Err.Raise TPD.hr
End Function


'Called after a thread is created to provide a mechanism
'for stopping execution and retrieving initial data for
'running the thread.  Should be called in ThreadLaunch_Go
'with: Controller.RegisterNewThread _
'  ThreadDataCookie, VarPtr(m_Notify), Controller, InputData
Public Sub RegisterNewThread( _
  ByVal ThreadDataCookie As Long, _
  ByVal ThreadSignalPointer As Long, _
  ByRef ThreadControl As ThreadControl, _
  Optional InputData As Variant)
Dim ThreadData As ThreadData
Dim fInCriticalSection As Boolean
    Set ThreadData = m_RunningThreads( _
      CStr(ThreadDataCookie))
    ThreadData.ThreadSignalPointer = ThreadSignalPointer
    ThreadData.GetData InputData

    'The new thread should not own the controlling thread
    'because the controlling thread has to teardown after
    'all the worker threads are done running code. This
    'can't happen if we happen to release the last reference
    'to ThreadControl in a worker thread.  ThreadData
    'already holds an extra reference on this object, so
```

```
'it is guaranteed to remain alive until ThreadData is
'signaled.
Set ThreadControl = Nothing
If m_fStoppingWorkers Then
    'This happens only when StopWorkerThreads is called
    'almost immediately after CreateWorkerThread. We could
    'just let this signal happen in the StopWorkerThreads
    'loop, but this allows a worker thread to be signalled
    'immediately. See note in SignalThread about
    'CriticalSection usage.
    ThreadData.SignalThread m_pCS, fInCriticalSection
    If fInCriticalSection Then LeaveCriticalSection m_pCS
End If
End Sub


'Call StopWorkerThreads to signal all worker threads
'and spin until they terminate. Any calls to an object
'passed via the Data parameter in CreateWorkerThread
'will succeed.
Friend Sub StopWorkerThreads()
Dim ThreadData As ThreadData
Dim fInCriticalSection As Boolean
Dim fSignal As Boolean
    If m_fStoppingWorkers Then Exit Sub
    m_fStoppingWorkers = True
    fSignal = True
    Do
        For Each ThreadData In m_RunningThreads
            If ThreadData.ThreadCompleted Then
                m_RunningThreads.Remove _
                    CStr(ObjPtr(ThreadData))
            ElseIf fSignal Then
                'See SignalThread about CriticalSection usage.
                ThreadData.SignalThread _
                    m_pCS, fInCriticalSection
            End If
        Next
        If fInCriticalSection Then
            LeaveCriticalSection m_pCS
            fInCriticalSection = False
        Else
```

```vb
                    'We can turn this off indefinitely because
                    'new threads that arrive at RegisterNewThread
                    'while stopping workers are signalled
                    'immediately.
                    fSignal = False
            End If
            If m_RunningThreads.Count = 0 Then Exit Do

                    'We need to clear the message queue here in order
                    'to allow any pending RegisterNewThread messages to
                    'come through.
                    SpinOlehWnd False
                    Sleep 0
        Loop
        m_fStoppingWorkers = False
End Sub


'Releases ThreadData objects for all threads
'that are completed. Cleaning happens automatically
'when you call SignalWorkerThreads, StopWorkerThreads,
'and RegisterNewThread.
Friend Sub CleanCompletedThreads()
Dim ThreadData As ThreadData
    For Each ThreadData In m_RunningThreads
        If ThreadData.ThreadCompleted Then
            m_RunningThreads.Remove CStr(ObjPtr(ThreadData))
        End If
    Next
End Sub


'Call to tell all running worker threads to terminate. If the
'thread has not yet called RegisterNewThread, it will
'not be signaled. Unlike StopWorkerThreads, this does not
'block while the workers actually terminate. StopWorker
'Threads must be called by the owner of this class before the
'ThreadControl instance is released.
Friend Sub SignalWorkerThreads()
Dim ThreadData As ThreadData
Dim fInCriticalSection As Boolean
    For Each ThreadData In m_RunningThreads
        If ThreadData.ThreadCompleted Then
```

```vb
                        m_RunningThreads.Remove CStr(ObjPtr(ThreadData))
                Else
                    'See SignalThread about CriticalSection usage.
                    ThreadData.SignalThread m_pCS, fInCriticalSection
                End If
        Next
        If fInCriticalSection Then LeaveCriticalSection m_pCS
    End Sub


    Private Sub Class_Initialize()
        Set m_RunningThreads = New Collection
        m_EventHandle = CreateEvent(0, 0, 0, vbNullString)
        If m_EventHandle = 0 Then
            Err.Raise &H80070000 + Err.LastDLLError
        End If
        m_pCS = VarPtr(m_CS)
        InitializeCriticalSection m_pCS
    End Sub


    Private Sub Class_Terminate()
        'Just in case: This generally does nothing.
        CleanCompletedThreads
        If m_EventHandle Then CloseHandle m_EventHandle
        If m_pCS Then DeleteCriticalSection m_pCS
    End Sub
```

```vb
    'ThreadStart procedure, ThreadProc.Bas
    Public Type ThreadProcData
        pMarshalStream As Long
        EventHandle As Long
        CLSID As CLSID
        hr As Long
        ThreadDataCookie As Long
        ThreadDonePointer As Long
        pCritSect As Long
    End Type
    Private Const FailBit As Long = &H80000000
    Public Function ThreadStart( _
      ThreadProcData As ThreadProcData) As Long
    Dim hr As Long
    Dim pUnk As IUnknown
```

```vb
Dim TL As ThreadLaunch
Dim TC As ThreadControl
Dim ThreadDataCookie As Long
Dim IID_IUnknown As VBGUID
Dim pMarshalStream As Long
Dim ThreadDonePointer As Long
Dim pCritSect As Long
    'Extreme care must be taken in this function to
    'not execute normal VB code until an object has been
    'created on this thread by VB.
    hr = CoInitialize(0)
    With ThreadProcData
        ThreadDonePointer = .ThreadDonePointer
        If hr And FailBit Then
            .hr = hr
            PulseEvent .EventHandle
            Exit Function
        End If
        With IID_IUnknown
            .Data4(0) = &HC0
            .Data4(7) = &H46
        End With
        hr = CoCreateInstance(.CLSID, Nothing, _
          CLSCTX_INPROC_SERVER, IID_IUnknown, pUnk)
        If hr And FailBit Then
            .hr = hr
            PulseEvent .EventHandle
            CoUninitialize
            Exit Function
        End If
        'If we made it this far, we can start using
        'normal VB calls because we have an initialized
        'object on this thread.
        On Error Resume Next
        Set TL = pUnk
        Set pUnk = Nothing
        If Err Then
            .hr = Err
            PulseEvent .EventHandle
            CoUninitialize
            Exit Function
```

```
End If
ThreadDataCookie = .ThreadDataCookie
pMarshalStream = .pMarshalStream
pCritSect = .pCritSect

'The controlling thread can continue at this point.
'The event must be pulsed here because
'CoGetInterfaceAndReleaseStream blocks if
'WaitForSingleObject is still blocking the
'controlling thread.
PulseEvent .EventHandle
Set TC = CoGetInterfaceAndReleaseStream( _
  pMarshalStream, IID_IUnknown)

'An error is not expected here.  If it happens,
'we have no way of passing it out because the
'structure may already be popped from the stack,
'meaning that we can't use ThreadProcData.hr.
If Err Then
    'Note: Incrementing the ThreadDonePointer call
    'needs to be protected by a critical section once
    'the ThreadSignalPointer has been passed to
    'ThreadControl. Before that time, there is no
    'conflict.
    InterlockedIncrement ThreadDonePointer
    Set TL = Nothing
    CoUninitialize
    Exit Function
End If

'Launch background processing and wait for it to
'finish. Note: TC is released by ThreadControl.
'RegisterNewThread
ThreadStart = TL.Go(TC, ThreadDataCookie)
'Tell the controlling thread that this thread is done.
EnterCriticalSection pCritSect
InterlockedIncrement ThreadDonePointer
LeaveCriticalSection pCritSect
'Release TL after the critical section. This
'prevents ThreadData.SignalThread from
'signalling a pointer to released memory.
```

```vb
        Set TL = Nothing
    End With
    CoUninitialize
End Function
```

```vb
'ThreadData class, ThreadData.cls
Private m_ThreadDone As Long
Private m_ThreadSignal As Long
Private m_ThreadHandle As Long
Private m_Data As Variant
Private m_Controller As ThreadControl
Friend Function ThreadCompleted() As Boolean
Dim ExitCode As Long
    ThreadCompleted = m_ThreadDone
    If ThreadCompleted Then
        'Since code runs on the worker thread after the
        'ThreadDone pointer is incremented, there is a chance
        'that we are signaled but the thread hasn't yet
        'terminated.  In this case, just claim we aren't done
        'yet to make sure that code on all worker threads is
        'actually completed before ThreadControl terminates.
        If m_ThreadHandle Then
            If GetExitCodeThread(m_ThreadHandle, ExitCode) _
              Then
                If ExitCode = STILL_ACTIVE Then
                    ThreadCompleted = False
                    Exit Function
                End If
            End If
            CloseHandle m_ThreadHandle
            m_ThreadHandle = 0
        End If
    End If
End Function
Friend Property Get ThreadDonePointer() As Long
    ThreadDonePointer = VarPtr(m_ThreadDone)
End Property
Friend Property Let ThreadSignalPointer(ByVal RHS As Long)
    m_ThreadSignal = RHS
End Property
Friend Property Let ThreadHandle(ByVal RHS As Long)
```

```vb
        'This takes over ownership of the ThreadHandle.
        m_ThreadHandle = RHS
    End Property
    Friend Sub SignalThread( _
      ByVal pCritSect As Long, ByRef fInCriticalSection As
      Boolean)
        'm_ThreadDone and m_ThreadSignal must be checked/modified
        'inside a critical-section because m_ThreadDone could
        'change on some threads while we are signalling. This
        'causes m_ThreadSignal to point to invalid memory, as
        'well as other problems. The parameters to this function
        'are provided to ensure that the critical section is
        'entered only when necessary. If fInCriticalSection is
        'set, the caller must call LeaveCriticalSection on
        'pCritSect. This is left up to the caller because
        'this function is designed to be called on multiple
        'instances in a tight loop. There is no point in
        'repeatedly entering/leaving the critical section.
        If m_ThreadSignal Then
            If Not fInCriticalSection Then
                EnterCriticalSection pCritSect
                fInCriticalSection = True
            End If
            If m_ThreadDone = 0 Then
                InterlockedIncrement m_ThreadSignal
            End If
            'No point in signalling twice.
            m_ThreadSignal = 0
        End If
    End Sub
    Friend Property Set Controller(ByVal RHS As ThreadControl)
        Set m_Controller = RHS
    End Property
    Friend Sub SetData( _
      Data As Variant, ByVal fStealData As Boolean)
        If IsEmpty(Data) Or IsMissing(Data) Then Exit Sub
        If fStealData Then
            CopyMemory ByVal VarPtr(m_Data), ByVal _
                VarPtr(Data), 16
            CopyMemory ByVal VarPtr(Data), 0, 2
        ElseIf IsObject(Data) Then
```

```
        Set m_Data = Data
    Else
        m_Data = Data
    End If
End Sub
Friend Sub GetData(Data As Variant)
    'This is called only once. Always steal.
    'Before stealing, make sure there's
    'nothing lurking in Data.
    Data = Empty
    CopyMemory ByVal VarPtr(Data), ByVal VarPtr(m_Data), 16
    CopyMemory ByVal VarPtr(m_Data), 0, 2
End Sub


Private Sub Class_Terminate()
    'This shouldn't happen, but just in case.
    If m_ThreadHandle Then CloseHandle m_ThreadHandle
End Sub
```

Workers Without Cross-Thread Object Support

The first architecture works well regardless of whether you call marshaled
objects from the worker thread. However, many parts of the architecture are
overkill if you never pass an object. The second architecture uses shared memory to not only signal from one thread to the other, but also to pass input and
output data between threads. Sharing memory in this fashion may sound risky,
but is actually completely safe if you are careful never to write to the same block
of memory from both threads at the same time and only read data that you know
the other thread has finished writing. There is no STA restriction on sharing data
with other threads in the same process, just with calling methods on STA objects
from a nonnative thread.

When you scratch object support from the list of requirements, you also
scratch the need to marshal the InputData from the main object to the worker.
Marshaling the input data with the InputData parameter was the only reason
that RegisterNewThread was a Public method, which in turn was the only reason that ThreadControl was a PublicNotCreatable class. With RegisterThread
gone, there is no need to explicitly marshal and unmarshal the ThreadControl
object, so you can also eliminate the CoVeryLongAPIName functions from an

object-free architecture. Since there is no danger of a worker calling the main thread during teardown for either RegisterNewThread or another custom method, there is also no need to spin the OLE window during StopWorkerThreads.

In addition to removing all of the object support calls, the second architecture also removes the event synchronization object from the controlling thread. This event object immediately returned an error result during thread creation, but it had the nasty side effect of blocking the controlling thread. Without the Event object, you get no immediate feedback if you pass an invalid CLSID or cause another immediate problem. However, you can get error information—a number only—with the GetWorkerOutput function added to the ThreadControl object for the second architecture.

The Event object ensured that the ThreadProcData structure on the CreateWorkerThread function's stack stayed on the stack until the worker thread had gleaned all the necessary information. If you don't use the Event to block the controlling thread in CreateWorkerThread, the only other choice is to allocate the data in a memory block that lives longer than the stack. To simplify matters by using a single heap allocation, all the data required for the controlling and worker threads has been moved into ThreadData, which is now a structure instead of a class. Cross-thread interactions for this new system are shown in Figure 13.4. The memory for each ThreadData structure is allocated directly with CoTaskMemAlloc. The role of each field in the structure is shown in the following code snippet.

```
'Key for ThreadData comments
' WT:R = Read by worker thread
' CT:W = Written by controlling thread
' CT:RW = Written and read by controlling thread
' WT:RW = Written and read by controlling thread

Public Type ThreadData
    CLSID As CLSID          'CLSID to create (CT:W, WT:R)
    hr As Long              'An error code (WT:W, CT:R)
    pCritSect As Long       'Critical-section pointer
                            '(CT:W, WT:R)
    ThreadDone As Long      'Increment on completion
                            '(WT:W, CT:R)
    InputData As Variant    'Input for the worker(CT:W, WT:R)
```

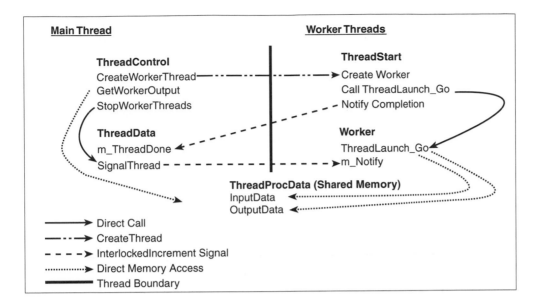

Figure 13.4. Eliminating cross-thread object support and the object creation event removes all cross-thread COM calls from the system. All the remaining cross-thread interaction occurs with direct memory access.

```
    OutputData As Variant 'Output from the worker
                            '(WT:W, CT:R)
    ThreadSignalPtr As Long 'Memory in worker (WT:W, CT:R)
    fSignaled As Boolean '*TB.ThreadSignalPtr changed (CT:RW)
    fKeepData As Boolean 'Cache output after completion
                            '(CT:RW)
    ExitCode As Long        'The threads exit code  (CT:RW)
    ThreadHandle As Long 'Handle to the current thread (CT:RW)
    Controller As ThreadControl 'Reference to controller
                            '(CT:RW)
End Type
```

The data's integrity is maintained by carefully following the read/write rules on each of the ThreadData structure's fields. The only fields that the worker class sees are InputData, OutputData, and ThreadSignalPtr. The ThreadLaunch interface has been modified and is shown in use below. The only requirement on a worker thread is that it must set ThreadSignalPtr as early as possible, and it can't put object data in the OutputData Variant.

```
Implements ThreadLaunch
Private m_Notify As Long

Public Function Go(InputData As Variant, _
    OutputData As Variant, ThreadSignalPtr As Long) As Long
    ThreadSignalPtr = VarPtr(m_Notify)
    'TODO: Process InputData while
    'regularly calling HaveBeenNotified to
    'see if the thread should terminate.
    If HaveBeenNotified Then
        'Clean up and return.
    End If
    'Fill in OutputData.
End Function
Private Function HaveBeenNotified() As Boolean
    HaveBeenNotified = m_Notify
End Function
```

You can retrieve the OutputData for the thread after the thread has completed by calling GetWorkerOutput with a special cookie value. The cookie is actually the allocated address of the ThreadData structure associated with the worker thread and is returned via the new OutputDataCookie parameter on the CreateWorkerThread function. You must also set the new fKeepOutputData parameter to True to force the controller to cache the output values. If you decide to keep the output, the ThreadData structure is transferred between the m_RunningThreads and m_FinishedThreads collections rather than destroyed. The memory is cleaned up during the call to GetWorkerOutput.

GetWorkerOutput takes the cookie value and returns the thread's ExitCode, any failing HRESULT from launching the worker class or from running ThreadLaunch_Go, and the OutputData Variant that you returned from the worker thread. With memory sharing techniques, you can also return this data directly to custom memory designated for output by passing a pointer to that memory block. The GetWorkerOutput mechanism is provided as a convenient way of retrieving data, but it is not the only way.

Listing 13.2. ThreadLaunch, ThreadStart, and Thread Data for lean-and-mean (non-object) architecture

```vb
'ThreadLaunch interface definition, ThreadLaunch.cls
'Instancing = PublicNotCreatable
Public Function Go(InputData As Variant, _
  OutputData As Variant, ThreadSignalPtr As Long) As Long
End Function
```

```vb
'ThreadControl class, ThreadControl.cls
'Instancing = Private

'Collection to hold ThreadData objects
'for each running thread
Private m_RunningThreads As Collection
'Collection to hold ThreadData objects
'for each finished thread
Private m_FinishedThreads As Collection
'Critical section to avoid conflicts
'when signalling threads
Private m_CS As CRITICAL_SECTION
'Pointer to m_CS structure
Private m_pCS As Long


'Called to create a new worker thread.
'CLSID can be obtained from a ProgID via CLSIDFromProgID
'InputData contains the data for the new thread. This
'  should never be an object reference.
'fKeepOutputData should be True if you want to retrieve
'  output data with GetWorkerOutput. This must be set for
'  a valid cookie to be returned in OutputDataCookie.
'OutputDataCookie retrieves a cookie that can be used
'  later to retrieve the exit code and output variant
'  from a completed worker thread.
'fStealInputData should be True if the data is large. If
'  this is set, Data will be Empty on return.
'fReturnThreadHandle must be explicitly set to True to
'  return the created thread handle. This handle can be
'  used for calls like SetThreadPriority and must be
'  closed with CloseHandle.
Friend Function CreateWorkerThread( _
  CLSID As CLSID, InputData As Variant, _
  Optional ByVal fKeepOutputData As Boolean = False, _
```

```vb
        Optional OutputDataCookie As Long, _
        Optional ByVal fStealInputData As Boolean = False, _
        Optional ByVal fReturnThreadHandle As Boolean = False) _
        As Long
    Dim InitThreadData As ThreadData
    Dim ThreadID As Long
    Dim ThreadHandle As Long
    Dim hProcess As Long
    Dim pThreadData As Long
        'We need to clean up sometime, this is as good a time
        'as any.
        CleanCompletedThreads
        With InitThreadData
            .CLSID = CLSID
            .pCritSect = m_pCS
            Set .Controller = Me
            If fStealInputData Then
                VBoost.MoveVariant .InputData, InputData
            'ElseIf IsObject(Data) Then
                'Don't support this case: No objects allowed
                'in data.
            Else
                .InputData = InputData
            End If
            .fKeepData = fKeepOutputData
        End With
        pThreadData = modThreadData.NewThreadData(InitThreadData)
        m_RunningThreads.Add pThreadData, CStr(pThreadData)
        If fKeepOutputData Then
            OutputDataCookie = pThreadData
        End If
        ThreadHandle = CreateThread(0, 0, _
          AddressOf ThreadProc.ThreadStart, _
          pThreadData, 0, ThreadID)
        If ThreadHandle Then
            'Turn ownership of the thread handle over to
            'the ThreadData object.
            modThreadData.ThreadHandle(pThreadData) = ThreadHandle
            If fReturnThreadHandle Then
                hProcess = GetCurrentProcess
                DuplicateHandle hProcess, ThreadHandle, hProcess, _
                  CreateWorkerThread
```

```
        End If
    End If
End Function


'Call StopWorkerThreads to signal all worker threads
'and spin until they terminate.
Friend Sub StopWorkerThreads()
    modThreadData.StopThreads _
        m_RunningThreads, m_FinishedThreads, m_pCS
End Sub


'Releases ThreadData objects for all threads
'that are completed. Cleaning happens automatically
'when you call SignalWorkerThreads, StopWorkerThreads,
'and GetWorkerOutput.
Friend Sub CleanCompletedThreads( _
  Optional ByVal fTossCompletedData As Boolean = False)
Dim Iter As Variant
    modThreadData.CleanThreads _
        m_RunningThreads, m_FinishedThreads
    If fTossCompletedData Then
        With m_FinishedThreads
            Do While .Count
                modThreadData.DestroyThreadData .Item(1)
                .Remove 1
            Loop
        End With
    End If
End Sub

'Call to tell all running worker threads to
'terminate. If the thread hasn't set its
'ThreadSignalPtr yet, it can't be signaled.
'Unlike StopWorkerThreads, this does not block
'while the workers actually terminate.
'StopWorkerThreads must be called by the owner
'of this class before the ThreadControl instance
'is released.
Friend Sub SignalWorkerThreads()
    modThreadData.SignalThreads m_RunningThreads, _
        m_FinishedThreads, m_pCS
End Sub
```

```vb
'Call to retrieve the data and exit code from
'a worker thread launched with CreateWorkerThread.
'This returns False if the thread has not
'yet completed. You get one call to GetWorkerOutput
'for each cookie.
Friend Function GetWorkerOutput( _
  ByVal OutputDataCookie As Long, hr As Long, _
  ExitCode As Long, OutputData As Variant) As Boolean
Dim DataKey As String
    CleanCompletedThreads
    DataKey = CStr(OutputDataCookie)
    On Error Resume Next
    m_FinishedThreads.Item DataKey
    If Err Then
        On Error GoTo 0
        Exit Function
    End If
    On Error GoTo 0
    modThreadData.GetOutputData _
      OutputDataCookie, hr, ExitCode, OutputData
    modThreadData.DestroyThreadData OutputDataCookie
    m_FinishedThreads.Remove DataKey
    GetWorkerOutput = True
End Function


Private Sub Class_Initialize()
    Set m_RunningThreads = New Collection
    Set m_FinishedThreads = New Collection
    m_pCS = VarPtr(m_CS)
    InitializeCriticalSection m_pCS
End Sub


Private Sub Class_Terminate()
    'Just in case: This generally only cleans completed data.
    CleanCompletedThreads True
    If m_pCS Then DeleteCriticalSection m_pCS
End Sub


'ThreadStart procedure, ThreadProc.bas
'ThreadData structure defined earlier
Public Function ThreadStart(ThreadData As ThreadData) As Long
```

```vb
Dim pUnk As IUnknown
Dim TL As ThreadLaunch
Dim IID_IUnknown As VBGUID
    'Extreme care must be taken in this function to
    'run normal VB code until an object has been
    'created on this thread by VB.
    With ThreadData
        .hr = CoInitialize(0)
        If .hr And FailBit Then
            .ThreadDone = 1
            Exit Function
        End If
        With IID_IUnknown
            .Data4(0) = &HC0
            .Data4(7) = &H46
        End With
        .hr = CoCreateInstance(.CLSID, Nothing, _
          CLSCTX_INPROC_SERVER, IID_IUnknown, pUnk)
        If .hr And FailBit Then
            .ThreadDone = 1
            CoUninitialize
            Exit Function
        End If


        'If we've made it this far, we can start using
        'normal VB calls because we have an initialized
        'object on this thread.
        On Error Resume Next
        Set TL = pUnk
        Set pUnk = Nothing
        If Err Then
            .hr = Err
            .ThreadDone = 1
            CoUninitialize
            Exit Function
        End If


        'Launch the background thread and wait for it to
        'finish.
        ThreadStart = TL.Go( _
          .InputData, .OutputData, .ThreadSignalPtr)
```

```
        .hr = Err

        'Tell the controlling thread that this thread is done.
        'Note that the critical section coordinates between
        'ThreadSignalPtr and ThreadDone. ThreadSignalPtr isn't
        'set before TL.Go, so we don't need a critical
        'section to increment ThreadDone until now.
        EnterCriticalSection .pCritSect
        .ThreadDone = 1
        LeaveCriticalSection .pCritSect

        'Release TL after the critical section. This
        'prevents ThreadData.SignalThread from
        'signalling a pointer to released memory.
        Set TL = Nothing
    End With
    CoUninitialize
End Function
```

```
'modThreadData module, in ThreadData.bas
Private Type OwnedThreadData
    Owner As ArrayOwner
    pSA() As ThreadData
End Type
Private m_Data As OwnedThreadData

'Allocate a ThreadData object on the heap and transfer the
'bits from the incoming structure.
Public Function NewThreadData(InitData As ThreadData) As Long
    With m_Data
        If .Owner.SA.cDims = 0 Then
            InitArrayOwner .Owner, LenB(.pSA(0)), _
                FADF_AUTO Or FADF_FIXEDSIZE, False
        End If
        NewThreadData = CoTaskMemAlloc(LenB(.pSA(0)))
        If NewThreadData = 0 Then Err.Raise 7 'Out of memory
        CopyMemory ByVal NewThreadData, _
          InitData.CLSID, LenB(.pSA(0))
        ZeroMemory InitData.CLSID, LenB(.pSA(0))
    End With
End Function
```

```vb
Public Sub DestroyThreadData(ByVal pThreadData As Long)
    With m_Data
        .Owner.SA.pvData = pThreadData
        With .pSA(0)
            'This shouldn't happen, but a safety valve
            'is good.
            If .ThreadHandle Then CloseHandle .ThreadHandle
        End With
        'Frees any leftover Variant information and
        'the controller.
        Erase .pSA
    End With
    CoTaskMemFree pThreadData
End Sub


Public Property Let ThreadHandle( _
  ByVal pThreadData As Long, ByVal RHS As Long)
    'This takes over ownership of the ThreadHandle.
    With m_Data
        .Owner.SA.pvData = pThreadData
        .pSA(0).ThreadHandle = RHS
    End With
End Property


Public Sub GetOutputData(ByVal pThreadData As Long, _
  hr As Long, ExitCode As Long, OutputData As Variant)
    With m_Data
        .Owner.SA.pvData = pThreadData
        With .pSA(0)
            VBoost.MoveVariant OutputData, .OutputData
            ExitCode = .ExitCode
            hr = .hr
        End With
    End With
End Sub


Private Function ThreadCompleted( _
  ThreadData As ThreadData) As Boolean
Dim ExitCode As Long
    With ThreadData
        'See comments in first listing.
```

```
                    ThreadCompleted = .ThreadDone
                If ThreadCompleted Then
                    If .ThreadHandle Then
                        If GetExitCodeThread( _
                            .ThreadHandle, ExitCode) Then
                            If ExitCode = STILL_ACTIVE Then
                                ThreadCompleted = False
                                Exit Function
                            End If
                        End If
                        CloseHandle .ThreadHandle
                        .ThreadHandle = 0
                        .InputData = Empty
                        .ExitCode = ExitCode
                    End If
                End If
            End With
        End Function


        Private Sub SignalThread(ThreadData As ThreadData, _
            ByRef fUnregistered As Boolean, _
            ByVal pCritSect As Long, _
            ByRef fInCriticalSection As Boolean)
            'See comments in first listing.
            With ThreadData
                If Not .fSignaled Then
                    If .ThreadSignalPtr Then
                        If Not fInCriticalSection Then
                            EnterCriticalSection pCritSect
                            fInCriticalSection = True
                        End If
                        If .ThreadDone = 0 Then
                            InterlockedIncrement .ThreadSignalPtr
                        End If
                        'No point in signalling twice.
                        .fSignaled = True
                    Else
                        'The worker hasn't set ThreadSignalPtr.
                        fUnregistered = True
                    End If
                End If
```

```vb
        End With
End Sub


Public Sub StopThreads(RunningThreads As Collection, _
    FinishedThreads As Collection, ByVal pCritSect As Long)
Dim fInCriticalSection As Boolean
Dim fSignal As Boolean
Dim fUnregistered As Boolean
Dim Iter As Variant
Dim pThreadData As Long
Dim DataKey As String
    fSignal = True
    With m_Data
        Do
            fUnregistered = False
            For Each Iter In RunningThreads
                pThreadData = Iter
                .Owner.SA.pvData = pThreadData
                If ThreadCompleted(.pSA(0)) Then
                    DataKey = CStr(pThreadData)
                    RunningThreads.Remove DataKey
                    If .pSA(0).fKeepData Then
                        Set .pSA(0).Controller = Nothing
                        FinishedThreads.Add pThreadData, _
                          DataKey
                    Else
                        'Don't call DestroyThreadData while
                        '.pSA(0) is a current With context.
                        DestroyThreadData pThreadData
                    End If
                    DataKey = vbNullString
                ElseIf fSignal Then
                    SignalThread .pSA(0), fUnregistered, _
                      pCritSect, fInCriticalSection
                End If
            Next
            If fInCriticalSection Then
                LeaveCriticalSection pCritSect
                fInCriticalSection = False
            Else
                'We can turn this off indefinitely if
```

```vb
                             'fUnregistered is False because all threads
                             'will have been signaled at this point.
                             fSignal = fUnregistered
                    End If
                    If RunningThreads.Count = 0 Then Exit Do
                    'Give up the rest of our time slice.
                    Sleep 0
           Loop
       End With
End Sub


Public Sub CleanThreads(RunningThreads As Collection, _
    FinishedThreads As Collection)
Dim pThreadData As Long
Dim Iter As Variant
Dim DataKey As String
       With m_Data
           For Each Iter In RunningThreads
               pThreadData = Iter
               .Owner.SA.pvData = pThreadData
               If ThreadCompleted(.pSA(0)) Then
                   DataKey = CStr(pThreadData)
                   RunningThreads.Remove DataKey
                   If .pSA(0).fKeepData Then
                       Set .pSA(0).Controller = Nothing
                       FinishedThreads.Add pThreadData, DataKey
                   Else
                       'Don't call DestroyThreadData while
                       '.pSA(0) is a current With context.
                       DestroyThreadData pThreadData
                   End If
                   DataKey = vbNullString
               End If
           Next
       End With
End Sub


Public Sub SignalThreads(RunningThreads As Collection, _
    FinishedThreads As Collection, ByVal pCritSect As Long)
Dim pThreadData As Long
Dim Iter As Variant
```

```
Dim fInCriticalSection As Boolean
Dim fUnregistered As Boolean  'Dummy
Dim DataKey As String
    With m_Data
        For Each Iter In RunningThreads
            pThreadData = Iter
            .Owner.SA.pvData = pThreadData
            If ThreadCompleted(.pSA(0)) Then
                DataKey = CStr(pThreadData)
                RunningThreads.Remove DataKey
                If .pSA(0).fKeepData Then
                    Set .pSA(0).Controller = Nothing
                    FinishedThreads.Add pThreadData, DataKey
                Else
                    'Don't call DestroyThreadData while
                    '.pSA(0) is a current With context.
                    DestroyThreadData pThreadData
                End If
                DataKey = vbNullString
            Else
                SignalThread .pSA(0), fUnregistered, _
                    pCritSect, fInCriticalSection
            End If
        Next
        If fInCriticalSection Then _
            LeaveCriticalSection pCritSect
    End With
End Sub
```

Worker Thread Recycling

The most expensive aspect of worker threads is their creation and destruction. Creating the thread, initializing COM, and initializing the VB thread and project data are not free. The thread initialization overhead is insignificant if you create worker threads that run long background computations. However, if you run many relatively short operations, the overhead becomes more significant.

This final variation on the threading architecture simply puts threads to sleep when they are done working rather than letting them terminate. While the worker is sleeping, the controlling thread returns all the ThreadData members to an initialized state, provides new input data, and then wakes the thread in response to a new request for a worker thread. The thread recycling code is similar to that of the previous architecture, but there are some fundamental changes.

The first change is the addition of a Win32 event object to each ThreadData structure. When the worker thread has finished processing its data, it calls Wait-ForSingleObject on ThreadData's event object, which is created as a nonsignaled synchronization object. The worker thread is then in a suspended state until the controlling thread calls PulseEvent to wake it. When the worker thread wakes up, it checks to see if the ThreadDone field in ThreadData is still set. If Thread-Done is True, ThreadStart knows to exit ThreadStart and finish the thread.

A worker always blocks before it exits, so the critical section used in the earlier architectures is no longer needed to guarantee the validity of ThreadSignalPtr as the worker unwinds. The worker also makes no efforts to clean the Worker class. You have to clean up any data, such as the m_Notify member, between sessions.

The ThreadControl functions for this architecture are the same as those for the second architecture. This poses a small dilemma in that the OutputData-Cookie returned by the object can no longer serve as a pointer to a ThreadData object because ThreadData is also used by the worker thread, which may be busy running another call when other code gets around to calling GetWorker-Output. The solution is to create a new structure, called ThreadDataOuput, that holds the hr, ExitCode, and OutputData fields previously found in the Thread-Data structure. A single ThreadData object can own multiple ThreadDataOutput objects over its lifetime. The OutputDataCookie returned by CreateWorkerThread is now a pointer to a ThreadDataOutput structure rather than a pointer to a complete ThreadData structure.

Listing 13.3.   ThreadControl, ThreadStart, and ThreadData for recycling architecture

```
'ThreadControl class, in ThreadControl.cls
Private m_RunningThreads As Collection
Private m_FinishedThreads As Collection


'Same comments as previous architecture
Friend Function CreateWorkerThread( _
  CLSID As CLSID, InputData As Variant, _
```

```vb
        Optional ByVal fKeepOutputData As Boolean = False, _
        Optional OutputDataCookie As Long, _
        Optional ByVal fStealInputData As Boolean = False, _
        Optional ByVal fReturnThreadHandle As Boolean = False) _
        As Long
Dim InitThreadData As ThreadData
Dim ThreadID As Long
Dim ThreadHandle As Long
Dim hProcess As Long
Dim pThreadData As Long
Dim pThreadDataOutput As Long
Dim pIdleThreadData As Long
    pIdleThreadData = modThreadData.CleanThreads( _
        m_RunningThreads, m_FinishedThreads)
    With InitThreadData
        .CLSID = CLSID
        Set .Controller = Me
        If fStealInputData Then
            VBoost.MoveVariant .InputData, InputData
        Else
            .InputData = InputData
        End If
        .fKeepData = fKeepOutputData
    End With
    If pIdleThreadData Then
        ThreadHandle = modThreadData.WakeSleepingThread( _
            pIdleThreadData, InitThreadData, pThreadDataOutput)
    Else
        pThreadData = modThreadData.NewThreadData( _
            InitThreadData, pThreadDataOutput)
        m_RunningThreads.Add pThreadData, CStr(pThreadData)
        ThreadHandle = CreateThread(0, 0, _
            AddressOf ThreadProc.ThreadStart, _
            pThreadData, 0, ThreadID)
        If ThreadHandle Then
            'Turn ownership of the thread handle over to
            'the ThreadData object.
            modThreadData.ThreadHandle(pThreadData) = _
                ThreadHandle
        End If
    End If
```

```
            If fKeepOutputData Then
                OutputDataCookie = pThreadDataOutput
            End If
            If ThreadHandle Then
                If fReturnThreadHandle Then
                    hProcess = GetCurrentProcess
                    DuplicateHandle hProcess, ThreadHandle, _
                        hProcess, CreateWorkerThread
                End If
            End If
        End Function
```

```
'Other functions in ThreadControl are the same except that
'there is no critical section, and the OutputData cookies
'are destroyed with modThreadData.DestroyThreadDataOutput
'instead of modThreadData.DestroyThreadData.
```

```
'ThreadStart procedure, ThreadProc.bas
Public Type ThreadDataOutput
    hr As Long                 'An error code (WT:W, CT:R)
                               '(keep first)
    ExitCode As Long           'The thread's exit code  (CT:RW)
    OutputData As Variant      'Output from the worker (WT:W, CT:R)
End Type
Public Type ThreadData
    CLSID As CLSID             'CLSID to create (CT:W, WT:R)
    ThreadDone As Long         'Increment on completion (WT:W, CT:R)
    InputData As Variant       'Input for the worker(CT:W, WT:R)
    ThreadSignalPtr As Long    'Memory in worker (WT:W, CT:R)
    fSignaled As Boolean       '*TB.ThreadSignalPtr changed (CT:RW)
    fKeepData As Boolean       'Cache output after completion (CT:RW)
    ThreadHandle As Long       'Handle to the current thread (CT:RW)
    Controller As ThreadControl 'Reference to controller
                                        '(CT:RW)
    pRecycleEvent As Long      'Synchronization handle (CT:RW)
    pOutput As Long            'ThreadDataOutput pointer
                               '(CT:RW, WT:R)
End Type
Private Const FailBit As Long = &H80000000
Public Function ThreadStart(ThreadData As ThreadData) As Long
Dim pUnk As IUnknown
```

```vb
Dim TL As ThreadLaunch
Dim IID_IUnknown As VBGUID
Dim SA1D As SafeArray1d
Dim pOutputData() As ThreadDataOutput
Dim hr As Long
    With ThreadData
        hr = CoInitialize(0)
        If hr And FailBit Then
            .ThreadDone = 1
            CopyMemory .pOutput, hr, 4
            Exit Function
        End If
        With IID_IUnknown
            .Data4(0) = &HC0
            .Data4(7) = &H46
        End With
        hr = CoCreateInstance(.CLSID, Nothing, _
          CLSCTX_INPROC_SERVER, IID_IUnknown, pUnk)
        If hr And FailBit Then
            .ThreadDone = 1
            CopyMemory .pOutput, hr, 4
            CoUninitialize
            Exit Function
        End If

        On Error Resume Next
        Set TL = pUnk
        Set pUnk = Nothing
        If Err Then
            hr = Err
            CopyMemory .pOutput, hr, 4
            .ThreadDone = 1
            CoUninitialize
            Exit Function
        End If

        'Launch the background thread and wait for it to
        'finish.
        With SA1D
            .cDims = 1
            .cElements = 1
```

```
                      .cbElements = LenB(pOutputData(0))
              End With
              CopyMemory ByVal VarPtrArray(pOutputData), _
                  VarPtr(SA1D), 4
      Recycle:
              SA1D.pvData = .pOutput
              With pOutputData(0)
                  .ExitCode = TL.Go(ThreadData.InputData, _
                      .OutputData, ThreadData.ThreadSignalPtr)
                  .hr = Err
              End With

              'Flag this pass as done.
              ThreadData.ThreadDone = 1

              'Wait until the event is pulsed to enable us to
              'recycle our data. If .ThreadDone is still set
              'after we clear this event, we should terminate.
              WaitForSingleObject .pRecycleEvent, INFINITE
              If .ThreadDone = 0 Then GoTo Recycle

              'Use VarPtrArray before releasing TL so that
              'the runtime is still with us.
              ZeroMemory ByVal VarPtrArray(pOutputData), 4

              Set TL = Nothing
          End With
          CoUninitialize
      End Function
```

```
  'modThreadData module, in ThreadData.Bas
  Private Type OwnedThreadData
      Owner As ArrayOwner
      pSA() As ThreadData
  End Type
  Private Type OwnedThreadDataOutput
      Owner As ArrayOwner
      pSA() As ThreadDataOutput
  End Type
  Private m_Data As OwnedThreadData
```

```vb
Private m_DataOutput As OwnedThreadDataOutput

'Allocate a ThreadData object on the heap and transfer the
'bits from the incoming structure.
Public Function NewThreadData(InitData As ThreadData, _
  pThreadDataOutput As Long) As Long
Dim TDO As ThreadDataOutput 'Dummy for LenB
    With m_Data
        If .Owner.SA.cDims = 0 Then
            'Establish flags so we can call Erase
            'to destroy data.
            InitArrayOwner .Owner, LenB(.pSA(0)), _
                FADF_AUTO Or FADF_FIXEDSIZE, False
            With m_DataOutput
                'fFeatures of 0 is OK because we
                'never Erase ThreadDataOutput.
                InitArrayOwner _
                    .Owner, LenB(.pSA(0)), 0, False
            End With
        End If
    End With
    With InitData
        .pRecycleEvent = CreateEvent(0, 0, 0, vbNullString)
        If .pRecycleEvent = 0 Then _
          Err.Raise &H80070000 + Err.LastDLLError

        On Error GoTo Error
        .pOutput = CoTaskMemAlloc(LenB(TDO))
        If .pOutput = 0 Then Err.Raise 7 'Out of memory
        pThreadDataOutput = .pOutput
        ZeroMemory ByVal .pOutput, LenB(TDO)

        NewThreadData = CoTaskMemAlloc(LenB(InitData))
        If NewThreadData = 0 Then Err.Raise 7 'Out of memory

        CopyMemory ByVal NewThreadData, .CLSID, LenB(InitData)
        ZeroMemory .CLSID, LenB(InitData)
    End With
    Exit Function
Error:
```

```
        With InitData
            If .pRecycleEvent Then CloseHandle .pRecycleEvent
            If .pOutput Then CoTaskMemFree .pOutput
        End With
        With Err
            .Raise .Number
        End With
    End Function


    'A new function to reinitialize and pulse a sleeping thread.
    Public Function WakeSleepingThread( _
        ByVal pThreadData As Long, InitData As ThreadData, _
        pThreadDataOutput As Long) As Long
    Dim TDO As ThreadDataOutput 'Dummy for LenB
        pThreadDataOutput = CoTaskMemAlloc(LenB(TDO))
        If pThreadDataOutput = 0 Then Err.Raise 7
        ZeroMemory ByVal pThreadDataOutput, LenB(TDO)
        With m_Data
            .Owner.SA.pvData = pThreadData
            With .pSA(0)
                .fSignaled = False
                .ThreadDone = 0
                .fKeepData = InitData.fKeepData
                VBoost.MoveVariant .InputData, InitData.InputData
                Set .Controller = InitData.Controller
                .pOutput = pThreadDataOutput
                PulseEvent .pRecycleEvent
            End With
        End With
    End Function


    Public Sub DestroyThreadData(ByVal pThreadData As Long)
        With m_Data
            .Owner.SA.pvData = pThreadData
            With .pSA(0)
                'This shouldn't happen, but a safety valve is
                'good.
                If .ThreadHandle Then CloseHandle .ThreadHandle
                'Clean up the event handle: This is expected.
                If .pRecycleEvent Then CloseHandle .pRecycleEvent
```

```vb
            'Clean any remaining ThreadDataOutput.
            If .pOutput Then DestroyThreadDataOutput .pOutput
        End With
        'Frees any leftover Variant information and
        'the controller.
        Erase .pSA
    End With
    CoTaskMemFree pThreadData
End Sub


Public Sub DestroyThreadDataOutput( _
  ByVal pThreadDataOutput As Long)
    With m_DataOutput
        .Owner.SA.pvData = pThreadDataOutput
        .pSA(0).OutputData = Empty
    End With
    CoTaskMemFree pThreadDataOutput
End Sub


Public Property Let ThreadHandle( _
  ByVal pThreadData As Long, ByVal RHS As Long)
    With m_Data
        .Owner.SA.pvData = pThreadData
        .pSA(0).ThreadHandle = RHS
    End With
End Property


Public Sub GetOutputData(ByVal pThreadDataOutput As Long, _
  hr As Long, ExitCode As Long, OutputData As Variant)
    With m_DataOutput
        .Owner.SA.pvData = pThreadDataOutput
        With .pSA(0)
            VBoost.MoveVariant OutputData, .OutputData
            ExitCode = .ExitCode
            hr = .hr
        End With
    End With
End Sub


Private Function ThreadCompleted( _
  ThreadData As ThreadData) As Boolean
```

```vb
    Dim ExitCode As Long
        With ThreadData
            ThreadCompleted = .ThreadDone
            If ThreadCompleted Then
                If .ThreadHandle Then
                    If GetExitCodeThread( _
                        .ThreadHandle, ExitCode) Then
                        If ExitCode = STILL_ACTIVE Then
                            'Wake the thread without clearing
                            'ThreadDone, forcing it to terminate.
                            PulseEvent .pRecycleEvent
                            ThreadCompleted = False
                            Exit Function
                        End If
                    End If
                    CloseHandle .ThreadHandle
                    .ThreadHandle = 0
                End If
            End If
        End With
    End Function


    Private Sub SignalThread(ThreadData As ThreadData, _
        ByRef fUnregistered As Boolean, ByRef fSignaled As Boolean)
        With ThreadData
            If Not .fSignaled Then
                If .ThreadSignalPtr Then
                    fSignaled = True
                    If :ThreadDone = 0 Then
                        InterlockedIncrement .ThreadSignalPtr
                    End If
                    'No point in signalling twice.
                    .fSignaled = True
                Else
                    'The worker hasn't set ThreadSignalPtr.
                    fUnregistered = True
                End If
            End If
        End With
    End Sub
```

```vb
Public Sub StopThreads(RunningThreads As Collection, _
  FinishedThreads As Collection)
Dim fSignal As Boolean
Dim fSignaled As Boolean
Dim fUnregistered As Boolean
Dim Iter As Variant
Dim pThreadData As Long
    fSignal = True
    With m_Data
        Do
            fUnregistered = False
            fSignaled = False
            For Each Iter In RunningThreads
                pThreadData = Iter
                .Owner.SA.pvData = pThreadData
                If ThreadCompleted(.pSA(0)) Then
                    RunningThreads.Remove CStr(pThreadData)
                    With .pSA(0)
                        If .fKeepData Then
                            FinishedThreads.Add .pOutput, _
                              CStr(.pOutput)
                            .pOutput = 0
                        End If
                    End With
                    DestroyThreadData pThreadData
                ElseIf fSignal Then
                  SignalThread .pSA(0), fUnregistered, _
                    fSignaled
                End If
            Next
            If Not fSignaled Then
                'We can turn this off indefinitely if
                'fUnregistered is False because all threads
                'will have been signaled at this point.
                fSignal = fUnregistered
            End If
            If RunningThreads.Count = 0 Then Exit Do
            'Give up the rest of our time slice.
            Sleep 0
        Loop
    End With
End Sub
```

```vb
Public Function CleanThreads(RunningThreads As Collection, _
    FinishedThreads As Collection) As Long
Dim pThreadData As Long
Dim Iter As Variant
Dim DataKey As String
    With m_Data
        For Each Iter In RunningThreads
            pThreadData = Iter
            .Owner.SA.pvData = pThreadData
            With .pSA(0)
                If .ThreadDone And CBool(.pOutput) Then
                    Set .Controller = Nothing
                    If .fKeepData Then
                        FinishedThreads.Add .pOutput, _
                            CStr(.pOutput)
                    Else
                        DestroyThreadDataOutput .pOutput
                    End If
                    'Clear most everything, but leave
                    'ThreadDone so signalling the sleeping
                    'thread without providing new data
                    'will cause it to terminate instead of
                    'loop.
                    .pOutput = 0
                    .fKeepData = False
                    .fSignaled = True
                    .ThreadSignalPtr = 0
                    .InputData = Empty
                    If CleanThreads = 0 Then
                        CleanThreads = pThreadData
                    End If
                ElseIf CleanThreads = 0 Then
                    If .pOutput = 0 Then
                        CleanThreads = pThreadData
                    End If
                End If
            End With
        Next
    End With
End Function
```

```
Public Sub SignalThreads(RunningThreads As Collection, _
  FinishedThreads As Collection)
Dim pThreadData As Long
Dim Iter As Variant
Dim fUnregistered As Boolean  'Dummy
Dim fSignaled As Boolean  'Dummy
    With m_Data
        For Each Iter In RunningThreads
            pThreadData = Iter
            .Owner.SA.pvData = pThreadData
            SignalThread .pSA(0), fUnregistered, fSignaled
        Next
    End With
End Sub
```

Modeless Forms and Worker Threads

VB5 added the capability of showing modeless (also called non-modal) forms in ActiveX DLLs. In reality, support for modeless forms also had to be added to a variety of hosts of ActiveX DLLs. An executable that loads an ActiveX DLL must cooperate with the DLL by exposing its message loop for use by the form. This negotiation process is nontrivial and completely undocumented (except as part of the licensed VBA host SDK).

If you create a worker thread in a DLL, you can't show a modeless form because there is no cooperative message loop above you on the worker thread. You must show any forms from a DLL modally. This isn't actually as bad as it sounds because modality applies only to the current thread, not the entire application. Two modal forms on different threads actually appear to be modeless with respect to each other.

Now I have to convey some bad news. There is a nasty bug in the runtime for VB6 SP3 and earlier: The data behind the App.NonModalAllowed flag is corrupted by worker threads. This flag *should* be stored in TLS, but it is actually stored in global data. The flag assumes the modality setting of the latest thread to have been created. The result is that a standard or ActiveX EXE can't show a new modeless form after you create a worker thread. This bug has nothing to do with how the thread is created; you can also see the problem if you create new threads from C++ and the new threads use VB DLL-created objects.

I know of one workaround for this problem, but it requires a workaround in the calling EXE, not the DLL. This puts you in the highly unfortunate situation of fixing a DLL bug in each EXE that uses the DLL. To enable a modeless form again, you must create a thread that does allow modeless forms to get the global setting back where it should be. Explicit thread-creation requires an ActiveX EXE, so you can't do this in a Standard EXE. Here are the steps.

1. Turn the Standard EXE into an ActiveX EXE.

2. In Project|Properties, set the Startup Object to Sub Main and the Threading Model to Thread per Object.

3. Use the ThreadCheck class shown earlier to recognize the first thread.

4. Add a MultiUse class called "Dummy" to the ActiveX EXE.

5. Add the following ShowNonModal procedure to a BAS file (adjust the ProgID as appropriate).

```
Public Sub ShowNonModal(ByVal Form As Form)
    If Not App.NonModalAllowed Then
        CreateObject "MyApp.Dummy"
    End If
    Form.Show
End Sub
```

6. You can now call ShowNonModal New Form1 instead of using the Show method directly.

You will see two limitations when you switch from a Standard EXE to a Thread-per-Object ActiveX EXE. First, you can no longer have MDI Forms in your project. There is no workaround for this limitation. Second, you can't build UserControls into the project. There *is* a workaround for this limitation: Use a companion ActiveX OCX project. You have some work to do if you have CTL files in your project and you need to switch the EXE type. I'd recommend that you first create the companion OCX, then create a dummy project with a form that contains one of each type of control. Make sure binary compatibility is set for the OCX. Now, hand-edit any FRM in the original project to switch the type of the control, using the dummy FRM file as a reference for the control names and guids. This is a hassle, but is much easier in the long run than deleting and resetting each control individually. Now for the good news: The App. NonModalAllowed bug is fixed in the SP4 release of msvbvm60.Dll.

Chapter 14

Strings in VB

I've never encountered a VB program that didn't use strings. After all, programs are designed to interact with users or to produce some other output, both of which invariably require text. As more programs are written for the Internet, strings play an even bigger role in the code we write. HTML, XML, and other Internet formats are very string-intensive, and they often require the generation of large strings. This makes the performance of String operations central to the performance of your application. This chapter looks at how VB defines and interacts with strings with the intent of increasing string performance. Although I will introduce several useful helper classes, this chapter is not an attempt to provide a complete library of string functions. Rather, this chapter will give you the tools to write your own highly optimized string routines.

You need to understand the underlying structure of a VB String before you can perform useful operations on it. A String in VB is equivalent to a BSTR type in C or C++. BSTR in turn is defined as a pointer to an unsigned short. In practice, a

BSTR is a length-prefixed UNICODE string with a built-in NULL terminator that is generally allocated and freed by OLE Automation (OleAut32.Dll). Let's break that statement down a bit. A *length-prefix* is extra memory that is allocated with every string to store its length. This size is a long value stored at the location four bytes before the value returned as the string pointer. The value is equivalent to the number of bytes in the string, not including the four bytes for the length prefix and the two bytes for the NULL termination character. After the length prefix comes a series of UNICODE characters, each of which take two bytes. A NULL UNICODE character (two 0 bytes) finishes the BSTR. The trailing NULL enables a BSTR to be used wherever a NULL-terminated string is called for. The memory layout of the string "BSTR" is shown in Figure 14.1.

The length-prefix enables a BSTR to do several things that a normal NULL-terminated string cannot. First, the length-prefix allows the String to be duplicated without any additional information. This is especially important when strings are used in public interfaces that are used across thread or process boundaries. Second, the length-prefix allows the BSTR to contain embedded NULL characters. Third, the length of a BSTR is very easy to calculate. The Len function, which returns the number of characters in a string, occupies a whopping total of six assembly instructions in the VB runtime. LenB is even smaller, coming in at five instructions (LenB doesn't need to divide the byte count by two to get the character count). This is why, comparing Len(string) or LenB(string) with 0 is the preferred mechanism for determining whether a string contains data. Comparing to "" or vbNullString generates a string-comparison call, which is much more expensive than simply reading the length from memory.

```
Dim strTest As String
'Worst test
```

| 8 | 0 | 66 | 83 | 84 | 82 | 0 |

Figure 14.1. **The memory layout of a String containing the word BSTR. The String variable is a pointer to the 3rd 2-byte slot, which holds a B (66).**

ADVANCED VISUAL BASIC 6

```
If strTest = "" Then Beep
'Not much better
If strTest = vbNullString Then Beep
'Very good
If Len(strTest) = 0 Then Beep
'Best
If LenB(strTest) = 0 Then Beep
```

The comparison with "" is considered worse that the comparison with vbNullString because "" occupies six bytes of memory; vbNullString is simply a NULL string-pointer. The two types are functionally equivalent in VB, but vbNull-String is preferred because it doesn't require any memory. You should always use vbNullString instead of "" to clear a string variable. You can occasionally get in trouble with assorted API calls by passing a true NULL instead of an empty string. If you must use an API call that actually requires a string buffer instead of NULL, you should use the StrPtr function to check an incoming string for 0 and replace the zero with "". StrPtr is the only way to differentiate between vbNull-String and "".

```
If StrPtr(strData) = 0 Then strData = ""
```

Varieties of the term *null* cause a great deal of confusion because in C, "NULL" always means the value 0. VB has five built-in keywords and constants that include null. First off, VB's *Null* keyword indicates a Variant with no valid data. The VarType of such a Variant is *vbNull,* which has a value of 1. The runtime function *IsNull* checks a Variant for this VarType. It is very common for programmers new to VB to incorrectly use vbNull in place of 0, Nothing, vbNull-String, or other concepts. The other null variants are both strings. vbNullString is a string constant with value 0, and vbNullChar is a string constant with a length of 1 that contains a single NULL character.

The fully capitalized form of NULL does not appear in VB. When you see this form of NULL, give it the meaning it has in C, which is 0. A NULL character is a character with the numeric value 0, and a NULL-terminated string is a string of characters that ends in a NULL character.

UNICODE Conversions

A BSTR is a UNICODE beast. The UNICODE string standard uses two bytes for every character, whereas the ANSI standard generally uses one byte per character. The fundamental difference between ANSI and UNICODE is that a code page is required to interpret an ANSI string, so the same bytes form a different string on a Cyrillic code page and on a western-European code page. The UNICODE standard maps the code pages into a single character range; you needn't specify a code page in order to uniquely identify a UNICODE character.

Another difference with UNICODE is that all the characters have the same width. Some ANSI code-pages use certain byte values as *lead bytes.* The lead byte and the trail byte(s) that follow determine the actual character. So although ANSI characters may consist of only one byte, they may also consist of more than one byte. ANSI is sometimes called the "multibyte character set," and UNICODE is sometimes called "wide characters." You can see this in the Win32 API set, which has MultiByteToWideChar and WideCharToMultiByte functions. Although it stores strings in UNICODE, VB often converts them to ANSI and vice-versa. Any automatic conversion always uses the code page of the current system.

> Writing a truly globalized application (that is, an app that runs in multiple languages regardless of the language of the machine's operating system) is a non-trivial problem. The heart of the problem is that globalization requires that you have explicit control of the code page used for any ANSI/UNICODE conversion. You can generally work around this in the code's language elements by performing explicit conversions, but VB's Forms package uses ANSI internally and offers no mechanism for specifying the code page used for string conversions. This lack of explicit code-page control means that even if you have a language-compatible font installed and loaded, you won't be able to assign text to a Label or TextBox control without jumping through some nasty hoops. Refer to Michael Kaplan's body of work for more information on using VB6 to create globalized applications.[1]

---

[1] *Black Belt Programming: Solve Cross-Codepage Problems* in the August 1999 edition of *Visual Basic Programmer's Journal* (http://www.vbpj.com). You can find additional information at http://www.trigeminal.com.

Implicit string conversion is very common in VB, and you often have no idea it has actually happened. However, string conversion is expensive and you should avoid it when possible. There are some simple steps you can take to minimize the number of string conversions. The first step is to use the W versions of the Asc and Chr$ functions. Asc must first convert a native UNICODE string into ANSI before it returns the value; AscW simply reads the number currently stored in the string. Similarly, Chr$ must convert the number you give it into a UNICODE number. The result is that AscW and ChrW$ are much faster than Asc and Chr$.

You should always use the $ versions of string functions whenever they are available. If a $ version of a function is available, then its non-$ counterpart actually returns a Variant rather than a String. Although the VB compiler is smart enough to avoid duplicating the string when assigning the return value of a Variant function to a String variable, a significant amount of overhead and code generation is involved in using the non-$ functions. If you think the extra character is too much trouble, one look at the generated code will cure your laziness. Search for $ in the Object Browser to get a list of the $ functions.

The best-known place where VB performs automatic ANSI/UNICODE conversion is when you send String or fixed-length string variables to Declare functions. To seamlessly handle an external world that is often ANSI from within an internal world that is always UNICODE, the VB brain trust decided that all API calls would be considered ANSI. When you *want* an ANSI API call, this situation is wonderful from a coding perspective because you don't have to do any work to make an ANSI API call from VB. But from a performance perspective, you add string-conversion overhead at runtime. If you write an application exclusively for Windows NT or Windows 2000, which have full UNICODE API support, string conversions for API calls are a waste.

The downside of implicit conversion is that there is no way to make a Declare statement treat all strings as UNICODE and leave them alone. Articles in the VB4 timeframe advocated a ridiculously heavy and complex workaround for calling UNICODE API functions. The technique involved copying strings to and from Byte arrays and passing the first element of the Byte array ByRef to the API call. As if the multiple string copies required with this technique weren't bad enough, many people got it wrong because they didn't explicitly NULL-terminate the Byte-array's copy of the String. Although VB lets you assign a String to a Byte array, it does not copy the NULL termination-character. Many people who attempted UNICODE API calls actually passed strings without a NULL terminator. VB5 and VB6 allow you to simply change the declared type to ByVal As Long from ByVal As String and pass StrPtr(String) instead of making a deep copy of the string.

```
'Deprecated method using a Byte array.
Public Declare Function FindWindowW Lib "user32" ( _
  ByVal lpClassName As Long, lpWindowName As Byte) As Long
Public Function LocateWindow(strWindowName As String) As Long
Dim bTmpBuf() As Byte
    'The vbNullChar is required. This actually generates
    'two copies of the string: one to concatenate
    'the NULL character and one to copy into the byte array.
    bTmpBuf = strWindowName & vbNullChar
    LocateWindow = FindWindowW(0, bTmpBuf(0))
End Function


'The preferred mechanism with StrPtr.
Public Declare Function FindWindowW Lib "user32" ( _
  ByVal lpClassName As Long, _
  ByVal lpWindowName As Long) As Long
Public Function LocateWindow(strWindowName As String) As Long
    LocateWindow = FindWindowW(0, StrPtr(strWindowName))
End Function
```

Clearly, it is much better to use the extremely fast StrPtr function than it is to copy the string twice. However, *As String* parameters are only half the problem. You can pass strings to a Declare function directly or as a field in a structure. StrPtr does not help with embedded strings or fixed-length strings. In order to pass a structure without converting it, simply change the ByRef As MyType declaration to ByVal As Long and put a VarPtr around the structure when you make the call. See "String Types" in Chapter 15 for a discussion of using type-library function declarations with explicit string typing (instead of StrPtr) for UNICODE API calls.

You can also use StrPtr with ANSI API calls to prevent VB from repeatedly applying the same string conversion to multiple calls. For example, if you call a Declare function that takes the same ByVal ANSI String inside a loop, it is more efficient to convert the string manually using StrConv, declare the parameter ByVal As Long, and use StrPtr to make the call.

```
Dim strANSIName As String
Dim pANSIName As Long
    strANSIName = StrConv(strName, vbFromUnicode)
    pANSIName = StrPtr(strANSIName)
    'You can now pass pANSIName multiple times with a
    'single conversion.
```

String Allocation

Like objects and arrays, strings are pointer types, so a String variable contains a pointer to a memory block that has the characteristics of a BSTR. All BSTRs are allocated by OleAut32.Dll (via SysAllocString, SysAllocStringLen, or SysAllocStringByteLen) and freed using the SysFreeString API. The VB runtime uses these API calls for string management when you assign and free strings, so you don't normally have to call them on your own. However, if you are passed a pointer to a NULL-terminated string and need to read it in VB, you can use the API set yourself to allocate your own string. All the OleAut32 string APIs are declared in the VBoostTypes typelib.

```
'Create a VB-readable string from a UNICODE pointer.
Dim strReadable As String
    strReadable = SysAllocString(pUNICODEString)
```

You have a little more work to do to get a readable string from an ANSI pointer, but it's still quite easy to do if you specify the byte length and let VB convert the string for you.

```
'Create a VB-readable string from an ANSI string pointer.
Dim strReadable As String
    strReadable = StrConv( _
      SysAllocStringByteLen(pANSIString, _
        lstrlen(pANSIString)), _
      vbUnicode)
```

VB always lets you assume that the memory in a String variable is writable. This can be both a good and a bad thing. It's a good thing because the string can always be modified dynamically without using new memory (as described in the next section), but it also means that the VB compiler has no notion of a read-only string. There are two immediate drawbacks to the lack of a read-only string type. First, VB must make a copy of a constant string any time you pass it to a ByRef string parameter. Second, VB automatically makes a copy of every string it receives via a ByVal String parameter to ensure that it can actually write to it. The copy is made because the string pointer that comes in on the stack points to the location from which the string was passed, which shouldn't be changed in a ByVal pass. Changing the data in the string causes a crash in a compiled EXE if a constant string is modified without first being copied. To be on the safe side, VB simply copies the incoming string into a local variable that you can edit without modifying the passed string.

Using a ByRef String is the easiest way to avoid the string copy for functions in the same project. However, if you are implementing an existing interface that takes potentially large strings as parameters, there is no way to avoid the string copy: You are forced to use a ByVal String. To handle this situation, you can Implement a "VB-ized" copy of the interface that takes a ByVal Long instead of a ByVal String and simply borrow the string pointer. This is easily done with a lightweight object that uses structure-termination code to change the string variable to a NULL value before VB gets a chance to call SysFreeString (see "Termination Code on Structures" in Chapter 8). The full code for the StringRef class is in StringRef.Bas.

Passing a string ByRef is fastest when the data is not being marshaled across a thread or process boundary. However, ByRef As String translates to an [in,out] BSTR* and tells the marshaling engine to copy the string both into the destination thread and back to the calling thread after the call. A ByVal pass is often recommended for marshaled strings to eliminate the overhead of copying the string back to the calling thread. If you need to use public objects from both marshaled and same-thread clients, you can get the in-thread benefits of a ByRef string without the marshaling penalty by using the PowerVB Post-Build Type Library Modifier to change the marshaling signature on the ByRef string to [in] BSTR*. (See Chapter 15 for more information.)

```
'VTable structure declarations omitted

Public Type StringRef
    pVTable As Long
    pThisObject As IUnknown
    Ref As String
End Type


Public Sub InitStringRef ( _
   SR As StringRef, ByVal pString As Long)
    'Initialize the VTable (omitted)
    With SR
        .pVTable = m_pVTable
        VBoost.Assign .pThisObject, VarPtr(.pVTable)
        VBoost.Assign .Ref, pString
    End With
End Sub


'QueryInterface and AddRef omitted
Private Function Release(This As StringRef) As Long
    'Clear the string pointer before VB gets hold of it.
    VBoost.AssignZero This.Ref
End Function
```

```
'Calling code
Public Sub IFoo_DisplayString(ByVal pString As Long)
Dim SR As StringRef
    InitStringRef SR, pString
    MsgBox SR.Ref
End Sub
```

For all but very short strings (fewer than 30 characters in my tests) it is actually faster to pass StrPtr to a ByVal Long and initialize a StringRef structure than it is to pass a String to a ByVal String parameter and allow the string copy to take place. Even for very short strings, StringRef is never more than 40 percent slower than a ByVal pass; however, it is orders of magnitude faster for large strings. The problem with a string copy is that the overhead is a function of the string's length, whereas StringRef has a constant overhead. You must be very disciplined when you use StringRef. The calling code must pass the pointer to a valid BSTR, and you must absolutely not modify the data in StringRef.Ref in any way.

The best way to optimize string performance is to minimize first the number and then the size of the strings you allocate. You need to be particularly aware of the number of strings you allocate if your application runs in a heavily threaded server environment. BSTR's are allocated by OLE Automation using the COM allocator, which in turn gets its memory from the default process heap. The heap is a shared resource, so only one thread can use it at a time. The more strings you allocate, the better chance you'll have of forcing threads to wait in line for their string (or any other) memory.

There are several things you can do to minimize string allocations. The first thing is to be aware if the string you're copying from ever needs to be used again. If it doesn't, you can simply steal it from the source variable using the VBoost.AssignSwap function. AssignSwap exchanges the values in two four-byte variables, so swapping between two string variables simply exchanges the string pointers without allocating data. For example, the right-hand side parameter of a Property Let function is generally passed ByVal, which automatically gives you a local copy of the string. In fact, even if you declare it ByRef, VB passes a copy of the string, so you might as well use ByVal to save VB the extra work and make the ByVal behavior official. This leaves you with a copy of the string that you can steal with no side effects.

```
Private m_strName As String
Public Property Let Name(ByVal RHS As String)
    VBoost.AssignSwap m_strName, RHS
    'The previous m_strName value will be freed
    'when RHS goes out of scope.
End Property
```

Stealing strings can eliminate a number of unnecessary string copies, which satisfies the goal of reducing the number of allocations. The second way to reduce string allocations is to use the Join function, which is new to VB6. Join combines an array of strings into a single string with one allocation. It is much more efficient to use Join to combine a number of strings than by appending them to the current value in a loop. Really bad string concatenation code is all too easy to write in VB. Here's a routine that reads lines from a file and rebuilds the string using the standard string concatenation operator.

```
Public Function ReadFile(strFileName As String) As String
Dim fNum As Integer
Dim strLine As String
    fNum = FreeFile
    Open strFileName For Input As #fNum
    'Note: ReadFile = Input(LOF(fNum), fNum) is sufficient,
    'here, but doesn't help with a concatenation demo.
    Do Until EOF(fNum)
        Line Input #fNum, strLine
        ReadFile = ReadFile & strLine & vbCrLf
    Loop
    Close #fNum
End Function
```

This code is intentionally poor, but you might be surprised at just *how* badly it runs. Running this loop against VBoost.Bas (approximately 110K) takes about 21 seconds on my machine. Using the alternative concatenation techniques we're about to discuss decreases that time to one-tenth of a second: a 21,000 percent performance gain.

The problem with this routine is that strings become increasingly expensive to allocate as they get larger. If you just keep appending small pieces onto a larger string, you are actually allocating large strings for every & operator. The test file (VBoost.Bas) has approximately 2,800 lines, and the function creates two cumulative strings per line for a total of 5,600 allocations. By first concatenating the smaller strings and then adding them to the total string, you can reduce the size of the allocations and speed up the function. You can give VB a big boost by adding parentheses to indicate which strings to combine first. A simple change to the concatenation line decreases the time from 21 to 8.5 seconds. This is still unacceptably slow, but it does show the importance of the allocation size in the performance equation. The addition of the parentheses does not change the number of allocations, but has a large effect on performance.

```
ReadFile = ReadFile & (strLine & vbCrLf)
```

OLE Automation has a string cache for small strings, so many small strings are pulled from the cache of previously allocated strings rather than from a new system allocation. However, no string caching takes place above 64K. The string cache essentially guarantees that you can't mess up too badly with small strings, no matter how bad the code is. However, the derivative of the concatenation cost-curve is discontigous at the point at which strings become larger than the cache. Code that runs with acceptable performance on 30K- or even 60K-strings, suddenly performs atrociously when you exceed the cache boundary. A more-systematic approach to string concatenation is required as strings get larger.

The Join function, introduced in VB6, is a great tool for reducing the number of string concatenations. Join concatenates an array of strings with a single call, optionally inserting a delimiter between each item in the array. Join first steps through all the strings in the array to determine the size of the final string, then makes a single allocation before copying the string data across. This greatly reduces the number of allocations required for concatenating strings, but Join on its own does not provide a full solution to the concatenation problem.

Join has two drawbacks. First, if you don't know the number of allocations you need when you start, it's hard to choose a reasonable size for the array. Second, the function does not take a Count parameter, so you are forced to ReDim Preserve the array to a smaller size or specify vbNullString as the Delimiter parameter so as not to get extra delimiter sequences appended to the resulting string. The alternative to using ReDim Preserve is to use VarPtrStringArray to obtain a reference to the cElements field in the array structure, and then temporarily modify this value for the duration of the Join call. This is demonstrated with the following snippet.

```
Dim Strings() As String
Dim pElemCount As Long
Dim cElems As Long
Dim strTotal As String
    With VBoost
        pElemCount = .UAdd( _
          .Deref(VarPtrStringArray(Strings)), 16)
        .AssignSwap ByVal pElemCount, cElems
        strTotal = Join(Strings, vbCrLf)
        .AssignSwap ByVal pElemCount, cElems
    End With
```

This book provides a helper class, called SmartConcat, to help you optimize concatenation performance without having to deal with Join directly.

SmartConcat uses a two-step approach with the Join function. When you call the AddString or AddStringSteal methods, SmartConcat places the string in a m_SmallStrings array. When the array is full or the total string length reaches a certain limit, the array is concatenated with the Join function and the resulting string stored in an intermediate array, m_MediumStrings. m_MediumStrings is made larger several items at a time as needed (with ReDim Preserve) until the GenerateCurrentString method is called. This method performs a final Join on all of the strings in the m_MediumStrings array. The result is a concatenation scheme that uses a small number of small allocations, a limited number of medium-sized allocations, and a single large allocation. The following code shows SmartConcat used in a modified version of the ReadFile function. This version loads the test file in .1 seconds; this compares very favorably with the 21 and 8.5 seconds of the two previous versions.

```vb
Public Function ReadFile(strFileName As String) As String
Dim fNum As Integer
Dim strLine As String
Dim Concat As SmartConcat
    fNum = FreeFile
    Open strFileName For Input As #fNum
    Set Concat = New SmartConcat
    Concat.Separator = vbCrLf
    Do Until EOF(fNum)
        Line Input #fNum, strLine
        Concat.AddStringSteal strLine
    Loop
    Close #fNum
    Concat.AddString vbNullString
    ReadFile = Concat.GenerateCurrentString
End Function
```

Strings as Numbers

A string is a set of individual characters in which every character is actually a number. As a general programming principle, you should treat strings as arrays of numbers rather than as autonomous units to get optimal performance from string routines. Unfortunately, VB offers no built-in mechanism for treating a String as a simple array of Integer numbers. This forces VB programmers to use string allocations for operations that *could* be numeric. This section looks at treating a VB String as an array of Integer values, allowing you to apply string algorithms that operate on numbers instead of normal string variables. I will rely heavily on the SafeArray techniques discussed in Chapter 2 and the ArrayOwner lightweight techniques from Chapter 8.

Visual Basic officially exposes the number of a string with the Asc and AscW functions. These functions read the numerical value of the first character in a String; AscW returns the UNICODE number, and Asc returns the ANSI number. AscW can be very useful for determining the first character in a string during an optimized Select Case statement. The following snippets are functionally equivalent, but the code generated is radically different.

```
'Snippet1
Select Case Left$(TestString, 1)
    Case "@"
        'etc
    Case "!"
        'etc
    Case Else
        'etc
End Select


'Snippet2
Select Case AscW(TestString)
    Case 64 '@
        'etc
    Case 33 '!
        'etc
    Case Else
        'etc
End Select
```

In snippet one, VB first allocates a new string then walks through a series of generated If/ElseIf statements, comparing strings in each case statement. Snippet2 has no string allocation, and VB generates a switch table using constant Long values. This is much more efficient than the If clauses generated by Snippet1. In short, Snippet1 loses hands down on all fronts. Note that you can type ?AscW("@") in the debug window at any time during design mode to get the correct string values. The comments are optional, but you'll thank yourself for including them the next time you read the code.

AscW works well for the first character in a string, but it doesn't help with subsequent characters. The easiest way to use the numerical values of subsequent characters is to point an Integer array at the memory owned by the string. This is shown in Figure 14.2. The following class, FastMid, generates a one-character string that you can dynamically update to hold the value of character in a second string, all without reallocation. Generally, reading a single character requires a call to the Mid$ function, which allocates a new string for every character. But FastMid allows you to step through a string one character at a time without actually allocating a new string for each character. This constitutes a huge savings when used with a large string.

```vb
'Requires: ArrayOwner.Bas or ArrayOwnerIgnoreOnly.Bas
Private Type OwnedInteger
    Owner As ArrayOwner
    pSA() As Integer
End Type
Private m_FullString As OwnedInteger
Private m_SingleChar As OwnedInteger

Public Function GetMidString(FullString As String) As String
    GetMidString = String$(1, 0)
    m_SingleChar.Owner.SA.pvData = StrPtr(GetMidString)
    With m_FullString.Owner.SA
        .pvData = StrPtr(FullString)
        .cElements = Len(FullString)
    End With
End Function
Public Sub SetMidPosition(ByVal Index As Long)
    m_SingleChar.pSA(0) = m_FullString.pSA(Index)
End Sub
Private Sub Class_Initialize()
    With m_FullString
        InitArrayOwner .Owner, 2, 0
        'FastMid is 1-based to map directly to the Mid$
        'function.
        .Owner.SA.lLbound = 1
    End With
```

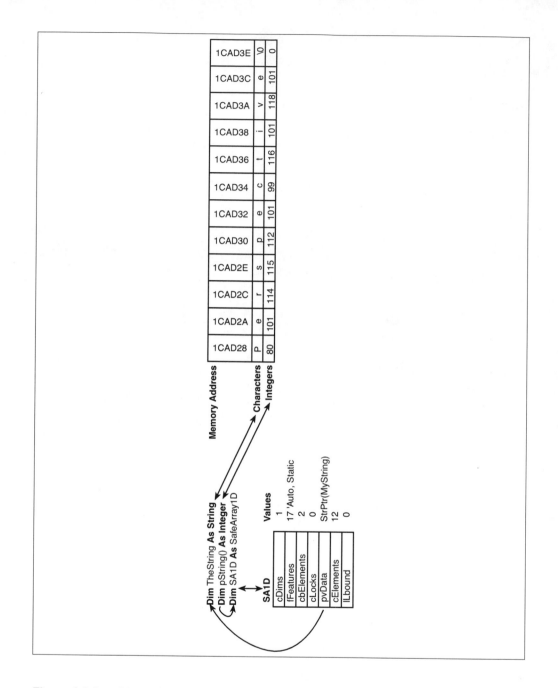

Figure 14.2. Use a SafeArray structure to manipulate the characters in a String via numbers in an Integer array. In this situation, StrPtr(TheString) = VarPtr(pString(0)).

```
        InitArrayOwner m_SingleChar.Owner, 2, 0
End Sub
```

```
'Use of FastMid, gives the same output as
'Debug.Print strWalkMe.
Dim strWalkMe As String
Dim strMid As String
Dim i As Long
    With New FastMid
        strMid = .GetMidString(strWalkMe)
        For i = 1 To Len(strWalkMe)
            .SetMidPosition i
            Debug.Print strMid;
        Next i
        Debug.Print
    End With
```

Clearly, if you call FastMid.SetMidPosition after the string you're examining or the MidString has been released or reallocated, the program crashes immediately. However, FastMid can outlive the strings to which it points as long as there is no call to SetMidPosition. FastMid works by treating a character in a string as an entry in an Integer array, enabling the character to be changed without using any of VB's string functions.

The second numeric-processing example uses Integer arrays attached to Strings to create a simple Tokenizer class. This class takes a set of single-character delimiters that are used to break a string into multiple fields. The Tokenizer class supports three classes of delimiters: delimiters that are removed from the final set, characters that act as delimiters but which remain in the final set of fields, and characters that indicate that processing should end. This Tokenizer class can be used to parse simple equations. Recognition of quoted strings is built-in. I'll show usage first, followed by the code listing for the class.

```
'A snippet to tokenize a line of Basic code and strip all
'spaces.
Dim strFields() As String
Dim iStoppedAt As Integer
Dim iFields As Integer
```

```
        With New Tokenizer
            .SetDelimiters " ", "^&:;*,/\-+=<>.()", "'"
            For iFields = 0 To _
                .TokenizeLines(strLine, iStoppedAt, strFields) - 1
                Debug.Print strFields(iFields)
            Next iFields
            If iStoppedAt Then _
                Debug.Print Mid$ (strLine,iStoppedAt)
        End With
```

```
    'Tokenizer Class from Tokenizer.cls
    'Requires: ArrayOwner.Bas or ArrayOwnerIgnoreOnly.Bas
Private Type OwnedInteger
    Owner As ArrayOwner
    pSA() As Integer
End Type


    'The complete set of tokens
Private m_Tokens As String
    'An owned integer array pointing to m_Tokens
Private m_RefTokens As OwnedInteger
    'The last end-of-line token: stop processing if tokens
    'before this are hit.
Private m_LastEOLToken As Integer
    'The last token that is a delimiter we should keep.
    'All tokens after this one are tossed out.
Private m_LastKeepToken As Integer
    'An owned integer array pointing to the line being processed.
Private m_RefLine As OwnedInteger
Private Const iDoubleQuote As Integer = 34


Public Sub SetDelimiters(TossDelimiters As String, _
    KeepDelimiters As String, StopAt As String)
    m_LastEOLToken = Len(StopAt)
    m_LastKeepToken = m_LastEOLToken + Len(KeepDelimiters)
    m_Tokens = StopAt & KeepDelimiters & TossDelimiters
    With m_RefTokens.Owner.SA
        .pvData = StrPtr(m_Tokens)
        .cElements = Len(m_Tokens)
    End With
End Sub
```

```vb
Public Function TokenizeLine(strLine As String, _
  iStoppedAt As Integer, strReturn() As String) As Integer
Const RedimIncrement = 20   'The grow size of the return array
Dim iRetArrSize As Integer  'The current size of the return
                            'array
Dim iPos As Integer         'The current position in strLine
Dim iMaxLen As Integer      'Cache for Len(strLine)
Dim iTestChar As Integer    'Character in the line being
                            'tested
Dim iStartPos As Integer    'Starting position of current
                            'field
Dim iFieldLength As Integer 'Length of current field
Dim iToken As Integer
Dim cTokens As Integer
Dim fHaveNextToken As Boolean


    TokenizeLine = 0

    iMaxLen = Len(strLine) 'Cache the length
    With m_RefLine
        With .Owner.SA
            'Plug the string into our SafeArray structure
            .pvData = StrPtr(strLine)
            'Go to +1 so trailing NULL terminator is in array
            .cElements = iMaxLen + 1
        End With
        iStoppedAt = 0
        cTokens = Len(m_Tokens)


        'The main processing loop
        Do While iPos < iMaxLen
            iStartPos = iPos 'Keep the current position
            iTestChar = .pSA(iPos)

            'See if we've hit any tokens
            If fHaveNextToken Then
                fHaveNextToken = False
            Else
                For iToken = 0 To cTokens - 1
                    If m_RefTokens.pSA(iToken) = _
                      iTestChar Then
```

```
                    Exit For
                End If
            Next iToken
        End If
        If iToken = cTokens Then
            'Not a token character: check for double-
            'quote and next token
            If iTestChar = iDoubleQuote Then
                'Consider quoted strings a single field.
                Do
                    iPos = iPos + 1
                    If iPos >= iMaxLen Then
                        Erase strReturn
                        Err.Raise 5
                    Else
                        iTestChar = .pSA(iPos)
                        If iTestChar = iDoubleQuote Then
                            'Check for 2 double quotes.
                            'Note that this won't look
                            'beyond the end of the array
                            'because the array length for
                            'the line includes the
                            'trailing NULL.
                            If .pSA(iPos + 1) = _
                               iDoubleQuote Then
                                iPos = iPos + 1
                            Else
                                Exit Do
                            End If
                        End If
                    End If
                Loop
                iPos = iPos + 1
                iFieldLength = iPos - iStartPos
            Else
                'Walk until the next token is hit.
                Do
                    iPos = iPos + 1
                    If iPos = iMaxLen Then Exit Do
                    iTestChar = .pSA(iPos)
                    For iToken = 0 To cTokens - 1
```

```vb
                            If m_RefTokens.pSA(iToken) = _
                               iTestChar Then
                                    fHaveNextToken = True
                                    Exit Do
                            End If
                        Next iToken
                    Loop
                    iFieldLength = iPos - iStartPos
            End If
        ElseIf iToken < m_LastEOLToken Then
            iStoppedAt = iPos + 1
            Exit Do
        ElseIf iToken < m_LastKeepToken Then
            iPos = iPos + 1
            iFieldLength = 1
        Else 'Toss token
            iFieldLength = 0
            iPos = iPos + 1
        End If


        If iFieldLength Then
            'Return this field
            'Grow the array if necessary
            TokenizeLine = TokenizeLine + 1
            'Increment the size of the array in blocks to
            'avoid Redim Preserve every time.
            If TokenizeLine > iRetArrSize Then
                iRetArrSize = iRetArrSize + RedimIncrement
                ReDim Preserve strReturn(iRetArrSize - 1)
            End If
            'Save the field to return.
            strReturn(TokenizeLine - 1) = _
              Mid$(strLine, iStartPos + 1, iFieldLength)
        End If
    Loop
End With
If TokenizeLine Then
    'Remove unused array elements.
    ReDim Preserve strReturn(TokenizeLine - 1)
Else
    Erase strReturn
```

```
        End If
End Function

Private Sub Class_Initialize()
    InitArrayOwner m_RefTokens.Owner, 2, 0
    InitArrayOwner m_RefLine.Owner, 2, 0
End Sub
```

TokenizeLine runs well in the IDE, but you don't see the full performance benefits until you run it in a compiled executable. To get maximum performance, be sure to disable integer overflow and array bounds-checking in the Advanced section of the Compile Options dialog. There are many requirements you can place on a tokenizing routine: this is just one example. However, it does show you how easy it is to point an Integer array at a string buffer and edit the buffer dynamically. You can now switch standard VB code to numeric processing any time you need to reduce the number of allocations, string comparisons, and other costly string operations. This gives your strings a big performance boost.

Chapter 15

Type Libraries and VB

Type libraries form the binary description language VB uses to consume objects and to describe the objects it generates. Your project must reference a type library that defines the types you want to use before you can compile against the contained objects. VB also generates a type library when you create an ActiveX component. In short, you can't write your first line of code in VB or produce custom ActiveX components without type libraries.

The VB IDE gives you no way of getting a low-level view of a type library, not to mention creating a new one or editing one that VB produces with your project. Most of the time, the fact that you have only a high-level (Object Browser) view of the libraries is beneficial. As a good high-level language, VB should hide as much complexity as it can. However, just as understanding the binary layout of a COM object enables you to greatly enhance what VB can do, control over the typelibs VB consumes and creates extends what you can do with VB and helps you produce a more professional product.

This discussion of typelibs addresses four areas. First, I'll take a quick look at the typelibs that VB generates for you. Second, I'll examine the benefits you can realize by creating custom libraries for consumption by your project. Third, I'll look at the binary compatibility file and discuss when and why you would want to modify it. And finally, I'll describe reasons for modifying the VB-created typelib generated with ActiveX components.

The goal of this chapter is to discuss typelibs as they relate directly to VB. It is not a reference manual for the use of typelib compilation tools, such as MkTypLib or MIDL. These are well-documented in MSDN and in numerous samples. To complement the typelib compilers that ship with Visual Studio, the book's CD contains three typelib manipulation add-ins that you can use to accomplish everything discussed in this chapter. The PowerVB Type Library Editor (EditTlb.Dll) allows you create and edit typelibs from within VB's IDE, PowerVB Binary Compatibility Editor (EditCompat.Dll) lets you make a restricted set of modifications to a project's compatibility file, and PowerVB Post-Build Type Library Modifier (PostBuild.Dll) lets you modify the VB-generated typelib. This chapter focuses on the need for these tools as opposed to how you can use them: You'll find documentation with the tools on the CD.

Type-library editing is possible on any Win32 development platform. However, editing the binary compatibility file and the built executable requires full support for the resource replacement API set, which is available only on the NT 4.0 and Windows 2000 operating systems.

VB-Generated Type Libraries

As the name "*type library*" implies a typelib includes a number of types. However, this means absolutely nothing until the types themselves are defined. Just as in VB and other languages, a typelib uses a starting set of intrinsic types grouped together to define functions and form complex types. In typelib jarbon, a complex type is known as a *record,* and a structure or user-defined type (UDT) in other contexts. The functions are grouped in either a strictly ordered set (an *interface*) or a loosely ordered set (a *module*). This definition is similar to what you do when coding in a normal programming language, except that a typelib produces a description but no implementation. To form a link between the type descriptions and implementations provided by an executable, a typelib contains a secondary grouping called a *coclass* (Component Object class), which is a combination of interfaces. A COM object, whether created by VB or another language, is defined as the implementation of a coclass. To round out the picture, a typelib can also define an *enum* type (which corresponds directly to its

Table 15.1 The layout of a type library. The elements in each column are defined using items from the column to its left. An asterisk (*) by an item indicates that it can be added to the custom types in the first column, producing a spiraling type system.

Step 1	Step 2	Step 3	Step 4
Intrinsic Types	Functions	Interfaces*	CoClasses*
Custom Types	Functions	Modules	
	Constants		
	Records*		
	Enums*		
	Aliases*		

VB counterpart) and an *alias* type (an alternate name for another type that has no VB equivalent.)

Elements of the VB language map to corresponding typelib elements. VB types form a true subset of typelib types, so all descriptive elements of the VB language (as opposed to the implementation elements) have a corresponding entry in typelib land. Many of the remaining typelib elements can be consumed by VB although they cannot be defined in the language.

An example is in order. The following VB snippet is part of a MultiUse class object, which means that not only the class but also the Public Enum and Public Type entries are written to the generated typelib. The equivalent structure is shown with the code in Object Definition Language (ODL). You can clearly see the progression from intrinsic type to custom type to function in both the VB and ODL snippets. The additional progression from function to interface to class is visible only in the ODL because VB automatically generates a default interface and an event interface for the class.

Listing 15.1. A VB class module and equivalent ODL

```
'VB code in a MultiUse class module. Several miscellaneous
'types are shown for demonstration purposes.
Public Enum Style
```

```vb
        All = 0
        Style1 = 1
        Style2 = 2
End Enum
Public Type Entry
    Name As String
    Data(0 To 2) As String
End Type
Public Type Entries
    Style As Style
    Entries() As Entry
End Type

'Event declarations
Event EntriesChanged()

'Methods and properties
Public Function GetEntries( _
  ByVal Style As Style, Entries() As Entries) As Boolean

End Function
```

```odl
//The equivalent ODL
[
  uuid(0983F45D-C5F6-11D3-BC23-D41203C10000),
  version(1.0)
]
library EntriesProject
{
    importlib("stdole2.tlb");

    typedef [uuid(0983F460-C5F6-11D3-BC23-D41203C10000)]
    enum EntryStyle {
        All = 0,
        Style1 = 1,
        Style2 = 2
    } EntryStyle;

    typedef [uuid(0983F461-C5F6-11D3-BC23-D41203C10000)]
    struct Entry {
```

```
        BSTR Name;
        BSTR Data[3];
    } Entry;


    typedef [uuid(0983F462-C5F6-11D3-BC23-D41203C10000)]
    struct Entries {
        EntryStyle Style;
        SAFEARRAY(Entry) Entries;
    } Entries;


    [
      uuid(0983F45E-C5F6-11D3-BC23-D41203C10000),
      hidden, dual, nonextensible
    ]
    interface _EntriesClass : IDispatch {
        HRESULT GetEntries(
                        [in] EntryStyle Style,
                        [in, out] SAFEARRAY(Entries)* Entries,
                        [out, retval] boolean* retVal);
    };


    [
      uuid(0983F463-C5F6-11D3-BC23-D41203C10000),
      hidden, nonextensible
    ]
    dispinterface __EntriesClass {
        properties:
        methods:
            [id(1)]
            void EntriesChanged();
    };


    [
      uuid(0983F45F-C5F6-11D3-BC23-D41203C10000)
    ]
    coclass EntriesClass {
        [default] interface _EntriesClass;
        [default, source] dispinterface __EntriesClass;
    };
};
```

Table 15.2   A mapping between VB types and elements and the corresponding type library element

VB Type	Typelib Equivalent
Integer	short
Long	long
Single	float
Double	double
Currency	currency
Date	DATE
String	BSTR
Object	IDispatch*
Boolean	boolean
Variant	VARIANT
Byte	unsigned char
Array of type x as a Parameter	SAFEARRAY(x)*
Type/End Type	record
Variable-size Array in a UDT	SAFEARRAY(x)
Fixed-Size Array in a UDT	x FieldName[2]
Declare and Const in a standard module	module
Class Module	coclass
Enum/End Enum	enum

The ODL version of the type system exposes several VB behaviors that are common to all VB-produced type libraries.

- There are three typelib entries for the single class. The EntriesClass coclass is the class itself, which is comprised of the _EntriesClass interface and the __EntriesClass source interface. If the class had had additional Implements statements, you would also have seen an additional interface listed before the event interface for each Implements statement.

- VB requires that the object that receives events expose an IDispatch-bound object to receive events. The event interface is marked with the *source* attribute in the list of coclass interfaces and indicates that this interface is consumed, not provided, by the specified class. A *dispinterface* specifies that a vtable is supported only through the IDispatch::Invoke method, so all calls to the object must go through IDispatch.

- VB produces objects that have dual interfaces. A dual interface is a vtable-bound interface that masquerades as a dispinterface. Tools that do not support vtable binding can treat and view the interface as a dispinterface, while newer tools (VB5 and later versions) can interact with the vtable. VB4, VBA versions before the Office 97 release, and all scripting languages (VBScript, JavaScript, and so on) use IDispatch binding only. The dual attribute also implies the oleautomation attribute, which means that all marshaling can be accomplished using the type description in the typelib. All the public classes produced are dual interfaces, so they all support IDispatch, and all are 100 percent dependent on a properly registered typelib to marshal objects across thread, process, and machine boundaries.

- All VB objects are nonextensible, which means that the VB compiler generates errors at compile time if it can't find a method or property in the typelib. Since IDispatch::GetIDsOfNames and IDispatch::Invoke can theoretically dynamically add properties and methods that are not in the typelib, VB must switch from vtable binding to late binding if it can't vtable bind a specific call. This is rarely done in practice, and it is not supported by VB objects (unless you are adept at using VBoost to provide a custom IDispatch implementation). The nonextensible attribute is usually added to objects to force a compilation error if properties, methods, or parameters can't be identified from the type information.

- All VB methods and properties on nonevent interfaces return an HRESULT, which is the COM mechanism for returning an error code. The oleautomation specification actually allows a void or an HRESULT return, but VB does not allow you to code a non-event function that can't return an error. See "To Err or Not to Err" in Chapter 8 for a more extensive discussion of methods that don't return in an HRESULT.

- A VB ByVal parameter translates into a simple type rather than a pointer type (long instead of long*), and it always uses the [in] parameter attribute. [in] tells the marshaling engine to copy data only to the stub object that receives the method call, never back to the caller. A ByRef parameter always translates to an [in, out] parameter with a pointer type, so ByRef Long is [in,out] long* in ODL. Note that objects, arrays, and strings are inherently pointer types, so a ByVal MyObject parameter is an [in] MyObject*, and a ByRef MyObject is [in,out] MyObject**. VB passes only pointers for object types; it never actually passes the underlying data. VB can't pass a ByVal array or structure, although the oleautomation standard supports both of these concepts.

- With the exception of a return value from a function (which is really a parameter because the true return value is an HRESULT), there is no way VB can specify an [out] only parameter. This is unfortunate: Data might be marshaled when it doesn't need to be. You'll learn more about [out] parameters later in this chapter.

- VB assigns GUIDs (specified with the uuid attribute in ODL) to all the elements it defines. The typelib compilers require GUIDs for all interfaces, dispinterfaces, and coclasses; the marshaler requires GUIDs for all structures. However, neither the compilers nor the marshaler require GUIDs on enums. After all, an enum is treated just like a Long at compilation and marshaling time. You'll see the negative side effects of enum versioning in the discussion on binary compatibility files.

You will find elements and attributes very similar to those shown above in all the typelibs VB produces when it creates an ActiveX component. The advantage to this standardized approach is that you don't have to worry about the typelib generation or ODL definition when you create public classes. The disadvantage is that you cannot control what VB produces. For example, there is no way to directly control the marshaling flags on parameters, the packing level on structures, the version of the typelib, or the GUIDs used on the interfaces and classes.

You need to take a three pronged approach to gain this low-level of control of the typelibs you use in your project and the ones you produce. If you want to define types that VB can't describe, you need to write your own typelib. If you have explicit requirements (such as existing coclass or interface identifiers that VB needs to know about to match the binary implementation to the typelib description), you need to modify the typelib and other resources in the binary compability file so that VB can reproduce these settings when it recompiles your project. Finally, if you need to change settings that only the consumer of your object cares about (such as parameter marshaling information), you need to modify the typelib contained in your executable after VB has finished writing it.

VB-Friendly Custom Type Libraries

Although VB produces highly standardized typelibs, it can consume a much greater range of functions and interfaces that it can produce. It is a common misconception that VB can consume only dual interfaces. This is simply not true. VB can call nearly any interface, and the number of interfaces that it can't call can be reduced to almost zero by redefining, or "VB-izing," the interface for VB consumption. Note that calling an interface falls strictly within the consumption category; implementing an interface with Implements implies that VB both consumes the interface and produces code for it, meaning that the interface requirements for Implements are much stricter than those for calling member functions on an interface.

There is only a limited set of typelib elements that VB can't handle at all. You can work around these limitations if you are willing to write a little extra code or define a VB-ized interface.

Typelib Elements That VB Can't Use
ByVal Arrays in Parameter Lists
VB handles only a SAFEARRAY(elementtype)* array (corresponding to a SAFEARRAY** in C++). To call this type, redefine it as a ByVal Long and use VarPtrArray combined with VBoost.Deref to pass the type. With Implements,

you can work around this limitation by changing the parameter to a ByVal Long and using the SafeArray dereferencing techniques discussed in Chapter 2. The ArrayOwner lightweight object is particularly useful in this and other pointer situations.

ByVal Structures in Parameter Lists

ByVal structures in parameter lists are very difficult to work around, but they are also extremely rare. If you need to implement a function that receives a ByVal structure, you must provide a series of Long parameters to correctly fill the stack. You can use ByVal Long for all parameters and recompose the object four bytes at a time, or you can use a ByRef Long for the parameter that corresponds to the first element in the structure and dereference the VarPtr of the first element into a SAFEARRAY to read the structure. You can use a similar process to call a function that takes a ByVal structure.

Pointer Fields in Structures

VB cannot handle structures that contain pointer-type fields (long*, long**, IDispatch**, MyStruct*, and so on). In order to call these types, you must use a Long field and dereference it using VBoost.Deref or SafeArray techniques. Fields that include native pointer types (objects, strings, variable-size arrays) are also pointer types in structures.

Unsigned Types

VB refuses to use structures that include unsigned long and unsigned short types. The one case in which VB *does* use an unsigned type is with the Byte type, which corresponds to an unsigned char. In this case, the signed, one-byte type (char) is not accessible from VB. Fortunately, the workaround here is easy, but it often requires a VB-ized library. VB can consume an alias to an unsigned type, but not the type itself. The ODL line *typedef [public] unsigned long ULONG;* defines an alias type called ULONG, which you can use in your typelib. Simply replace any unsigned long or unsigned short types with aliases and your work is done. VB treats an unsigned long as a long in all arithmetic operations, so be sure to use VBoost's unsigned arithmetic functions if you need true unsigned arithmetic. You can also skip the alias definition and simply replace unsigned long with long.

However, the alias provides useful Intellisense information when it comes time to call the function. VB cannot call aliases to the char or unsigned int types.

Fixed-Length Strings in Structures

See "String Types" below.

Union Types

Union is the one element in a structure that VB does not consume. I've never actually seen one in production code, so I don't consider this a big loss.

You may have found the brevity of the list of negatives a pleasant surprise, and the good stuff is still to come. I'll concentrate on a few highly beneficial typelib types and attributes that VB can consume but not define.

[out] Parameters

Visual Basic maps ByVal MyType to [in] MyType and ByRef MyType to [in, out] MyType*. There is no way to make VB produce an [out] parameter without attaching the [in] baggage as well. These flags are primarily for marshaling interfaces, Any ByRef type is copied from the caller's process to the callee's process even if the parameter is only used to retrieve data. The easiest way to get an [out] parameter is to use the function's return value, but this only works if you try to retrieve a single value.

There is a side effect of [out] that is useful even without the marshaling layer. The [out] specification indicates that no incoming data exists, and the callee should make no attempt to read or free the data in the parameter. When combined with the fact that [out] parameters are always ByRef, the required lack of incoming data means that VB must free any data in the variable passed to the [out] parameter before the function is called. VB uses a temporary variable with an [out, retval] parameter so it can verify that the function succeeded before it clears the assigned variable, but it does not use a temporary with an [out] parameter. The variable is cleared before the function is called. An example of this usage is VBoost.MoveVariant, which puts an [out] on the varDst parameter to force VB to clear the incoming parameter before VBoost sees it.

If all your callers pass empty variables to your functionally out-only ByRef parameters, you don't gain much from the auto-free behavior: The cost of marshaling an empty Array, String, Variant, or Object is minimal. However, if the caller passes an array that already contains data, the marshaling layer duplicates all the data into the apartment just so that you can completely ignore it. In addition, you get a nasty error if the caller passes a fixed-size array and you try to ReDim the array. Just as VB won't let you assign a fixed-size array to a function's return value, it also won't let you pass a fixed-size array to an [out] parameter. Simply by setting the [out] flag, the callee can guarantee that the incoming data is empty and the marshaling layer won't waste resources by duplicating unneeded data.

Now that you see some of the benefits of [out] parameters, you may want to use them on your VB objects. VB won't let you do this, either directly or on your Implements interface, but there are several ways you can fake it. With Implements, you can simply make a VB-ized version of the interface that has no [out] parameter (see "VB-izing Implements Interfaces"). For functions on your primary interface, you need to make a post-build modification to change the parameter attribute (see "Post-Build Type Library Modifications" in this chapter). In either of these cases, you need to prepare your code up front to accept an [out] parameter rather than an [in, out].

The first problem occurs because [out] parameters can be defined to accept a zero pointer value, which never happens with [in,out]. The zero pointer is very informative because it tells the callee that the data that corresponds to this parameter does not have to be generated and returned. However, if you simply VB-ize an interface by turning an [out] to an [in,out], a zero crashes VB, which assumes that the incoming [in,out] parameter contains a valid, nonzero pointer. To accept an [out] with a zero pointer, you need to redefine the parameter as an [in] long. This allows you to test the incoming pointer value. You can then define a local of the expected type and copy it to the output parameter before the function returns. You can use an alias instead of a Long to indicate the true type of the parameter in the Intellisense Quick Tip window.

```
'The pData parameter is an [out] SAFEARRAY(long)*.
Private Function IVBizedInterface_UseOutParam( _
   ByVal pData As LongArrayPtr) As Long
Dim Data() As Long
   If pData Then
```

```
            'See next paragraph.
            VBoost.AssignZero ByVal pData
            'Fill Data
            VBoost.AssignSwap ByVal pData, _
               ByVal VarPtrArray(Data)
        End If
End Function
```

Although the next problem is theoretically an issue, I haven't actually seen it in practice. Unlike an [in, out] parameter, an [out] parameter provides no guarantee that it will receive a properly initialized value. With an [in, out], the pointer and the data it contains must be valid. The pointer for an [out] parameter is guaranteed to be valid or zero, but the data is undefined. If you leave this data undefined and use VB to assign to the parameter, you might free undefined data and crash the program. For example, if an incoming String parameter contains garbage data, assigning new data to that parameter frees the bad data. To account for this state, I always explicitly zero out any [out] parameters at the top of the function. VB also zeroes these values before the call, and the typelib-driven marshaling code does as well. This is done as a courtesy by the calling code, and it comes with no guarantee.

HRESULT Returns on API Calls

When you use the VB's Declare statement, you can't control the type of error handling VB produces for the function call. With a Declare function, VB always calls the GetLastError API and stores the value in Err.LastDllError after you call a Declare function. There are several disadvantages to this approach. First, there is the overhead of this extra call, which adds approximately 15 to 20 percent to the overhead of calling a declared function. Second, many functions return an HRESULT value directly to specify an error condition rather than using the SetLastError/GetLastError mechanism to return failure information. Third, functions that return an HRESULT need to be declared with a Long return value, which then needs to be explicitly checked after the function call.

Unfortunately for Declare statements, HRESULTs are the basis of VB's built-in error-handling mechanism. You can make use of this error-handling mechanism by using a module section in a typelib in place of a Declare statement. Typelibs let you declare an HRESULT return type and explicitly determine whether VB calls GetLastError after the function call. Let's look at the CoCreateGuid API as an example of using an HRESULT. VB can't use the system-defined GUID type because it uses unsigned types, so the VBoostTypes typelib defines the VB-compatible VBGUID type used here.

```
'Code for calling VB-declared CoCreateGuid.
Public Declare Function CoCreateGuid _
    Lib "ole32.dll" (NewGuid As VBGUID) As Long


'Calling code
Public Function NewGuid() As VBGUID
Dim hr As Long
    hr = CoCreateGuid(NewGuid)
    If hr Then Err.Raise hr
End Function


'Equivalent code using a Module section in a typelib.
[Dllname("ole32.Dll")]
module Ole32
{
    [entry("CoCreateGuid")]
    HRESULT CoCreateGuid([out,retval] VBGUID* retVal);
}


'Calling code using typelib definition.
Public Function NewGuid() As VBGUID
    NewGuid = CoCreateGuid
End Function
```

This calling code shows you that CoCreateGuid is much easier to call when you use the typelib declaration. If the API call happens to return an error, VB's error-handling mechanism picks it up automatically. The HRESULT returned also enables you to specify the parameter as a retval, so you simply see a function that returns a VBGUID and not a function with one parameter that returns a Long. To enable automatic population of the Err.LastDllError field, add the *usesgetlasterror* attribute to the entry attribute when you define the typelib function.

The other difference between a Declare statement and a typelib module entry is that typelib functions are all resolved when the executable loads and

Declare functions are bound the first time they are called. Forcing Windows to bind a large number of functions when the program launches has two disadvantages: It adds extra time to startup, and you can't even launch the executable if the DLL or the entrypoint can't be found. Consult MSDN when you declare API functions in a typelib to make sure they are available on all the target platforms.

When you use typelib declarations, the DLL you call is locked in memory for the entire life of the program. When you use a Declare statement, the DLL is locked as soon as the first function call made to it succeeds. If you want to explicitly unload a DLL, either for memory reasons or to upgrade it dynamically, you need to perform your own LoadLibrary and FreeLibrary calls. This is possible using a FunctionDelegator object (described in Chapter 11). Because a function delegator uses a typelib-defined function, you get the same type and HRESULT advantages as you do with a normal call. Unfortunately, there is no way to force VB to make an explicit GetLastError call after the FunctionDelegator completes its call.

String Types

Visual Basic's String variables are always BSTRs, but there are three string types in a typelib. BSTR indicates BSTR, LPSTR indicates a NULL-terminated ANSI string, and LPWSTR indicates a NULL-terminated UNICODE string. By specifying the exact string type, you can make the expected string type explicit and avoid using StrPtr with a ByVal Long just to make a UNICODE API call.

To specify that a function requires a NULL-terminated ANSI string, use an [in] LPSTR for a ByVal String and an [in,out] LPSTR* for a ByRef String equivalent. VB takes care of all remaining ANSI/UNICODE conversion. You can also use LPWSTR to indicate a NULL-terminated UNICODE string that needn't be a length-prefixed BSTR. All three string types are displayed As String in the Object Browser and IntelliSense windows. [out] LP[W]STR* parameters are handled slightly different than [out] BSTR* parameters: The BSTR passed to these parameters is considered a required output buffer and is not freed before the function call.

If you need a string type in a typelib-declared structure, you get to do some extra work. A BSTR is the only string-type VB can handle in a record. LPWSTR and LPSTR don't compile, and there is no way to define a fixed-length string in a typelib. You can provide equivalents for all these types, but you won't get seamless integration. Let's start with LPWSTR and LPSTR.

LPWSTR and LPSTR are just pointers to NULL-terminated strings. A BSTR is also a pointer to a NULL-terminated string, so you can replace the LPWSTR or LPSTR with BSTR and just treat the field as a normal string (LPWSTR) or assign the value with StrConv(, vbFromUnicode) for an LPSTR. This simple modification works very well for structures that you use as input parameters, but it is disastrous if the called function modifies the input structure or is responsible for populating it in the first place. In such an instance, you should simply change the type to long instead of LPWSTR or LPSTR and use the SysAllocString* functions to turn the string pointer into a VB-readable BSTR.

When you use fixed-length string fields, you must use an embedded array of type short (Integer in VB) for UNICODE strings or type unsigned char (Byte in VB) for ANSI strings. Then you need to copy the data to and from the structures yourself using CopyMemory. Such a technique is not pretty, and it is a miserable use of memory. But it *is* feasible.

```vb
'VB type
Public Type FLStringField
    TheString As String * 38
End Type


'Typelib equivalent, UNICODE
record TLibFLStringField
{
    short[38] TheString;
} TLibFLStringField;


'Calling code, UNICODE
Dim FLSF As TLibFLStringField
Dim strData As String
Dim cBytes As Long
    'Write to the field.
    cBytes = LenB(strData)
    If cBytes > 38 Then cBytes = 38
    CopyMemory FLSF.TheString(0), ByVal strData, cBytes
    'Read from the field.
    strData = SysAllocString(VarPtr(FLSF.TheString(0)))
```

```
'Typelib equivalent, ANSI
record TLibFLStringField
{
    unsigned char[38] TheString;
} TLibFLStringField;

'Calling code, ANSI
Dim FLSF As TLibFLStringField
Dim strData As String
Dim strDataA As String
Dim pStringA As Long
Dim cBytes As Long
    'Write to the field.
    strDataA = StrConv(strData, vbFromUnicode)
    cBytes = LenB(strData)
    If cBytes > 38 Then cBytes = 38
    CopyMemory FLSF.TheString(0), ByVal strDataA, cBytes
    'Read from the field.
    pStringA = VarPtr(FLSF.TheString(0))
    strData = StrConv( _
      SysAllocStringByteLen(pStringA, lstrlen(pStringA), _
        vbUnicode)
```

Alias Definitions

Visual Basic can't define alias types, but it can consume them quite well, provided they are not aliases to enums. An alias is simply a different name for the same type. There are several reasons to use aliases. Aliases provide guidelines for how the type should be used. For example, although a VARIANTArrayPtr is just a long, it tells the caller to pass the VarPtr of the first element in a Variant array. In addition, a typedef allows VB to declare a type from an unreferenced typelib. The OCXDirect add-in discussed in the "VTable Binding Custom Control Interfaces" section of Chapter 4 uses aliases to allow you to use types from an arbitrary number of OCXs without any project reference to the OCXs themselves.

```
// ODL syntax, some aliases in a typelib.
[version(1.0),
 uuid(FEB67C60-CDC2-11d3-BC2E-D41203C10000)]
library AliasLib
{
```

```
importlib("stdole2.Olb");
importlib("mscomctl.Ocx");

// Provide a more-instructive type than long.
// The [public] attribute is required to actually
// get the type in the typelib.
// The uuid attribute is not required for an alias.
typedef [public] long VARIANTArrayPtr;

// Enable use of Node type without referencing
// mscomctl.Ocx.
typedef [public] MSComtlLib.Node Node;
}
```

The VB compiler handles aliases by fully resolving them to their underlying type, so it treats VARIANTArrayPtr just like VB's Long type and Node as if it were the Node declared in mscomctl.Ocx. There are some differences between aliases to intrinsic types and aliases to user-defined types, however. First, you can't see the intrinsic aliases as types in VB's Object Browser. This makes it pointless to add a helpstring attribute to the alias, and it encourages you to make the names themselves descriptive. Second, if you use aliases in public methods or properties, intrinsic aliases are written to the VB-generated typelib, but aliases to all other types are resolved before they are written.

This difference in behavior is significant when it comes time to redistribute typelibs. If you want the typelib to be useful on a different machine, you must redistribute the typelib that contains the intrinsic alias. Alternately, you can perform a post-build typelib modification to make the alias type part of the executable's typelib (as discussed later in this chapter). Users of the typelib see descriptive types in the Object Browser and IntelliSense windows. The fact that aliases to custom types are never written to a public typelib means you can use them within your project without broadcasting that implementation detail to the whole world. This is especially important when you program against the native vtable interfaces of custom controls (see Chapter 4).

There is a bug in OLE Automation and VB's handling of aliases to Enums. This bug will likely never be fixed because it could break backwards-compatibility. Aliases to enums bind correctly in the type namespace (after an As in VB), but not in the normal namespace. If MyEnumAlias is an alias to MyEnum, MyEnum.FirstValue compiles correctly, but MyEnumAlias.FirstValue does not. You can still use the values from the alias; you just can't qualify them with the alias name. You need to be especially wary of this limitation when you use MIDL to build your typelibs: MIDL likes to generate aliases to enums. I'll show you how to get around this default behavior later in the chapter.

Constant Definitions

Enum definitions in type libraries are very similar to the Enum structures used in VB. However, enums are not the only constant types that you can put in a typelib. In fact, you can define constants for strings, date values, currency, and any other numeric type. MkTypLib won't let you define constants of type LPWSTR or VARIANT. MIDL lets you define these, but VB refuses to use an LPWSTR, and it crashes when it accesses a VARIANT constant. All typelib constants must be declared in a module, which is also used for API-style function declarations.

```
// mktyplib requires Dllname to compile a module.
[DLLname("bogus")]
module MyConstants
{
    const double PI = 3.14159265358979;
    const DATE NothingHappened = "2000-01-01";
    const LPSTR Description = "About this library";
}
```

Both MkTypLib and MIDL recognize escape sequences in string definitions. You're probably familiar with these if you've programmed in C or C++, but you might not be if you've used only VB strings. An escape sequence is an embedded character-sequence within a string definition that indicates a special character. An escape sequence always begins with the backslash (\) character, followed by other data. For example, a "\t" inserts a tab, an "\r" inserts carriage return, and a "\n" inserts a line feed. In addition to the standard escape names, "\" can also specify a character number. These numbers are entered in hexadecimal (\x##) or octal (\0###) formats. (Note that mktyplib supports the octal escape sequences only).

```
// Three representations of carriage return/line feed.
const LPSTR CRLF = "\r\n";
const LPSTR CRLFOctal = "\015\012";
const LPSTR CRLFHex = "\xd\xa"; // MIDL only

// Other escape sequences.
const LPSTR EmbeddedBackslash = "DLLs\\MyDll.Dll";
const LPSTR DoubleQuote = "\"";
const LPSTR TwoTabs = "\t\t";
```

Aligned Structures

All VB-defined structures are aligned on a four-byte boundary; structures often contain unused space, called *padding,* that places structure elements on a reasonable boundary. For example, a structure that contains an Integer and a Long is eight bytes long and not the expected six because two bytes of padding after the Integer place the Long on a four-byte boundary. This alignment policy provides very efficient code: The CPU has to work much harder to process unaligned data than aligned data. However, padding can cause problems if you consume data from external sources that use a different alignment. For example, data coming from a communications port is often byte aligned, making it difficult to read with a four-byte aligned, VB-declared structure.

The VB compiler can consume structures with any alignment, even though it can't define them. Typelibs also allow you to specify structure alignment, so working around the byte-alignment problem is not difficult. You can use any typelib-defined structure in code, a publicly exposed function, or Implements interface as long as you ensure that the defining typelib is redistributed and registered with the application (see "Registry Effects and Side Effects" in this chapter). If the type is used only for compilation, you should not specify the uuid attribute on the structure.

You can specify a type library's default structure alignment with the command line /align # switch. For example, the following command uses MkTypLib to generate byte-aligned structures.

```
mktyplib /align 1 StructLib.Odl
```

In addition to the default alignment, MIDL also supports the pragma pack directive, which you can use to align a single structure to a nondefault alignment.

```
#pragma pack(2)
typedef struct PackedStruct
{
    short Field1;
    long Field2;
};
#pragma pack()
```

VB-izing Implements Interfaces

There is a considerable difference between simply calling methods on an interface and actually providing an implementation for that interface. VB can call just
about anything, but it is not as adept at implementation as it is at interpretation.
If you combine the lightweight objects and aggregation techniques discussed
earlier in this book, it is possible to construct an implementation of absolutely
any interface and aggregate it into the controlling IUnknown of any VB class.
However, you can often use a much simpler approach of modifying the interface
so that VB can work with it directly. This is known as "VB-izing" the interface,
and it requires a typelib created solely for the VB compiler.

There are three issues you can't address simply by VB-izing the interface, and
they all involve the HRESULT return value. You cannot convince VB to implement
an interface with a function that does not return an HRESULT, nor can you implement an interface that returns a success HRESULT. A success HRESULT return
code does not indicate failure, but it provides additional information about a
successful function call. For example, the IOleInPlaceActiveObject interface's
TranslateAccelerator function returns 0 (S_OK) if it actually does something with
the message and 1 (S_FALSE) otherwise. There is no way to return this value from
VB. Finally, you cannot return any HRESULT value that VB maps to a standard VB
error number. For example, you can't return E_NOINTERFACE (&H80004002)
because it is mapped to VB's *Type mismatch* error (&H800A000D). You need to
use VBoost or another vtable construction or modification mechanism to handle
these cases.

You can solve all other incompatibility problems by VB-izing the interface
you implement. The most common problems arise from the use of types that VB
can't define, such as unsigned types and the VT_UNKNOWN type. The other
incompatibilities arise from [out] parameters and interfaces that aren't derived

directly from either IUnknown or IDispatch. You can VB-ize stubborn interfaces by taking a few simple steps.

1. Copy the interface, including the IID, into a new ODL. You can get an official interface description from the OleView.Exe utility or from MSDN.

2. Make sure that the dual and oleautomation attributes are not set. You must add the ODL attribute as well.

3. Flatten the interface as needed by adding methods from base classes other than IUnknown and IDispatch to the top of the function list.

4. Check for unsigned types, and add typedefs or simply replace them with their signed siblings (DWORD becomes long).

5. Check for [out] parameters. If there is only one [out] parameter and it is the last parameter, simply turn it into an [out, retval]. If you can't do that, turn it into an [in,out] type* p1 or an [in] long p1. Refer to the discussion on [out] parameters to decide how to handle these parameters in the implementation.

6. Change IUnknown to stdole.IUnknown.

7. If that doesn't work, keep playing with the interface until VB agrees to compile the Implements statement and all its methods. If you're not sure where the trouble comes from, comment out all the methods in the ODL and add them back one at a time. This can be a bit tedious (you have to close the referencing project to rebuild the typelib), but you will fix the problem in a reasonable amount of time.

A simple implementation of the IPersistHistory interface provides a good example of the process required to VB-ize an interface. Internet Explorer (versions 4.0 and later) uses IPersistHistory to cache information for a custom control so the control can be restored to its current state when the user navigates with the Forward or Back buttons. IPersistHistory maintains its state by reading and writing from an IStream implementation provided by IE. Although you can call streams with a VB-ized version of the IStream interface, there is no need in this case because the IPersistStreamInit interface is already supported by VB. You can defer all stream operations to VB's implementation of this interface. In fact, I'll make both interfaces pass [in] long parameters instead of [in] IStream* parameters. This allows the stream pointer to be passed through the IPersistHistory implementation to VB's IPersistStreamInit implementation without considering how its real type looks.

The MSDN description of IPersistHistory looks like this.

```
[
    uuid(91A565C1-E38F-11d0-94BF-00A0C9055CBF),
    object, pointer_default(unique)
]
interface IPersistHistory : IPersist
{
    typedef [unique] IPersistHistory *LPPERSISTHISTORY;

    HRESULT LoadHistory(
            [in] IStream *pStream,
            [in] IBindCtx *pbc);

    HRESULT SaveHistory(
            [in] IStream *pStream);

    HRESULT SetPositionCookie(
            [in] DWORD dwPositioncookie);

    HRESULT GetPositionCookie(
            [out] DWORD *pdwPositioncookie);
}
```

There are several things to modify here. First, the IPersist interface is flattened into the VB-ized interface by including its GetClassID function. GetClassID takes an [out] parameter typed as CLSID; this turns into an [in] long parameter so it can be forwarded to the simplified IPersistStreamInit definition. The IStream* and IBindCtx* parameters turn into [in] long, DWORD becomes long, and [out] DWORD* becomes [out,retval] long*. The MIDL-specific attributes (object, pointer_default) and the typedef are also not needed. The resulting typelib, which also includes a simplified redefinition of the IPersistStreamInit interface, looks like this.

```
[
    uuid(6FBB99C0-D342-11d3-BC39-D41203C10000),
    helpstring("IPersistHistory: Simplified Types"),
    lcid(0x0),
    version(1.0)
]


library PersistHistory
{
    importlib("stdole2.tlb");
    [
        uuid(7FD52380-4E07-101B-AE2D-08002B2EC713),
        odl
    ]
    interface IPersistStreamInit : IUnknown
    {
        HRESULT GetClassID([in] long pClassID);
        // IsDirty returns S_OK or S_FALSE. VB can't
        // distinguish between these values, so we
        // change the return type to long.
        long IsDirty();
        HRESULT Load([in] long pStream);
        HRESULT Save([in] long pStream,
                     [in] long fClearDirty);
        HRESULT GetSizeMax([in] long pcbSize);
    }
    [
        uuid(91A565C1-E38F-11d0-94BF-00A0C9055CBF),
        odl
    ]
    interface IPersistHistory : IUnknown
    {

        HRESULT GetClassID([in] long pClassID);
        HRESULT LoadHistory([in] long pStream,
                            [in] long pbc);
        HRESULT SaveHistory([in] long pStream);
        HRESULT SetPositionCookie([in] long
                                      dwPositionCookie);
        HRESULT GetPositionCookie([out,retval] long*
                                      pdwPositionCookie);
```

```
            }
        }
```

When this definition is in place, the control's actual implementation is surprisingly simple. In addition to helping the compiler, you can also simplify the implementation by using a heavy hand when you VB-ize the interface. The sample control has a single TextBox, called txtData, which maintains its value while walking through the browser's history. (This project is contained in the Samples\PersistHistory directory on the CD.)

```vb
Implements IPersistHistory

'The three functions we care about simply defer to the
'IPersistStreamInit implementation
Private Sub IPersistHistory_GetClassID( _
  ByVal pClassID As Long)
Dim pPSI As IPersistStreamInit
    Set pPSI = Me
    pPSI.GetClassID pClassID
End Sub
Private Sub IPersistHistory_LoadHistory( _
  ByVal pStream As Long, ByVal pbc As Long)
Dim pPSI As IPersistStreamInit
    Set pPSI = Me
    pPSI.Load pStream
End Sub
Private Sub IPersistHistory_SaveHistory( _
  ByVal pStream As Long)
Dim pPSI As IPersistStreamInit
    Set pPSI = Me
    pPSI.Save pStream, 0
End Sub


'These both return E_NOTIMPL, as indicated in MSDN.
Private Sub IPersistHistory_SetPositionCookie ( _
  ByVal dwPositionCookie As Long)
    Err.Raise E_NOTIMPL
End Sub
Private Function IPersistHistory_GetPositionCookie() As Long
```

```
        Err.Raise E_NOTIMPL
End Function

'Property bag procedures are called by the control's native
'IPersistStreamInit implementation.
Private Sub UserControl_InitProperties()
    txtData.Text = "<No Data>"
End Sub
Private Sub UserControl_ReadProperties
  (PropBag As PropertyBag)
    txtData.Text = PropBag.ReadProperty("Data")
End Sub
Private Sub UserControl_WriteProperties( _
  PropBag As PropertyBag)
    PropBag.WriteProperty "Data", txtData.Text
End Sub

Private Sub UserControl_Resize()
    txtData.Move 0, 0, ScaleWidth, ScaleHeight
End Sub
```

Registry Effects and Side Effects

Type libraries are tightly coupled with the registry. When you register a type library, you add a key to the HKEY_CLASSES_ROOT\TypeLib section registry. But this key is not the only one added: Typelib registration also adds keys to the HKCR\Interface section. This section plays the pivotal role that allows you to call COM methods across thread, process, and machine boundaries. When you register a VB-created ActiveX server, VB automatically registers the contained typelib resource, including changes to the Interface section.

```
HKEY_CLASSES_ROOT
    Interface
        {39719D96-9A7A-11D3-BBEC-D41203C10000}
            (Default) = IMyInterface
            ProxyStubClsid
                (Default) = {00020424-0000-0000-C000-
                            000000000046}
            ProxyStubClsid32
```

```
          (Default) = {00020424-0000-0000-C000-
                         000000000046}
     TypeLib
          (Default) = {39719D93-9A7A-11D3-BBEC-
                         D41203C10000}
          Version = 1.0
```

If you track down the ProxyStubClsid32 key in the CLSID section, you'll find the following.

```
HKEY_CLASSES_ROOT
   CLSID
      {00020424-0000-0000-C000-000000000046}
          (Default) = PSOAInterface
          InProcServer
              (Default) = ole2disp.Dll
          InProcServer32
              (Default) = oleaut32.Dll
              ThreadingModel = Both
```

Together, these keys indicate that the methods and properties of the IMyInterface interface are marshaled using OleAut32.Dll, which in turn looks up the interface in the specified TypeLib to find out how to perform the marshaling. If COM can't find the Interface or TypeLib keys, you can't marshal the interface. This key is added for all interfaces marked with the *oleautomation* or *dual* attributes, which tell OLE Automation to marshal based on the type library. These keys are written to the registry whenever a typelib is registered, even if they are already present. This is usually the desired effect, but it means that you have to be extremely careful with VB-ized interfaces to avoid overriding the system settings. For example, the settings for IObjectSafety look like this

```
HKEY_CLASSES_ROOT
   Interface
      {CB5BDC81-93C1-11CF-8F20-00805F2CD064}
          (Default) = IObjectSafety
          NumMethods
              (Default) = 5
          ProxyStubClsid32
```

```
        (Default) = _
            {B8DA6310-E19B-11D0-933C-00A0C90DCAA9}

HKEY_CLASSES_ROOT
    CLSID
        {B8DA6310-E19B-11D0-933C-00A0C90DCAA9}
            (Default) = PSFactoryBuffer
            InProcServer32
                (Default) = "C:\WINNT\System32\ACTXPRXY.Dll"
                ThreadingModel = Both
```

If you create a VB-ized version of the IObjectSafety interface and override the registry setting, the IObjectSafety interface no longer functions on your machine. You also lose all the information about the Interface key's former contents, so restoring your system is nontrivial. Interface key corruption is a nasty bug to track: It often doesn't manifest itself until weeks or months after the injury has occurred. You must be very careful not to not use the *oleautomation* or *dual* attributes when you VB-ize interfaces. Note that there is a relatively new flag, *proxy,* that disables the Interface key modifications regardless of the other flags, but most MkTypLib and MIDL versions do not recognize this attribute.

You might think that VB-izing an interface can cause problems with marshaling. However, there is no problem whatsoever in practice. The customized interfaces affect only the code in your project. As soon as you leave the project boundary, you turn control over to the system to perform any necessary marshaling. The only information the system has about the interface is its IID, which is the same in both the native and the VB-ized versions of a system interface. The system uses the object specified with the registered ProxyStubClsid32 entry for all marshaling, which means that the VB-ized interface is completely out of the picture once you get to the marshaling layer.

The introduction of public structures in VB6 introduced another twist to VB's dependence on correctly registered typelibs. Public structures allow you to declare a Public Type in any public class module and correctly marshal that type. You have to worry about registry settings only when you marshal interfaces, but you must deal with correctly registered record types in your local project as well. Typelib-driven marshaling of structures requires a typelib just like that required by interface marshaling but the retrieval mechanism does not require an Interface setting. Structure marshaling occurs as part of the interface marshaling through the typelib description of a record type. However, marshaling a simple type is only one consideration.

In addition to passing a simple record type, you can also pass a record in a Variant or in an array. Both require an attached description of the record, called an IRecordInfo. VB uses the GetRecordInfoFromGuids API to retrieve an IRecordInfo reference to attach to a Variant or SafeArray. GetRecordInfoFromGuids takes a LIBID to identify the typelib and the record's GUID to identify the type in that library. Although the IRecordInfo is needed only for marshaling, there is no way to know if marshaling will be required when the array or Variant is created. VB always tries to locate the typelib and record whenever you use an array or Variant with a Public structure, even if you never marshal it.

As a result of all of these considerations, the typelib that contains the record must be correctly registered if you want to marshal it or use it in a Variant or array. If you just want an array, there is one simple workaround: Omit the uuid attribute when you define the type. Without the uuid, the VB compiler makes no attempt to locate the IRecordInfo, so you don't need a registered typelib. However, you can't put the structure in a Variant, and you can't marshal an array of structures when you don't specify the IID.

You should also pay attention to typelib dependencies when you define public interfaces because all dependencies of a given interface must be correctly registered to support marshaling. For example, the VBoostTypes typelib defines a VBGUID record type without a uuid parameter. You must have VBoostTypes6.Olb registered on all machines that use the public interface if you want to use VBGUID

Table 15.3.   Rules for using public records

Desired Feature	Requirement
Marshal simple type	Registered typelib, no uuid required
Marshal array or variant	Registered typelib, uuid required
Assign to variant	Registered typelib, uuid required
Assign to array	Registered typelib only required if uuid specified
Pass simple type in same thread	Registered typelib not required

and have the interface marshal correctly. However, you don't need VBoostTypes registered to create an array of VBGUIDs because the uuid attribute is not specified. Similarly, you can't use the intrinsic alias type, such as DWORD and ULONG, in public interfaces that you ship because this adds a typelib dependency. This causes problems with VBoostTypes6.Olb and other typelibs that are designed for development use only, so you should use the Post-Build Type Library Modifier add-in described later to move external typelib dependencies into the shipping product.

MkTypLib Versus MIDL Versus Direct API Calls

Microsoft has officially replaced MkTypLib.EXE with MIDL.EXE as its preferred typelib compiler. However, I've found—through hard experience—that MkTypLib works better for producing typelibs designed strictly for VB. MIDL is a much more powerful general-purpose tool than MkTypLib. The primary purpose of MIDL is the generation of custom-marshaling DLLs, while the primary purpose of MkTypLib is the generation of type libraries. MIDL introduces complexity that you just don't need to create typelibs for VB's compiler. There are also several quirks in MIDL that make it difficult to use for VB typelib generation.

- MIDL always resolves stdole.IUnknown to the type VT_UNKNOWN instead of the VT_USERDEFINED type with a GUID of IID_IUnknown. There is no way to use MIDL to satisfy the common requirement of specifying an IUnknown type for use in VB-ized Implements interfaces.

- MIDL doesn't let you redefine an IID that has already been used in an imported library. You can't create a VB-ized version of an interface that is defined in an importlib, forcing you to fully redefine (not just alias) the other types the interface needs as well.

- MIDL requires additional syntax to prevent it from generating alias types for enums and records. In MIDL, the first piece of ODL shown below generates two types: an enum called something like __MIDL___MIDL _itf_filename_0000_0001, and an alias to that enum called MyEnum. You must use the second variation to force MIDL to make a single type.

I mentioned earlier that aliases to enums are bad news for the compiler, so you should always use the second syntax with MIDL.

```
// Generates an enum and an alias.
typedef [public] enum
{
    Value1
} MyEnum;

// Just generates an enum.
typedef [public] enum MyEnum
{
    Value1
} MyEnum;
```

- MIDL requires extra path information to compile correctly. In particular, it requires the include path to contain the VC98\Include subdirectory of the Visual Studio installation.

- MkTypLib.EXE ships with the standalone VB product; MIDL does not.

- MIDL and MkTypLib use different syntaxes for a Boolean type. MkTypLib uses boolean, which maps to a one-byte type in MIDL rather than the two-byte OLE Automation standard. To allow the ODL to work with both compilers, you should use VARIANT_BOOL instead of boolean in the body of the library and include the following lines near the top of the ODL file.

```
#ifdef __MKTYPLIB__
#ifdef VARIANT_BOOL
#undef VARIANT_BOOL
#endif
#define VARIANT_BOOL boolean
#endif //__MKTYPLIB__
```

MkTypLib and MIDL are not the only options available for typelib creation. In fact, these compilers are just wrappers that call the ICreateTypeLib2 and ICreateTypeInfo2 interfaces. You can get an ICreateTypeLib2 interface from the

CreateTypeLib2 API in OleAut32.Dll or simply by calling QueryInterface on any ITypeLib reference. Similarly, you can get an ICreateTypeInfo2 interface from an ITypeInfo reference. All the type library interfaces and functions are defined in TLBTypes.olb (VBoost: Type Library Types and Interfaces) included with this book. In addition, there is a type library editor add-in, called PowerVB Type Library Editor, that allows you to define and modify referenced typelibs from within VB's IDE. (Source code for this and all other tools is included.)

There are several reasons to use the typelib API directly. First, the API enables a friendly graphical interface that isn't available with ODL. Second, it enables you to duplicate or edit existing typelibs. Third, there are several things you can do with the API that aren't possible with the compilers. For example, you can specify multiple help files for a single typelib, use a nonzero base for a fixed-size array, and explicitly lay out the vtable order (complete with holes in the vtable if you like). The API also supports the use of types before they have been defined in the typelib (forward referencing). VB generates typelibs with strange ordering. For example, enums and records are defined *after* the functions that use them. If you dump the ODL for a VB-generated typelib and try to compile, compilation often fails. The only way to reliably edit the compatibility file or other VB-generated typelibs is with the direct ICreateType* interfaces.

You may not think that the type ordering is important. But if you use your libraries from VBA and change the type ordering, you must also increase at least the minor version number of the library. If you don't, your VBA project crashes when it attempts to recompile against the new library. I don't know of any other tools that care about the type ordering in a library, but there may be others as well.

Binary Compatibility

COM component upgrades are a frequent requirement of most systems. After all, one of the main reasons for using components is the ability to update a single component without updating the entire application. You might want to upgrade a DLL or OCX to fix a bug or add new features. In either case, you generally want to be sure that code designed to run against the old version also runs correctly against the new version. This is the goal of a VB project's compatibility settings.

VB provides three options for compatibility. The first option, *No compatibility,* makes VB regenerate all externally visible elements of your executable for every recompile. The typelib's LIBID changes, as do the CLSIDs, IIDs, vtable order, DISPIDs, and any other ID you can think of. The next compatibility level, *Project Compatibility,* locks the LIBID and CLSID values, but everything else is vulnerable. This allows persistent cross-project references during the development cycle. When *No Compatibility* is set, you must constantly edit the project references for any consuming project. Project Compatibility is a convenient setting for early development, but it does not offer nearly enough version control for upgrading components robustly. You should always select the maximum level of compatibility checking—*Binary Compatibility*—before a component leaves your machine.

You will generally set the compatibility file to a compiled version of the executable. Although VB lets you set compatibility against the target executable, you should avoid doing this for two reasons. First, if there are references between types, (such as a method in ClassX that returns an object of type ClassY) the Make EXE step fails because VB is using the file. Second, if you point your compatibility file to the constantly updating target executable, your compatibility file ends up containing information about builds that you no longer care about. A typical development cycle involves many intermediate builds, but very few ever make it to a machine outside your development and quality-assurance organizations. You care only about compatibility with previous versions you've actually deployed to real customers—not the versions they've never seen. But VB doesn't distinguish between intermediate and shipping versions and it happily makes sure that the program is compatible with not only the official versions, but with all of the garbage in between as well.

How Compatibility Saves You

You've already seen that VB handles all typelib generation. Compatibility adds a new twist to these automatically generated typelibs because they need to work with previous versions as well as the current version. The typelib's layout is based partially on the compatibility file and partially on the current project. For every interface, VB makes sure that all methods and properties of the interface as defined in the compatibility file are also present in the new project. If the interface is binary compatible but VB finds new methods or properties, it does five things, all without notifying you of a change.

- VB gives the interface a new IID.

- VB adds an alias type to the typelib. The alias is given the IID of the original interface, and it points back at the current interface. The alias is a hidden type, and is called something like Class1___v0, with the same version number as the previous interface version.

- VB increments the minor version number on the interface. Note that this version number is never actually used for marshaling or compiling: It is simply a bookkeeping mechanism.

- VB increments the minor version number of the typelib. This number *is* used, in particular by VBA. If the minor version of a referenced typelib changes, VBA automatically recompiles code that references that library. Note that incrementing the version number is critical if the order of types in the library changes. VBA crashes during recompilation if you change the type ordering but not the version number.

- VB modifies the _IID_CLASS1 resource. VB builds one of these resources for each interface defined in the project. The binary format of an IID resource is simple: The first four-byte long indicates the number of IIDs in the list, and this number is followed by a list of IIDs (the newest listed last).

If the new file is saved as your compatibility file, this whole process is repeated if you add one or more methods before you recompile. If you don't update the compatibility file, VB keeps using it as a base to construct the new typelib. In practice, this means that the actual IID of your interface changes frequently and turns into a moving target for anyone who uses it. For example, consider the following sequence.

1. You have an ActiveX DLL with a binary compatible file set, and you need a new method on one of your classes.

2. You add the method and compile the DLL.

3. You close your DLL project and work on another project, which calls the DLL. You may or may not need the new method. You compile the project.

4. The next day, you fix a bug in the new method and recompile the DLL.

5. Your compiled EXE now fails with a *Type mismatch* error when it trys to retrieve the interface.

The step you missed here is that the new method wasn't found in the compatibility file, so VB regenerated a new IID each time you rebuilt the executable. Note that depending on the number and type of edits you made between compiles, the IID might not change if you compile twice in the same IDE session. You must copy the DLL that contains the new method as your compatibility file in order to lock down the IID. The dilemma here is that the amount of baggage in the compatibility file—and hence in your finished product—grows every time you add a method.

Visual Basic requires all the extra information about old interface IIDs to make the DLL a binary replacement for the previous versions of the typelib. VB uses the IID resources to provide marshaling support for all the previous interfaces, and uses the resources to enable the QueryInterface function to respond correctly to a request for a previous interface identifier. To support marshaling on a legacy interface, VB replaces the Interface\{…}\TypeLib key with an Interface\{…}\Forward key that points to the primary interface. The Forward key instructs the typelib-driven marshaling engine to treat the interface the same as the currently implemented primary interface.

You get to carry all this compatibility information around in your finished product. The resources get bigger and you add to registry overhead as you extend interfaces, the typelib grows as more and more aliases are added, and the data-driven QueryInterface implementation behind the publicly exposed objects has ever-more data to check before it can reply yes or no to an interface request. Fortunately, any client compiled against a new version of the DLL won't be able to get the interface it expects from an old DLL and call a method that is not supported on the old version of the vtable.

Watching the changes that VB makes to a specific interface offers a lot of insights into the way VB lays out a typelib and the type of conditions against which it tries to protect you. The following exercise looks at three versions of a simple class file. I'll build a binary compatibility file against the first version, then modify the class by adding a function and then renaming the first function. I'll ignore IID changes and look at three other fields. The first relevant number is the vtable offset; the second is the DISPID, and the third is the order in which the function is listed in the typelib.

```
'The starting class
Public Function F1() As Long
End Function
Public Function F2() As Long
End Function

'Add a function
Public Function F1() As Long
End Function
```

Table 15.4.   Function layout in the starting class

Function	VTable Offset	DISPID (hex)	Function Number
F1	28	60030000	1
F2	32	60030001	2

Table 15.5.   Function layout with a compatible edit

Function	VTable Offset	DISPID (hex)	Function Number
F1	28	60030000	1
F2	32	60030001	3
F3	36	60030002	2

Table 15.6.   Function layout with the compatibility broken

Function	VTable Offset	DISPID (hex)	Function Number
F1Ex	28	60030003	1
F2	36	60030005	3
F3	32	60030004	2

```
Public Function F3() As Long
End Function
Public Function F2() As Long
End Function


'Rename the first function, accepting the warning that you
'are breaking binary compatibility.
Public Function F1Ex() As Long
End Function
Public Function F3() As Long
End Function
Public Function F2() As Long
End Function
```

There are several pieces of information you can glean from this data. First, the function order in the typelib is always the same as the function order in the module. Second, vtable order is based first on binary-compatibility function order and then on the function order in the CLS file. Third, breaking compatibility can reorder the vtable (this is a corollary to the first and second observations). Fourth, VB goes out of its way to make sure that the DISPIDs in the new interface don't overlap the DISPID values in the binary-compatible interface. This is done because both the old and the new versions have the same CLSID, and both support IDispatch binding. You can make IDispatch calls on the interface without querying for the newly generated IID. Generating new DISPIDs along with the new IID effectively blocks a call against the previous version of the interface.

Part of the problem with breaking binary compatibility is that all the information about previous interfaces is lost, not only for the broken interface, but also for the other interfaces in the project. When compatibility is broken, the compatibility aliases are lost for all interfaces—not just the one you broke. The major version of the typelib is also incremented. VB essentially reverts to project compatibility, preserving only the LIBID and CLSID values.

Development Compatibility Requirements
The compatibility protection offered by VB is very strong, but you also need to consider how much is actually gained by changing the IID of an interface when

Table 15.7. Compatibility requirements as a function of calling code

Calling code	VTable	DISPID	Member Name	Interface Name
VTable bound	Yes	No	No	-
DISPID bound	No	Yes	No	-
Late bound	No	No	Yes	-
New	-	-	-	No
CreateObject	-	-	-	Yes

you add new methods to it. The interface identifier is used during the Set statement to verify that the running objects support the IID promised by its design-time typelib description. If a new client calls an old DLL that doesn't support the latest and greatest interface, the Set statement fails. If you simply add new methods to the end of the vtable and leave the IID the same, the Set statement succeeds, but a subsequent method call might call a function off the end of the vtable (which almost always results in a crash). In either case, your program can't continue if the client code calls a method that isn't supported by the current version of the ActiveX DLL. VB's IID modification process provides a kindler, gentler fatal error, but it's still a fatal error.

Constantly churning IIDs during rebuilds makes the individual components moving targets. This can cause a number of problems during the development cycle. This doesn't just create the bloat I've already described: It also forces you to recompile all the pieces of your application that consume a modified component, even if the calling code doesn't use the modified methods. This problem is compounded when you work in a development team or if you call components from C++, which is forced to regenerate header files whenever the target typelib changes. You want some level of compatibility control during the development process, but you rarely want the iron-clad protection that VB offers. The full armor certainly doesn't hurt the shipping versions, but it is excessively cumbersome if you have to wear it all the time.

If you want the IID to remain the same when you modify an interface, you must pick and choose among three types of compatibility. The type of compatibility you need depends entirely on how current versions of calling applications bind to your object. If the calling code is vtable bound, you need to maintain the vtable order and function signatures for all existing functions. However, the actual names of the functions and the DISPID values can change because they are not used. If your code is early-id bound, the vtable and names can change, but the DISPID values must remain the same. If calling code is fully late-bound, you must keep the names the same. In addition to these member changes, you can also change the class's name if existing code uses the New keyword exclusively instead of CreateObject.

Binary Compatibility Editing

The PowerVB Binary Compatibility Editor (EditCompat.Dll), documented on the book's CD, provides complete control over the binary compatibility file.

- You can make any direct edit to the file, provided it is compatible with VB-generated code. This includes changing member names, changing IIDs, deleting entire types, deleting secondary interfaces (produced by Implements statements), adding members, and other similar actions. Note that you should need this direct-editing capability only if you can't choose the Preserve Compatibility option when you compile your project. Some of these edits might produce a change in the IID resources of the compatibility file. Note that this leaves the resources of the compatibility file inconsistent with the compiled code: You can still use the file for compatibility reasons, but you won't be able to use it as an executable.

- You can back out any IID updates generated by adding new members to an interface. This takes place after a build has succeeded without compatibility errors by generating a new compatibility file (based on the typelib from the new EXE) and IIDs from the old compatibility file.

- You can automatically remove all the aliasing baggage from your compatibility file. Just provide a directory that contains copies of all the previously shipped versions of your executable. All the versions are analyzed to determine which of the intermediate interfaces must actually be supported. Any aliased interfaces not found in previous versions are eliminated.

In short, the binary-compatibility add-in puts you in full control of component versioning. You can make edits that add or remove compatibility support from the compatibility file, and then let VB regenerate the executable against the current settings. This allows you to make simple edits, such as changing a member name, adding a new member, or removing an Implements interface, without creating problems in existing code. Although this is a great tool for development, it gives you the opportunity to mess things up pretty badly. You should always verify that you can set your binary compatibility file to the last-shipped version and build without receiving compatibility errors.

Post-Build Type-Library Modifications

VB puts a great deal of information in a component's type library, but there is often more typelib-resident information that you need to distribute before your application can run. If your component requires such information, you must distribute and administer extra files along with your VB-built binary. When you register a VB component, the VB runtime automatically registers its typelib for you. You can make VB register more (or less) typelib information by modifying the original typelib and replacing the original typelib with the customized version. There are several common scenarios in which you will find this technique very useful. All the edits mentioned here are possible with the PowerVB Post-Build Type Library Modifier (PostBuild.Dll), documented on the book's CD. This section simply looks at some of the reasons why you might want to use it.

- If you've described an interface for Implements by using a typelib, and you need that interface to be accessible across thread, process, or machine boundaries, you must register a typelib that contains the interface definition. This generally means that you must ship and register a TLB file in addition to the component. You can eliminate the extra file dependency by importing the external types into your executable's typelib resource and redirecting all the external references to the internal copy.

- If you've used Implements as an internal (intra-thread) design construct, and you don't want to broadcast this information, you have two options. First, you can simply leave the interface definition attached to the class and orphan it by not shipping the referenced typelib. This is a benign solution unless the binary is an OCX and you need it to work with VB5. In this case, you must ship the referenced library or end up with a control that has no events in the IDE (this OCA-generation bug has been fixed in VB6). Second, you can modify the typelib and delete the rogue interface reference. Note that the solution you really want here is support for Private Implements in VB, which would allow a class to support an interface without writing it to the typelib.

- If you implement an interface using the VBoost aggregation objects, the interface is not shown on the coclass. If you want to publicize your implementation of this interface, you must add it to the list of implemented interfaces.

- If you've VB-ized a typelib-defined interface to help with Implements, the typelib has a reference to the VB-ized typelib, not the original typelib. If you don't ship and register the VB-ized library, this reference dangles and its interface identifier can't be read. Some applications verify a component by searching for an implemented interface on a coclass. If you want a VB-generated component to be identifiable, you need to redirect the interface to the true typelib instead of the VB-ized version.

- There are some types of data that you can't define in VB. For example, you may want to include string constants or aliases with your executable. With post-build modification, you can define the types in an external library and merge them into the executable's library before you ship.

- You may find it easier to define structures and enums in a typelib instead of as public entries in a class module. This gives you the freedom to modify enums without causing binary-compatibility changes, and it enables alignment capabilities on your public structures. If you merge these into your main typelib before you ship, you don't have to redistribute the external libraries.

- If you want to change the default interface of a class, you need to edit the typelib. The VBoost objects enable you to redirect a QueryInterface request for the IDispatch object to a secondary interface, but this doesn't help you if you never receive a QI for IID_IDispatch. By modifying the typelib *and* redirecting the QI call, you can keep the object implementation and the typelib description of your object in sync. This enables you to put a standard default interface on multiple objects and also to build VB objects with methods such as Open, Close, Input, Output, Stop, and so on. In general, you can't use these names because VB won't let you use a method or property name that conflicts with a keyword.

- You can help the marshaler by changing [in,out] parameter settings to either [in] or [out]. Changing [in,out] to [in] on an array or structure type can save an entire array copy when the function call returns. Changing an array parameter's attribute to [out] guarantees that you always have an empty array to work with when it is called from an external source.

The typelib tools provided with the book are meant to enhance but not replace VB's automatic typelib generation. Most of the time, VB does what you want. These tools just provide a few enhancements you need to ease your development process and produce a highly professional finished product.

Chapter 16

Controlling Windows

Although VB6 uses COM objects extensively, it is generally viewed as primarily a Window's development tool. Your first VB project was most likely a Standard EXE that had a form or two, not an ActiveX DLL. When you participate in the Windows environment, you devote a lot of development time to creating and interacting with forms, controls, and other VB elements that have a graphical representation. After all, the best back-end engine in the world is worthless if you can't display the results to a user. This chapter focuses on applying technologies from this book to the specific problems of subclassing and window creation. Subclassing allows you to interact with the stream of messages sent from the operating system to a window object. Window creation allows you to create custom windows from scratch rather than adopt them after VB has created them for you.

A window is like a COM object in many ways. Window objects use memory, encapsulate an implementation behind a set of publicly defined functions, and have a specific type, a unique identity, and a well-defined lifetime. But a window differs from a COM object in that it has a single owner, is manipulated through API functions rather than methods, and it receives all event notifications through a single function. Just as external calls to a COM object use a pointer to the object, calls to window objects use a *window handle,* or HWND (Handle to WiNDow). You can think of an HWND as a weak reference to a window object. Storing an HWND does not imply that you own the window object in the same sense that holding a strong reference on a COM object guarantees that the object remains alive. Windows itself owns every window object and ultimately controls the lifetime of them all.

External manipulation of a window object takes place through the subset of the Windows API that takes an HWND as the first parameter or that returns an HWND value. The collection of API functions provided for manipulating an HWND is loosely coupled and randomly ordered: a stark contrast with the tightly defined world of COM vtables, interfaces, and methods. All HWND functions are declared in the User32 part of the Win32 API. The other two core groups of functions are Kernel32, which handles the core OS operations such as process and thread creation, and GDI32, which contains drawing functions. A User32-controlled window lives within a process created by Kernel32, and it is drawn using GDI32.

You will see a number of API calls in this chapter. Although I briefly discuss the API functions that are directly applicable to the core concepts presented here I'm leaving you on your own to research the other calls. There are a number of good API books that address several different skill levels. I also recommend keeping your MSDN CDs up to date to get the most complete API information.

I have not tried to create a comprehensive set of TypeLib-declared API calls because this book is not a comprehensive (or even partial) overview of using the Win32 API with VB. The projects referenced in this chapter rely on Declare statements to access the Window's API, but you could also use a type library if you like. I'd recommend using the API typelib from Bruce McKinney's *Hardcore Visual Basic* (Microsoft Press). Bruce has chosen not to complete a third edition of his book and is no longer updating this typelib. You need not fret, however, because some very able hands still maintain the typelib. You can find an up-to-date version of the typelib, complete with source, at http://www.TheMandelbrotSet.com.

The two most common HWND functions are SendMessage, which sends a synchronous message to a window and doesn't return until the message is processed, and PostMessage, which adds a pending message to the target window's message queue and returns immediately. Windows pulls messages from the message queue one at a time and sends them to the current "window procedure" for the window object. The window procedure is the single entry point for all events that come into a window. Almost all API calls made against an HWND wind up as one or more messages sent to the window procedure. The WM_PAINT message is a good example of a message received by a window procedure. Processing the WM_PAINT message provides full control over what is painted in the client area of a window. Clearly, whoever controls the window procedure controls the window.

Subclassing

You must control the window procedure to customize a window's response to the messages it receives. This is easy because Windows lets you replace the current window procedure of any window in your process with a new procedure. The window procedure is simply a function pointer that you can replace with a different function pointer, using the SetWindowLong API with the GWL_WNDPROC index. Subclassing is conceptually equivalent to the IUnknown hooking techniques that VBoost uses, but it is much easier because you have to replace only a single function instead of a multi-function entire vtable. When you replace the window procedure, SetWindowLong returns the previous function pointer. Your procedure should handle the messages it wants to and then forward all other calls to the previous window procedure with the CallWindowProc API function. To ensure proper window termination, you should restore the original value of the window procedure before the window is destroyed. The most basic window procedure simply defers to the next window procedure in the chain.

```
Function WindowProc(ByVal hWnd As Long, ByVal uMsg As Long, _
    ByVal wParam As Long, ByVal lParam As Long) As Long
    'Debug.Print Hex$(uMsg) 'Put useful code here.
    WindowProc = CallWindowProc(m_wndprcNext, hWnd, uMsg, _
                        wParam, lParam)
End Function
```

This function has one big problem: The m_wndprcNext variable is undefined. This leads to the first issue you must address whenever you subclass: How do you associate a window procedure, which must be in a BAS module so you can apply the AddressOf operator, with a m_wndprcNext value, which must be stored separately for each window you subclass. If you declare m_wndprcNext in the same BAS module as the window procedure, you can use that BAS module to subclass only a single window. A subclassing system that scales reliably to only one window is clearly not a complete solution.

The m_wndprcNext value is the tip of the iceberg when it comes to the data you need for a real window procedure. If you subclass to customize the painting of a control window, you need the current settings of the control instance associated with the given HWND value. Ideally, you want to have the window procedure defined as a function in a UserControl module itself so you can access private member variables to accurately draw the control.

The identifying HWND parameter is the only unique value that Windows hands your window procedure. For this reason, mapping a window procedure to instance data has traditionally involved storing a weak reference to the instance using API calls and the HWND itself. The instance data can be stored by using the GWL_USERDATA index and the SetWindowLong function, or by using the GetProp and SetProp API calls. These techniques were first discussed by William Storage and myself in the February 1997 edition of *Visual Basic Programmers Journal*. These techniques work well, but they are no longer necessary.

What you *really* want with subclassing is a function pointer that can call a Friend function in a class module without having to perform extra processing to locate the associated instance. I introduced the concept of a PushParamThunk in the "Pointers to Class Functions" section of Chapter 11. This little piece of dynamically-generated assembly code eliminates the need to associate any data with an HWND because the instance data is built into the custom-generated window procedure. Subclassing is just a special case of using a pointer to call an instance-based function.

You can now easily subclass a window by using the SetWindowLong and CallWindowProc API functions and a PushParamThunk-generated window procedure. The only missing ingredient is the HWND itself, which is provided by the hWnd property on VB's windowed objects (Form.hWnd, Text1.hWnd,

UserControl.hWnd, and so on). Subclassing in Listing 16.1 consists of helper functions from SubClass.bas (found in the Code directory on the book's CD), calls to those functions, a Friend window procedure in a Form, and a simple BAS function that redirects calls to the form instance.

Listing 16.1. **Subclassing is easy when you use a PushParamThunk and redirection in a BAS module to call a window procedure in a CLS, FRM, or CTL module.**

```
'Support code from SubClass.Bas
'Requires: PushParamThunk.bas
'This listing does not show the debugging support
'discussed later in the chapter.
Public Type SubClassData
    wndprocNext As Long
    wndprocThunk As PushParamThunk
End Type


Public Sub SubClass( _
   Data As SubClassData, ByVal hWnd As Long, _
   ByVal ThisPtr As Long, ByVal pfnRedirect As Long)
      With Data
         'Make sure we aren't currently subclassed.
         If .wndprocNext Then
             SetWindowLong hWnd, GWL_WNDPROC, .wndprocNext
             .wndprocNext = 0
         End If

         'Generate the window procedure function.
         InitPushParamThunk .wndprocThunk, ThisPtr, pfnRedirect

         'Establish the new window function.
         .wndprocNext = SetWindowLong _
           (hWnd, GWL_WNDPROC, .wndprocThunk.pfn)
      End With
End Sub
Public Sub UnSubClass( _
   Data As SubClassData, ByVal hWnd As Long)
      With Data
         'Restore the window procedure to its original value.
         If .wndprocNext Then
```

```
                    SetWindowLong hWnd, GWL_WNDPROC, .wndprocNext
                    .wndprocNext = 0
                End If
            End With
        End Sub
```

```
    'Code in Form1
    Private m_SubClassMain As SubClassData

    Private Sub Form_Load()
        'Use the helper function to establish the subclass.
        SubClass m_SubClassMain, _
            Me.hWnd, ObjPtr(Me), AddressOf RedirectForm1WindowProc
    End Sub

    Private Sub Form_Unload(Cancel As Integer)
        UnSubClass m_SubClassMain, Me.hWnd
    End Sub

    Friend Function WindowProc( _
        ByVal hWnd As Long, ByVal uMsg As Long, _
        ByVal wParam As Long, ByVal lParam As Long) As Long
        'Watch the messages (add real code here).
        Debug.Print Hex$(uMsg)
        'Defer to the original window procedure.
        WindowProc = CallWindowProc(m_SubClassMain.wndprocNext, _
            hWnd, uMsg, wParam, lParam)
    End Function
```

```
    'Code in a BAS module.
    Public Function RedirectForm1WindowProc(ByVal This As Form1, _
        ByVal hWnd As Long, ByVal uMsg As Long, _
        ByVal wParam As Long, ByVal lParam As Long) As Long
        'Redirect to the Form1 instance provided by the thunk.
        RedirectForm1WindowProc = _
            This.WindowProc(hWnd, uMsg, wParam, lParam)
    End Function
```

From a pure API perspective, subclassing a window object is straight-forward. Introducing a new window procedure into the current procedure chain also adds very little overhead to your program. The entire operation shown in Listing 16.1 amounts to four additional calls to very fast functions (Windows→Thunk→Redirect→WindowProc→CallWindowProc→original window procedure). The calls are direct, meaning that none requires a vtable lookup. You generally code a window procedure by using a Select Case statement to determine which message you're examining. A Select Case statement with constant Long-type Case values is also very fast. The bottom line is that a properly written window procedure does not add significant overhead to processing window messages—except for the messages you actually care about and process.

There are several third-party controls that claim to make subclassing easier. Before the introduction of AddressOf in VB5, subclassing required external help. But you no longer need to add the overhead of an external control to meet your basic subclassing needs. If you do decide to use an external component to subclass, there are several things you should know.

- The cost of instantiating a control is significantly higher than the cost of using subclassing directly. A PushParamThunk is a small embedded structure (28 bytes) allocated with the memory for the UserControl instance. Loading a separate control involves heap allocations by both VB and the control. There is no way the control can initialize the subclass faster than you can with the API.

- If you use an ActiveX DLL object instead of a control to do your subclassing, the overhead is less, but you have to write just as much code in each form or control as you would to use the SubClass.Bas helper functions.

- Subclassing controls generally require a list of messages to look for and a set of flags to indicate when you should be notified that the message has fired. This approach requires a lookup for every message. No matter how good the lookup is, it will not be faster than the code generated by the simple, compiled VB Select Case statement. You have to write the Select Case anyway if you're interested in more than one message.

- You should never use a control that notifies you of a message via an event procedure. Events are IDispatch-based, and they are much slower than direct function calls or vtable calls. But performance isn't the only issue. If you subclass with events and show a MsgBox or modal form while debugging in the IDE, all the events in the modally-blocked part of the application stop firing. If you are subclassing with event procedures, you don't get window message notifications, and your control doesn't function properly. This is unacceptable for a commercial-quality control, especially when it doesn't have to happen. Frozen events are generally not a problem in a compiled application.

- Controls that use an Implements-interface callback instead of an event procedure are a big improvement, but they still involve control-instantiation, the lookup costs for every message, and vtable-call overhead for the relevant message. This does not compare favorably with SubClass.Bas.

- SubClass.Bas is compiled into your project. You needn't rely on external files. No one needs to know which technologies you're using to make your application tick.

- You already own SubClass.Bas.

- If you can't figure out the API work necessary for subclassing, you are kidding yourself if you think you'll be able to do any meaningful API work within your window procedure. This is not meant to discourage you from using subclassing: I'm just pointing out that subclassing is one of the easiest things you can do with the Win32 API.

Debugging Subclassed Windows

Despite the disadvantages inherent in subclassing controls, there is one legitimate perceived advantage: If you subclass using a control, you can actually hit a breakpoint while debugging. The problem with subclassing directly to an AddressOf procedure is that VB doesn't actually give you a function pointer to the code itself, but rather to a small thunk procedure. This procedure prevents you from running the AddressOf function when you're in break mode. This thunk is out of the picture after you compile your executable, but it wreaks havoc when you're in the IDE.

VB doesn't actually crash if you enter break mode while a direct subclass is in place. Instead, you confuse Windows just enough that you can't use either the

IDE or the form you're trying to debug. Windows requires that a window procedure take certain actions before it returns control, but the AddressOf blocking thunks do nothing and return 0. If you're lucky, you'll be able to hit F5 and continue. But if not, you have to kill the VB process and start over.

Fortunately, there is a way out of this situation. The solution is built into SubClass.Bas. The approach is straightforward: If VB is in break mode, you defer to the original window procedure directly instead of calling the AddressOf-supplied function first. In break mode, the project will run as if the subclass didn't exist. A DLL, DbgWProc.Dll, makes this possible. DbgWProc was first written for the February 1997 article I mentioned earlier, and it is also mentioned in MSDN as an available download. The original version supports only 100 concurrent subclasses, but the version with the book uses the PushParamThunk code to remove this limitation.

DbgWProc is easy to use, and it is designed to add no additional runtime overhead to subclassing code. Take the following steps to get painless debugging with direct API subclassing.

1. Add a project reference to Debug Object for AddressOf Subclassing. If this entry is not available in the References dialog, Browse to the PowerVB\Tools directory to add the reference.

2. On the Project Properties Dialog's Make tab, add the conditional compilation value DEBUGWINDOWPROC = 1.

3. Use SubClass and UnSubClass from SubClass.Bas just as you did before.

4. Change the DEBUGWINDOWPROC conditional value to 0 before you choose File/Make Exe. If you fail to do this and load DbgWProc.Dll when the IDE is not loaded, then you'll get a message box that says, "WindowProc debugging isn't required outside the Visual Basic design environment." This is a benign message (you can continue running the application), but you probably don't want to show it to your customers. You should not distribute DbgWProc.Dll with your application.

You can refer to SubClass.Bas on the CD for the code that enables debugging with an active subclass. Of course, SubClass.Bas does all the work for you,

Table 16.1. Call order for a subclassed window in different debugging and subclass states. Windows calls the first function.

Function Visited	No subclass	No hook	Hook (run)	Hook (break)
WindowProcHook function	-	-	1	1
PushParamThunk assembly	-	1	2	-
Bas module redirection	-	2	3	-
Replacement WindowProc	-	3	4	-
Original WindowProc	1	4	5	2

so you'll probably never have to duplicate this code. Just remember that the code now takes different execution paths depending on whether VB is in break mode or in run mode.

Now that the debugging hook is in place, you're ready to start programming your window procedure. If you use subclassing, you should always save the project before you run. The project will usually be more stable if you disable Compile On Demand on the Tools|Options dialog's General tab. You should also get out of the habit of performing a rude shutdown during a debug session with the Stop button or the End statement. If you follow these simple steps, you will enjoy many hours of crash-free subclass debugging ahead of you, assuming that you code all your API functions correctly the first time.

WM_GETMINMAXINFO Sample

Now that you have control of the window procedure, you can interact with any message you like. The Samples\SubClass directory on the CD contains four basic subclassing samples. Minimal contains the code above for use as a starting point. SystemMenu demonstrates the addition of an item to the system menu and a response to the message. DrawItem demonstrates catching the WM_DRAWITEM message to add pictures to a CheckBox style ListBox, and MinMaxInfo contains the code for the project shown here. The basic techniques are the same in all projects: The differences lie in the API code within the window procedure.

Windows sends the WM_GETMINMAXINFO message to a window procedure when the user attempts to resize or maximize a window. Setting values in the associated MINMAXINFO structure allows you to specify the minimum and maximum sizes for the window and to customize the size and position of a maximized window. The most common usage of the WM_GETMINMAXINFO message involves setting lower limits for the dimensions of your form. The Form_Resize event generally contains a lot of error-trapping code to handle the case where a user shrinks the window so much that it can no longer accommodate all the controls. Handling the WM_GETMINMAXINFO message allows you to greatly reduce the Form_Resize pain by calculating a minimum width and height for your form.

The biggest issue with coding against the WM_GETMINMAXINFO message is that you get a pointer to the MINMAXINFO structure in the window procedure's lParam argument. In C and C++, you simply cast the lParam to a MINMAXINFO* and access the memory directly. However, casting is not possible in straight VB. The most common approach is to use CopyMemory to copy the data to a local MINMAXINFO structure, modify the local, and then copy it back. Instead of relying on two CopyMemory calls, the MinMaxInfo sample uses an ArrayOwner to allow direct access to the pointer. It is easy to apply direct memory access techniques to this and other messages to interpret the ByVal Long lParam as an arbitrary type.

Listing 16.2. Use the WM_GETMINMAXINFO message to ensure that a window can't be resized to cover the lower right corner of a label control.

```
'modMinMaxInfo (SubClass\MinMaxInfo\MinMaxInfo.bas).
'External dependencies:
'   ArrayOwner.Bas or ArrayOwnerIgnoreOnly.Bas
'   PushParamThunk.Bas
'   SubClass.Bas

'API declares omitted

'Type and variable to allow direct access to
'a pointer to a MINMAXINFO structure.
Public Type OwnedMinMaxInfo
    Owner As ArrayOwner
```

```
            pSA() As MINMAXINFO
End Type
Public g_DerefMinMaxInfo As OwnedMinMaxInfo


'Project/Properties/General/Startup Object: = Sub Main
Public Sub Main()
    With g_DerefMinMaxInfo
        InitArrayOwner .Owner, LenB(.pSA(0)), 0
    End With
    frmMinMaxInfo.Show
End Sub


'Redirection function for PushParamThunk.
Public Function RedirectMinMaxInfoWindowProc( _
  ByVal This As frmMinMaxInfo, _
  ByVal hWnd As Long, ByVal uMsg As Long, _
  ByVal wParam As Long, ByVal lParam As Long) As Long
    RedirectMinMaxInfoWindowProc = _
       This.WindowProc(hWnd, uMsg, wParam, lParam)
End Function
```

```
'frmMinMaxInfo (SubClass\MinMaxInfo\MinMaxInfo.frm)
'This form has a single Label control (lblMessage)
'dropped somewhere in the middle of the form.
Private m_SubClassMain As SubClassData
Private m_MinTrackSize As POINTAPI
Private Sub Form_Load()
    'Find the minimum tracking size by using the
    'Label.AutoSize property to determine the size of the
    'control, then calculate the pixel offset of the lower
    'right corner of the label from the upper left corner of
    'the window. Note that the Left property of a control is
    'relative to the client area of the window, which needs
    'be adjusted by Width - ScaleWidth to get the position
    'relative to the actual corner of the window. The
    'equivalent vertical calculation is done against the
    'Top property.
    With lblMessage
        .AutoSize = True
        .Caption = _
          "Try to resize the form to cover this text."
```

```
            m_MinTrackSize.x = (.Left + .Width + _
                Width - ScaleWidth) \ Screen.TwipsPerPixelX
            m_MinTrackSize.y = (.Top + .Height + _
                Height - ScaleHeight) \ Screen.TwipsPerPixelY
        End With
        SubClass m_SubClassMain, Me.hWnd, ObjPtr(Me), _
            AddressOf RedirectMinMaxInfoWindowProc
    End Sub
    Private Sub Form_Unload(Cancel As Integer)
        UnSubClass m_SubClassMain, Me.hWnd
    End Sub
    Friend Function WindowProc( _
        ByVal hWnd As Long, ByVal uMsg As Long, _
        ByVal wParam As Long, ByVal lParam As Long) As Long
        Select Case uMsg
            Case WM_GETMINMAXINFO
                With g_DerefMinMaxInfo
                    .Owner.SA.pvData = lParam
                    'Read off the cached minimum tracking size.
                    'All other values are preset by Windows.
                    .pSA(0).ptMinTrackSize = m_MinTrackSize
                End With
                Exit Function 'Return 0 per MSDN.
            'Add other messages here.
        End Select
        WindowProc = CallWindowProc(m_SubClassMain.wndprocNext, _
            hWnd, uMsg, wParam, lParam)
    End Function
```

Custom Window Creation

Subclassing an existing window gives you full control over every action that the
window is asked to take. However, fully controlling the message stream does not
let you modify the type of the window or the attributes with which it was created. You must actually create the window yourself with the CreateWindowEx
API call to dictate every aspect of a window. Calling CreateWindowEx is relatively easy, but VB doesn't expect you to create your own windows. VB makes no
effort to help a custom-created window interact with the window objects that it
creates itself. Coercing VB into playing well with a window it didn't create is the
hard part of custom window creation.

You might wonder why you would ever want to call CreateWindowEx yourself when VB's intrinsic controls, combined with ability to create your own ActiveX controls, provide so much flexibility already (especially when you add subclassing to the equation). Despite the choices already available, there are three main areas where the lack of control over the CreateWindowEx call leaves you hanging.

- Most intrinsic control properties that are read-only at runtime correspond to style settings on the underlying windows that must be set when the window is created. For example, you can't change the Multi-Line property of a TextBox control after it has been created, and you can't change the MultiSelect, Style, or Sorted properties of a ListBox in code. There are many fundamental control properties that are read-only at runtime (even though VB6 eliminated a number of these). This is especially restrictive when using the new Controls.Add feature because you can't add an intrinsic control with anything but the default property values. Creating your own LISTBOX- or EDIT-style windows instead of using the intrinsic ListBox and TextBox controls also allows you to destroy and recreate the windows when you need to change read-only window styles.

- Even if all the VB control properties were writable at runtime, not all window styles have a corresponding property on the VB objects. For example, the system's LISTBOX window class supports an LBS_NODATA style that allows it to be completely virtual. With a virtual list, you can display a practically unlimited number of items without first copying all the data into the LISTBOX. However, the VB ListBox control does not have a NoData property, and VB does not provide an interface definition for populating a virtual ListBox control. Similarly, the common shell controls allow you to create a fully virtual ListView control. You can't get to either of these settings from VB. CreateWindowEx lets you use advanced features in the OS to create incredibly efficient controls tuned specifically for your applications.

- All of VB's controls are ANSI-based. Some Windows versions provide full UNICODE support for each of these controls. If you want a UNICODE-enabled app to run in Windows NT or Windows 2000, you run into a lot of problems when you use the intrinsic ANSI controls.

Once you've created your own window, controlling it requires the same code that you use to subclass windows that you didn't create. You call SetWindowLong on the new window to establish your window procedure, skim the relevant messages from the incoming message stream, and forward the ones you don't handle downstream with the CallWindowProc or DefWindowProc APIs. All the extra work for custom-created windows involves interactions with the parent window. You will generally have no need to create top-level windows, such as forms. There just aren't many things you can customize in this area. You're more likely to create windows with the WS_CHILD style for use with a VB-created parent window.

In addition to using a VB-created parent window, you also need a window that VB knows about to interact correctly with VB-created controls on the form. If you can't associate yourself with a window that VB knows about (which by definition, is one that it created), there is no way to put your control in the form's tab order. The most natural way to satisfy the requirement for these two windows is to make all of your CreateWindowEx calls from within a UserControl. Wrapping custom creation with a UserControl lets you use the single UserControl window for both the tab-order-dictated and the required VB-created parent window.

You should always be aware of both the runtime and the design-time requirements of a UserControl object. You need to show a fully functional control at design time. In particular, there is little need to actually create an extra window or put a subclassing hook in place. The problem is that you don't know in UserControl_Initialize if you are actually currently running in design or run mode. This information is available only from the Ambient object, which is not available until much later in the control-creation process.

The UserControl_InitProperties and UserControl_ReadProperties events provide the first reliable entry points in which the Ambient property is actually available. One of these functions is called whenever the control is created: InitProperties for a new control, and ReadProperties for a control with a cached set of properties. To avoid duplicate code in these two events, you need to create a helper routine that does the work appropriate for Class_Initialize but not for

UserControl_Initialize. Listing 16.3 shows the starting point for all of the book's control samples. It provides a design-mode check and code for printing the current control name on the design-time control.

Listing 16.3.   The beginning code needed by a UserControl to correctly handle both Design and Run modes

```
Private m_fDesign As Boolean

Private Sub UserControl_InitProperties()
    InitializeMode
End Sub
Private Sub UserControl_ReadProperties(PropBag As PropertyBag)
    InitializeMode
End Sub

Private Sub SetDesignMode()
    On Error Resume Next
    m_fDesign = Not Ambient.UserMode
    If Err Then m_fDesign = True
    On Error Goto 0
End Sub
Private Sub InitializeMode()
    SetDesignMode
    If Not m_fDesign Then
        'Subclassing and aggregation calls go here.
    End If
End Sub

Private Sub UserControl_Paint()
    If m_fDesign Then
        With UserControl
            'Assume a scalemode of Pixels.
            .CurrentX = 4
            .CurrentY = 2
            UserControl.Print .Ambient.DisplayName
        End With
    End If
End Sub
Private Sub UserControl_AmbientChanged(PropertyName As String)
    If m_fDesign Then
```

```
        If PropertyName = "DisplayName" Then _
            UserControl.Refresh
    End If
End Sub
```

You are now ready to create a window within a UserControl at runtime. The CreateWindowEx call is the next step, followed by calls that subclass the custom window and the UserControl window. You need both subclasses in place to make sure that focus always travels to the custom window by way of the VB-recognized UserControl window. There are two cases to consider. The first case occurs when the UserControl receives focus via the keyboard with a Tab or other accelerator key. Here you need to process the WM_SETFOCUS message on the main window, and then use the SetFocus API call to turn control over to the custom window. The second case occurs when the user activates the control by clicking directly on the custom window. This is handled by refusing the WM_MOUSEACTIVATE message and setting focus to the UserControl so that the custom window is activated using the same code path as the first case. The details are shown in Listing 16.4.

You can get a full framework for minimal custom-window creation in the CD's Samples\CreateWindow\MinimalEdit directory. This example creates a User-Control with a single EDIT window. All the public properties and methods you would generally expect on a control have been omitted from this sample to give you a starting point for your own projects. The Samples\CreateWindow\LBoxEx sample provides a highly scaleable virtual listbox control. The LBoxEx sample is an update to the project first shown in the June 1997 issue of *Visual Basic Programmer's Journal.* The original LBoxEx incarnation crashed in IE (their bug, my problem) and did not work correctly on an MDI child form (my bug *and* my problem). These problems have been fixed with the techniques shown in this chapter.

Listing 16.4. Code to play hot-potato between the UserControl's window and the do-it-yourself window. This is a partial listing from the MinimalEdit sample.

```
Private m_SubClassEdit As SubClassData
Private m_hWndEdit As Long
```

```vb
Private m_SubClassParent As SubClassData
Private m_hWndParent As Long


Friend Function WindowProcParent( _
  ByVal hWnd As Long, ByVal uMsg As Long, _
  ByVal wParam As Long, ByVal lParam As Long) As Long
    Select Case uMsg
        'Special code to get the correct background
        'color on an edit control.
        Case WM_CTLCOLOREDIT
            'Bypass VB on this message. It doesn't let it
            'drop through.
            If lParam = m_hWndEdit Then
                WindowProcParent = DefWindowProc( _
                    hWnd, uMsg, wParam, lParam)
            Exit Function
            End If
    End Select


    'Note: You can achieve something similar here without the
    'parent window subclass by calling SetFocusAPI m_hWndEdit
    'in UserControl_GotFocus. However, with the subclass, the
    'focus is set correctly on the child window before
    'you reach any of its events, and you will generally need
    'to handle other messages in the parent window anyway.
    WindowProcParent = CallWindowProc( _
      m_SubClassParent.wndprocNext, _
      hWnd, uMsg, wParam, lParam)
    'Bounce focus to the child edit window.
    If uMsg = WM_SETFOCUS Then SetFocusAPI m_hWndEdit
End Function


Friend Function WindowProc( _
  ByVal hWnd As Long, ByVal uMsg As Long, _
  ByVal wParam As Long, ByVal lParam As Long) As Long
    Select Case uMsg
        Case WM_MOUSEACTIVATE
            If GetFocus <> m_hWndEdit Then
                'Bounce focus back to the UserControl window
                'so that VB knows where the focus is. The
                'parent window will then bounce control right
```

```vb
                            'back to us.
                            SetFocusAPI m_hWndParent
                            WindowProc = MA_NOACTIVATE
                            Exit Function
                    End If
            End Select
            WindowProc = CallWindowProc(m_SubClassEdit.wndprocNext, _
                hWnd, uMsg, wParam, lParam)
    End Function


    Private Sub InitializeMode()
        SetDesignMode
        If Not m_fDesign Then
            If m_hWndEdit Then Exit Sub
            With UserControl
                m_hWndEdit = CreateWindowEx( _
                    WS_EX_CLIENTEDGE, "EDIT", vbNullString, _
                    WS_CHILD Or WS_CLIPSIBLINGS Or WS_TABSTOP, _
                    0, 0, .ScaleWidth, .ScaleHeight, .hWnd, 0, _
                    App.hInstance, ByVal 0&)
                If m_hWndEdit Then
                    SubClass m_SubClassEdit, m_hWndEdit, _
                        ObjPtr(Me), AddressOf RedirectEditProc
                    m_hWndParent = .hWnd
                    SubClass m_SubClassParent, m_hWndParent, _
                        ObjPtr(Me), AddressOf RedirectEditProcParent
                    ShowWindow m_hWndEdit, SW_SHOW
                End If
            End With
        End If
    End Sub
    Private Sub UserControl_Terminate()
        If Not m_fDesign Then
            If m_hWndParent Then _
                UnSubClass m_SubClassParent, m_hWndParent
            If m_hWndEdit Then _
                UnSubClass m_SubClassEdit, m_hWndEdit
            m_hWndParent = 0
            m_hWndEdit = 0
        End If
    End Sub
```

Put the Brakes on Message Acceleration

If you run a simple test of a control with only this much code, you might think you're done. In fact, if your control is the only one on a form, then everything works correctly. You don't actually run into problems until you drop a second control onto the form. At this point, you find that hitting the arrow keys actually moves focus to the next control on the form instead of navigating within the current control. Since you have a subclass in place, you can easily watch the WM_KEYDOWN message and determine that you never actually see these keystrokes.

The problem here is that all these precious keystrokes are lost during accelerator translation, which happens before any window procedures are called. You created the EDIT window yourself, so VB is clueless as to the window's existence. Therefore, VB thinks there are no constituent controls on the UserControl. This means that the arrow keys are essentially equivalent to a tab key and they move focus to the next control. You need to get a call during the keystroke preprocessing in order to have a chance to respond to the arrow keys. In an ActiveX control, this means that you need control over the TranslateAccelerator method on the IOleInPlaceActiveObject interface.

Support for IOleInPlaceActiveObject is built into the VB UserControl implementation, and you can retrieve this interface with a Set statement. This would generally involve using a VBoost aggregate object or QIHook to override the implementation of the interface. Unfortunately, VB does not call QueryInterface to retrieve the active object. It relies instead on a direct internal cast, so hooking the IUnknown does not help the situation. If VB actually queried for this interface, you could hook the call when you first created the window and not worry about it again. Without the IUnknown hook, you have to go behind VB's back when you get a WM_SETFOCUS message and replace the active object with a custom implementation. The override remains in use until the control is deactivated, at which point you are back at ground zero.

An override of the IOleInPlaceActiveObject interface is provided in the Code\InPlaceActiveObjectHook.Bas file on this book's CD. IPAOHook is a straightforward lightweight object that defers to the native implementation for all functions except the TranslateAccelerator method. TranslateAccelerator defers to the TranslateAccelerator function defined on the IHookAccelerator interface in

OleTypes.Olb (VBoost: Ole Type Definitions). You need to implement this interface and initialize the IPAOHook object to use the IHookAccelerator implementation. The required additions to your code are shown in Listing 16.5.

Listing 16.5. Additional code required to get a shot at accelerated messages before VB gets hold of them. This code requires a reference to OleTypes.Olb and InPlaceActiveObjectHook.Bas.

```
Implements OleTypes.IHookAccelerator
Private m_IPAOHook As IPAOHook


Friend Function WindowProc( _
  ByVal hWnd As Long, ByVal uMsg As Long, _
  ByVal wParam As Long, ByVal lParam As Long) As Long
    Select Case uMsg
        Case WM_SETFOCUS
            OverrideActiveObject m_IPAOHook, Me
        Case WM_MOUSEACTIVATE
    'Other code as in Listing 16.4.
End Function
Private Sub IHookAccelerator_TranslateAccelerator( _
  lpmsg As OleTypes.MSG, hrReturnCode As Long)
    'Return code defaults to S_FALSE (1).
    With lpmsg
        If .message = WM_KEYDOWN Then
            Select Case LOWORD(lpmsg.wParam)
                Case vbKeyUp, vbKeyDown, vbKeyLeft, _
                     vbKeyRight, vbKeyPageDown, vbKeyPageUp, _
                     vbKeyHome, vbKeyEnd
                    'Process now.
                    DoMsg .message, .wParam, .lParam
                    'Indicate that we've handled the message.
                    hrReturnCode = 0
            End Select
        End If
    End With
End Sub
Private Function DoMsg(ByVal uMsg As Long, _
  Optional ByVal wParam As Long = 0, _
  Optional ByVal lParam As Long = 0) As Long
    'Go straight to the previous window procedure instead of
```

```
        'calling SendMessage. This prevents unnecessarily stepping
        'through our window procedure.
        DoMsg = CallWindowProc(m_SubClassEdit.wndprocNext, _
            m_hWndEdit, uMsg, wParam, lParam)
    End Function
    Private Sub InitializeMode()
        'Other code as in Listing 16.4.
        If Not m_fDesign Then
            InitializeIPAOHook m_IPAOHook, Me
        End If
    End Sub
```

Now that you have full control of the accelerated messages as well as the window procedures of both the custom window and its parent, you're ready to expand your control by adding methods, properties, and events that interact with the custom hWnd and respond to its messages. The only unfortunate part of this situation is the number of resources required to create your custom window. You've actually created twice as many windows as you want. If the project runs on Windows 95 or 98 and you use a lot of windowed controls on multiple forms, you could very easily run out of resources: These operating systems have a relatively low system-wide limit on the total number of window and device-context handles.

You should be familiar with a window handle, but you might not be as familiar with a device context. A device context is an object that represents a drawing surface, such as a printer or a region on the screen. Windows lets you use temporary device context objects (created as needed and then returned to the system) or a device context that is created and destroyed with each HWND. VB defaults to the latter, but using the default value means that each Form and UserControl you create uses two handles from the precious resource store. To combat this problem, VB6 introduced the HasDC property. This property tells VB to borrow device contexts as needed instead of caching them, thereby cutting the number of persistent handles in half. The cost is that the painting is slightly slower, but you are very unlikely to notice a difference in most situations. I recommend setting the HasDC property to False for all new forms and UserControls to reduce the handle overhead. While you're at it, change the ClipControls value to False from its unfortunate True setting to improve your form's drawing performance.

Windowless Controls

HasDC includes one of the two properties added to controls in VB6 to reduce resource usage. The second property is the WindowLess property. A WindowLess control allows you to create a UserControl that doesn't use an HWND at all. Instead, it exists only as a region within another window. Windowless controls were first seen in VB2 with the lightweight Label and Image controls. You could also make windowless VBX controls for 16-bit applications. However, the 32-bit ActiveX control specification that arrived with VB4 did not account for windowless controls. Windowless support was added to the ActiveX specification around the time of VB5, and VB5 can host windowless controls but not create them. VB6 is the first release that can actually create windowless UserControl objects.

The ability to create controls without window handles enables you to use many more controls on a single form. The lack of an HWND shouldn't lead you to assume that windowless controls are significantly lighter than windowed controls. Windowless controls incur roughly the same startup costs as a windowed control. That said, however, you are not penalized for using them, and there is no reason to create windows that aren't actually needed.

Windowless controls are most useful for providing custom drawing in a control. Fancy drawing is done best with the Windows API, but windowless controls immediately provide some API challenges that you don't encounter with normal controls. First, you need to understand how to draw on the control's surface without spilling over the edge of control's region. Second, you don't have direct access to the stream of window messages. Third, there is no native VB way to receive reliable notifications when the control is activated. The third issue in particular makes it very difficult to create a windowless control that uses normal UI elements, such as a caret or a highlighted selection rectangle. You can solve all of these problems with direct access to the IOle* interfaces—and a little help from VBoost.

Finding the Rectangle

Before you can even begin to draw with the Windows API, you need the HWND, the rectangle you're drawing in, and access to a device context. In a windowless control, the UserControl.hWnd property always returns 0, so you must use the UserControl.ContainerHwnd property instead to determine the window you're in. Of course, this is only half the story because you should use only your part of the window, not the whole thing. Drawing outside this region is considered extremely bad manners. You can determine the rectangle within the container's HWND using the short helper functions shown here.

```
'A helper function to retrieve the in-place site. This is
'in a helper function because this interface is useful for
'more than just finding the rectangle.
Private Function WindowlessSite() As IOleInPlaceSiteWindowless
Dim pOleObject As IOleObject
    Set pOleObject = Me
    Set WindowLessSite = pOleObject.GetClientSite
End Function


'Given the site, find the rectangle relative to
'the container's window.
Private Function CtlRect( _
  pSite As IOleInPlaceSiteWindowless) As RECT
Dim pFrame As IOleInPlaceFrame
Dim pDoc As IOleInPlaceUIWindow
Dim ClipRect As RECT
Dim FrameInfo As OLEINPLACEFRAMEINFO
    FrameInfo.cb = LenB(FrameInfo)
    pSite.GetWindowContext _
        pFrame, pDoc, CtlRect, ClipRect, FrameInfo
End Function


'Calling code
Dim rct As RECT
    rct = CtlRect(WindowlessSite)
```

You now have the control's rectangle, but you need a device context to call the GDI drawing APIs. If you've done a lot of API programming, your first reaction at this point would be to call the GetDC function on the container's HWND and ReleaseDC when you're done. But you should never do this because this DC lets you draw all over the container's window and makes no consideration of controls that overlap yours. Instead of the GetDC/ReleaseDC API calls, use the GetDC and ReleaseDC methods on the IOleInPlaceSiteWindowless interface. The DC you get from the GetDC method is properly clipped, so you can draw without worrying about leaving visible footprints in places you're not allowed to tread. The DC you get from this function has its origin at the left corner of the window, not of the control, so you need to use the CtlRect function to get the correct rectangle.

The GetDC/ReleaseDC exercise may seem a bit extreme because the UserControl provides a built-in hDC property. The built in DC is also properly clipped, but its origin is relative to the corner of the control, not the container. If the ScaleMode is set to Pixels, the rectangle to use with the hDC has corners {{0,0},{ScaleWidth, ScaleHeight}}. To draw in a region that isn't clipped, you need to use the correct rectangle with the correct DC. The built-in DC is sufficient for your basic needs, but is not necessarily performance-tuned for everything you need to do.

- The GetDC has several options that aren't available with the hDC property. GetDC lets you specify a rectangle that can be smaller than the entire control. It also gives you three DC options not available with the hDC property: OLEDC_NODRAW, OLEDC_PAINTBKGND, OLEDC_OFFSCREEN. The container has the option of honoring these flags or not. VB appears to honor only the OLEDC_NODRAW flag, which is a great optimization if you are using the DC only to get information, such as text width, instead of drawing.

- In stress tests that use multiple overlapping lightweight controls, I've found that the GetDC approach generates less screen flash. It is very hard to judge this type of performance with the naked eye, so I'm offering this as an observation, not as a scientific conclusion.

- If the BackStyle property of your control is set to Transparent, you will see no output if you use GetDC in the UserControl_Paint event. You must draw with the hDC property and associated rectangle.

Getting Messages

You can't subclass a windowless control the way you can a windowed control. However, the ActiveX control specification does allow a windowless control to see messages that occur in its region via the OnWindowMessage method on the IOleInPlaceObjectWindowless interface. As with the normal message stream, VB doesn't give you automatic access to these messages, but you can see them by providing a custom implementation for this interface. Unlike IOleInPlace-ActiveObject, which must be rehooked whenever the control gets focus, VB's control container retrieves IOleInPlaceObjectWindowless via QueryInterface. You can use the VBoost aggregator with the interface-overriding techniques discussed in Chapter 12 to get access to this message.

The Code\InPlaceObjectWindowLessHook.Bas file defines a type called WindowlessSubclass and exposes a single public function called Initialize-WindowlessSubclass (modeled on the "Aggregating Lightweight Objects" section in Chapter 8). All the flags and objects necessary for aggregation are done for you; you simply pass an element from the AggregateData and IID arrays that you will pass yourself to the VBoost.AggregateUnknown call. This lets you aggregate additional objects with a single UnknownHook. The code uses a lightweight implementation of the IDelayCreation interface, so you get thin interface wrapping with no hassle. See Listing 16.6 for a sample implementation.

I have not been able to successfully debug a control while an active WindowlessSubclass object runs on the VB VBoost implementation. If VB crashes during debugging, you may want to set the VBOOST_INTERNAL conditional setting to 0.

The most pressing need for the subclass hook comes as a result of a hole in the event model for windowless controls. If you tab to or click on a windowless control, you get a GotFocus event. However, if you switch to another application or window and then reactivate the form, you will *not* receive a GotFocus (or any other) event. This makes it impossible to use the GotFocus and LostFocus events to show the active state of a control. However, if you watch the message stream coming into OnWindowMessage, you will get WM_KILLFOCUS and WM_SETFOCUS events when the form itself is deactivated and reactivated in addition to when the user selects the controls as the active control on the form. This enables you to take actions like showing and hiding a caret or focus rectangle. You can give your windowless control the look and feel of a normal windowed control that visibly changes when it receives and loses focus only if you have access to the message stream.

Listing 16.6. Use a WindowlessSubclass object to get an activation notification that is more reliable than the GotFocus event. You can leverage the WM_SETFOCUS message to install an accelerator hook just as you would with the WM_SETFOCUS message in a normal subclass.

```
'Member variables to get OnWindowMessage.
Implements OleTypes.IHookWindowlessMessage
Private m_WLSC As WindowlessSubclass
Private m_Hook As UnknownHook
Private Type HookData
    AggData(0) As AggregateData
    IIDs(0) As IID
End Type


'Member variables to get accelerator notifications.
Implements OleTypes.IHookAccelerator
Private m_IPAOHook As IPAOHook


'Called from InitProperties and ReadProperties.
Private Sub InitializeHooks()
Dim HookData As HookData
    If Ambient.UserMode Then
        InitializeIPAOHook m_IPAOHook, Me
        With HookData
            'Notify the hook after forwarding the message
            'to VB's implementation.
            InitializeWindowlessSubclass m_WLSC, Me, _
              nmNotifyAfter, .AggData(0), .IIDs(0), 0
            VBoost.AggregateUnknown Me, .AggData, .IIDs, m_Hook
        End With
    End If
End Sub


Private Sub IHookWindowlessMessage_OnWindowMessage( _
  ByVal fBefore As Boolean, _
  ByVal uMsg As VBoostTypes.UINT, _
  ByVal wParam As VBoostTypes.wParam, _
  ByVal lParam As VBoostTypes.lParam, _
  plResult As OleTypes.LRESULT, _
  hrReturnCode As Long)
    'This is always called with fBefore False because the
    'hook was established with nmNotifyAfter. nmNotifyBefore
    'can also be used to get the first shot at the message.
```

```vb
            'If fBefore is true, an hrReturnCode of 0 stops
            'further processing.
            If uMsg = WM_SETFOCUS Then
                OverrideActiveObject m_IPAOHook, Me
            End If
End Sub
Private Sub IHookAccelerator_TranslateAccelerator( _
    lpmsg As OleTypes.MSG, hrReturnCode As Long)
Dim plResult As LRESULT
Dim pIPOWL As IOleInPlaceObjectWindowless
        'Return code defaults to S_FALSE (1).
    With lpmsg
        If .message = WM_KEYDOWN Then
            Select Case .wParam And &HFFFF& 'LOWORD of wparam
                Case vbKeyUp, vbKeyDown, vbKeyLeft, _
                    vbKeyRight, vbKeyHome, vbKeyEnd
                    'Forward directly to the control instead
                    'of the usual window handle.
                    Set pIPOWL = Me
                    hrReturnCode = pIPOWL.OnWindowMessage( _
                        .message, .wParam, .lParam, plResult)
            End Select
        End If
    End With
End Sub
```

With the OnWindowMessage and TranslateAccelerator hooks in place, you have enough control to make your windowless controls do whatever you like. There are two sample projects on the CD that use these techniques. The first, in the Samples\CreateWindow\MinimalEditWindowLess directory, is a modified version of the MinimalEdit project that uses CreateWindowEx to use a windowless UserControl as the host for a windowed EDIT control. This accomplishes the task of creating a custom window in VB with a single window handle. The second sample, in Samples\WindowLess\LightEdit is a completely windowless edit control. This control gives you a UNICODE editing surface that you can use transparently over any background. This control can easily be extended to support multiline text and other features. With the activation and accelerator hooks in place, there is no way to distinguish a windowed control from a windowless control without using the SpyXX utility to scan for window handles.

Appendix

VBoost Reference

The VBoost objects are a set of objects and functions that provide capabilities not possible in straight VB. VBoost objects fall into three categories:

- Functions to handle arithmetic and assignment operations that are not native to VB.
- Objects to provide alternate memory-allocation schemes.
- Objects to facilitate aggregating objects.

In addition to the functions and their code, I've provided many more function declarations that facilitate the creation of the VBoost objects in VB and provide sufficient declarations for the coding topics covered in this book. For example, all the SafeArray API functions are included, as are GUID-manipulation functions and memory-allocation functions.

The type descriptions for the VBoost objects are separate from the implementation of the objects. All type descriptions are in VBoostTypes6.olb, while the C++ implementation of the VBoost objects is in VBoost6.Dll. You are free to redistribute the DLL. However, you are not free to redistribute the OLB (unless you send a gift copy of the book along with it).

In addition to the implementation provided in VBoost6.Dll, there is a full VB implementation provided for the VBoost objects as well. You can choose whether to compile the objects into your project or to redistribute the DLL with your projects. The VB implementation comes with fine-grained conditional-compilation switches to minimize the size of the code generated by your project.

You need to initialize a global variable called VBoost somewhere in your project's startup code to enable calling the VBoost functions as they are shown in the book's samples. You should explicitly instantiate the VBoost variable instead of using As New VBoostRootImpl syntax for two reasons, both of which minimize the cost of using the VBoost functions. First, the As New declaration works for the C++ implementation only because the VBoostRoot object is implemented as a lightweight in VB and can't be instantiated with New. Second, even if you are using the C++ implementation exclusively, you can avoid the extra code-generation required wherever the VBoost variable is used by not using As New.

The following steps enable both the C++ and VB implementations of VBoost and make it very easy to switch between them.

1. Open the Project|References dialog and add a reference to VBoost Object Types (6.0) and VBoost Object Implementation (6.0). These libraries are contained in VBoostTypes6.Olb and VBoost6.Dll, respectively.

2. Open the Project|Properties dialog.

3. On the General tab, select the Sub Main as Startup Object.

4. On the Make tab, add a VBOOST_INTERNAL = 0 value to the Conditional Compilation Constants field. Note that multiple values in this field are separated with a colon.

5. Add the VBoost.Bas file to your project.

6. Call the InitVBoost function from the Sub Main procedure.

7. Change the VBOOST_INTERNAL value to 1 to use the VB implementation instead of the DLL. If you use the VB implementation, you do not need to distribute VBoost6.Dll with your application. You should *never* distribute VBoostTypes6.Olb.

If you don't want a Sub Main, you can call InitVBoost from any object that uses it. There is no penalty for calling multiple times. However, many of the files included with the book assume an instantiated VBoost reference, so you should call InitVBoost early. If you plan on distributing VBoost6.Dll, you can skip the addition of VBoost.Bas to your project and instantiate a VBoostRoot object yourself with the following code.

```
Public VBoost As VBoostTypes.VBoostRoot
Sub Main()
    Set VBoost = New VBoost6.VBoostRootImpl
    'Other project specific code here.
End Sub
```

If you're using the VB implementation, you can add additional conditional compilation constants to reduce the amount of code generated. You can reduce the number of vtable entries supported by the blind vtable delegator using the VBOOST_BLIND_# constants, where # is in the set {1024, 512, 256, 128, 64, 32}. For finer-grained control of the vtable size, make a local copy of VBoost.Bas and edit the cBlindVTableEntries constant. You can also remove support for most functions by setting the VBOOST_CUSTOM constant to a nonzero value. In the following table of conditional compilation constants, all values below VBOOST_CUSTOM are ignored if VBOOST_CUSTOM is 0 or not defined. If you set VBOOST_CUSTOM only, the code is so small that you probably won't even see the VBoost presence reflected in the size of the EXE.

Calling a function that is not included causes a break in the IDE via a Debug.Assert call. If you hit the assert, you can use the View|Call Stack dialog to determine which function is missing. You must avoid the temptation to hit the Stop button at this point. Step out of the assert function and use the Set Next Statement (Ctrl-F9) and Step over error (Alt-F8) commands to gracefully exit the failing function or functions. Much of the code in this book, including VBoost, can crash the IDE or leave it in a useless state if you skip normal termination code.

Whether you've chosen to use the VB or the C++ implementation, you can now proceed with using the VBoost objects. The C++ objects can be more stable during debugging, so you may want to use the C++ objects during development and switch to the VB version before you build your final executable. It's now time to look at all the functions on the VBoostRoot object, as well as the structures and enums associated with the functions.

Assignment and Arithmetic Functions

Use the first group of functions for unsigned arithmetic and assignment between different types. Although some of these functions are possible in straight VB, the VBoost entries are much faster than anything you can write in VB. In the VB

Table A.1.   VBoost.Bas Conditional Compilation Constants.

Conditional Constant	Action
VBOOST_INTERNAL	Use the VB implementation instead of New VBoostRootImpl
VBOOST_BLIND_#	Limit the size of the generated blind vtable to {1024, 512, 256, 128, 64, 32}
VBOOST_CUSTOM	Remove all but the Assignment and Arithmetic functions
VBOOST_Aggregates	Support both AggregateUnknown and CreateAggregate
VBOOST_AggregateUnknown	Support AggregateUnknown only
VBOOST_CreateAggregate	Support CreateAggregate only
VBOOST_Hooks	Support both HookQI and HookQIAR
VBOOST_HookQI	Support HookQI only
VBOOST_HookQIAR	Support HookQIAR only
VBOOST_Memory	Support CreateFixedSizeMemoryManager with or without compaction
VBOOST_Memory_Simple	Support CreateFixedSizeMemoryManager with fCompactible False
VBOOST_Memory_Compactible	Support CreateFixedSizeMemoryManager with fCompactible True
VBOOST_BLIND	Support CreateDelegator and BlindFunctionPointer

version, all these functions, except AssignAddRef and SafeUnknown, are simply pointers into an array of asm bytes.

Assign(pDst As Any, pSrc As Any)

The Assign function is essential to the code in this book. Assign is functionally equivalent to CopyMemory pDst, pSrc, 4, but it is much faster. The most common size for assignment is 4. You can still use CopyMemory for other sizes. Assign transfers data between two variables without any type checking. The four ways you can call Assign are shown here with the C equivalent preceding it.

```
Dim pDst As Long, pSrc As Long
'(void*)pDst = (void*)pDst
VBoost.Assign pDst, pSrc
'*(void**)pDst = (void*)pSrc
VBoost.Assign ByVal pDst, pSrc
'(void*)pDst = *(void**)pSrc
VBoost.Assign pDst, ByVal pSrc
'*(void**)pDst = *(void**)pSrc
VBoost.Assign ByVal pDst, ByVal pSrc


'Equivalent statements
pDst = pSrc
VBoost.Assign pDst, pSrc
VBoost.Assign ByVal VarPtr(pDst), ByVal VarPtr(pSrc)


'More equivalent statements. This demonstrates an assignment
'across types. Note that Assign is faster because it doesn't
'perform an AddRef/Release on the Me object.
pDst = ObjPtr(Me)
VBoost.Assign pDst, Me


'Assign a 10-element array directly to an array variable.
'SafeArrayCreateVectorEx returns a Long value which is
'assigned directly to the array variable's memory.
Dim x() As Long
VBoost.Assign ByVal VarPtrArray(x), _
  SafeArrayCreateVectorEx(vbLong, 0, 10)
```

Since Assign directly references memory, you can cause a crash very easily if you use it incorrectly. Be sure to save your work often. The third syntax (which dereferences a pointer value) is very common, so VBoost has a special function to help with this operation.

Deref(ByVal Ptr As Long) As Long

Dereference the memory in Ptr and return the value. This is the functional inverse of the VarPtr function.

```
Dim lVal As Long
Dim Ptr As Long
Ptr = VarPtr(lVal)
Debug.Print VBoost.Deref(Ptr) = lVal 'Prints True

'Use Deref in line to get the dimensions of an array.
Dim cDims As Long
Dim x(0, 0) As Long
cDims = SafeArrayGetDim(VBoost.Deref(VarPtrArray(x)))
'cDims = 2
```

AssignZero(pDst As Any)

AssignZero is used to zero out pointer. This is functionally equivalent to Assign pDst, 0&, but AssignZero generates far less code because VB doesn't have to construct a temporary variable to hold the 0& constant (and you don't have to remember the trailing ampersand on the 0).

AssignAddRef(pDst As Any, pSrc As Any)

AssignAddRef is a special version of Assign that assumes the incoming data is an object. The AddRef function is called before the function returns. Since pDst is flagged as an [out] only parameter, you are not responsible for setting pDst to Nothing before calling AssignAddRef. Because of the As Any types, this function never performs a QI; only an AddRef. You can assign references from either a long value (provided it is a pointer to an object) or from another object.

```
Dim Me1 As Class1
Dim Me2 As Class1
Dim pUnk As stdole.IUnknown
VBoost.AssignAddRef Me1, Me
VBoost.AssignAddRef Me2, ObjPtr(Me)
VBoost.AssignAddRef pUnk, Me

'This outputs four equivalent values.
Debug.Print ObjPtr(Me), ObjPtr(Me1), ObjPtr(Me2), _
  ObjPtr(pUnk)
```

One underhanded but highly convenient use of AssignAddRef is possible with UserControl variables. UserControl is what VB calls a "private base class," which means the members of the base class don't end up on the Me object. This is why there are no members on the Me object of an empty UserControl object, but you get all the Form members on a Form object's Me. VB's compiler does not allow you to assign the private base class to variable or pass it to a normal parameter. The compiler makes this check when it determines whether an assignment should generate an AddRef or a QueryInterface. This check is skipped when passing to a ByRef As Any parameter, so you can get a UserControl reference into a variable by using AssignAddRef. You can use this loophole to write helper functions that operate against any UserControl object in projects with multiple controls. However, you are responsible for ensuring that the UserControl reference does not outlive the UserControl itself.

```
Dim UC As UserControl
    'Failing Code
    Set UC = UserControl
    'Succeeding code
    VBoost.AssignAddRef UC, UserControl
```

AssignSwap(pLeft As Any, pRight As Any)

AssignSwap lets you exchange the current values in two variables that are four-byte types (Long, String, object, and so on). None of the incoming data is modified or freed. AssignSwap is not a generic swap routine. If you pass two Variants, you will corrupt your variants by exchanging the Variant types, but no data. If you pass two Integer values, the results are undefined. If you use AssignSwap instead of Assign to transfer heap-allocated data between two variables of the same type, you don't have to worry about clearing the destination variable before the call.

```
'Exchange two String values.
Dim str1 As String, str2 As String
str1 = "ped"
str2 = "Swap"
VBoost.AssignSwap str1, str2
Debug.Print str1; str2
'Output: Swapped

'Swap an array variable into a function name.
Private m_Cache() As Long
```

```
Public Function FillArray() As Long()
    'Call helpers to fill m_Cache.
    'Set return value with AssignSwap.
    VBoost.AssignSwap _
      ByVal VarPtrArray(FillArray), _
      ByVal VarPtrArray(m_Cache)
    'Equivalent code without AssignSwap. Note that AssignSwap
    'into an empty variable is faster than Assign/AssignZero.
    Erase FillArray
    VBoost.Assign _
      ByVal VarPtrArray(FillArray), _
      ByVal VarPtrArray(m_Cache)
    VBoost.AssignZero ByVal VarPtrArray(m_Cache)
End Function
```

MoveVariant(pDst As Variant, pSrc As Variant)

MoveVariant allows you to assign one Variant to another, regardless of the Variant type. Normally, when assigning arbitrary Variants, you have to branch to either a Set statement or a normal assignment using IsObject as the criterion. If you assign an object type Variant without using a Set statement, VB tries to assign the default value of the object, not the object itself. MoveVariant frees any data in the pDst Variant by using the [out] attribute on the parameter, moves all 16 bytes of data from pSrc into pDst, and then flags pSrc as Empty. Handling variants in this fashion not only avoids type checking, it also eliminates data duplication.

```
Public Function GetData() As Variant
    VBoost.MoveVariant GetData, HelperFunc
End Function
```

Without MoveVariant, you would have to know the return type of HelperFunc before it was even called, or you would have been forced to write HelperFunc with an output parameter instead of a direct return type. If you're moving large arrays or strings in Variants, MoveVariant is a great tool for avoiding unnecessary duplication of the data.

SafeUnknown(ByVal pUnknown As Unknown) As stdole.IUnknown

VB always generates a QueryInterface call for IID_IUnknown when assigning an object to an IUnknown variable. Wrapping the assignment with SafeUnknown stops the QueryInterface call and assigns the current pointer, not its controlling IUnknown.

```
Dim pUnk1 As stdole.IUnknown
Dim pUnk2 As stdole.IUnknown
Set pUnk1 = Me
Set pUnk2 = VBoost.SafeUnknown(Me)

Debug.Print ObjPtr(pUnk1) = ObjPtr(pUnk2) 'False
```

[UAdd|UDif|UDiv](ByVal x As Long, ByVal y As Long)

Returns the result of adding (UAdd), subtracting (UDif), or dividing (UDiv) the x and y values using unsigned integer arithmetic. The UAdd and UDif functions are used primarily for safe pointer arithmetic, while UDiv is rarely used but is included for the sake of completion. UAdd and UDif do not do overflow checking. A multiplication function is not provided: Any multiplication operation (other than multiplying by 1 against an unsigned value above &H7FFFFFFF) results in an overflow, meaning that the function would never be useful.

```
'Add 1 to the maximum positive signed long value.
Debug.Print Hex$(VBoost.UAdd(&H7FFFFFFF, 1) '80000000
```

[UGT|UGTE](ByVal x As Long, ByVal y As Long) As Boolean

Compares the x and y values as unsigned longs using greater-than (UGT) or greater-than-or-equal (UGTE) comparison operators. ULT and ULTE are not provided; just switch the parameter order.

Memory Allocation Objects

VBoost provides two versions of a fixed-size memory manager. The base model, FixedSizeMemoryManager, does not free memory until the object itself is released. You can recycle memory during the memory manager's lifetime, but there is no way to get this memory back to the system. The second memory manager, CompactibleFixedSizeMemoryManager, allocates and frees memory somewhat slower than its noncompactible sibling, but you don't have to destroy the memory object to return resources to the system heap. There is one function on VBoostRoot, CreateFixedSizeMemoryManager, that creates both types of objects.

CreateFixedSizeMemoryManager

CreateFixedSizeMemoryManager takes three parameters and returns a Fixed-SizeMemoryManager object. If you specify compactible memory, you can assign the returned object to a CompactibleFixedSizeMemoryManager variable to get the additional methods and properties needed for compaction. First, let's look at the three parameters used to create the object.

ElementSize (Long) specifies the amount of memory (in bytes) required by each allocation. For performance reasons, this value is adjusted up to a four-byte boundary, so the value you read from the ElementSize property may be larger than the value you specify here.

ElementsPerBlock (Long) is the number of elements for which you want to reserve space in a single allocation. Memory is allocated from the heap Element-Size * ElementsPerBlock bytes at a time.

fCompactible (Boolean) indicates whether you want to support compaction. The default for this value is False. If the value is True, the returned object supports both the FixedSizeMemoryManager and the CompactibleFixedSizeMemory-Manager interfaces.

The following methods and properties are supported by both memory manager interfaces.

Alloc takes no parameters and returns a pointer to memory. In a heap allocation, the alloc function takes a size parameter, but that isn't needed here because each of these objects provides memory blocks with a uniform size. If all previously allocated memory is in use, Alloc goes to the heap to get enough memory for another ElementsPerBlock objects. Alloc can raise an out-of-memory error.

Free takes a pointer returned by Alloc as a parameter and makes it available for a subsequent call to Alloc. Free does not validate the incoming pointer and does not return an error, so make sure you give it a valid pointer to avoid a crash.

ElementSize is a read-only property that returns the size of an allocation returned by Alloc. This may be the same as the ElementSize parameter passed to CreateFixedSizeMemoryManager, but is always adjusted up to a four-byte boundary. For example, a request for 10 bytes actually gives you an ElementSize of 12. Maintaining four-byte alignment makes life a lot easier on your processor and is worth the extra padding memory.

ElementsPerBlock is a read-only property that returns the number of items created per heap allocation.

The remaining properties apply only to the compactible object.

CompactOnFree is a read-write property that indicates whether you want to give memory back to the heap during a call to Free or if you want the object to wait for an explicit Compact call. CompactOnFree defaults to False.

BufferBlocks is a read-write property that indicates how many empty blocks you want to keep when Compact is called. If you alternate Alloc and Free calls, you may end up on the boundary of a block. When this happens, a Free call frees a block of memory, and the next Alloc call requires more memory and reallocates a block of the same size that it just freed. Clearly, this happens only if CompactOnFree is True. To prevent thrashing memory in this fashion, you can specify that the allocator should not give the last BufferBlocks blocks back to the heap during a compaction. Changing BufferBlocks does not automatically trigger a compact; you must explicitly call Compact to actually free any empty blocks. BufferBlocks defaults to 1.

Compact is called when you want to give memory back to the heap. The amount of memory actually freed depends on the BufferBlocks setting. If CompactOnFree is True and you haven't recently reduced the value of BufferBlocks, you don't need to call Compact explicitly. BufferBlocks = 0 followed by Compact releases all blocks of memory which are no longer in use by any allocated object.

Aggregation Functions

Functions and objects that support aggregation form the bulk of the VBoost code. VTable delegation and IUnknown hooking are the two core technologies that VBoost uses to make one object appear like many. Although VBoost exposes the HookQI, HookQIAR, and CreateDelegator functions for your enjoyment, it is expected that you will usually call AggregateUnknown and CreateAggregate as these automatically handle all the QueryInterface interactions and delegator creation based on the data you specify. Aggregating objects by hand with just HookQI and CreateDelegator is cumbersome and nontrivial.

Since I'm expecting you to spend most of your time with the two aggregation functions, let's look at them first and then go back and look at HookQI, HookQIAR, and CreateDelegator. Every COM object has a controlling IUnknown interface. In fact, having the same controlling IUnknown is what identifies two different interface references as parts of the same object. Aggregation combines two or more COM objects into a single COM object by giving them all the same controlling IUnknown. The consumers of the composite object can't tell that it is an aggregate composed of multiple objects.

Since the controlling IUnknown plays such a central role in aggregation and defines COM object identity, getting a controlling IUnknown is the first step in aggregating. The reason there are two aggregation functions is that one, AggregateUnknown, hooks an existing IUnknown and builds an aggregate around it. The second function, CreateAggregate, takes the same data but creates a controlling IUnknown object from scratch. The most important parameters for each of these functions are the pData and pIIDs arrays. The AggregateData structure and its corresponding flags are the heart of VBoost aggregation.

The AggregateData Structure

The aggregation functions take an array of AggregateData structures to determine the objects and IIDs to be supported by the composite object. The FirstIID and LastIID fields in AggregateData are (0-based) indices into the pIIDs array passed with the pData array. The pObject field holds the object to compose into the controlling IUnknown. The Flags field, of type ADFlags, determines how the aggregators interpret the other three fields.

adIgnoreIIDs   (default, 0) specifies that the FirstIID and LastIID fields are not used. At runtime, VBoost steps through the list of items with explicit IIDs, then walks the objects that specified adIgnoreIIDs and sends the QueryInterface request to each object in turn. The first object to respond successfully is wrapped in a very thin windbreaker and sent out into the rain. Objects that don't specify a filter for the IID requests they respond to are called "blind aggregates."

adUseIIDs   specifies that FirstIID to LastIID, inclusive, is a range of identifiers that maps to the object specified in pObject. LastIID is ignored if it is less than FirstIID. If you want to guarantee that pObject maps to a specific IID by putting it early in the list, you can still include the same object as a blind aggregate in a later AggregateData array entry.

adMapIID   specifies that the IID indexed by FirstIID maps to the IID specified by LastIID. IID mapping allows you to correctly implement multiple derived interfaces with a single implements statement. For example, if IFooEx derives from IFoo, your object should respond to both IID_IFooEx and IID_IFoo. However, this requires an Implements statement for both IFooEx and IFoo. By pointing FirstIID to IID_IFoo in the pIIDs array and LastIID to IID_IFooEx, you can eliminate the hassle of supporting extraneous interface with Implements. pObject should always be Nothing when you use adMapIID.

adBlockIIDs   specifies that a set of IIDs should never be acknowledged. This is a rare requirement, but is supported nonetheless. pObject should be Nothing, and LastIID is ignored if it is less than FirstIID.

adPrimaryDispatch   gives the object of this element the first chance at any incoming IID_IDispatch QI. Since multiple interfaces can derive from IDispatch but a COM object can return a reference to only one of these interfaces in response to a QueryInterface call, you need a QI hook to change the interface that acts as the primary dispatch. (See IUnknown discussion in Chapter 3.) This flag lets you specify an aggregated object rather than the controlling IUnknown as the primary dispatch for your interface. A special feature of adPrimary-Dispatch: If you don't set the pObject, set adUseIIDs, and set FirstIID, the aggregator uses FirstIID retrieved from the controlling IUnknown as the primary dispatch. This allows you to point the primary IDispatch to an interface that you implement directly in your class. You can redirect IID_IDispatch with adPrimaryDispatch, with adMapIIDs, or in the QIHook function on the IQIHook interface. adPrimaryDispatch is the easiest because I do all the work for you.

(See "Post-Build Type Library Modifications" in Chapter 15 to see how to change your primary interface. Setting the primary IDispatch is a critical step.)

adBeforeHookedUnknown   tells the aggregator to send QI calls to pObject before sending them to the primary object. By default, the hooked object is first in the QI chain, and processing stops on success. This flag lets you override supported interfaces before VB sees them. This flag has no effect when used with CreateAggregate because there is no specified controlling IUnknown.

adDontQuery   specifies that the object should be referenced but never queried. This flag greatly simplifies the creation of composite objects in which a strong reference is required. See the "Hierarchical Object Models" section of Chapter 6 for an example of using this flag.

adNoDelegator   tells the aggregator not to put a blind delegator around the returned interface. Of course, the delegator provides the QueryInterface override to redirect calls back to the controlling IUnknown, so this means that COM identity is lost. Not generating a delegator has three advantages. First, there is no delegation overhead. Second, the object is now a native VB object, so Friend functions work. Third, for the same reason, the debugger recognizes the returned object as a VB object and can show the private variables within the implementing class. If you're using aggregation on a public COM object, be a good COM citizen and allow the delegator to be built for all publicly available interfaces. However, using the aggregators with adNoDelegator for internal objects gives you direct Set statement support for nonnative interfaces.

adDelayCreation   tells the aggregator that the passed object is actually an IDelayCreation interface. IDelayCreation has one function, Create, which takes an iid parameter and returns a resolved object. Delayed creation allows you to create supporting objects as needed instead of creating the object before creating the aggregator. For delayed creation, you must also specify adUseIIDs and at least the FirstIID. If LastIID is also set, the object returned by IDelayCreation_ Create is expected to support all of the given IIDs. VBoost supports implementing IDelayCreation on the aggregated controlling unknown's object without causing object-lifetime problems by automatically handling the circular reference.

```
'IFoo is delay created by AggObj.
Dim IFoo As IFoo
'Calls IDelayCreation_Create.
Set IFoo = AggObj
Set IFoo = Nothing
'IDelayCreation_Create is not called a second time
'because the reference is cached.
Set IFoo = AggObj
```

adDelayDontCacheResolved tells the aggregator not to cache the object returned by IDelayCreation_Create. With adDelayCreation, IDelayCreation is used once, and the entry then reverts to a normal object. The aggregator holds a reference to the delay-created object until the object terminates. You may want to opt for the adDelayDontCacheResolved flag if the interface is used rarely, if maintaining the validity of the interface over time is difficult, or if the returned implementation holds an extra reference on the controlling object. adDelayDontCacheResolved implies adDelayCreation, so you don't have to specify both flags. As the name implies, adDelayDontCacheResolved stops the aggregator from keeping the resolved reference, so IDelayCreation_Create is called multiple times for multiple requests for the same IID, even if a reference for this IID is currently in use. There is rarely a reason to use this flag when aggregating an object that will be marshaled because the COM marshaler always caches interfaces, so you see only one request.

adFullyResolved tells the aggregator not to call QueryInterface after an item has been retrieved. adFullyResolved is ignored if adUseIIDs is not set, and only one IID can be specified. When you wrap an interface of a given object, you never want to QI the object for the wrapped interface because you'll get the unwrapped interface. By telling the aggregator to skip the QI, you can aggregate against wrapped objects. You can use this flag as an optimization for other interfaces, but you must be extremely cautious when setting the pObject field. Generally, you'll want to use VBoost.AssignAddRef to eliminate any chance of a QueryInterface call. Any object returned from IDelayCreation_Create must also respect this flag.

adWeakRefBalanced tells the aggregator that the object being added already holds a reference to the controlling IUnknown. In this circular reference situation, the UnknownHook object itself ends up owning a reference to its parent class and can't shut down properly. To break the circular reference without holding an unsafe reference on the aggregated object itself, the aggregate releases a reference on the controlling IUnknown and puts the reference count back during teardown before releasing the aggregated object. (See "Safe Weak Referencing of Secondary Interfaces" in Chapter 10 for more information on balanced weak references). It is very dangerous to combine adNoDelegator with adWeakRefBalanced because the returned reference holds no reference count on the controlling IUnknown and can easily cause a crash.

adWeakRefRaw tells the aggregator to simply hold the reference as a raw weak reference. The controlling IUnknown should hold a reference on weakly referenced objects. The same comments regarding adNoDelegator apply to adWeakRefRaw as to adWeakRefBalanced.

AggregateUnknown

The AggregateUnknown function builds an aggregate on top of an existing IUnknown by hooking the vtable of the controlling IUnknown. The hook remains in place until the UnknownHook object returned by AggregateUnknown is set to Nothing. Generally, the UnknownHook object itself is owned by the controlling IUnknown, which can teardown correctly even if the hook is still active. This enables you to aggregate with code in Class_Initialize only. Here are the parameters for AggregateUnknown.

pUnk (ByVal stdole.IUnknown) is the object that should act as the controlling IUnknown. Do not use SafeUnknown when passing to this parameter; the IUnknown QI resulting from the pass to IUnknown is expected and required. You will generally pass Me to this parameter.

pData (AggregateData array) is the array of AggregateData items that specifies the layout of the aggregate.

pIIDs (VBGUID array) is the list of IIDs pointed to by the FirstIID and LastIID fields in pData. This array may be empty, but you must provide it.

ppOwner (UnknownHook, out parameter) takes a member variable declared as UnknownHook and gives it ownership of the hook. The hook remains in place as long as UnknownHook remains in scope. You can remove the hook at any time by setting the variable to Nothing.

```
'Aggregate a Form with a collection object, then retrieve
'the collection from the form and display an item.
Private m_Hook As UnknownHook
Private Sub Command1_Click()
Dim Coll As Collection
    Set Coll = Me
    MsgBox Coll(1)
    If TypeOf Coll Is Form Then
        MsgBox "(with a new identity)"
    End If
End Sub


Private Sub Form_Initialize()
Dim Coll As Collection
Dim pIIDs() As VBGUID
Dim AggData(0) As AggregateData
    Set Coll = New Collection
    Coll.Add "I'm alive!"
    With AggData(0)
        Set .pObject = Coll
        .Flags = adIgnoreIIDs
    End With
    VBoost.AggregateUnknown Me, AggData, pIIDs, m_Hook
End Sub
```

CreateAggregate

CreateAggregate aggregates using the same data as AggregateUnknown, but it creates a new controlling IUnknown object instead of hooking an existing one. CreateAggregate returns a stdole.IUnknown reference, which you can then assign to a more specific object type.

pData   same as AggregateUnknown.

pIIDs   same as AggregateUnknown.

pOwner (Optional, ByVal Long)   is an optional parameter that lets you track whether your aggregate object is still alive. Specifying pOwner lets you return an existing aggregate rather than creating a new one on every request. If you want such a capability, pass the VarPtr of a member variable of one of the objects you specify in a pObject field in the pData array. When the aggregate object is destroyed, this memory address is zeroed. Since the aggregate holds a reference on the pObject objects you send with pData, this memory address is guaranteed to be valid during the lifetime of the aggregate.

```
'CreateExternal is a specific version of the function shown in
'in "Hierarchical Object Models" section of Chapter 6. In
'this scenario, a Child object has a weak reference on its
'parent object. When the Child object is passed to an
'external client, it needs to protect its parent. This is
'easily done with CreateAggregate by establishing the child
'as a blindly aggregated object and the parent as a reference
'that isn't queried.
'Child is the main object, ParentPtr is the ObjPtr of its
'parent, and ExternalPtr is a member variable of Child. This
'function is in ExternalChild.Bas on the CD.
Function CreateExternal(ByVal Child As IUnknown, _
  ByVal ParentPtr As Long, ExternalPtr As Long) As IUnknown
Dim AggData(1) As AggregateData
Dim IIDs () As VBGUID
    If ExternalPtr Then
        VBoost.AssignAddRef CreateExternal, ExternalPtr
    Else
        'Defer all QueryInterface calls to the child.
        With AggData(0)
            Set .pObject = Child
            .Flags = adIgnoreIIDs
        End With

        'Let the aggregator hold the parent reference for us,
        'but don't forward QueryInterface calls to it.
        With AggData(1)
            VBoost.AssignAddRef .pObject, ParentPtr
            .Flags = adDontQuery
        End With

        Set CreateExternal = VBoost.CreateAggregate( _
          AggData, IIDs, VarPtr(ExternalPtr))
```

```
      End If
End Function
```

HookQI Function, IQIHook Interface

HookQI allows you to watch and modify the QueryInterface calls yourself instead of letting the provided aggregators do it for you. Interface requests are monitored through the IQIHook interface. HookQI is extremely useful if you want to monitor the QueryInterface requests that come into your object and see if they were successful. QI monitoring can be very useful while debugging, where a failing QI request that immediately precedes an error is often an indication that you have another interface to implement. You can identify most interfaces by looking up their IIDs in the HKEY_CLASSES_ROOT\Interfaces section in the registry.

Here are the parameters for HookQI.

pUnk (ByVal stdole.IUnknown)   is the object whose controlling IUnknown you are hooking. Do not use SafeUnknown when passing to this parameter; the IUnknown QI resulting from the pass to IUnknown is expected and required. You will often pass Me to this parameter.

pQIHook (ByVal IQIHook)   is a reference to an IQIHook implementation. pQIHook can have the same controlling IUnknown as pUnk, allowing you to hook yourself.

uhFlags (ByVal UnkHookFlags)   is a combination of none, some, or all the values uhBeforeQI, uhAfterQI, and uhMapIIDs. The values specified indicate which IQIHook functions to call and when. This parameter provides the initial Flag settings; you can modify them at any time to use the Flags property on the returned UnknownHook object. Note that Flags, the only property on UnknownHook, is read-only when the UnknownHook object is created by AggregateUnknown instead of HookQI or HookQIAR.

ppOwner (UnknownHook, out parameter)   On return, this parameter holds the object that owns the hook. The hook remains in place until the variable goes out of scope or you set it to Nothing. The variable passed here is usually a member variable of the hooked unknown.

The IQIHook interface has two functions: MapIID and QIHook. The number of calls to these functions depends on the current setting of the UnknownHook.Flags property. If uhMapIIDs is currently specified, the MapIID function is called very early during the QueryInterface call, giving you the chance to swap in a different IID or to block the call altogether. If uhBeforeQI is set, the QIHook function is called before QueryInterface is attempted against the controlling IUnknown, allowing you to preempt the object for certain IIDs. If uhAfterQI is set, the QIHook is called after the QueryInterface call, allowing you to verify or change the returned object. During all of these calls, the IUnknown hook is deactivated, so the hooked IUnknown is temporarily in its native state.

MapIID takes a single IID As VBGUID parameter. You can either change the IID used during the rest of the QueryInterface call or block the call completely by raising any error. You will rarely want to block an IID, but mapping by changing the IID parameter is used in two scenarios. First, you can map the IID_IDispatch IID to an implemented interface instead of the primary interface on the controlling IUnknown. Second, if one interface corresponds to multiple IID values, the easiest way to support all IIDs is with an IID map. (This was addressed earlier in the discussion of the adMapIID flag.)

QIHook allows you to view and modify the reference returned by the QueryInterface function on the controlling IUnknown. QIHook has four parameters.

- *IID* is the requested IID. If MapIID modified the IID, this is the modified version. You should never change the value of IID during this call.

- *uhFlags* (ByVal UnkHookFlags) is either uhBeforeQI or uhAfterQI, indicating when the QIHook function is being called.

- *pResult* (ByRef stdole.IUnknown) is the value to be returned by the QI function. For a uhBeforeQI call, pResult always starts with a Nothing value. If you set it before returning, the QI function on the native object is not called. pResult might be set at the beginning of a uhAfterQI call, but you are free to modify the value. If pResult is Nothing at the end of the uhAfterQI call, QueryInterface fails with an E_NOINTERFACE return. If you set the value of pResult, make sure you assign the value with SafeUnknown or AssignAddRef. Otherwise, assigning to the IUnknown variable will cause a QueryInterface call that returns the wrong interface, resulting in a likely crash. The CreateDelegator function, often used to create a result object, returns an stdole.-IUnknown that can be assigned directly to pResult with set.

- *HookedUnknown* (ByVal stdole.IUnknown) is the controlling IUnknown of the hooked object. The hook is not in place during the call. HookedUnknown is provided to make it easier to create a vtable delegator that defers to the controlling IUnknown.

```
'Watch all QueryInterface calls coming into this object and
'whether they succeeded.
Implements IQIHook
Private m_Hook As UnknownHook
Private Sub Class_Initialize()
    VBoost.HookQI Me, Me, uhAfterQI, m_Hook
End Sub
Private Sub IQIHook_MapIID(IID As VBoostTypes.VBGUID)
    'Not called
End Sub

Private Sub IQIHook_QIHook(IID As VBoostTypes.VBGUID, _
  ByVal uhFlags As VBoostTypes.UnkHookFlags, _
  pResult As stdole.IUnknown, _
  ByVal HookedUnknown As stdole.IUnknown)
Dim GuidString As String * 38
    StringFromGUID2 IID, GuidString
    Debug.Print "QI for " & GuidString;
    If pResult Is Nothing Then
        Debug.Print " failed."
    Else
        Debug.Print " succeeded."
    End If
End Sub
```

HookQIAR Function, IQIARHook Interface

HookQIAR is an extension of HookQI. The AR indicates that you get notifications for the AddRef and Release functions as well as for QueryInterface. AddRef and Release monitoring is generally not useful in production code, but it can be extremely useful during development. If you're able to watch the AddRef and

Release calls as they happen, you can track when your object is being referenced and released.

Here are the parameters for HookQIAR.

pUnk　Same as HookQI.

pQIARHook (ByVal IQIARHook)　is a reference to an IQIARHook implementation. IQIARHook adds the AfterAddRef and AfterRelease functions to the IQIHook interface. As with IQIHook, you can implement IQIARHook as part of the object you're watching. However, you won't see the final Release notification if you take this approach. You don't actually need a final release in this case because Class_Terminate is an equivalent notification to the final release call.

uhFlags　supports up to five different values. In addition to the three flags supported by the IQIHook interface, IQIARHook adds uhAddRef and uhRelease. As you can with HookQI, you can use the Flags property on the return UnknownHook object to dynamically change the current flags during the lifetime of the object. You cannot switch between a QIHook and a QIARHook by changing flag values; a HookQI-established UnknownHook ignores these flag values.

ppOwner　Same as HookQI.

The IQIARHook interface adds the AfterAddRef and AfterRelease notification functions to the QIHook and MapIID functions. Unlike the QI functions, these are strictly notification functions: you cannot use them to modify the behavior of the object. The IUnknown hook is deactivated during calls into the IQIARHook interface.

AfterAddRef　takes two ByVal Long parameters: Result and pHookedUnknown. Result is the value returned by the AddRef call on the hooked object. pHookedUnknown is equivalent to the ObjPtr of the HookedUnknown parameter passed to the QIHook function. You can use these values for tracking purposes during debugging.

AfterRelease　takes the same parameters as AfterAddRef. Of course, the Result value comes from Release instead of from AddRef. If you get a Result of 0, the pHookedUnknown is the pointer to the object that was just destroyed. To actually see the O Result, you must implement IQIARHook on an object other than the one you are hooking.

```
'Output all object creation and destruction as well as all
'QueryInterface, AddRef, and Release calls.
Implements IQIARHook
Private m_Hook As UnknownHook
Private Sub Class_Initialize()
Dim pUnk As IUnknown
    Set pUnk = Me
    Debug.Print "Initialize: " & Hex$(ObjPtr(pUnk))
    Set pUnk = Nothing
    VBoost.HookQIAR _
      Me, Me, uhAfterQI Or uhAddRef Or uhRelease, m_Hook
End Sub
Private Sub Class_Terminate()
Dim pUnk As IUnknown
    Set m_Hook = Nothing
    Set pUnk = Me
    Debug.Print "Terminate: " & Hex$(ObjPtr(pUnk))
End Sub
Private Sub IQIARHook_AfterAddRef( _
  ByVal Result As Long, ByVal pHookedUnknown As Long)
  Debug.Print "AddRef="; Result; " on: "; _
    Hex$(pHookedUnknown)
End Sub
Private Sub IQIARHook_AfterRelease( _
  ByVal Result As Long, ByVal pHookedUnknown As Long)
  Debug.Print "Release="; Result; " on: "; _
    Hex$(pHookedUnknown)
End Sub
Private Sub IQIARHook_MapIID(IID As VBoostTypes.VBGUID)
    'Not called
End Sub
Private Sub IQIARHook_QIHook(IID As VBoostTypes.VBGUID, _
  ByVal uhFlags As VBoostTypes.UnkHookFlags, _
  pResult As stdole.IUnknown, _
  ByVal HookedUnknown As stdole.IUnknown)
    If Not pResult Is Nothing Then
```

```
        Debug.Print "QI Successful on: ";
        Debug.Print Hex$(ObjPtr(HookedUnknown))
    End If
End Sub
```

In addition to its use for instance tracking, HookQIAR is also very useful for watching VB's interaction with the IUnknown interface. For example, as you step out of the HookQIAR function itself, you'll see two Release calls. These calls come from the temporary variables used to cast Me to the IUnknown and IQIARHook interface references required by HookQIAR. You'll also see AddRef/Release sequences as you step over a Public or Friend function in a class, but not when stepping over a Private function.

CreateDelegator

The CreateDelegator function is used to create a blind vtable delegator around an inner object and a controlling IUnknown. You can use this function in IQI-Hook_QIHook to aggregate an object into the controlling IUnknown on the fly. There are two required parameters; three optional ones provide advanced use of the delegator.

punkOuter (ByVal stdole.IUnknown) is the controlling IUnknown that the QueryInterface call in the blind delegator should defer to.

punkDelegatee (ByVal Unknown) is the interface to be wrapped. Note that the type of this parameter is Unknown, so VB doesn't perform a QueryInterface call when passing an object to this parameter.

pIID (Optional, ByVal VBGUIDPtr) is an optional parameter that specifies an IID to query the delegatee for to determine the correct interface to wrap. If your punkDelegatee is a reference to the object you want to wrap but not necessarily the correct interface, pass VarPtr(IID_Wanted) to the pIID parameter.

pEmbedded (Optional, ByVal BlindDelegatorPtr) allows the vtable delegator to be allocated as part of a larger structure. To use this parameter, include a member of type BlindDelegator in your structure and pass VarPtr(.BDMember). If you pass pEmbedded, you can also specify a function address in pfnDestroyEmbedded.

pfnDestroyEmbedded (Optional, ByVal Long) is the function called when the blind delegator is destroyed. If pEmbedded is not specified, standard allocation is used to allocate a blind delegator structure. This structure is deleted when the delegator reference is released. The destructor is stored in the pfnDestroy field in the BlindDelegator structure and can be modified during the lifetime of the object. For example, the AggregateUnknown aggregator can easily hand out delegators that outlive the hook object. When the hook sees that it has outstanding objects on teardown, it gives outstanding IID table entries a reference to the FixedSizeMemoryManager used to allocate them and changes the pfnDestroy field in the BlindDelegator structure to release the memory object on teardown. Although this is an advanced feature, it is required to enable writing the VBoost objects in VB and custom-population of the BlindDelegator structure. See "Interface Wrapping" and "Wrapping Your Own Interface" in Chapter 12 for an example.

BlindFunctionPointer

The BlindFunctionPointer function lets you use vtable delegation with lightweight objects to override functions of existing interfaces. For example, when you use CreateWindowEx to build highly customized controls, you must override the IOleInPlaceActiveObject.TranslateAccelerator function. This is the only relevant function. However, you have to provide delegation code for all the other functions in the vtable as well. BlindFunctionPointer lets you use the vtable delegation code so you don't have to provide implementations for each function. To use BlindFunctionPointer, the inner object must be placed immediately after the vtable pointer in the structure.

```
Public Type IPAOHookStruct
    lpVTable As Long 'VTable pointer
    IPAOReal As IOleInPlaceActiveObject 'Inner object, offset
    'four
    'Other fields
End Type


Private Type IPAOVTable
    VTable(9) As Long
End Type
```

```
Private m_IPAOVTable As IPAOVTable

'VTable layout without BlindFunctionPointer.
With m_IPAOVTable
    .VTable(0) = FuncAddr(AddressOf QueryInterface)
    .VTable(1) = FuncAddr(AddressOf AddRef)
    .VTable(2) = FuncAddr(AddressOf Release)
    .VTable(3) = FuncAddr(AddressOf GetWindow)
    .VTable(4) = FuncAddr(AddressOf ContextSensitiveHelp)
    .VTable(5) = FuncAddr(AddressOf TranslateAccelerator)
    .VTable(6) = FuncAddr(AddressOf OnFrameWindowActivate)
    .VTable(7) = FuncAddr(AddressOf OnDocWindowActivate)
    .VTable(8) = FuncAddr(AddressOf ResizeBorder)
    .VTable(9) = FuncAddr(AddressOf EnableModeless)
End With


'VTable layout with BlindFunctionPointer.
With m_IPAOVTable
    .VTable(0) = FuncAddr(AddressOf QueryInterface)
    .VTable(1) = FuncAddr(AddressOf AddRef)
    .VTable(2) = FuncAddr(AddressOf Release)
    .VTable(3) = VBoost.BlindFunctionPointer(3)
    .VTable(4) = VBoost.BlindFunctionPointer(4)
    .VTable(5) = FuncAddr(AddressOf TranslateAccelerator)
    .VTable(6) = VBoost.BlindFunctionPointer(6)
    .VTable(7) = VBoost.BlindFunctionPointer(7)
    .VTable(8) = VBoost.BlindFunctionPointer(8)
    .VTable(9) = VBoost.BlindFunctionPointer(9)
End With
```

Note that the first three entries in the delegation vtable interact directly with the members of the BlindDelegator structure. For this reason, you generally want to provide your own IUnknown vtable functions or use a BlindDelegator structure directly as shown in the "Thinner Interface Wrapping" section of Chapter 12. You can pass the special value −1 to BlindFunctionPointer to get a pointer to the entire blind vtable instead of an entry in the vtable. You can use this value in the CopyMemory call to duplicate a large number of blind vtable entries with a single call. For example, the previous code can be modified as follows.

```vb
'VTable layout with BlindFunctionPointer(-1).
With m_IPAOVTable
    CopyMemory .VTable(0), _
        ByVal VBoost.BlindFunctionPointer(-1), _
        LenB(.VTable(0)) * (UBound(.VTable) + 1)
    .VTable(0) = FuncAddr(AddressOf QueryInterface)
    .VTable(1) = FuncAddr(AddressOf AddRef)
    .VTable(2) = FuncAddr(AddressOf Release)
    .VTable(5) = FuncAddr(AddressOf TranslateAccelerator)
End With
```

Index

G

los angeles · boston · london · portland, OR

A DEVELOPER SERVICES COMPANY

developmentor

www.develop.com

ABOUT DEVELOPMENTOR

DevelopMentor is a distinct educational resource providing advanced technical information through training, publications, conferences, and software. DevelopMentor is comprised of passionate developers who offer insight and leadership in areas such as XML, JAVA, and COM. The DevelopMentor Technical Staff have authored more than 24 technical books and are regular contributors to *MSDN, Java Developer Connection, Visual Basic Programmer's Journal,* and other publications. DevelopMentor training facilities are located in Los Angeles, Boston, London, and Portland.

HELPING DEVELOPERS WITH TRAINING, SOFTWARE, AND PUBLICATIONS.

COM+ · OLE DB · ATL · C++ · WDM
MFC · MTS · MSMQ · ADO · SECURITY
JAVA · XML · WEB APPS · RMI · EJB
3D GRAPHICS · VB · WIN 32

FOR MORE INFORMATION:

www.develop.com

IN THE US
800.699.1932

WITHIN THE UK
01242.525.108

WITHIN EUROPE
+44.1242.525.108

Register Your Book

at www.aw.com/cseng/register

You may be eligible to receive:

- Advance notice of forthcoming editions of the book
- Related book recommendations
- Chapter excerpts and supplements of forthcoming titles
- Information about special contests and promotions throughout the year
- Notices and reminders about author appearances, tradeshows, and online chats with special guests

Contact us

If you are interested in writing a book or reviewing manuscripts prior to publication, please write to us at:

Editorial Department
Addison-Wesley Professional
75 Arlington Street, Suite 300
Boston, MA 02116 USA
Email: AWPro@aw.com

Addison-Wesley

Visit us on the Web: http://www.aw.com/cseng

CD-ROM Warranty

Addison-Wesley warrants the enclosed disc to be free of defects in materials and faulty workmanship under normal use for a period of ninety days after purchase. If a defect is discovered in the disc during this warranty period, a replacement disc can be obtained at no charge by sending the defective disc, postage prepaid, with proof of purchase to:

Editorial Department
Addison-Wesley Professional
Pearson Technology Group
75 Arlington Street, Suite 300
Boston, MA 02116
Email: AWPro@awl.com

Addison-Wesley and Matthew Curland make no warranty or representation, either expressed or implied, with respect to this software, its quality, performance, merchantability, or fitness for a particular purpose. In no event will Matthew Curland or Addison-Wesley, its distributors, or dealers be liable for direct, indirect, special, incidental, or consequential damages arising out of the use or inability to use the software. The exclusion of implied royalties is not permitted in some states. Therefore, the above exclusion may not apply to you. This warranty provides you with specific legal rights. There may be other rights that you may have that vary from state to state. The contents of this CD-ROM are intended for non-commercial use only.

More information and updates are available at:
http://www.awl.com/cseng/titles/0-201-70712-8